RECORDS OF
THE HISTORIAN

*Prepared for the Columbia College Program of
Translations from the Oriental Classics*
WM. THEODORE DE BARY, *Editor*

Records of the Historian

Chapters from the Shih chi
of Ssu-ma Ch'ien

translated by
BURTON WATSON

COLUMBIA UNIVERSITY PRESS

NEW YORK

Copyright © 1958, 1961, 1962, 1969 Columbia University Press
The account of Ching K'o in "The Biographies of the
Assassin-Retainers" first appeared in the *Anthology
of Chinese Literature,* edited by Cyril Birch (Copyright © 1965
by Grove Press, Inc.).

UNESCO COLLECTION OF REPRESENTATIVE WORKS
CHINESE SERIES
This book
has been accepted
in the Chinese Series
of the Translations Collection
of the United Nations
Educational, Scientific and Cultural Organization
(UNESCO)

ISBN 0–231–03321–4
Library of Congress Catalog Number: 70-89860
Printed in the United States of America

10 9 8 7 6 5 4

Clothbound editions of Columbia University Press books are
Smyth-sewn and printed on permanent and durable acid-free
paper.

FOREWORD

The *Records of the Historian* by Ssu-ma Ch'ien is one of the Translations from the Oriental Classics by which the Committee on Oriental Studies has sought to transmit to Western readers representative works of the major Asian traditions in thought and literature. Our intention is to provide translations based on scholarly study but written for the general reader rather than primarily for other specialists.

Professor Watson's two-volume translation of a major portion of the *Records of the Historian* inaugurated this series in 1961. Since then he has contributed substantially to the more than twenty titles which have appeared. In the present paperbound edition of the *Records of the Historian* he has made a selection of key chapters in the original two-volume work and added new translations which would help to give, though in smaller compass, a sense of Ssu-ma Ch'ien's work as a whole. We hope that this may fulfill one of the aims of the series: to put these translations within the reach of ordinary readers and students. Professor Watson has distinguished himself and put us all in his debt by his devoted labors in this cause.

CONTENTS

INTRODUCTION

The present volume consists of eighteen chapters and one brief excerpt translated from the *Shih chi* or *Records of the Historian* of Ssu-ma Ch'ien. Thirteen of these are taken from the translator's two-volume *Records of the Grand Historian of China* (Columbia University Press, 1961), which contains material relating to the Han dynasty (206 B.C.– A.D. 220). To these have been added five chapters dealing with the preceding Chou (*ca.* 1123–256 B.C.) and Ch'in (221–207 B.C.) dynasties. One of these chapters appeared, in a slightly different version, in the translator's *Ssu-ma Ch'ien: Grand Historian of China* (Columbia University Press, 1958), and part of another in the *Anthology of Chinese Literature* edited by Cyril Birch (Grove Press, 1965). The purpose of the selection is to suggest to the reader something of the form and content of this first, and in many ways most important, of the great Chinese works of history, to indicate the type of material presented by the historian and his methods of presentation, and to allow the reader to enjoy some of the more famous and highly praised passages in the work.

Not much is known about the life of Ssu-ma Ch'ien outside of the little information he gives us in the autobiography appearing at the end of his life work, the *Shih chi,* or *Records of the Historian.* Most scholars place his birth in 145 B.C. and agree that he died around 90 B.C., so that his lifetime more or less parallels that of Emperor Wu, the vigorous, strong-willed ruler who brought the Han dynasty to its peak of power and at whose court Ssu-ma Ch'ien spent most of his life.

Ssu-ma Ch'ien's father, Ssu-ma T'an, was given the position of grand historian at the court of Emperor Wu shortly after that ruler's accession in 141 B.C., and at Ssu-ma T'an's death in 110 B.C., Ssu-ma Ch'ien succeeded to the post. The official duties of the grand historian seem to have been largely connected with astrology and divination, though Ssu-ma T'an, perhaps on his own initiative, planned to write a work of history and began to collect material for it. In accordance with his father's dying request, Ssu-ma Ch'ien took up the task when he became grand historian and spent the next twenty-some years bringing it to completion. Midway in his work he aroused the ire of Emperor Wu and was condemned to suffer castration. Although it was customary under such circumstances for men of honor to commit suicide, Ssu-ma Ch'ien chose to bear the indignity in order to complete his manuscript and justify himself in the eyes of posterity. Two thousand years of admiring readers have amply rewarded his bitter decision.

The result of his labors is a monumental work in 130 chapters covering the history of the Chinese people, as well as of the foreign peoples known to China, from the earliest times down to the lifetime of the historian. In our present version of the work, at least one chapter is missing altogether and several others appear to be fragmentary or incomplete. Compared to the sad state in which the works of some of Ssu-ma Ch'ien's Western contemporaries such as Polybius or Livy have come down to us, however, we can only marvel at the excellent condition of the text.

The *Shih chi* is divided into five large sections. The first section, entitled "Basic Annals," comprises twelve chapters devoted to the histories of the earlier dynastic houses or, in the case of the reigning Han dynasty, to the lives of individual emperors. These are followed by ten "Chronological Tables" listing in graph form the important events of the past with their dates. Next come eight "Treatises" on such subjects as rites, music, astronomy, religious affairs, and economics. These are followed by thirty chapters entitled "Hereditary Houses," which for the most part deal with the histories of the various feudal states of pre-Ch'in China. The work ends with seventy chapters entitled "Biographies" or "Accounts," devoted to the lives of famous men of history, or to the foreign peoples and countries with which China had contact. Within each section the chapters are arranged chronologically, but the grouping of the material into sections and the essentially biographical approach of most of the chapters necessitates considerable scattering of the data pertaining to any given period, as well as frequent recapitulation in the narrative.

Early histories in chronicle form, notably the famous *Spring and Autumn Annals* of the state of Lu, traditionally supposed to have been edited by Confucius, as well as collections of speeches and historical anecdotes, had existed before the time of Ssu-ma Ch'ien. But the form of the *Shih chi,* with its division of material into "Annals," "Treatises," "Biographies," etc., seems to have been Ssu-ma Ch'ien's own creation. In spite of certain obvious drawbacks, it has been regarded by Chinese historians as a masterpiece of form, and was adopted in the twenty-four "Dynastic Histories," the official accounts compiled to cover all of the dynasties from the time of Ssu-ma Ch'ien to the present century.

According to tradition, Chinese rulers employed historiographers at their courts as early as a thousand years before the time of Ssu-ma Ch'ien, and no doubt a vast number of chronicles and similar historical materials came into existence during this early period. Unfortunately, most of these were lost in the wars and uprisings that accompanied the unification of China under the Ch'in dynasty, and its successor, the Han, or were deliberately destroyed by the Ch'in's notorious "burning of the books." As a result, Ssu-ma Ch'ien in his account of pre-Ch'in history was forced to rely heavily on two or three well-known sources, such as the *Tso chuan,* or the *Intrigues of the Warring States,* and in places had to piece out his narrative with legend and popular romance. With the treatment of Ch'in and Han times, however, Ssu-ma Ch'ien's narrative takes on depth and verisimilitude; his characters cease to be moral stereotypes and become fully rounded personalities. These chapters, dealing with events close to or contemporary with his own lifetime, form the heart of his history and display the most original and important aspects of his genius. Accordingly it is for the most part these later sections which I have chosen to present here.

The exploits of mankind being basically much the same in any age or clime, the English reader, I expect, will find little in Ssu-ma Ch'ien's account of the emperors, generals, and statesmen of the Han dynasty that is not already familiar to him from the history of the Classical West. Indeed, Ssu-ma Ch'ien's whole approach to history—his concern with the didactic import of his story, his emphasis upon the life and importance of the individual, his skepticism and relative lack of interest in the supernatural—shows a striking similarity to that of the historians of ancient Greece and Rome. Even the literary devices which he uses to create his dramatic effects resemble those of his Western contemporaries. Though there is no evidence that he intended his work to be declaimed in public as did the Greek or Roman historians, he was hardly less concerned than they with rhetoric and questions of style. Like Thucydides or Tacitus, he relies heavily upon elaborate and probably fictitious speeches put into the mouths of his characters to explain and advance the action and to delineate personality, speeches composed with the same balanced periods, the hyperboles, the erudite allusions and homely metaphors familiar to us in the Western rhetorician's art.

In addition to these formal speeches, however, the Chinese historian makes very free use of direct discourse. The past is visualized as a series of dramatic episodes in which, instead of describing the action, the historian makes his characters speak aloud. Repeatedly we find the narrative serving only to set the scene, while the burden of the story is carried forward by the discourse of the participants. If, in the pages that follow, the reader from time to time has a distinct impression that he is reading a novel rather than a work of history, it is because of this characteristic Chinese fondness for direct speech.

Classical Chinese, it should be noted, is capable of a breathtaking economy and vigor of expression. Chinese historians in particular prize terseness above almost any other quality of style, and though the *Shih chi* is relatively verbose compared to other early historical works, its narrative still maintains a swiftness and leanness that can seldom be reproduced in another language. There are few passages of pure description, few of the disgressions and leisurely asides we are accustomed to in the works of Greek and Roman historians. All is speech and action, the two traditional components of Chinese history.

In the two thousand years since its appearance, the *Shih chi* has been widely and affectionately read not only by educated Chinese but by men of learning in Korea and Japan, as well. The reason for its continued popularity and the incalculable influence it has had upon the literatures of these countries lies undoubtedly in its moving portraits of the great men of the past, its dramatic episodes and deft anecdotes. Accordingly, it is these aspects of the *Shih chi*—giving it interest as a collection of good stories—which I have been most concerned to reproduce in the translation.

I have avoided the use of Chinese technical terms or titles which might prove distracting, or of awkward sounding translations of such titles and terms, no matter how faithfully they might reproduce the meaning of the originals. Again, I have used as few Chinese weights and measures as possible, employing English substitutes in cases where the exact value of the measurement did not seem of great importance to the sense of the narrative. I have occasionally translated place names, such as White Horse Ford, where the original meaning of the name is still immediately apparent in the Chinese.

In another important respect I have sacrificed strict fidelity to readability. Most of the major figures appearing in the *Shih chi* have two given names, a familiar and a polite one, and a variety of military, official, and noble titles by which they are referred to at various times. Some commentators insist that Ssu-ma Ch'ien, by the particular way he chooses to refer to his characters at particular times, is attempting to convey subtle moral judgments on their worth and dignity. I have grave doubts about this theory, but, however valid it may be, I have felt compelled to sacrifice such subtleties to considerations of intelligibility. The Western reader, to whom the profusion of unfamiliar names which follows will be trial enough, can hardly be expected to carry in his head a complicated set of titles and ranks, while continual bracketing to assist identification would prove tiresome. As far as possible I have therefore chosen one name to refer to a person and used it throughout, regardless of how the original reads. The one exception is Liu Chi, the founder of the Han dynasty, who in the course of his rise to power is variously known as "governor of P'ei," "king of Han," and finally "Emperor Kao-tsu."

In addition to such titles, the Chinese language employs an elaborate set of pronouns and polite terms of address in direct discourse. English, to be sure, possesses acceptable equivalents such as "Your Majesty" or "Your Lordship." But too frequent use of such terms would, I fear, give a labored and archaic tone to the translation, and nothing could be farther from the style of the original. I have consequently used honorific expressions only occasionally to set the tone of a discourse, and hope that the reader will imagine that the appropriate air of humility is sustained throughout. Again I have attempted to vary in the translation some of the set formulas of the original, such as the ubiquitous "he said" or "he asked saying." Good Chinese permits such formulas where good English demands variety, and it seems pointless, merely for the sake of literalness, to make Ssu-ma Ch'ien sound like a clumsy schoolboy. Where proper names or historical allusions are used metaphorically, I have, as Robert Graves would say, "brought up" into the translation whatever information is necessary to make their meaning comprehensible. I have avoided footnotes wherever possible; in most cases what is not clear at first will, I believe, become so as the reader proceeds to later chapters. I have occasionally enclosed in parentheses one or two sentences of the original which appear to be in the nature of an aside.

In making selections from a work covering such a lengthy span of time, it is impossible to present a detailed picture of any one age. I have therefore tried instead to select chapters that, though carefully dovetailed with other chapters in the original, can nevertheless be read as separate entities, examples of the historian's art that, even without the fuller context, possess the kind of depth and meaning one expects of true literature.

The selection opens with *Shih chi* 61, "The Biography of Po Yi and Shu Ch'i," the first chapter in the *lieh-chuan* or "Biography" section, which serves as an introduction to the section and sets forth the historian's views on such fundamental questions as the criteria for judging historical reliability, the fate of goodness in the world, and the special role which the historian plays in singling out the man of virtue for praise and insuring that his fame will be handed down to posterity. This is followed by several chapters relating the lives of eminent statesmen and military leaders of middle and late Chou times, when China was divided into a number of feudal states, all acknowledging nominal fealty to the Chou king while engaging one another in a ceaseless struggle for gain or survival. This struggle was brought to an end when the state of Ch'in, situated in the northwest, finally conquered all its rivals and united China under one central administration, a process completed in 221 B.C. when the Ch'in ruler assumed the title of Shih-huang-ti or First Supreme Emperor. The full account of this great process of conquest and the revolutionary measures instituted by the new dynasty is too lengthy to be presented here; instead the reader is let in on a secret concerning the First Emperor's true parentage, and told of a daring attempt on his life which, had it been successful, might have changed the entire course of the nation's development.

The chapters that follow deal with one of the most colorful periods of Chinese history, the founding of the Han dynasty, when two heroes, Hsiang Yü and Liu Chi, rose to overthrow the faltering Ch'in and then fell upon one another in a fight to the death. Following the biographies of the protagonists, called *pen-chi* or "Annals" because both at one time exercised *de facto* rule over the empire, are chapters relating the lives of the men who aided Liu Chi in his rise to power and helped him to create the laws and institutions for his new dynasty.

The last age to be covered in this selection is that of Emperor Wu (r. 140–87 B.C.), the fifth Han ruler and one of the most renowned of Chinese sovereigns, the age of the historian himself. It was a time of intense activity. At home the government built roads, dug canals, and embarked upon other great public works; abroad it vigorously attacked the Hsiung-nu tribes to the north and extended Chinese power east into Korea, south toward Vietnam and Burma, and west into Central Asia, activities which are reflected in the present selection in "The Treatise on the Yellow River and Canals," "The Account of Ta-yüan," and "The Biography of General Li Kuang." To accomplish such feats, Emperor Wu drove his people hard, taxing heavily, imposing huge labor and military conscriptions, and stifling all opposition through stern and repressive laws, as "The Biographies of the Harsh Officials" eloquently testifies.

The selection closes with "The Biographies of the Money-makers," a chapter which describes the careers of the great merchants of the historian's time and earlier, as well as presenting several recipes for making a fortune and a geographical survey of the occupations, principal products, and life styles of the various regions of China. It also serves neatly to sum up what is in the end the central theme of Ssu-ma Ch'ien's entire 130-chapter history: the indefatigable will of man. The *Shih chi,* like most histories, is full of grisly battles, appalling natural disasters, executions, plagues, poverty, and distress. But through it all Ssu-ma Ch'ien is careful to stress that, whatever the men of history may have been forced to suffer, whatever frustrations and calamities they may have encountered, they could never be robbed of their determination, their freedom to make moral choices. It was they who made history, not the other way around, as so often seems to be the case in the historiography of our own time. As Ssu-ma Ch'ien remarks at the end of his "Biographies of the Assassin-Retainers," "some succeeded in carrying out their duty and some did not. But it is perfectly clear that they had determined upon the deed. They were not false to their intentions. Is it not right, then, that their names should be handed down to later ages?"

TRANSLATOR'S NOTE ON THE TEXT

On the whole I have followed the text of the *Shih chi* as it appears in the edition entitled *Shiki kaichū kōshō* (Tokyo, 1934), edited and with a commentary in Chinese by Takikawa Kametarō, which was reprinted several years ago. Fuller information on translations and other works consulted in the preparation of the Han sections may be found in the Translator's Note in *Records of the Grand Historian of China,* vols. 1 and 2. In preparing the translation of the five pre-Han chapters I have consulted with profit the translations of parts of this material by Professors Derk Bodde, Frank Kierman, and Richard Rudolph. I wish to thank Grove Press for permission to use the Ching K'o section of "The Biographies of the Assassin-Retainers," which appeared earlier in Cyril Birch's *Anthology of Chinese Literature.*

In order to avoid confusion between the names of feudal states which, though written with different characters, appear the same in romanized form, I have, in the sections pertaining to Chou times, romanized the name of the older state of Wei, founded at the beginning of the Chou dynasty and situated in western Shantung, as Wey; and the state created in the fifth century out of the old territory of Chin, as Wei. In the Han sections I have romanized the name of the state created, like Wei, out of the old territory of Chin, as Hann, in order to distinguish it from the area on the upper reaches of the Han River in which Liu Chi was first enfeoffed and from which he took the name of his dynasty.

Shih chi 61: The Biography of Po Yi and Shu Ch'i

While a degenerate age scrambled for profit, they alone hastened to righteousness, relinquishing a state, starving to death, and for this the whole world praised them. Thus I made The Biography of Po Yi and Shu Ch'i.[1]

Although in the world of learning there exist a large number and variety of books and records, their reliability must always be examined in the light of the Six Classics.[2] In spite of deficiencies in the *Odes* and *Documents,* we can nevertheless know something about the culture of the times of Emperor Shun and the Hsia dynasty. When, for instance, Emperor Yao wished to retire from his position, he yielded the throne to Shun, and Shun in turn yielded it to Yü. But in each case the high court officials first unanimously recommended these men for the position and they were given the throne for a period of trial. Only after they had discharged the duties of the imperial office for twenty or thirty years, and their merit and ability had become manifest, was the rule finally ceded to them. This proves that the empire is a precious vessel, its ruler part of a great line of succession, and that its transmission is a matter of extreme gravity. Yet there are theorists who say that Yao tried to yield the empire to Hsü Yu and that Hsü Yu was ashamed and would not accept it but instead fled into hiding. Again, for the time of the Hsia dynasty we have similar stories of men called Pien Sui and Wu Kuang. Where do people get stories like this?

The Grand Historian remarks: When I ascended Mount Chi I

[1] The summaries which head the chapters are taken from Ssu-ma Ch'ien's table of contents in *Shih chi* 130.

[2] The six Confucian Classics, the *Book of Odes, Book of Documents, Book of Changes, Spring and Autumn Annals, Book of Rites,* and *Book of Music.* The *Music* was lost long ago.

found at the top what is said to be the grave of Hsü Yu. Confucius, we know, eulogizes the ancient sages and men of wisdom and virtue, and quite specifically mentions such figures at T'ai-po of Wu and Po Yi. Now I am told that Hsü Yu and Wu Kuang were men of the highest virtue, and yet in the Classics there appears not the slightest reference to them. Why would this be?

Confucius said, "Po Yi and Shu Ch'i never bore old ills in mind and hence seldom had any feelings of rancor." "They sought to act virtuously and they did so; what was there for them to feel rancor about?"[3]

I am greatly moved by the determination of Po Yi. But when I examine the song that has been attributed to him,[4] I find it very strange.

The story of these men states that Po Yi and Shu Ch'i were elder and younger sons of the ruler of Ku-chu. Their father wished to set up Shu Ch'i as his heir but, when he died, Shu Ch'i yielded in favor of his elder brother Po Yi. Po Yi replied that it had been their father's wish that Shu Ch'i should inherit the throne and so he departed from the state. Shu Ch'i likewise, being unwilling to accept the rule, went away and the people of the state set up a middle brother as ruler. At this time Po Yi and Shu Ch'i heard that Ch'ang, the Chief of the West, was good at looking after old people, and they said, "Why not go and follow him?" But when they had gone they found that the Chief of the West was dead and his son, King Wu, had taken up the ancestral tablet of his father, whom he honored with the posthumous title of King Wen, and was marching east to attack the emperor of the Yin dynasty. Po Yi and Shu Ch'i clutched the reins of King Wu's horse and reprimanded him, saying, "The mourning for your father not yet completed and here you take up shield and spear—can this conduct be called filial? As a subject you seek to assassinate your sovereign—can this conduct be called humane?" The king's attendants wished to strike them down, but the

---

[3] *Analects* V, 22; VII, 14.

[4] *Yi-shih,* a poem attributed to ancient times but not included in the *Book of Odes;* for this reason alone, it would be suspect. In addition, as we shall see, the spirit of the song conflicts with what Confucius said about Po Yi.

king's counselor, T'ai-kung, interposed, saying, "These are righteous men," and he sent them away unharmed.

After this, King Wu conquered and pacified the people of the Yin and the world honored the house of Chou as its ruler. But Po Yi and Shu Ch'i were filled with outrage and considered it unrighteous to eat the grain of Chou. They fled and hid on Shou-yang Mountain, where they tried to live by gathering ferns to eat. When they were on the point of starvation, they composed a song:

> We climb this western hill
>   and pick its ferns;
> replacing violence with violence,
>   he will not see his own fault.[5]
> Shen Nung, Yü, and Hsia,
>   great men gone so long ago—
> whom shall we turn to now?
> Ah—let us be off,
>   for our fate has run out!

They died of starvation on Shou-yang Mountain. When we examine this song, do we find any rancor or not?

Some people say, "It is Heaven's way to have no favorites but always to be on the side of the good man."[6] Can we say then that Po Yi and Shu Ch'i were good men or not? They piled up a record for goodness and were pure in deed, as we have seen, and yet they starved to death.

Of his seventy disciples, Confucius singled out Yen Hui for praise because of his diligence in learning, yet Yen Hui was often in want, never getting his fill of even the poorest food, and in the end he suffered an untimely death. Is this the way Heaven rewards the good man?

Robber Chih day after day killed innocent men, making mincemeat of their flesh. Cruel and willful, he gathered a band of several thousand followers who went about terrorizing the world, but in the end he lived to a ripe old age. For what virtue did he deserve this?

---

[5] "He" refers to King Wu, who replaced the violence of Yin with his own brand of violence.

[6] *Tao-te-ching* 79.

These are only the most obvious and striking examples. Even in more recent times we see that men whose conduct departs from what is prescribed and who do nothing but violate the taboos and prohibitions enjoy luxury and wealth to the end of their lives, and hand them on to their heirs for generations without end. And there are others who carefully choose the spot where they will place each footstep, who "speak out only when it is time to speak," who "walk no bypaths" [7] and expend no anger on what is not upright and just, and yet, in numbers too great to be reckoned, they meet with misfortune and disaster. I find myself in much perplexity. Is this so-called Way of Heaven right or wrong?

Confucius said, "Those whose ways are different cannot lay plans for one another." [8] Each will follow his own will. Therefore he said, "If the search for riches and honor were sure to be successful, though I should become a groom with whip in hand to get them, I would do so. But as the search might not be successful, I will follow after that which I love." [9] "When the year becomes cold, then we know that the pine and cypress are the last to lose their leaves." [10] When the whole world is in muddy confusion, then is the man of true purity seen. Then must one judge what he will consider important and what unimportant.

"The superior man hates the thought of his name not being mentioned after his death." [11] As Chia Yi has said:

> The covetous run after riches,
> the impassioned pursue a fair name;
> the proud die struggling for power,
> and the people long only to live.

Things of the same light illumine each other; things of the same class seek each other out. Clouds pursue the dragon; the wind follows the tiger. The sage arises and all creation becomes clear.

Po Yi and Shu Ch'i, although they were men of great virtue, became, through Confucius, even more illustrious in fame. Though Yen Hui was diligent in learning, like a fly riding the tail of a swift horse, his attachment to Confucius made his deeds renowned. The hermit-

---

[7] *Analects* XIV, 14; VI, 12.   [8] *Analects* XV, 39.   [9] *Analects* VII, 11.
[10] *Analects* IX, 271.   [11] *Analects* XV, 19.

scholars hiding away in their caves may be ever so correct in their givings and takings, and yet the names of them and their kind are lost and forgotten without receiving a word of praise. Is this not pitiful? Men of humble origin living in the narrow lanes strive to make perfect their actions and to establish a name for themselves, but if they do not somehow attach themselves to a great man, a "man of the blue clouds," how can they hope that their fame will be handed down to posterity?

Prince Chien met with slander and the trouble spread to Wu She; Wu Shang went to his father's rescue, while Wu Yün fled to Wu. Thus I made The Biography of Wu Tzu-hsü.

Wu Tzu-hsü was a native of Ch'u; his personal name was Yün. His father was named Wu She; his elder brother, Wu Shang. One of his forebears, Wu Chü, had won renown for the frankness with which he offered advice when he was in the service of King Chuang of Ch'u, and accordingly the family in later generations enjoyed fame in the state of Ch'u.

King P'ing of Ch'u [r. 528–516] had a son named Chien whom he had designated as crown prince and to whom he appointed Wu She as Grand Tutor and Fei Wu-chi as Lesser Tutor. Fei Wu-chi, however, felt no loyalty to Prince Chien and, when King P'ing sent him to the state of Ch'in to fetch a bride for the prince, he hurried back and reported to King P'ing, saying "The Ch'in woman is of extraordinary beauty! Your Majesty should take her for yourself and let me go look for someone else to be a bride for the prince." King P'ing in the end took the Ch'in woman for himself. He treated her with extreme favor and affection and she bore him a son named Chen. Another bride was found for the prince.

Fei Wu-chi, having used the Ch'in woman to ingratiate himself with King P'ing, then left the service of the prince and entered that of the king. But he feared that, if some morning the king should pass away and the crown prince come to the throne, the latter would kill him, and so he set about slandering the prince. The prince's mother was a woman of Ts'ai[1] and no longer enjoyed the favor of the king. The king grew increasingly cold toward the crown prince, dispatching

---

[1] A small state on the northern border of Ch'u; see p. 22.

him to guard the region of Ch'eng-fu and see that the troops along the border were kept up to strength.

Before long Fei Wu-chi was at the king again, day and night telling him of the prince's shortcomings. "Because of the business of the woman of Ch'in," he said, "it is impossible that the prince should be without feelings of resentment and anger. I hope Your Majesty will take some small precautions to protect yourself. Ever since the prince has been residing in Ch'eng-fu and has had command of the troops there, he has been in contact with the lords of other states abroad. It would almost seem as though he is preparing to enter the capital and start a revolt!"

King P'ing thereupon summoned the Grand Tutor Wu She and subjected him to examination. Wu She, aware that Fei Wu-chi had been speaking ill of the crown prince to King P'ing, exclaimed, "How can Your Majesty let some petty, slandering villain of a minister estrange you from your own flesh and blood!"

But Fei Wu-chi said, "If Your Majesty does not block the prince now, the plot may be brought off and you will very likely end up a prisoner!" In anger King P'ing thereupon had Wu She thrown into prison and ordered Fen Yang, the marshal of Ch'eng-fu, to go and kill the crown prince. Fen Yang set out, but before arriving he sent a man ahead to inform the crown prince, urging him to leave immediately. "If not, you will be put to death!" he warned. Prince Chien fled and took refuge in the state of Sung.

Fei Wu-chi said to King P'ing, "Wu She has two sons, both worthy men. If you do not put them to death, they are likely to cause trouble for the state of Ch'u. It would be best to use the father as a hostage and summon them to court. If not, they will be a worry to Ch'u!" The king sent a messenger to Wu She to inform him, "If you can make your two sons come to court, you may live; if not, you die."

Wu She said, "Shang is a man of goodness. If I call him, he is sure to come. But Yün is a man of fierce determination, willing to bear disgrace and capable of accomplishing great things. When he sees that, if he comes, he will only be taken prisoner along with his brother, he will be bound under the circumstances not to come!"

The king, heedless of his words, sent a messenger to summon the two sons, saying, "If you come, I will spare your father. If you do not come, I will kill him this instant!"

Wu Shang wanted to go, but Yün said, "The ruler of Ch'u is not summoning the two of us because he wants to spare our father's life. He is afraid that, if we get away, we will make trouble later on and so he is using our father as a hostage and is summoning us under false pretenses. If both of us go, then father and sons will all end up dead. How will this make our father's death any less terrible? Our going will only assure that the injustice of it will never be avenged! It would be better to flee to some other state, enlist outside help, and in that way wipe out our father's disgrace. If we are all destroyed, nothing can be done!"

Wu Shang said, "I know that even if I go I can never hope to save my father's life. It is just that I would hate to think that he called me to save his life and I failed to obey. Later, if I should be unable to wipe out the disgrace, I would end as the laughing stock of the world and nothing more!" Then he said to Wu Tzu-hsü, "You must go away, for you are capable of avenging the wrong of our father's murder. I will go to the death that awaits me."

Wu Shang accordingly gave himself up to arrest but, when the envoys tried to seize Wu Tzu-hsü as well, he drew his bow, snatched an arrow, and stood facing them so that they did not dare advance. Eventually he was able to escape and, hearing that Prince Chien was in Sung, went there to become his follower.

When Wu She heard that Tzu-hsü had escaped, he said, "It will not be long before the ruler and subjects of the state of Ch'u taste the bitterness of war!" When Wu Shang arrived at the Ch'u court, the ruler put both him and his father Wu She to death.

Wu Tzu-hsü had reached the state of Sung when the revolt of the Hua family broke out there and he and Prince Chien accordingly fled together to Cheng, where the people of Cheng treated them very well. The prince also journeyed to Chin, where Duke Ch'ing of Chin said to him, "You are already on good terms with Cheng and the men of Cheng trust you. If you were willing to work on my behalf from inside the state of Cheng, while I attacked from the outside, we could be certain of wiping it out, and with Cheng wiped out, I could grant you a fief!" The prince accordingly returned to Cheng. The time had not yet come to carry out the plot, however, when it happened that, for private reasons, the prince decided to put to death one of his followers. The man knew of the plot and informed the men of Cheng of it, whereupon Duke Ting of Cheng and his prime minister Tzu-ch'an put Crown Prince Chien to death in punishment.

Prince Chien had a son named Sheng. Wu Tzu-hsü, alarmed by what had happened, joined Sheng and together they fled to the state of Wu. When they reached the Chao Pass, the keeper of the pass wanted to arrest them but Wu Tzu-hsü, separating from Sheng and fleeing on foot alone, just managed to escape, his pursuers following close behind. When he reached the Yangtze, he found a solitary fisherman in a boat who, recognizing that he was in a desperate situation, ferried him across. When they had reached the other shore, Wu Tzu-hsü unfastened his sword and said, "This sword is worth a hundred pieces of gold. I will make you a present of it." But the fisherman said, "According to the command of the state of Ch'u, anyone who captures Wu Tzu-shü will receive fifty thousand piculs of grain and be honored with the title of Holder of the Jade Baton! If I had reward in mind, why would I settle for a mere hundred-gold-piece sword?" He refused to accept the gift.

Before Wu Tzu-hsü reached the state of Wu, he fell sick and had to stop along the road to beg for food.

When he arrived in Wu, the state was under the rule of King Liao, with Prince Kuang commanding the army. Through the good offices of Prince Kuang, Wu Tzu-hsü was able to gain an interview with the king. Sometime later, the women of Chung-li, a town on the Ch'u border that engaged in sericulture, and those of Pi-liang, a town on the Wu border with a like occupation, quarreled over their mulberry trees and the two towns attacked one another. King P'ing of Ch'u was enraged, and it reached the point where both states called out their armies to prepare for battle. Wu dispatched Prince Kuang to attack Ch'u and he captured Chung-li and Chü-ch'ao before returning. Wu Tzu-hsü advised King Liao of Wu, saying, "Ch'u is ripe for conquest! I beg you to send Prince Kuang into the field once more." But Prince Kuang said to the king, "This Wu Tzu-hsü's

father and elder brother were both put to death by Ch'u. He en-
courages Your Majesty to attack Ch'u only because he wishes to
avenge their deaths. An attack on Ch'u is not at all certain to end in
conquest!"

Wu Tzu-hsü realized that Prince Kuang had ambitions within the
state—that he hoped to kill the king and set himself up as ruler—
and that it was useless to talk to him about campaigns abroad. He
therefore recommended Chuan Chu to Prince Kuang, while he himself, along with Sheng, the son of Crown Prince Chien, retired to a
life of farming in the countryside.[2]

Five years later, King P'ing died. Earlier, the woman of Ch'in
whom King P'ing had taken away from his son, Crown Prince Chien,
had given birth to a son named Chen. When King P'ing died, Chen
was eventually set up as his successor and is known as King Chao.
King Liao of Wu took advantage of the funeral in Ch'u to dispatch
two princes to lead troops in a surprise attack against Ch'u. Ch'u
called out its own troops to cut off the Wu army from the rear and
prevent it from returning. With the state of Wu now empty of
troops, Prince Kuang ordered Chuan Chu to surprise and assassinate
King Liao, after which he took the throne himself. He is known as
King Ho-lü.

Ho-lü, having realized his ambitions and gained the throne, summoned Wu Tzu-hsü and made him his foreign envoy, consulting with
him on matters of state policy. Ch'u meanwhile put to death its high
ministers Hsi Yüan and Po Chou-li. Po Chou-li's grandson Po P'i
escaped and fled to Wu, where in time he was granted high station.
The two princes whom King Liao had sent to lead the troops in an
attack on Ch'u first found their avenue of return cut off, and then
received word that Ho-lü had murdered his sovereign, King Liao,
and set himself up in his place. In the end they surrendered, along
with their troops, to Ch'u, which enfeoffed them in the region of Shu.

In the third year of his reign, Ho-lü called out his forces and,
with Wu Tzu-hsü and Po P'i, attacked Ch'u, seizing the region of
Shu and eventually taking prisoner the two Wu generals who had
earlier gone over to the enemy. The king wished to push on to Ying,

----

[2] For a fuller account of Chuan Chu, see p. 46.

the Ch'u capital, but General Sun Wu said, "The people are exhausted. The time has not yet come—let us wait a bit." Accordingly, they returned.

In the fourth year, Wu attacked Ch'u and seized the regions of Liu and Ch'ien. In the fifth year, it attacked the state of Yüeh and inflicted a defeat. In the sixth year, King Chao of Ch'u sent Prince Nang-wa to lead the troops in an attack on Wu. Wu dispatched Wu Tzu-hsü to meet and repulse the attack. He inflicted a major defeat on the Ch'u army at Yü-chang and seized Chü-ch'ao from Ch'u.

In the ninth year, King Ho-lü of Wu said to Wu Tzu-hsü and Sun Wu, "Earlier you told me that it was too soon to try to march on Ying. What do you say to that idea now?"

The two men replied, "The Ch'u general Nang-wa is greedy and the states of T'ang and Ts'ai are both enraged at him. If Your Majesty is determined to launch a major attack, you must secure the help of T'ang and Ts'ai. Then there will be some hope of success."

Ho-lü followed their advice and, calling out all his troops, joined T'ang and Ts'ai in an attack on Ch'u, the attackers drawing up on one side of the Han River, the Ch'u forces on the other. The king of Wu's younger brother, Fu-kai, led his troops and asked to be allowed to join in, but the king would not hear of it. In the end, he took the five thousand men under his command and made an attack on the Ch'u general Nang-wa, who fled in defeat to the state of Cheng. The Wu armies, pressing their advantage, moved forward and, after five battles, reached the city of Ying. On the day *chi-mao,* King Chao of Ch'u fled from the capital; the following day, *keng-ch'en,* the king of Wu entered it.[3]

When King Chao left the capital, he sought refuge in the marsh of Yün-meng but, being attacked by bandits there, he hurried on to the region of Yün. Huai, the younger brother of the lord of Yün, said, "King P'ing murdered our father, so it will surely be all right if we murder his son, will it not?" The lord of Yün, fearful that his younger brother would in fact kill the king, fled with the king to Sui. The Wu troops surrounded Sui and said to its inhabitants, "All the states along the Han River that belonged to the heirs of the Chou

---

[3] On the designations for the days, see p. 133, note 13.

have been wiped out by Ch'u!"[4] The men of Sui wantéd to kill the king, but Prince Ch'i, a member of the Ch'u royal family, concealed the king and prepared to pass himself off in his place, whatever might ensue. The men of Sui divined to see if they should hand the king over to Wu but, receiving an unfavorable answer, they conveyed their apologies to Wu and declined to hand over the king.

Earlier, Wu Tzu-hsü had been friendly with one Shen Pao-hsü. When Wu Tzu-hsü fled from the state of Ch'u, he said to Shen Pao-hsü, "I am determined to destroy Ch'u!" "And I am determined to preserve it!" replied Shen Pao-hsü. Later, when the Wu forces entered Ying, Wu Tzu-hsü searched for King Chao. Failing to find him, he proceeded to dig up the grave of King P'ing of Ch'u, expose the corpse, and inflict three hundred lashes upon it. Only then would he let the matter rest. Shen Pao-hsü, who had escaped to the mountains, sent word to Wu Tzu-hsü, "How harshly you avenge the wrongs of the past! I have heard that men, if their numbers are sufficient, may win out against Heaven, but that Heaven, once it has determined to do so, is likewise capable of destroying men. You were once a minister to King P'ing, facing north in the manner of a subject and serving him in person. Yet now you go so far as to inflict punishment upon a dead man! Do you suppose there is no limit to what Heaven will countenance?"

Wu Tzu-hsü replied, "My apologies to Shen Pao-hsü. Tell him that the day draws to a close and my journey is a long one. Therefore I stumble on as best I can and resort to any crooked means to gain my end."[5]

With this, Shen Pao-hsü hastened to the state of Ch'in to spread news of Ch'u's peril and beg help from Ch'in. Ch'in refused to grant his petition, but Shen Pao-hsü stood in the Ch'in court lamenting for seven days and seven nights, never once ceasing his cries, until Duke

---

[4] The tiny state of Sui, like T'ang, Ts'ai, and Wu itself, had been founded by descendants of the Chou royal house. Ch'u, a "barbarian" or non-Chou state, was threatening, or had already overthrown, these Chou lineage states in the south. The men of Wu are attempting to arouse the resentment of the men of Sui by reminding them of this fact.

[5] That is, Wu Tzu-hsü, fearful that he may die before he can seize the living king and carry out his vengeance in proper manner, resorts to the symbolic punishment of his dead predecessor. For the importance of such symbolic vengeance, see p. 50.

Ai of Ch'in took pity on him. "Though Ch'u may be unprincipled," he said, "if it has ministers like this one, how can it help but survive!" Then he dispatched five hundred war chariots to assist Ch'u in attacking the Wu forces. In the sixth month they inflicted a defeat on the Wu armies at Chi.

Meantime, while King Ho-lü continued to remain abroad in Ch'u to search for King Chao, his younger brother, Fu-kai, returned to Wu in secret and set himself up as king. When King Ho-lü received word of this, he abandoned Ch'u and went home to attack his brother Fu-kai. Fu-kai fled in defeat and in time made his way to Ch'u. King Chao of Ch'u, seeing that Wu was torn by internal strife, returned to his capital at Ying. He enfeoffed Fu-kai in T'ang-ch'i, making him lord of T'ang-ch'i. Ch'u fought once more with the Wu forces, inflicting a defeat, whereupon the king of Wu returned to his capital.

Two years later Ho-lü sent his son, Crown Prince Fu-ch'a, to lead the forces and attack Ch'u, where he seized control of P'an. Ch'u, fearful that Wu would invade in large numbers again, abandoned Ying and moved its capital to Jo.

At this time Wu, employing strategies suggested by Wu Tzu-hsü and Sun Wu, crushed the powerful state of Ch'u in the west, filled Ch'i and Chin to the north of it with awe, and in the south forced the people of Yüeh to submit. Four years later Confucius became prime minister of Lu.[6]

Four years after this, Wu attacked Yüeh. King Kou-chien of Yüeh came out to meet the attack, inflicted a defeat on the Wu army at Ku-su, and wounded King Ho-lü in the finger. The army was driven back and Ho-lü, ill from his wound, lay on the point of death. He said to Crown Prince Fu-ch'a, "Will you forget that Kou-chien killed your father?" to which Fu-ch'a replied, "I would not dare forget!" That evening Ho-lü died. Fu-ch'a, succeeding him as king of Wu, appointed Po P'i to be his chief minister and drilled his troops in archery.

---

[6] Confucius' brief term as prime minster of Lu, of doubtful historicity, was supposed to have taken place in 500 B.C. It is one of several key events which Ssu-ma Ch'ien uses in his narratives on the various feudal states as markers by which the reader may orient himself in time and relate local events to the overall chronology of China.

Two years later he attacked Yüeh and inflicted a defeat at Fu-chiao. King Kou-chien of Yüeh took his remaining soldiers, five thousand men, and encamped with them on top of K'uai-chi. He sent his High Official Chung with generous gifts to give to Wu's chief minister, Po P'i, and beg for peace, offering to surrender sovereignty of his state and declare his vassalage to Wu. The king of Wu was on the point of accepting the offer when Wu Tzu-hsü advised against it, saying, "The king of Yüeh is the kind of man who is willing to endure great shame and hardship. If you do not destroy him now, you will be sure to regret it later!" The king of Wu, however, ignored this advice and instead followed the recommendation of his chief minister Po P'i and made peace with Yüeh.

Five years later, word came to the king of Wu that Duke Ching of Ch'i had died and that his chief ministers were vying with one another to win favor with the new ruler, who was still a boy. He thereupon called out his armies and prepared to march north and attack Ch'i. Wu Tzu-hsü admonished him, saying, "Kou-chien eats the plainest food, consoles the families of the dead, and inquires after the ailing— it would seem that he has some task in store for his people. As long as this man continues to live, he will always be a threat to Wu! Yüeh is to Wu like a sickness in the belly or the heart of a man! Yet now Your Majesty does not first dispose of Yüeh, but concentrates instead upon Ch'i—is this not a mistake?"

The king of Wu would not listen but attacked Ch'i and inflicted a major defeat on the Ch'i army at Ai-ling. Then, having overawed the rulers of the neighboring states of Tsou and Lu with his might, he returned, and from this time on grew increasingly deaf to Wu Tzu-hsü's suggestions on policy.

Four years later, the king of Wu prepared to march north and attack Ch'i again. King Kou-chien of Yüeh, adopting a scheme recommended by Tzu-kung, led out his forces and went to assist Wu, meanwhile sending lavish gifts to the Wu chief minister Po P'i. Po P'i had already received bribes from Yüeh a number of times in the past and, favoring and trusting Yüeh implicitly, he day and night spoke on its behalf to the king of Wu, who in turn trusted Po P'i and followed his suggestions. Wu Tzu-hsü warned him, saying, "Yüeh is a sickness in the heart and belly! Now you put faith in its groundless words, its deceits and hypocrisies, and are greedy to acquire Ch'i. But even if you should conquer Ch'i, it would be to you like a stony field, something wholly without use! Moreover, does not the Announcement of P'an-keng say, 'If there are men who are perverse, insubordinate, and lacking in respect, I will cut off their noses, kill them, and wipe them out! I will not let their young ones live, I will not let them shift their seed to this new city!'[7] It was in this way that the Shang rose to glory. I beg Your Majesty to leave Ch'i alone and first dispose of Yüeh. If not, you will regret it later, and then it will be too late!"

The king of Wu refused to listen, but sent Wu Tzu-hsü as an envoy to Ch'i. When he was about to leave, Tzu-hsü said to his son, "I have again and again remonstrated with the king, but he will not heed me, and now I foresee only defeat for Wu. There is no use in your perishing along with it!" He thereupon took his son and entrusted him to Pao Mu of Ch'i before returning to Wu and reporting on his mission.

The chief minister Po P'i, having earlier had a falling out with Wu Tzu-hsü, took this opportunity to slander him, saying, "Wu Tzu-hsü is the kind of man who is stubborn and violent, showing little mercy for others, full of suspicion and malice. His hatred and resentment will, I fear, bring on some terrible disaster! Earlier, when Your Majesty wished to attack Ch'i, he insisted that it would not do, yet you carried out the attack and won great success. Ashamed that his advice and counsel were not heeded, he reacted with hatred instead of joy. Now you plan once more to attack Ch'i and Wu Tzu-hsü bends every effort to speak out against it, trying to upset and destroy the whole undertaking, only hoping that Wu will somehow be defeated so that his own advice will be vindicated. Your Majesty is preparing to go in person, leading every man in the nation who is capable of bearing arms, to carry out the attack on Ch'i. But Wu Tzu-hsü, since his admonitions are not heeded, will find some way to drop out, sending his apologies, feigning illness, and not joining in. Your Majesty must

[7] *P'an-keng* Pt. 2, a section of the *Book of Documents* which records the words of the Shang ruler P'an-keng to his people before and after moving to a new capital.

not fail to take precautions—disaster might easily arise from such a situation! What is more, I have sent men to spy on him and they report that, when he went as envoy to Ch'i, he entrusted his son to the Pao family of Ch'i. Now when a minister is unable to get what he wants within the state, he often looks for help from the feudal lords abroad. He regarded himself as chief consultant to the former king and now, when his advice is no longer heeded, he is in a constant fret of anger and resentment. I beg Your Majesty to deal with him as soon as possible!"

"Even if you had not spoken, I was beginning to grow suspicious of him!" said the king of Wu. He then dispatched a messenger to present Wu Tzu-hsü with the sword named Shu-lü, saying, "You will die with this."

Wu Tzu-hsü looked up to heaven and sighed, saying, "Ah, it is that slanderous minister Po P'i who is making trouble, and the king instead condemns *me* to death! I made your father a leader among the feudal lords, and before you had been designated heir, when the other princes were struggling to gain the throne, I risked my life battling for you with the former king, and even then you almost did not succeed in winning the throne. And once you had become ruler, you wanted to divide the state of Wu and give me part of it but, far from accepting, I said that it was more than I had any right to hope for. Yet now you heed the words of a sycophant and because of them inflict death upon a worthy man!" [8]

Then he said to his retainers, "You must plant my grave mound with catalpa trees—the wood will come in handy for making coffins. Pluck out my eyes and hang them over the eastern gate of Wu, so I may watch when the Yüeh invaders come to wipe out the state of Wu!" Then he cut his throat and died.

When the king of Wu heard of his dying words, he was filled with anger and proceeded to take Wu Tzu-hsü's corpse, stuff it into a leather wine sack, and set it adrift in the Yangtze River. The people of Wu, filled with pity, set up a shrine to Wu Tzu-hsü on the river bank, and thus the place came to be called the Hill of Hsü.

---

[8] Throughout this speech, in which Wu Tzu-hsü addresses the king as though he were present, he uses a familiar form of the pronoun "you" to show his contempt for the king.

After the king of Wu had put Wu Tzu-hsü to death, he carried out his attack on Ch'i. The Pao clan of Ch'i murdered their sovereign, Duke Tao, and set up Yang Sheng in his place. The king of Wu intended to punish the usurper but, failing to gain victory, he withdrew. Two years later the king of Wu summoned the rulers of Lu and Wey to a meeting with him at T'ao-kao. The following year he went a step farther by proceeding north and calling a great meeting of the other feudal lords at Yellow Lake, claiming that he was defending the authority of the royal house of Chou.[9] Meanwhile King Kou-chien of Yüeh made a surprise attack on Wu, killing the Wu crown prince and defeating the Wu armies. The king of Wu, hearing of this, returned home and sent envoys with generous gifts to buy peace with Yüeh.

Nine years later King Kou-chien of Yüeh finally destroyed Wu and killed King Fu-ch'a. He also put to death the chief minister Po P'i because he had been disloyal to his sovereign, accepting lavish bribes from abroad and allying himself with the king of Yüeh.

Sheng, the son of the former heir apparent of Ch'u, Crown Prince Chien, with whom Wu Tzu-hsü had originally fled from Ch'u, had remained in Wu. In the time of King Fu-ch'a of Wu, King Hui of Ch'u wanted to invite Sheng to return home to Ch'u, but the lord of She advised against it, saying, "Sheng sets great store by bravery and is secretly casting about for men who will be willing to die in his service. It would almost appear that he is up to something!" King Hui ignored the advice, however, and eventually summoned Sheng to come home and sent him to reside in Yen, a city on the Ch'u border, where he was given the title of lord of Po. Three years after he returned to Ch'u, Wu Tzu-hsü was put to death by the ruler of Wu.

After Sheng returned to Ch'u, because he hated the state of Cheng for having killed his father, he secretly gathered together a band of followers who would be willing to die for him, hoping to carry out vengeance against Cheng. Five years after returning to Ch'u he asked permission to attack Cheng. The Ch'u premier Tzu-hsi granted the

---

[9] Following the reading in the parallel passage in *Shih chi* 31. The king of Wu was attempting to set himself up as a *pa,* a dictator or hegemon who exerted authority over the other feudal lords, but pretended to be merely reasserting the sovereignty of the Chou king.

request but, before the troops had been dispatched, the state of Chin attacked Cheng. Cheng asked Ch'u to come to its aid, and Ch'u sent Tzu-hsi to assist it. He concluded an oath of alliance and returned home. Sheng, enraged, declared, "It is not Cheng who is my enemy— it is Tzu-hsi!" and set about sharpening his sword. When someone asked what he was doing, he replied, "I am preparing to kill Tzu-hsi!" On hearing of this, Tzu-hsi laughed and said, "Sheng is a mere infant—what can he do?"

Four years later Sheng, the lord of Po, and Shih Ch'i surprised and killed Premier Tzu-hsi and Marshal Tzu-ch'i at court. "We must not fail to kill the king as well!" said Shih Ch'i, and they accordingly forced the king to go with them to the Upper Treasury. Ch'ü Ku, a retainer of Shih Ch'i,[10] put King Hui on his back and fled with him to the palace of Lady Chao. Meanwhile the lord of She, hearing that the lord of Po had started a revolt, led the men of his territory in an attack. The lord of Po and his followers were defeated and he fled into the mountains, where he committed suicide. Shih Ch'i, however, was captured alive. Questioned as to the whereabouts of the body of the lord of Po, he would not speak. When preparations were made to boil him alive, he said, "If the affair succeeds, I become a high offi- cial; if it fails, I get boiled alive—that's the kind of business it is!" To the end he refused to tell them where the corpse was, and so they boiled him alive. Then they searched until they found King Hui and restored him to his throne.

The Grand Historian remarks: How terrible a thing is the poison of hatred in men! If a ruler must not arouse hatred among his min- isters and subjects, how much more important that he not do so among his equals! If Wu Tzu-hsü had joined his father She and died with him, he would have been of no more significance than a mere ant. But he set aside a small righteousness in order to wipe out a great shame, and his name has been handed down to later ages. How moving! At that time Wu Tzu-hsü suffered hardship by the riverside and begged for his food along the road, but in his determination he

---

[10] According to the more plausible reading in *Shih chi* 40, he was a retainer of King Hui.

did not for a moment forget Ying. He bore all secretly and silently, and in the end achieved merit and fame. Who but a man of burning intention could have accomplished such a deed?

If the lord of Po had not tried to set himself up as ruler, his deeds and schemes would hardly be important enough to mention.[11]

---

[11] According to the account in *Shih chi* 40, the lord of Po declared himself king of Ch'u and held the title for something over a month before being defeated by his enemies.

Shih chi 82: The Biography of T'ien Tan

When King Min had already lost his capital at Lin-tzu and had fled to Chü, T'ien Tan alone, leading the men of Chi-mo, was able to smash the invaders and send them running, and in the end to save Ch'i's altars of the soil and grain. Thus I made The Biography of T'ien Tan.

T'ien Tan was a member of one of the remoter branches of the great T'ien family of Ch'i. In the reign of King Min [323–284 B.C.] he served as a market place official in Lin-tzu, the Ch'i capital, but failed to attract any special notice.

When the state of Yen dispatched Yüeh Yi to attack and smash the Ch'i forces, King Min of Ch'i fled from the capital. In time he established himself at the stronghold in Chü, while the Yen armies embarked upon a lengthy campaign to bring all of Ch'i under their control. T'ien Tan had fled to An-p'ing, ordering all the members of his clan to make certain to cut off the ends of their carriage axles and cap them with iron. Later the Yen forces attacked An-p'ing and the city capitulated. The Ch'i people fled but, as they struggled to push ahead of one another on the road, the axle heads of the carriages snapped off, the carriages broke down, and the occupants were as a result taken prisoner by the Yen forces. Only the men of T'ien Tan's clan, because of the iron caps on their axle heads, were able to escape, fleeing east to refuge in the city of Chi-mo.

In time Yen forced almost all the cities of Ch'i to surrender, only Chü and Chi-mo holding out. When the Yen army learned that the king of Ch'i was in Chü, it massed all its resources for an assault, but Nao Ch'ih, having murdered King Min in Chü, proceeded to strengthen the defenses of the city and hold off the Yen army. Several years passed but the city did not capitulate, whereupon the Yen commander withdrew and led his troops east to lay siege to Chi-mo. The leaders of Chi-mo went out to do battle but were defeated and killed. The men left within the city then recommended T'ien Tan, saying, "At the battle of An-p'ing, the members of T'ien Tan's clan were able to escape because of the iron caps on their axles. He must be well versed in military matters!" They made him their general with the task of blocking the Yen advance at Chi-mo.

Some time later King Chao of Yen died and was succeeded by King Hui [r. 278–272], who was on bad terms with the Yen general Yüeh Yi. T'ien Tan, hearing of this, set about sowing dissension, spreading word to this effect: The king of Ch'i is dead and only two of his cities have failed to surrender. But Yüeh Yi, fearful that he may be put to death, does not dare to return home. He pretends that his purpose is to continue the attack on Ch'i, but in truth he hopes to drag out the campaign and eventually face south and declare himself king of Ch'i. He is uncertain whether the men of Ch'i will support him, however, and so for the time being he has eased the pressure on Chi-mo and is waiting to see how things develop. The only fear of the people of Ch'i at this point is that some other general will be sent in his place who will destroy Chi-mo.

The king of Yen, believing this account, ordered Ch'i Chieh to replace Yüeh Yi. Yüeh Yi thereupon went and offered his services to the state of Chao. These events caused much dissatisfaction among the officers and men of the Yen army.

Meanwhile, T'ien Tan gave orders to the people within the city that at each meal they were to offer sacrifices to their ancestors in their courtyards. Soon all the birds of the air were hovering over the city and swooping down to eat the food. When the soldiers of the Yen army began to wonder at this, T'ien Tan spread the rumor that it was the gods coming down to give instruction to the men of Chi-mo. Then he passed word among the people of the city, saying, "Surely some divine being will appear to be our commander!"

There was a soldier of the rank and file who shouted, "Maybe I can be commander!" and then turned about and tried to run away. But T'ien Tan dashed after the man and, dragging him back, made him take the seat of honor facing east and treated him as a leader. "I was only fooling you," the soldier protested; "I have no ability at all!"

But T'ien Tan replied, "Say no more!" So the man was made commander, and whenever orders were issued, they were always put out in the name of this so-called Divine Commander.

T'ien Tan then spread about word to this effect: My only fear is that the Yen forces will punish the Ch'i soldiers who have surrendered to them by cutting off their noses and forcing them to march in the vanguard when they attack us, for if they do so, Chi-mo will surely be defeated! The men of Yen, hearing this, did precisely what he had said, and when the men in the city saw that all the Ch'i soldiers who had surrendered to the enemy had had their noses cut off, they were enraged and fought all the harder to defend the city, only fearful that they themselves might be taken prisoner.

Once again T'ien Tan began working his deceptions by remarking, "I am terrified that the men of Yen may dig up the graves of our ancestors outside the city wall and inflict some outrage upon them. My heart grows cold at the thought!" The Yen army accordingly dug up all the grave mounds and burned the corpses. The men of Chi-mo, watching far off from the city walls, all began to weep and could scarcely wait to go out and fight, their hatred for the enemy having at once increased tenfold.

T'ien Tan, knowing now that his officers and men were ready for action, took up trowel and mortarboard and personally joined them in their work on the fortifications, at the same time assigning his own womenfolk to tasks among the ranks. Then he distributed to his soldiers what food and drink was still left. He ordered all the armed men into hiding and sent the old men, boys, and women to mount the walls. He dispatched a messenger with a promise of surrender to the Yen army, which, on receipt of the news, broke into shouts of rejoicing. He also collected a thousand taels of gold from among the people and had the rich men of Chi-mo send it as a gift to the Yen general, saying, "When Chi-mo surrenders, we hope that our families and womenfolk will not be robbed or taken prisoner, but will be assured of safety." The Yen general, greatly pleased, gave his word. As a result of these moves, the Yen army became increasingly lax in its guard.

T'ien Tan then rounded up a thousand or more oxen from within the city and had them fitted with coverings of red silk on which dragon shapes had been painted in five colors. He had knives tied to their horns and bundles of grease-soaked reeds to their tails, and then, setting fire to their tails, had them driven out into the night through some twenty or thirty openings which had been tunneled in the city wall. Five thousand of the best soldiers poured out after them. The oxen, maddened by the fires that burned their tails, rushed into the Yen encampment which, it being night, was filled with terror. The oxtail torches burned with a dazzling glare, and wherever the Yen soldiers looked, they saw nothing but dragon shapes. All who stood within the path of the oxen were wounded or killed. The five thousand soldiers, gags in their mouths so they would make no noise, moved forward to attack, while from within the city came an accompaniment of drumming and clamor, the old men and boys all beating on bronze vessels to make a noise until the sound of it shook heaven and earth. The Yen army, taken completely by surprise, fell back in defeat, and the men of Ch'i were able to capture and put to death its commander, Ch'i Chieh.

The Yen forces fled in disorder, the men of Ch'i pursuing those who tried to escape. The cities which the Yen army passed in its rout all turned against Yen and came over to the side of T'ien Tan, whose troops grew more numerous each day as he pressed his advantage. Yen's forces meanwhile day by day melted away in defeat until they at last reached the river that marked the boundary between Ch'i and Yen. By this time, all of Ch'i's seventy or more cities had been restored to Ch'i rule and a party was sent to Chü to greet the new ruler, King Hsiang, and escort him to the capital at Lin-tzu, where he assumed direction of the government. King Hsiang enfeoffed T'ien Tan with the title of lord of An-p'ing.

The Grand Historian remarks: In the use of arms, there are regular engagements and there are surprise victories. He who is good at warfare will come forward with an inexhaustible supply of surprise moves, so that surprises and regular maneuvers follow one another in unbroken succession like a ring that has no beginning or end. First to sit there like a shy maiden till the enemy comes forcing open the door, then to rush out like a rabbit on the loose when the enemy is no longer able to stop you—this might describe T'ien Tan and his tactics, might it not?

Early in the war, when Nao Ch'ih killed King Min, the people of Chü searched for King Min's son, Fa-chang, and found him in the home of the Grand Historian Chiao, working as a hired man and watering the garden. Earlier, Chiao's daughter, feeling sorry for him, had treated him with kindness and, after he had secretly told her who he was, they became lovers. Still later, when the people of Chü joined in setting up Fa-chang as King Hsiang of Ch'i and holding Chü against the Yen attacks, the daughter of the Grand Historian became his consort and is known as the Sovereign Queen.[1]

When the Yen forces first invaded Ch'i, they heard reports that Wang Chu of the city of Hua was a man of great worth. An order was accordingly issued to the army not to approach within a thirty-li radius of Hua out of respect for Wang Chu. Later the Yen leader sent a man to say to Wang Chu, "The people of Ch'i have often spoken of your lofty devotion to righteousness. I would like to make you a general and enfeoff you with ten thousand households." Wang Chu steadfastly refused, whereupon Yen sent word, "If you do not accept, I will lead my entire army of three divisions and massacre the inhabitants of Hua!"

To this Wang Chu replied, "A loyal subject does not serve two lords, a chaste wife does not take to herself two husbands. The king of Ch'i would not heed my reprimands and so I retired to the countryside and turned to the work of the fields. Now my country has been overwhelmed and destroyed and I have not been able to save it. If, on top of this, I should give in to the threat of arms and become a general for you, that would be to aid the tyrant Chieh in working his violence. I would rather be boiled in a pot than live with such unrighteousness!" With this he tied his head to the limb of a tree and flung himself about until he broke his own neck and died.

When the officials of Ch'i who had fled into hiding heard of this,

---

[1] In *Shih chi* 46 Ssu-ma Ch'ien mentions that her father, the Grand Historian, disowned her on the grounds that "any girl who picks out her own husband without going through a matchmaker is no daughter of mine!"

they said, "Wang Chu was no more than a coarse-robed commoner, and yet out of a sense of righteousness he refused to face north and serve the state of Yen. How much more so should we, then, who hold office and receive government stipend!" So they banded together and made their way to Chü, where they sought out the son of the former ruler and set him up as King Hsiang.

Shih chi 85: The Biography of Lü Pu-wei

He strengthened family ties between Tzu-ch'u and his royal kin and set the counselors of the feudal lords to vying with one another, seeing who could lend most eloquent support to his bid for power in Ch'in. Thus I made The Biography of Lü Pu-wei.

Lü Pu-wei was a great merchant of Yang-ti who, by traveling here and there, buying cheap and selling dear, had accumulated a fortune amounting to thousands in gold.

In the fortieth year of the reign of King Chao of Ch'in [267 B.C.] the crown prince died, and two years later, in the forty-second year of his reign, the king designated his second son, Lord An-kuo, as crown prince. Lord An-kuo had over twenty sons. He had a concubine of whom he was extremely fond and whom he had designated as his consort with the title of Lady Hua-yang, but she had borne him no sons. By another concubine, of the Hsia family, who no longer enjoyed his favor he had a son named Tzu-ch'u, one of the younger among his twenty or more sons. Tzu-ch'u had been sent by the state of Ch'in to be a hostage at the court of Chao,[1] and since, in spite of this, Ch'in had several times invaded Chao, the Chao court accordingly treated Tzu-ch'u with scant respect. Being merely a grandson of the king of Ch'in and the son of a concubine, and having been sent as hostage to one of the other feudal states, Tzu-ch'u was poorly provided with carriages and other equipment and had to live in straitened circumstances, unable to do as he pleased. Lü Pu-wei, visiting Han-tan, the capital of Chao, on business, saw him and was moved to pity. "Here is a rare piece of goods to put in my warehouse!" he exclaimed.

[1] Younger sons of rulers were often sent to reside at the courts of allied states where they acted as hostages to encourage the continuance of peaceful relations between the states.

He then went and called on Tzu-ch'u, remarking, "I know how to enlarge your gate for you!"

Tzu-ch'u laughed and said, "You'd better enlarge your own gate before you worry about mine!"

"You don't understand," said Lü Pu-wei. "The enlarging of my gate *depends* on the enlarging of yours!"

Tzu-ch'u, guessing what was in his mind, led him to a seat in an inner room and the two were soon deep in conversation. "The king of Ch'in is old and Lord An-kuo has been designated crown prince," Lü Pu-wei said. "I am told that Lord An-kuo is very much in love with Lady Hua-yang, and since she has no son of her own, it will be up to her alone to decide which son shall be appointed as the rightful heir. Now you have twenty or more brothers, and from the point of view of age, you are about halfway down the line. You enjoy no particular favor and have been a hostage at the court of one of the other feudal lords for a long time. If your grandfather, the old king, should pass away and Lord An-kuo become king, I'm afraid you would have little chance of competing for the position of crown prince with your elder brothers or with your other brothers who are there in person morning and evening to wait upon your father."

"True," said Tzu-ch'u. "But what can I do about it?"

Lü Pu-wei said, "You are poor and living in a foreign land. You have nothing to use as gifts to present to the members of your family or to attract a band of followers about you. I too am poor, but with your permission I would like to take a thousand measures of gold and travel west on your behalf to Ch'in, where I will wait upon Lord An-kuo and Lady Hua-yang and see to it that you are made the rightful heir."

Tzu-ch'u bowed his head and said, "If indeed it should turn out as you say, when the day comes I hope you will allow me to divide the state of Ch'in and share it with you!"

Lü Pu-wei accordingly took five hundred measures of gold and presented it to Tzu-ch'u to be used as expense money in attracting a band of followers, and with another five hundred he purchased various rare objects, trinkets, and toys, which he took with him west on a trip to Ch'in. There he sought an interview with the elder sister of Lady

Hua-yang and asked that the gifts he had brought be presented to Lady Hua-yang. He took the opportunity to mention how virtuous and wise Tzu-ch'u was, how he had friends among the followers of the various feudal lords all over the world, how he was constantly heard to exclaim, "Her Ladyship is as precious as Heaven itself to me!", and how he wept day and night with longing for his father, the crown prince, and Lady Hua-yang. Lady Hua-yang was very pleased with this message.

Lü Pu-wei then persuaded the elder sister to speak to Lady Hua-yang to this effect: "They say that one who has only beauty to offer a man will find, as beauty fades, that his love grows cold. Now you wait upon the crown prince but, though he loves you dearly, you have no son. Before it is too late, should you not take this opportunity to choose one of his sons whom you deem worthy and befriend him, seeing to it that he is elevated to the position of rightful heir and treating him as your own son? Then, as long as your husband lives, you will enjoy honor; and when his hundred years of life are ended and the one whom you call son becomes king, you need never fear any loss of position. This is what they call 'speaking one word that brings ten thousand years of gain.' But if now in blossom time you do not make certain that your roots are firm, then when beauty has faded and love grown cold, though you might hope for a chance to 'speak one word,' how could you gain a hearing? Now Tzu-ch'u is a worthy man and, being far down the line, knows that he cannot hope to become heir by the normal order of succession. In addition, his mother enjoys no favor, and so he offers all his devotion to you. If you were truly willing to use this moment to pluck him from the line of succession and make him the heir, then to the end of your days you would enjoy favor in the state of Ch'in!"

Lady Hua-yang, convinced of the truth of this argument, waited until her husband, the crown prince, was at leisure and then casually mentioned that Tzu-ch'u, who had been sent as hostage to Chao, was a man of outstanding worth and that everyone coming from abroad praised him highly. Then, with tears in her eyes, she said, "I have been fortunate enough to be assigned to your women's quarters, but not so fortunate as to bear a son. I beg you to give me Tzu-ch'u for a son and to set him up as the rightful heir so that I may have someone to entrust my fate to!"

Lord An-kuo gave his consent and had a jade tally engraved to this effect which he divided with Lady Hua-yang, promising that he would make Tzu-ch'u his rightful heir.[2] Then Lord An-kuo and Lady Hua-yang sent rich gifts to Tzu-ch'u and asked Lü Pu-wei to act as his tutor. As a result, Tzu-ch'u became increasingly renowned among the feudal lords.

Lü Pu-wei had selected from among the courtesans of Han-tan one of matchless beauty and great skill in dancing and had lived with her, and in time he learned that she was pregnant. Tzu-ch'u, joining Lü Pu-wei in a drinking bout, happened to catch sight of her and was pleased. Immediately he stood up, proposed a toast to Lü's long life, and asked if he might have her. Lü Pu-wei was enraged, but soon recalled that he had by now invested all of his family's wealth in Tzu-ch'u in hopes of fishing up some wonderful prize, and so in the end he presented the girl to him. She concealed the fact that she was pregnant, and when her time was up, she bore a son who was named Cheng. Tzu-ch'u eventually made her his consort.

In the fiftieth year of his reign King Chao of Ch'in sent Wang Ch'i to lay siege to Han-tan and, when the situation grew critical, the men of Chao wanted to kill Tzu-ch'u. Tzu-ch'u and Lü Pu-wei plotted together, however, and distributed six hundred catties of gold to the officers who were in charge of guarding them, and in this way managed to escape, make their way to the Ch'in army, and eventually return home. The men of Chao then proposed to kill Tzu-ch'u's wife and child, but because his wife was the daughter of a wealthy family of Chao, she was able to go into hiding; thus both mother and son escaped alive.

King Chao of Ch'in passed away in the fifty-sixth year of his reign. The crown prince, Lord An-kuo, succeeded him as king, Lady Hua-yang became queen, and Tzu-ch'u was made crown prince. The state of Chao obliged by sending Tzu-ch'u's wife and son Cheng to

[2] In such cases the tally was broken in two, the pieces to be held by the two parties to the agreement. Since Lord An-kuo was himself only crown prince, he could not at this time make public his decision.

their new home in Ch'in. The king of Ch'in passed away after one
year of rule and was given the posthumous title of King Hsiao-wen.
The crown prince Tzu-ch'u succeeded him and is known as King
Chuang-hsiang. Queen Hua-yang, whom King Chuang-hsiang had
come to treat as a mother, was given the title of Queen Dowager Hua-
yang, and his real mother, whose family name was Hsia, was called
Queen Dowager Hsia.

In the first year of his reign King Chuang-hsiang made Lü Pu-wei
his prime minister and enfeoffed him as marquis of Wen-hsin with
the revenue from one hundred thousand households in Lo-yang in
Ho-nan.

King Chuang-hsiang passed away after three years on the throne
and the crown prince Cheng became king. He honored Lü Pu-wei
with the position of premier and as a mark of respect addressed him
as Chung-fu or Uncle. The new king of Ch'in was still young and his
mother, the former concubine of Lü Pu-wei, who had now become
queen dowager, from time to time had sexual relations with Lü Pu-
wei in secret. Lü Pu-wei had some ten thousand male servants in his
household.

This was the period of Lord Hsin-ling of Wei, Lord Ch'un-shen
of Ch'u, Lord P'ing-yüan of Chao, and Lord Meng-ch'ang of Ch'i,
all men who were willing to humble themselves before others and who
delighted in gathering bands of followers about them, seeking in
this way to outdo one another. Lü Pu-wei felt that, since Ch'in was
a powerful state, it was disgraceful for it not to do likewise, and so
he too set about to attract gentlemen to his service with offers of
generous rewards and treatment, and in time gathered as many as
three thousand men who lived and ate at his expense. This was also
the period when there were many skilled debaters in the various
feudal states, men such as Hsün Ch'ing[3] who wrote books and
circulated them throughout the world. Lü Pu-wei accordingly ordered
each of his retainers to write down what he himself had learned, and
then collected and edited the results into a work comprising eight *lan*
or "surveys," six *lun* or "discussions," and twelve *chi* or "records,"

[3] The famous Confucian philosopher Hsün Tzu (fl. 250 B.C.), author of a
work in 32 sections.

totaling over two hundred thousand characters. It was intended to embrace all the affairs of Heaven, earth, the ten thousand things, yesterday, and today, and was entitled "The Spring and Autumn of Mr. Lü." [4] The text was posted on the market gate of Hsien-yang, the Ch'in capital, with a thousand pieces of gold suspended above it. An invitation to the wandering scholars and retainers of the various feudal lords informed them that the thousand in gold would be awarded to anyone who could add or subtract a single character from it.

The king of Ch'in, who was later to bear the title of First Emperor of the Ch'in,[5] in time grew to manhood, but his mother, the queen dowager, did not cease her wanton behavior. Lü Pu-wei began to fear that, if her conduct were ever brought to light, he himself would become involved in the scandal. He therefore searched about in secret until he found a man named Lao Ai who had an unusually large penis, and made him a servant in his household. Then, when an occasion arose, he had suggestive music performed and, instructing Lao Ai to stick his penis through the center of a wheel made of paulownia wood, had him walk about with it, making certain that the report of this reached the ears of the queen dowager so as to excite her interest. She received the report and, as had been expected, wanted to have the man smuggled into her quarters. Lü Pu-wei then presented Lao Ai, at the same time getting someone to pretend to accuse him of a crime for which the punishment was castration. Lü Pu-wei spoke to the queen dowager in private, pointing out that, if the man were subjected to a mock castration, he could then be taken into service in the queen's private apartments. The queen accordingly sent lavish gifts in secret to the official who was in charge of performing the castration, who then pretended to carry out the sentence, plucking out the man's beard and eyebrows and making him into a "eunuch." In this way he eventually came to wait on the queen, who carried on clandestine relations with him and grew to love him

---

[4] The work is still extant; see the translator's *Early Chinese Literature* (Columbia University Press, 1962), pp. 186–89.

[5] He assumed the title in 221 B.C., when he had completed his conquest of the other feudal states.

greatly. In time she became pregnant and, fearing discovery, pretended to conduct a divination that indicated that, in order to avoid a period of evil influences, she should move from the palace and take up residence in Yung. Lao Ai was constantly in attendance on her and received lavish gifts and awards. All decisions were made by Lao Ai, who was waited upon by an entourage of several thousand male servants. His followers numbered over a thousand, all men who flocked to him in hopes of attaining government office.

In the seventh year of the king's reign [240 B.C.] Queen Dowager Hsia, the mother of King Chuang-hsiang, passed away. Earlier Queen Dowager Hua-yang, the queen of King Hsiao-wen, had been buried with her husband, King Hsiao-wen, at Shou-ling, and Queen Dowager Hsia's son, King Chuang-hsiang, had been buried at Chih-yang. Accordingly, Queen Dowager Hsia was buried separately at a spot east of Tu where, in her words, "I may look eastward to my son and westward to my husband. And after a hundred years, a city of ten thousand households will surely grow up by my side."

In the ninth year of the king's reign someone reported that Lao Ai was not a real eunuch at all, but had constantly been engaging in secret misconduct with the queen dowager, and that she had borne him two sons, both of whom were being kept in hiding. "He and the queen dowager have agreed," said the report, "that, when the present king passes on, one of these sons shall succeed him."

The king thereupon referred the matter to his officials for investigation and all the facts were brought to light, including those that implicated the premier Lü Pu-wei. In the ninth month Lao Ai and his three sets of relatives were executed,[6] the two sons whom the queen dowager had borne him were put to death, and the residence of the queen was officially transferred to Yung. Lao Ai's followers were all deprived of their household goods and sent into exile in Shu.

The king of Ch'in wanted to put the premier Lü Pu-wei to death as well but, because he had won great distinction in the service of the former king, and because so many followers and men of eloquence came forward to speak in his behalf, the king could not bring himself to apply the death penalty. In the tenth month of the

---

[6] On the "three sets of relatives," see p. 138, note 20.

tenth year of his reign the king of Ch'in removed Lü Pu-wei from the office of premier.

Later Mao Chiao, a man of Ch'i, spoke to the king of Ch'in and persuaded him to send to Yung for his mother, the queen dowager, and allow her to return to residence in Hsien-yang. The king also ordered Lü Pu-wei, the marquis of Wen-hsin, to leave the capital and proceed to his fief in Ho-nan. A year or so later he learned that so many of the followers and envoys of the various feudal lords were traveling to Ho-nan to call on Lü Pu-wei that their carriages were never out of sight of each other on the road. Fearful that there might be some plot afoot, the king sent a letter to Lü Pu-wei saying, "What did you ever do for the state of Ch'in that Ch'in should enfeoff you in Ho-nan with the revenue from a hundred thousand households? What relation are you to the ruler of Ch'in that you should be addressed as 'Uncle'? Be so good as to take your family and retinue and move your residence to Shu!"

Lü Pu-wei judged that he would only have to suffer increasing insult and, fearing the death penalty,[7] he drank poison and died. With Lü Pu-wei and Lao Ai, the two men had been the butt of his anger, both dead, the king recalled Lao Ai's retainers who had been exiled to Shu. In the nineteenth year of his reign his mother, the queen dowager, passed away and was given the posthumous title of Empress Dowager. She was buried with her husband, King Chuang-hsiang, at Chih-yang.

The Grand Historian remarks: Lü Pu-wei and Lao Ai were both honored with fiefs, the former receiving the title of marquis of Wen-hsin [the latter that of marquis of Ch'ang-hsin].[8] When accusations were first made against Lao Ai, he received word of it. The king of Ch'in questioned those about him as to the truth of the charges but had not yet uncovered any definite evidence when he set off for Yung to perform the suburban sacrifice. Lao Ai, fearful that calamity was about to befall him, plotted with the members of his clique and,

---

[7] Because it would involve his family in the punishment.

[8] The words in brackets do not appear in the text but must be supplied to complete the sense.

using the queen dowager's seal of authority without her permission, called out troops and initiated a revolt in the Ch'i-nien Palace. The king dispatched officers to attack Lao Ai's forces and Lao Ai fled in defeat. He was pursued and cut down at Hao-chih, and eventually his whole clan was wiped out. This marked the beginning of Lü Pu-wei's fall from power. What Confucius said about the "man of fame" might well apply to this Master Lü, might it not? [9]

[9] Confucius, contrasting the true man of distinction with one who merely enjoys a good reputation, said, "The man of fame may be one who puts on the appearance of virtue but in practice acts quite differently" (*Analects* XII, 20).

Through Master Ts'ao's dagger Lu recovered its lands and Ch'i proved it could be trusted. Yü Jang did not consider it right to harbor treacherous intentions. Thus I made The Biographies of the Assassin-Retainers.

Ts'ao Mei

Ts'ao Mei was a native of Lu. Because of his daring and strength he was taken into service by Duke Chuang of Lu [r. 693–662], who had great admiration for physical might. Ts'ao Mei served as a general of Lu, engaging in battle with Ch'i, but he was three times defeated and forced to retreat. Duke Chuang, becoming apprehensive, handed over the city of Sui and the region around it in order to buy peace with Ch'i, but later he once more made Ts'ao Mei a general. Duke Huan of Ch'i consented to meet with the ruler of Lu at a place called K'o so that they might conclude the oath of agreement. When Duke Huan and Duke Chuang had finished swearing the oath at the top of the altar mound, Ts'ao Mei, brandishing a dagger, threatened Duke Huan of Ch'i. None of the duke's attendants dared to make a move, but merely asked, "What is it you want?"

"Ch'i is powerful and Lu is weak," said Ts'ao Mei. "You and your mighty state—how deeply have you penetrated into the territory of Lu! If the walls of the Lu capital were to collapse, they would come crashing down on the very borders of Ch'i! Perhaps, my lord, you would give this some thought!"

Duke Huan thereupon promised to return to Lu all the territory that Ch'i had seized in its incursions. When he had finished speaking, Ts'ao Mei threw down his dagger, descended from the altar mound, and faced north,[1] taking his place among the other officials.

---

[1] When conducting affairs of state the Chinese ruler faces south and his ministers face north. Ts'ao Mei is thus returning to his correct ritual position,

His face showed no sign of emotion and he spoke in his usual manner.

Duke Huan, enraged, wanted to repudiate the agreement, but his chief minister Kuan Chung said, "That will not do! In your greed for some petty gain with which to gratify yourself, you will alienate the trust of the other feudal lords and lose the good will of the world. It would be better to hand over the land." As a result, Duke Huan in the end returned to Lu all the territory which had been stripped from it by invasion, the territory which Ts'ao Mei had lost in his three battles.

Chuan Chu

One hundred and sixty-seven years later, in the state of Wu, there was the affair of Chuan Chu. Chuan Chu was a native of T'ang-yi in Wu. When Wu Tzu-hsü fled from Ch'u and came to Wu, he recognized that Chuan Chu was a man of ability. Wu Tzu-hsü had earlier had an audience with King Liao of Wu and had described to him the advantages of launching an attack on Ch'u. But Prince Kuang of Wu had said to the king, "The father and elder brother of this Wu Tzu-hsü were both put to death by the state of Ch'u. When he talks of an attack on Ch'u, it is simply that he wants the satisfaction of avenging his own private wrong. He has no time to think of the welfare of Wu!" The king of Wu accordingly put aside all thought of an attack. Wu Tzu-hsü knew that Prince Kuang was hoping to murder King Liao of Wu, and said to himself, "Since Kuang has ambitions here at home, it is useless to talk to him about undertakings abroad." He therefore recommended Chuan Chu to the service of Prince Kuang.

Kuang's father had been King Chu-fan of Wu. Chu-fan had three younger brothers, the first called Yü-chi, the second Yi-mei, and the third Chi-tzu Cha. Chu-fan knew that Chi-tzu Cha was a worthy man and so he did not designate his own son as crown prince but instead arranged that the throne should pass down to his younger brothers in succession, hoping that eventually the state would come into the hands of Chi-tzu Cha. When Chu-fan died, the succession accordingly

---

indicating that he has no desire to continue his insubordinate conduct now that he has exacted a promise from the duke.

passed to Yü-chi, and when Yü-chi died, it passed to Yi-mei. When Yi-mei died, it should have passed to Chi-tzu Cha, but Chi-tzu Cha withdrew from the state and declared himself unwilling to take the throne. The people of Wu thereupon set up Yi-mei's son Liao as king.

"If it were right for it to have passed from elder to younger brother," Prince Kuang said to himself, "then Chi-tzu ought to have been set up. And if it were intended for the son, then I was surely the rightful heir and should have become king!" He therefore secretly gathered about him men who he thought could assist him in plotting to gain the throne. When he had acquired the services of Chuan Chu, he treated him as a valuable retainer.

Nine years after this, King P'ing of Ch'u died. In the spring King Liao of Wu, hoping to take advantage of Ch'u's period of mourning, sent his two younger brothers, the princes Kai-yü and Chu-yung, to lead the troops and lay siege to the Ch'u city of Ch'ien. He also sent Chi-tzu Cha, who had been enfeoffed in Yen-ling, to the state of Chin to observe any shifts of alliance that might take place among the other feudal lords. Ch'u dispatched troops to cut off the avenue of retreat behind the Wu generals Kai-yü and Chu-yung so that the Wu troops could not return home.

At this point Prince Kuang said to Chuan Chu, "Here is an opportunity not to be missed! If we make no effort, what will we ever gain? Moreover, I am the rightful heir and should be given the throne. Even if Chi-tzu comes home, he will not try to take it away from me."

"It would be well to kill King Liao," said Chuan Chu. "His mother is old, his son still a boy, and his two younger brothers have led the troops in an attack on Ch'u, which has cut off their avenue of retreat. Now that Wu is embroiled in difficulties abroad and emptied of troops at home, with no outspoken ministers to stick like fish bones in the throat, there's no one who can do anything to stop us!"

Prince Kuang bowed his head and said, "I am in your hands."

In the fourth month, the day *chia-tzu,* Kuang, having concealed armed men in an underground room, set out wine and invited King Liao to his home. King Liao ordered his soldiers to form ranks stretching all the way from the palace to Kuang's house. On the left and right of each gateway and flight of stairs men were lined up in attendance, all of them supporters of King Liao, all of them bearing long knives. When the drinking had reached its height, Prince Kuang pretended that he had a pain in his leg and made his way to the underground room. Then he ordered Chuan Chu to place a dagger in the belly of a fish that had been roasted and offer the fish to the king. When Chuan Chu arrived in the king's presence, he ripped open the fish and stabbed the king with the dagger. The king fell dead on the spot. His attendants in turn killed Chuan Chu. While the king's men were milling about in confusion, Prince Kuang appeared with the soldiers who had been lying in wait and fell upon King Liao's followers, wiping them out to a man. Eventually Prince Kuang set himself up as king and is known as King Ho-lü. He enfeoffed Chuan Chu's son and made him a high-ranking minister.

Yü Jang

Some seventy years later there was the affair of Yü Jang in Chin. Yü Jang was a native of the state of Chin. He once served the Fan family, and later the Chung-hang family, but attracted no notice under either of them. He left and became a retainer of Chih Po, who treated him with great respect and honor. Later Chih Po attacked Hsiang-tzu, the lord of Chao. Hsiang-tzu plotted with the lords of Han and Wei, wiped out Chih Po and his heirs, and divided up his land among the three of them. Hsiang-tzu hated Chih Po intensely and had his skull lacquered and made into a drinking cup.[2]

Yü Jang fled and hid in the mountains. He sighed and said, "A man will die for one who understands him, as a woman will make herself beautiful for one who delights in her. Chih Po understood me. Before I die, I will repay him by destroying his enemy! Then my spirit need feel no shame in the world below."

He changed his name, became a convict laborer, and succeeded in entering the palace of the lord of Chao, where he was given the task

[2] Fan, Chung-hang, Chih, Chao, Han, and Wei were all high ministerial families of Chin. In the middle of the fifth century B.C., when these events took place, Chih Po wiped out the Fan and Chung-hang families and was in turn destroyed by Chao, Han, and Wei, who overthrew the ruling family of Chin and divided the state into three parts.

of replastering the privy. In his breast he concealed a dagger, hoping to stab Hsiang-tzu with it. Hsiang-tzu entered the privy but suddenly grew uneasy and ordered his men to seize and examine the convict laborer who was plastering the privy. It was Yü Jang who, clasping the knife to his breast, said, "I intended to avenge Chih Po's death!"

Hsiang-tzu's attendants were about to put him to death on the spot, but Hsiang-tzu said, "He is a righteous man. From now on I will simply take care to keep him at a distance. Chih Po and his heirs were all wiped out. If one of his retainers feels compelled to try to avenge his death, he must be a worthy man such as the world seldom sees." So he pardoned Yü Jang and sent him away.

After some time, Yü Jang painted his body with lacquer to induce sores like those of a leper, destroyed his voice by drinking lye, and completely changed his appearance until no one could recognize him. When he went begging in the market place, even his wife did not know him. But, as he was going along, he met a friend who recognized him and asked, "Aren't you Yü Jang?"

"I am," he said.

His friend began to weep. "With your talent, you could swear allegiance and take service under Hsiang-tzu, and he would be sure to make you one of his close associates. Once you got close to him, you would have a chance to accomplish your aim. Would that not be easier? Destroying your body and inflicting pain on yourself in order to carry out your revenge—is this not doing it the hard way?"

Yü Jang replied, "To seek to kill a man after you have sworn allegiance and taken service with him amounts to harboring traitorous thoughts against your own lord. I have chosen the hard way, it is true. But I have done so in order to bring shame to all men in future generations who think to serve their lords with treacherous intentions!" Then he took leave of his friend.

Sometime later, word got about that Hsiang-tzu was going out on an excursion, and Yü Jang accordingly went and hid under the bridge he was to pass over. When Hsiang-tzu came to the bridge, his horse suddenly shied. "This must be Yü Jang!" he said, and sent one of his men to investigate. It was indeed Yü Jang.

Hsiang-tzu began to berate him. "You once served both the Fan and Chung-hang families, did you not? And yet when Chih Po wiped them out, you made no move to avenge their deaths, but instead swore allegiance and took service under Chih Po. Now that Chih Po too is dead, why are you suddenly so determined to avenge his death?"

Yü Jang replied, "I served both the Fan and Chung-hang families, and both of them treated me as an ordinary man; therefore I repaid them as an ordinary man would. But when I served Chih Po, he treated me as one of the finest men of the land, and so I have determined to repay him in the same spirit."

Hsiang-tzu sighed a deep sigh and tears came to his eyes. "Ah, Yü Jang," he said, "the world already knows of your loyalty to Chih Po, and I have already pardoned you all I need to. You had best take thought for your end. I can pardon you no more!" He ordered his men to surround Yü Jang.

"They say that a wise ruler does not hide the good deeds of others," said Yü Jang, "and a loyal subject is bound to die for his honor. Formerly you were gracious enough to pardon me, and all the world praised you as a worthy man. For today's business I have no doubt that I deserve to be executed. But I beg you to give me your robe so that I may at least strike at it and fulfill my determination for revenge. Then I may die without regret. It is more than I dare hope for, yet I am bold to speak what is in my heart."

Hsiang-tzu, filled with admiration at Yü Jang's sense of duty, took off his robe and instructed his attendants to hand it to Yü Jang. Yü Jang drew his sword, leaped three times into the air, and slashed at the robe, crying, "Now I can go to the world below and report to Chih Po!" Then he fell on his sword and died. That day, when men of true determination in the state of Chao heard what he had done, they all wept for him.

Nieh Cheng

Some forty years later there was the affair of Nieh Cheng in Chih. Nieh Cheng was from the village of Deep Well in Chih. He killed a man and, in order to escape retaliation, went with his mother and elder sister to the state of Ch'i, where he made a living as a butcher. Some time later Yen Chung-tzu of P'u-yang, an official in the service of Marquis Ai of Han, had a falling out with Han Hsia-lei, the prime minister of Han. Fearful that he might be put to death, Yen Chung-tzu fled from the state and traveled about to other states searching for someone who would be willing to get back at Hsia-lei for him.

When he arrived in Ch'i, someone told him that Nieh Cheng was a man of valor and daring who, fleeing from his enemies, was hiding out among the butchers. Yen Chung-tzu went to his door and requested an interview, but was several times turned away. He then prepared a gift of wine which he asked to be allowed to offer in the presence of Nieh Cheng's mother. When the drinking was well under way, Yen Chung-tzu brought forth a hundred taels of yellow gold which he laid before Nieh Cheng's mother with wishes for a long life. Nieh Cheng was astounded at such generosity and firmly refused the gift. When Yen Chung-tzu just as firmly pressed it on him, Nieh Cheng repeated his refusal, saying, "I am fortunate enough to have my old mother with me. Though our family is poor and I am living in a strange land and earning my way as a dog butcher,[3] I am still able, come morning and evening, to find some sweet or tasty morsel with which to nourish her. She has everything she needs for her care and comfort—I could not be so bold as to accept your gift."

Yen Chung-tzu asked the others present all to withdraw and spoke to Nieh Cheng in private. "I have an enemy," he said, "and I have already traveled about to a great many states. When I reached Ch'i, however, I was privileged to learn that you, sir, are a man of extremely high principles. Therefore I have presented these hundred taels of gold, hoping that you may use them to purchase some trifling gift of food for your honored parent and that I may have the pleasure of your friendship. How would I dare hope for anything more?"

Nieh Cheng replied, "I have been content to humble my will and shame my body, living as a butcher here by the market place and well, only because I am fortunate enough to have my old mother to take care of. While she lives, I dare not promise my services to any man!"

Yen Chung-tzu continued every effort to persuade him, but to the

[3] Dogs were raised to be eaten.

end Nieh Cheng was unwilling to accept the gift. Yen Chung-tzu nevertheless did all that etiquette demands of a proper guest before taking his leave.

Some time later Nieh Cheng's mother died and, when she had been buried and the mourning period was over, Nieh Cheng said to himself, "Ah! I am a man of the market place and well, swinging a knife and working as a butcher, while Yen Chung-tzu is chief minister to one of the feudal lords. And yet he did not consider it too far to come a thousand miles, driving far out of his way just to make friends with me. I treated him very shabbily indeed! I have accomplished no great deeds for which I might be praised, yet Yen Chung-tzu presented a hundred taels of gold to my mother with wishes for her continued good health. Though I did not accept it, it is clear that he did so simply because he has a profound appreciation of my worth. Now a worthy gentleman, burning with anger and indignation, has offered friendship and trust to a poor and insignificant man. Can I bear to remain silent and let it end there? Earlier, when he made his request of me, I refused only because my mother was still alive. Now that her years have come to a close, I shall offer my services to one who truly understands me!"

Thereupon he journeyed west to P'u-yang in Wey and went to see Yen Chung-tzu. "The reason I would not agree earlier," he said, "was simply that my mother was still alive. Now, unfortunately, the years Heaven gave her have come to a close. Who is this enemy that you wish to take revenge on? I request permission to undertake the task!"

Yen Chung-tzu then related to him the whole story. "My enemy is Han Hsia-lei, the prime minister of Han. He is also the younger uncle of the ruler of Han. His clan is numerous and powerful and there are many armed guards stationed wherever he happens to be. I had hoped to send someone to stab him to death, but so far no one has been able to accomplish it. Now if you are so kind as not to reject my plea for help, I hope you will allow me to give you additional carriages and men to assist you in the job."

But Nieh Cheng said, "Han and Wey are near neighbors. Now if one is going to murder the prime minister of another state, and the prime minister also happens to be a close relative of the ruler, then the circumstances make it unwise to send a large party of men. If you try to use a lot of men, then there are bound to be differences of opinion on how best to proceed; if there are differences of opinion, then word of the undertaking will leak out; and if word leaks out, then the whole state of Han will be up in arms against you! What could be more dangerous?"

Nieh Cheng therefore declined to accept any carriages or attendants, but instead took leave and set off alone, disguising his sword as a walking stick,[4] until he reached Han. When he arrived, the Han prime minister Hsia-lei happened to be seated in his office, guarded and attended by a large body of men bearing lances and other weapons. Nieh Cheng walked straight in, ascended the steps, and stabbed Hsia-lei to death. Those about the prime minister were thrown into great confusion, and Nieh Cheng, shouting loudly, attacked and killed thirty or forty of them. Then he flayed the skin of his face, gouged out his eyes, and, butchering himself as he had once done animals, spilled out his bowels and in this way died.

The ruler of Han had his corpse taken and exposed in the market place, offering to reward anyone who could identify him, but no one knew who he was. The ruler then hung up the reward, promising to give a thousand pieces of gold to anyone who could say who it was that had killed Prime Minister Hsia-lei. A long time passed but no one came forward with the answer.

Meanwhile Nieh Cheng's elder sister Jung heard that someone had stabbed and killed the prime minister of Han, but that the blame could not be fixed since no one knew the culprit's name. His corpse had been exposed in the market place with a reward of a thousand pieces of gold hanging above it, she was told. Filled with apprehension, she said, "Could it be my younger brother? Ah—Yen Chung-tzu certainly knew what he was capable of!"

[4] This phrase is customarily taken simply to mean "using his sword as a walking stick," but this makes little sense here, in addition to being a rather foolish and disrespectful way to handle a sword. Examination of other passages where the phrase occurs shows that in all cases the person is traveling incognito and I therefore suggest the above translation. Nieh Cheng could hardly have approached the prime minister if his sword had been visible.

Then she set off at once and went to the market place of Han, where she found that the dead man was indeed Nieh Cheng. Throwing herself down beside the corpse, she wept in profound sorrow, crying, "This man is called Nieh Cheng from the village of Deep Well in Chih!"

The people passing back and forth through the market all said to her, "This man has committed an act of violence and treachery against the prime minister of our state and our king has posted a reward of a thousand gold pieces for anyone who can discover his name—have you not heard? How dare you come here and admit that you were acquainted with him?"

Jung replied, "Yes, I have heard. But Cheng was willing to accept shame and disgrace, throwing away his future and making a living in the market place, because our mother was still in good health and I was not yet married. After our mother had ended her years and departed from the world, and I had found a husband, then Yen Chung-tzu, recognizing my brother's worth, lifted him up from hardship and disgrace and became his friend, treating him with kindness and generosity. So there was nothing he could do. A gentleman will always be willing to die for someone who recognizes his true worth. And now, because I am still alive, he has inflicted this terrible mutilation upon himself so as to wipe out all trace of his identity. But how could I, out of fear that I might be put to death, allow so worthy a brother's name to be lost forever?"

Having astounded the people of the market place with these words, she cried three times in a loud voice to Heaven and then died of grief and anguish by the dead man's side. When the inhabitants of Chin, Ch'u, Ch'i, and Wey heard of this, they all said, "Cheng was not the only able one—his sister too proved herself a woman of valor!"

If Cheng had in fact known that his sister would be unwilling to stand by in silence but, heedless of the threat of execution and public exposure, would make her way a thousand miles over the steep passes, determined to spread his fame abroad, so that sister and brother would both end as criminals in the market place of Han, then he would surely never have agreed to undertake such a mission for Yen Chung-tzu. And as for Yen Chung-tzu, it can certainly be said that he knew how to recognize a man's ability and win others to his service.

Ching K'o

Some two hundred and twenty years later there was the affair of Ching K'o in Ch'in. Ching K'o was a native of Wey, though his family came originally from Ch'i. The men of Wey referred to him as Master Ch'ing, the men of Yen, as Master Ching. He loved to read books and practice swordsmanship. He expounded his ideas to Lord Yüan of Wey, but Lord Yüan failed to make use of him. Later, Ch'in attacked Wey, established the Eastern Province, and moved the collateral kinsmen of Lord Yüan of Wey to Yeh-wang.

Ching K'o once visited Yü-tz'u, where he engaged Kai Nieh in a discussion on swordsmanship. In the course of their talk, Kai Nieh got angry and glared fiercely at Ching K'o, who immediately withdrew. Someone asked Kai Nieh if he did not intend to summon Ching K'o back again. "When I was discussing swordsmanship with him a little while ago," said Kai Nieh, "we had a difference of opinion and I glared at him. Go look for him if you like, but I'm quite certain he has gone. He wouldn't dare stay around!" Kai Nieh sent a messenger to the house where Ching K'o had been staying, but Ching K'o had already mounted his carriage and left Yü-tz'u. When the messenger returned with this report, Kai Nieh said, "I knew he would go. I glared at him and frightened him away."

Again, when Ching K'o was visiting the city of Han-tan, he and a man named Lu Kou-chien got into a quarrel over a chess game. Lu Kou-chien grew angry and began to shout, whereupon Ching K'o fled without a word and never came to see Lu Kou-chien again.

In the course of his travels Ching K'o reached the state of Yen, where he became close friends with a dog butcher and a man named Kao Chien-li who was good at playing the lute. Ching K'o was fond of wine, and every day he would join the dog butcher and Kao Chien-li to drink in the market place of the Yen capital. After the wine had begun to take effect, Kao Chien-li would strike up the lute and Ching K'o would join in with a song. In the middle of the crowded market place they would happily amuse themselves, or if their mood changed they would break into tears, exactly as though there were no one else about. But, although Ching K'o spent his time with drunkards, he was a man of depth and learning. Whatever feudal state he traveled to, he always became close friends with the most worthy and influential men. When he went to Yen, Master T'ien Kuang, a gentleman of Yen who was living in retirement, treated him very kindly, for he realized that he was no ordinary man.

After Ching K'o had been in Yen some time, Prince Tan, the heir apparent of Yen, who had been a hostage in Ch'in, escaped and returned home. Prince Tan had previously been a hostage in the state of Chao. Cheng, the king of Ch'in, was born in Chao, and in his youth had been very friendly with Prince Tan; later, when Cheng became king, Prince Tan went as a hostage to the Ch'in court. But the king of Ch'in treated him very shabbily until, in anger, he escaped from the state and returned to Yen. After his return, he looked about for someone who would undertake to get back at the king of Ch'in for him; but because Yen was small and powerless, there was nothing he could do. Meanwhile, Ch'in day by day dispatched more troops east of the mountains, attacking Ch'i, Ch'u, Han, Wei, and Chao and gradually eating away at the lands of the other feudal lords, until it became obvious that Yen's turn would be next. The ruler of Yen and his ministers all feared imminent disaster, and Prince Tan likewise, worried by the situation, asked his tutor Chü Wu what could be done.

Chü Wu replied, "Ch'in's lands fill the world and its might overawes the rulers of Han, Wei, and Chao. To the north it occupies the strongholds at Sweet Springs and Valley Mouth, and to the south the fertile fields of the Ching and Wei river valleys; it commands the riches of Pa and Han and the mountain ranges of Lung and Shu to the west, and the vital Han-ku and Yao passes to the east. Its people are numerous and its soldiers well trained, and it has more weapons and armor than it can use. If it should ever decide to march against us, we could find no safety south of the Great Wall or north of the Yi River.[5] Angry as you are at the insults you have suffered, you surely would not want to brush against its bristling scales!"[6]

"Then what should I do?" said Prince Tan.

"Let me retire and think it over," replied Chü Wu.

Shortly afterwards the Ch'in general Fan Yü-ch'i, having offended

[5] The boundaries of the state of Yen.
[6] The deadly scales that protrude from the throat of the dragon.

the king of Ch'in, fled to Yen, where Prince Tan received him and assigned him quarters. Chü Wu admonished the prince, saying, "This will not do! Violent as the king of Ch'in is, and with the resentment he nurses against Yen because of your escape, it is already enough to make one's heart turn cold. And what will he be like when he hears where General Fan is staying? This is what men call throwing meat in the path of a starving tiger—there will be no help for the misfortune that follows! Even if you had ministers as wise as Kuan Chung and Yen Ying, they could think of no way to save you! I beg you to send General Fan at once to the territory of the Hsiung-nu barbarians [7] to get him out of the way. Then, after you have negotiated with Han, Wei, and Chao to the west, entered into alliance with Ch'i and Ch'u on the south, and established friendly relations with the leader of the Hsiung-nu to the north, we may be able to plan what move to make next."

"The scheme you propose will require a great deal of time," said Prince Tan. "As anxious as I feel at the moment, I am afraid I cannot wait that long! And that is not all. General Fan, having been hounded throughout the world, has come to entrust his fate to me. No matter how much I might be pressed by Ch'in and its power, I could never bear, when he is in such a pitiful plight, to betray his friendship and abandon him by sending him off to the Hsiung-nu! This is a matter of life and death to me. I beg you to consider the question once more."

Chü Wu said, "To pursue a dangerous course and hope for safety, to invite disaster while seeking good fortune; with too little planning and too much hatred to disregard a serious threat to the whole nation because of some lately incurred debt of friendship to one man—this is what is known as 'fanning resentment and abetting disaster'! Drop a swan's feather into a burning brazier and pff!—it is all over in an instant. And when Ch'in, like a ravening hawk, comes to vent its anger, will Yen be able to last any longer? However, there is a certain Master T'ien Kuang in Yen who is a man of deep wisdom and great daring. He would be a good person to consult."

[7] A nomadic people who occupied the area north of China; they are often identified with the Huns. *Shih chi* 110 relates the history of Chinese–Hsiung-nu relations.

"I would like you to introduce me to him," said Prince Tan. "Can you arrange it?"

"With pleasure," said Chü Wu, and went to see Master T'ien, informing him that the crown prince wished to consult him on matters of state. "I will be happy to comply," said Master T'ien. He went to call on the prince, who came out to greet him, politely led him inside, knelt, and dusted off a mat for him to sit on.

When T'ien Kuang was settled on his seat and those about them had retired, the prince deferentially moved off his mat and addressed his request to his visitor: "Yen and Ch'in cannot both stand! I beg you to devote your mind to this problem."

"They say," replied T'ien Kuang, "that when a thoroughbred horse is in its prime, it can gallop a thousand li in one day; but when it is old and decrepit, the sorriest nag will outdistance it. It appears that you have heard reports of how I was when I was in my prime, but you do not realize that my strength is by now wasted and gone. Nevertheless, though I myself would not venture to plan for the safety of the state, I have a friend named Master Ching who could be consulted."

"I would like you to introduce me to him," said Prince Tan. "Is it possible?"

"With pleasure," said T'ien Kuang and, rising from his mat, he hurried from the room. The prince escorted him as far as the gate and there warned him, "What we have been discussing is a matter of vital concern to the nation. Please do not let word of it leak out!"

T'ien Kuang lowered his gaze to the ground and replied with a laugh, "I understand."

Then, stooped with age, he made his way to the house of Master Ching. "Everyone in Yen knows that we are good friends," he said. "The crown prince, having heard reports of me when I was in my prime and unaware that by now my powers have failed, has told me that Yen and Ch'in cannot continue to exist side by side and begged me to devote my mind to the problem. Rather than refuse his request, I took the liberty of mentioning your name. May I ask you to go call on him at his palace?"

"I will be glad to comply," said Ching K'o.

"They say," T'ien Kuang continued, "that a worthy man does not act in such a way as to arouse distrust in others. Now the prince has warned me that the matter we discussed is of vital concern to the nation and begged me not to let word of it leak out. Obviously he distrusts me, and if my actions have aroused his distrust, then I am no gentleman of honor!" T'ien Kuang had decided to commit suicide in order to spur Ching K'o to action, and he continued: "I want you to go at once and visit the prince. Tell him I am already dead, so he will know that I have not betrayed the secret!" With this he cut his throat and died.

Ching K'o went to see the prince and informed him of T'ien Kuang's death and last words. The prince bowed twice and then, sinking to his knees, crawled forward, the tears starting from his eyes. After some time he said, "I only cautioned Master T'ien not to speak so that we could be sure of bringing our plans to a successful conclusion. Now he has actually killed himself to show me that the secret will never be betrayed—as though I could have intended such a thing!"

After Ching K'o had settled himself, the prince moved off his mat, bowed his head, and said, "Master T'ien, unaware of how unworthy a person I am, has made it possible for me to speak my thoughts to you. It is clear from this that Heaven has taken pity upon Yen and has not abandoned me altogether.

"Ch'in has a heart that is greedy for gain, and its desires are insatiable. It will never be content until it has seized all the land in the world and forced every ruler within the four seas to ackowledge its sovereignty. Now, having already taken captive the king of Han and annexed all his lands, Ch'in has mobilized its troops to strike against Ch'u in the south, while in the north it stands poised for an attack on Chao. Wang Chien, leading several hundred thousand troops, is holding Chang and Yeh, while Li Hsin leads another force against T'ai-yüan and Yün-chung. Chao, unable to withstand the might of Ch'in, will undoubtedly submit and swear allegiance to it. And when Chao has gone under, Yen will stand next in line for disaster!

"Yen is small and weak, and has often fared badly in war. Even if we were to mobilize the entire nation, we obviously could not stand against Ch'in; and once the other feudal lords have bowed to its rule, none of them will dare to become our allies. Nevertheless, I have a scheme of my own which, foolish as it may be, I would like to sug-gest—that is, to find a really brave man who would be willing to go as our envoy to the court of Ch'in and tempt it with some offer of gain. The king of Ch'in is greedy, and under the circumstances would surely listen to our offer. If this man could then somehow threaten the king, as Ts'ao Mei threatened Duke Huan of Ch'i, and force him to return to the feudal lords all the land he has seized, that would be the best we could ask for. And if that proved impossible, he might still be able to stab and kill the king. With the Ch'in generals free to do as they wished with the troops in the outlying areas, and the Ch'in court in a state of confusion, dissension would surely arise between ruler and subject. The feudal lords could then take advantage of the situation to band together once more, and in that case the defeat of Ch'in would be inevitable. This is what I would like to see more than anything else, but I do not know who could be entrusted with such a mission. I can only ask that you give it some thought!"

After some time Ching K'o said, "This is a matter of grave impor-tance to the state. I am a person of little worth and I fear I would be unfit for such a mission."

The prince moved forward and, bowing his head, begged and begged Ching K'o to accept the proposal and not to decline any longer, until at last Ching K'o gave his consent. The prince then honored him with the title of Highest Minister and assigned him the finest quarters in the capital. Every day the prince went to call at his mansion, pre-senting gifts of food, supplying him with all manner of luxuries, and from time to time pressing him to accept carriages, rider attendants, and waiting women, indulging his every wish so as to insure his cooperation.

Time passed, but Ching K'o showed no inclination to set out on the mission. Meanwhile the Ch'in general Wang Chien defeated Chao, took prisoner its king, and annexed its entire territory. Then he ad-vanced north, seizing control of the land as he went, until he reached the southern border of the state of Yen. Crown Prince Tan, filled with terror, begged Ching K'o to set off. "Any moment now the Ch'in forces may cross the Yi River, and if that happens, though I might wish to continue to wait upon you, how could I do so?"

"I intended to say something, whether you mentioned it or not," said Ching K'o. "The trouble is that, if I set off now, without any means of gaining the confidence of the king of Ch'in, I will never be able to get close to him. The king of Ch'in has offered a thousand catties of gold and a city of ten thousand households in exchange for the life of his former general, Fan Yü-ch'i. If I could get the head of General Fan and a map of the Tu-k'ang region of Yen, and offer to present these to the king of Ch'in, he would certainly be delighted to receive me. Then I would have a chance to carry out our plan."

But the prince replied, "General Fan has come here in trouble and distress and entrusted himself to me. I could never bear to betray the trust of a worthy man for the sake of my own personal desires. I beg you to think of some other plan."

Ching K'o realized that the prince would never bring himself to carry out his suggestion, and so he went in private to see Fan Yü-ch'i. "Ch'in's treatment of you has been harsh indeed!" he said. "Your father, your mother, and all the members of your family have been done away with; and now I hear that Ch'in has offered a reward of a thousand catties of gold and a city of ten thousand households for your head! What do you intend to do?"

Fan Yü-ch'i looked up to heaven and gave a great sigh, tears streaming down his face. "I think of nothing else, until the ache of it is in my very bones! But I do not know what I can do!"

"Suppose I said that one word from you could dispel the troubles of the state of Yen and avenge the wrong you have suffered?"

Fan Yü-ch'i leaned forward. "What is it?" he asked.

"Give me your head, so that I can present it to the king of Ch'in! Then he will surely be delighted to receive me. With my left hand I will seize hold of his sleeve, with my right I'll stab him in the breast, and all your wrongs will be avenged and all the shameful insults which Yen has suffered will be wiped out! What do you say?"

Fan Yü-ch'i bared his shoulder and gripped his wrist in a gesture of determination. Moving forward, he said, "Day and night I gnash my teeth and eat out my heart trying to think of some plan. Now you have shown me the way!" Then he cut his throat.

When the crown prince heard what had happened, he rushed to the spot and, throwing himself upon the corpse, wept in deep sorrow. But, since there was nothing that could be done, he took Fan Yü-ch'i's head and sealed it in a box. Earlier he had ordered a search for the sharpest dagger that could be found, and had purchased one from a man of Chao named Hsü Fu-jen for a hundred measures of gold. He ordered his artisans to coat the blade with poison and try it out on some men; though the thrust drew hardly enough blood to stain the robe of the victim, every one of the men dropped dead on the spot. The prince then began to make final preparations for sending Master Ching on his mission. There was a brave man of Yen named Ch'in Wu-yang who at the age of thirteen had murdered someone, and was so fierce that no one dared even to look at him crossly. This man the prince ordered to act as a second to Ching K'o.

There was another man whom Ching K'o wished to have along in his party, but he lived a long way off and had not yet arrived in Yen. Meanwhile preparations for the journey were completed but, though time passed, Ching K'o still did not set off. The prince began to fret at the delay and to suspect that Ching K'o had changed his mind. He therefore went to Ching K'o and pressed his request. "The day for departure has already passed, and I am wondering what you intend to do. Perhaps I should send Ch'in Wu-yang on ahead . . ."

"What do you mean, send Ch'in Wu-yang on ahead?" roared Ching K'o angrily. "Send that little wretch alone and you may be sure he'll never return successful—setting off with a single dagger to face the immeasurable might of Ch'in! The reason I have delayed is that I was waiting for a friend I wanted to go with me. But, if you feel it is growing too late, I beg to take my leave."

Then he set out. The crown prince and all his associates who knew what was happening put on white robes and caps of mourning to see the party off, accompanying them as far as the Yi River. After they had sacrificed to the god of the road and chosen their route, Kao Chien-li struck up his lute and Ching K'o joined in with a song in the mournful *pien-chih* mode. Tears streamed from the eyes of the company. Ching K'o came forward and sang this song:

> Winds cry *hsiao-hsiao,*
> Yi waters are cold.
> Brave men, once gone,
> Never come back again.

Shifting to the *yü* mode with its martial air, Ching K'o sang once more; this time the eyes of the men flashed with anger and their hair bristled beneath their caps. Then he mounted his carriage and set off, never once looking back.

In time he arrived in Ch'in, where he presented gifts worth a thousand measures of gold to the Counselor of the Palace Meng Chia, one of the king's favorite ministers. Meng Chia in turn spoke on his behalf to the king of Ch'in: "The king of Yen, trembling with awe before Your Majesty's might, has not ventured to call out his troops to oppose our forces, but requests that he and all his people may become vassals of Ch'in, so that he may be ranked among the other feudal lords and present tribute and perform labor services in the manner of a province; in this way he hopes to be allowed to continue the sacrifices at the temple of his ancestors, the former kings of Yen. In his terror he has not dared to come and speak in person, but has respectfully sent the severed head of Fan Yü-ch'i sealed in a box, along with a map of the Tu-k'ang region in Yen, to be presented to you. Bowing respectfully in his courtyard, he has sent these gifts, dispatching his envoys to inquire Your Majesty's pleasure. He awaits your command."

When the king of Ch'in heard this, he was delighted and, donning his court robes and ordering a full dress reception, he received the envoys of Yen in the Hsien-yang Palace. Ching K'o bore the box with Fan Yü-ch'i's head, while Ch'in Wu-yang carried the map case; step by step they advanced through the throne room until they reached the steps of the throne, where Ch'in Wu-yang suddenly turned pale and began to quake with fear. The courtiers eyed him suspiciously. Ching K'o turned around, laughed at Ch'in Wu-yang, and then stepped forward to apoligize: "This man is a simple rustic from the barbarous region of the northern border, and he has never seen the Son of Heaven. That is why he shakes with fright. I beg Your Majesty to pardon him for the moment and permit me to complete my mission here before you."

"Bring the map he is carrying!" said the king to Ching K'o, who took the map container from Ch'in Wu-yang and presented it to the king. The king opened the container, and when he had removed the map, the dagger appeared. At that moment Ching K'o seized the king's sleeve with his left hand, while with his right he snatched up the dagger and held it pointed at the king's breast, but he did not stab him. The king jerked back in alarm and leapt from his seat, tearing the sleeve off his robe. He tried to draw his sword, but it was long and clung to the scabbard and, since it hung vertically at his side, he could not, in his haste, manage to get it out.

Ching K'o ran after the king, who dashed around the pillar of the throne room. All the courtiers, utterly dumfounded by so unexpected an occurrence, milled about in disorder.

According to Ch'in law, no courtier or attendant who waited upon the king in the upper throne room was permitted to carry a weapon of any kind. The palace attendants who bore arms were ranged in the lower hall, and without a command from the king they were forbidden to ascend to the throne room. In his panic the king had no chance to give a command for the soldiers to appear, and thus Ching K'o was able to pursue him. Having nothing with which to strike at Ching K'o, the king in panic-stricken confusion merely flailed at him with his hands. At the same time the physician Hsia Wu-chü, who was in attendance, battered Ching K'o with the medicine bag he was carrying.

The king continued to circle the pillar, unable in his confusion to think of anything else to do. "Push the scabbard around behind you!" shouted the king's attendants, and, when he did this, he was at last able to draw his sword and strike at Ching K'o, slashing him across the left thigh. Ching K'o, staggering to the ground, raised the dagger and hurled it at the king, but it missed and struck the bronze pillar. The king attacked Ching K'o again.

Ching K'o, wounded now in eight places, realized that his attempt had failed. Leaning against the pillar, his legs sprawled before him, he began to laugh and curse the king. "I failed because I tried to threaten you without actually killing you and exact a promise that I could take back to the crown prince!" As he spoke, the king's attendants rushed forward to finish him off.

It was a long time before the king regained his composure. When at last he came to himself, he discussed with his ministers the question of who deserved a reward for his part in the incident, and who deserved punishment. To the physician Hsia Wu-chü he presented two hundred taels of gold, "because Hsia Wu-chü, out of love for me, hit Ching K'o with his medicine bag."

After this the king in a rage dispatched more troops to join his army in Chao and commanded Wang Chien to attack Yen. Ten months later the Ch'in army captured the city of Chi. King Hsi of Yen, Prince Tan, and the others of the court, leading their best troops, fled east to Liao-tung for safety. The Ch'in general Li Hsin pursued and attacked them with ever increasing fury.

King Chia of Tai sent a letter to King Hsi of Yen which read: "It is all because of Prince Tan that Ch'in is harassing you with such vehemence. If you would only do away with the prince and present his corpse to Ch'in, the king's anger would surely be appeased and he would leave you in peace to carry on the sacrifices to your altars of the soil and grain."

Shortly after this, Li Hsin pursued Prince Tan as far as the Yen River, where the prince hid among the islands in the river. Meanwhile the king of Yen sent an envoy to cut off the prince's head, intending to present it to Ch'in, but Ch'in dispatched more troops and reopened its attack on Yen. Five years later, Ch'in finally destroyed the state of Yen and took its ruler, King Hsi, prisoner. The following year [221 B.C.] the king of Ch'in united all the world under his rule and assumed the title of Supreme Emperor.

The Ch'in ruler then began a campaign to ferret out the associates of Prince Tan and Ching K'o, and as a result they all went into hiding. Kao Chien-li, who was among the group, changed his name, hired himself out as an indentured workman, and went into hiding in a household in the city of Sung-tzu, enduring for a long time the hardships of a laborer's life. Whenever he heard some guest of the family playing the lute in the main hall of the house, he would linger outside, unable to tear himself away, and after each performance he would say, "That man plays well" or "That man is not very good." One of the servants reported this to the master of the house, saying, "That hired man must know something about music, since he ventures to pass judgment on everyone's playing."

The master of the house summoned Kao Chien-li to appear and play the lute before his guests, and when he did so, everyone in the company praised his playing and pressed wine on him. Kao Chien-li thought of the long time he had been in hiding, and of the seemingly endless years of hardship and want that lay ahead; finally he went back to his room, got his lute and good clothes out of the trunk where he had stored them and, changing his clothes, appeared once more in the hall. The guests were overcome with surprise and, bowing and making room for him as an equal, they led him to the seat of honor and requested him to play the lute and sing. When the performance was over, there was not a guest who left the house dry-eyed.

Kao Chien-li was entertained at one home after another in Sung-tzu, and in time his fame reached the ears of the Ch'in emperor. The emperor summoned him to an audience, but, when he appeared, someone who had known him in the past exclaimed, "This is Kao Chien-li!" The emperor, unable to bring himself to kill such a skilled musician, ordered his eyes put out and commanded him to play in his presence. The emperor never failed to praise his playing and gradually allowed him to come nearer and nearer. Kao Chien-li then got a heavy piece of lead and fastened it inside his lute, and the next time he was summoned to play at the emperor's side, he raised his lute and struck at the emperor. He missed and was summarily executed, and after that the emperor never again permitted any of the former followers of the feudal lords to approach his person.

When Lu Kou-chien heard of Ching K'o's attempt to assassinate the king of Ch'in, he sighed to himself and said, "What a pity that he never properly mastered the art of swordsmanship! And as for me— how blind I was to his real worth! That time when I shouted at him in anger, he must have thought I was hardly human!"

The Grand Historian remarks: When people these days tell the story of Ching K'o, they assert that at the command of Prince Tan the heavens rained grain and horses grew horns.[8] This is of course a gross error. They likewise say that Ching K'o actually wounded the king of Ch'in, which is equally untrue. At one time Kung-sun Chi-

---

[8] An anonymous fictionalized version of the Ching K'o story, which contains this detail, has been handed down, in somewhat battered state, under the title "Prince Tan of Yen." It is translated in Wolfgang Bauer and Herbert Franke, eds., *The Golden Casket* (Harcourt, Brace & World, Inc., 1964), pp. 30–41.

kung and Master Tung were friends of the physician Hsia Wu-chü and they learned from him exactly what happened. I have therefore reported everything just as they told it to me.

Of these five men, from Ts'ao Mei to Ching K'o, some succeeded in carrying out their duty and some did not. But it is perfectly clear that they had all determined upon the deed. They were not false to their intentions. Is it not right, then, that their names should be handed down to later ages?

Ch'in failed in goodness and the great leaders rose to vex it. Hsiang Liang began the task and his nephew, Yü, carried it on. When the latter killed Sung I and rescued Chao, the feudal leaders made him their ruler; but when he executed Tzu-ying and rebelled against King Huai, the world joined in censuring him. Thus I made The Basic Annals of Hsiang Yü.

Hsiang Chi, whose polite name was Yü, was a native of Hsia-hsiang. He was twenty-four when he first took up arms. His father's youngest brother was Hsiang Liang. Hsiang Liang's father, Hsiang Yen, was a general of Ch'u who was driven to suicide by the Ch'in general Wang Chien. The Hsiang family for generations were generals of Ch'u and were enfeoffed in Hsiang; hence they took the family name Hsiang.

When Hsiang Yü was a boy he studied the art of writing. Failing to master this, he abandoned it and took up swordsmanship. When he failed at this also, his uncle, Hsiang Liang, grew angry with him, but Hsiang Yü declared, "Writing is good only for keeping records of people's names. Swordsmanship is useful only for attacking a single enemy and is likewise not worth studying. What I want to learn is the art of attacking ten thousand enemies!" With this, Hsiang Liang began to teach his nephew the art of warfare, which pleased Yü greatly. On the whole Yü understood the essentials of the art, but here again he was unwilling to pursue the study in detail.

Hsiang Liang was once implicated in some crime in Yüeh-yang but, obtaining a letter on his behalf from the prison warden of Chi, Ts'ao Chiu, he presented it to Ssu-ma Hsin, the prison warden of Yüeh-yang, and was released from the charge.

Later Hsiang Liang killed a man and, with Hsiang Yü, fled to the region of Wu to escape the vengeance of the man's family. All the worthy and renowned men of the region of Wu acknowledged Hsiang Liang as their superior and, whenever there was some major government construction work or a funeral in the area, Hsiang Liang was put in charge of the proceedings. In secret he formed a band of guests and retainers and trained them in the art of war so that he came to know the abilities of each.

Once the First Emperor of Ch'in came on a visit to K'uai-chi. When he was crossing the Che River, Hsiang Liang and Hsiang Yü went to watch the procession. "This fellow could be deposed and replaced!" Hsiang Yü remarked. Hsiang Liang clapped his hand over his nephew's mouth. "Don't speak such nonsense," he cautioned, "or we and all our family will be executed!" After this incident Hsiang Liang treated his nephew with peculiar respect.

Hsiang Yü was over eight feet tall [1] and so strong that with his two hands he could lift a bronze cauldron. In ability and spirit he far surpassed others, so that all the young men of the region of Wu were afraid of him.

In the first year of the Second Emperor of Ch'in [209 B.C.], during the seventh month, Ch'en She and his band began their uprising in the region of Ta-tse. In the ninth month T'ung, the governor of K'uai-chi, announced to Hsiang Liang, "All the region west of the Yangtze is in revolt. The time has come when Heaven will destroy the house of Ch'in. I have heard it said that he who takes the lead may rule others, but he who lags behind will be ruled by others. I would like to dispatch an army with you and Huan Ch'u at the head." (Huan Ch'u was at this time in hiding in the swamps.)

Hsiang Liang replied, "Huan Ch'u is in hiding and no one knows where he is. Only Hsiang Yü knows the place." Hsiang Liang left the room and went to give instructions to Hsiang Yü, telling him to hold his sword in readiness and wait outside. Then he returned and sat down again with the governor. "I beg leave to call in my nephew Yü, so that he may receive your order to summon Huan Ch'u," said Hsiang Liang. The governor consented, and Hsiang Liang sent for Hsiang Yü to come in. After some time, Hsiang Liang winked at his nephew and said, "You may proceed!" With this, Hsiang Yü drew his sword and cut off the governor's head. Hsiang Liang picked up the governor's head and hung the seals of office from his own belt. The governor's

---

[1] I.e., over six feet. The Han foot is about three fourths of our foot.

office was thrown into utter panic and confusion. After Hsiang Yü had attacked and killed several dozen attendants the entire staff submitted in terror, not a man daring to offer resistance.

Hsiang Liang then summoned a number of high officials whom he had known in the past and informed them of his reasons for starting a revolt. He called out all the troops of the region of Wu, sending men to recruit them from the various districts under his jurisdiction, until he had obtained a force of eight thousand picked men, and he assigned various distinguished and powerful men of Wu as his commanders, lieutenants, and marshals. One man, to whom no post had been assigned, went to Hsiang Liang and asked the reason. "In the past," replied Hsiang Liang, "at the time of So-and-so's funeral, I put you in charge of certain affairs, but you were unable to handle them properly. For this reason I have not assigned you a post." After this everyone accepted his assignments without argument. Hsiang Liang became governor of K'uai-chi and Hsiang Yü was made lieutenant general with the task of subduing the districts under the governor's jurisdiction.

Chao P'ing, a man of Kuang-ling, had been sent by Ch'en She to seize the district of Kuang-ling, but the district had not yet submitted. When Chao P'ing heard that Ch'en She had been defeated and fled and that the Ch'in forces were on their way, he crossed the Yangtze and, pretending that he was acting on orders from Ch'en She, conferred on Hsiang Liang the title of chief minister to the king of Ch'u. "Now that this region east of the Yangtze is under control," he said, "you must with all speed lead your troops west and attack Ch'in!"

Hsiang Liang took his eight thousand men, crossed the Yangtze, and proceeded west. When he heard that Ch'en Ying had already conquered Tung-yang he sent an envoy suggesting that the two of them join forces and proceed west together. Ch'en Ying had formerly been secretary to the district magistrate of Tung-yang. He was unfailingly honest and circumspect in all his duties in the district and was known as a man of exceptional worth. Some of the young men of Tung-yang had murdered the district magistrate and, gathering together a force of several thousand men, were looking for a leader. Failing to find anyone suitable, they asked Ch'en Ying. He refused, saying that he was unsuited for the job, but they finally forced him to become their leader.

When they had gathered a force of twenty thousand men from the district they decided to make Ch'en Ying a king, mark their forces off from the other rebel groups by wearing blue caps, and start their own uprising.

Ch'en Ying's mother advised him, saying, "From the time I first came into your household as a bride I have never heard of any of your ancestors who were noblemen. Now if you should suddenly acquire a great title, I fear it would bring ill luck. It would be better for you to place yourself under the command of someone else. If the undertaking is successful, you will still be made a marquis. And should the undertaking fail, it will be easy for you to go into hiding, for the world will not point you out by name."

As a result Ch'en Ying did not venture to become a king. Instead he told the leaders of his army, "The Hsiang family have for generations been generals, and are well known in Ch'u. If we wish now to begin a revolt, it is imperative that we have one of them as our general. If we put our trust in a family of such renown, there is no doubt that Ch'in can be destroyed." All agreed to follow his advice and put their troops under Hsiang Liang's command. When Hsiang Liang crossed the Huai River, both Ch'ing Pu and General P'u, as well, placed their troops under his command. In all he had a force of sixty or seventy thousand men, which he encamped at Hsia-p'ei.

At this time Ch'in Chia had already set up Ching Chü as king of Ch'u and was himself camped east of P'eng-ch'eng, intending to block Hsiang Liang's advance. Hsiang Liang addressed his officers, saying "Ch'en She, king of Ch'u, was formerly the leader of the uprising, but he was unsuccessful in battle and we do not know at present where he is. Now Ch'in Chia, acting in defiance of Ch'en She, has set up Ching Chü as king. This is a most outrageous act of treason!" Then he led his troops to attack Ch'in Chia, who fled in defeat. Hsiang Liang pursued him as far as Hu-ling, where Ch'in Chia turned and engaged in battle. At the end of the day Ch'in Chia was dead and his army had surrendered. Ching Chü fled to the region of Liang, where he died. Hsiang Liang then joined Ch'in Chia's army to his own and camped at Hu-ling, preparing to march west.

At this time the Ch'in army led by Chang Han had reached Li.

Hsiang Liang sent Chu Chi-shih and Yü Fan-chün as special generals to attack him there, but Yü Fan-chün was killed in battle and the army of Chu Chi-shih, defeated, fled back to Hu-ling. Hsiang Liang then led his forces into Hsieh and executed Chu Chi-shih.

Earlier, Hsiang Liang had sent Hsiang Yü with a special force to attack the city of Hsiang-ch'eng, but the city was strongly defended and would not submit. When he at last succeeded in capturing it Hsiang Yü had all the defenders butchered. He then returned and reported to Hsiang Liang. When Hsiang Liang received definite news that Ch'en She was dead he summoned all his various generals to a meeting at Hsieh to plan his next move. At this time Liu Chi, the governor of P'ei, who had also begun an uprising in P'ei, attended the meeting.

Also present was Fan Tseng of Chü-ch'ao, a man of seventy who lived in retirement and took no part in public affairs. He was very fond of peculiar plans and stratagems, and counseled Hsiang Liang, saying, "It is altogether natural and proper that Ch'en She should have met with defeat. Among all the six great kingdoms which Ch'in destroyed Ch'u was least deserving of its fate. Ever since the time when King Huai of Ch'u went to visit Ch'in and failed to return to his own land the people of Ch'u have never ceased to grieve. Therefore Master Nan, the seer of Ch'u, has said: 'Though but three houses be left in Ch'u, it is she who will destroy Ch'in!' When Ch'en She was head of the uprising he did not set up the heir to the royal house of Ch'u, but made himself king instead, and thus his power quickly waned. Now, since you have risen east of the Yangtze, the leaders of Ch'u swarm forth like bees, vying with one another to place themselves at your disposal. This is because the men of your family have for generations been generals of Ch'u and you have it in your power to reestablish the royal line of Ch'u."

Hsiang Liang, acknowledging the truth of his words, sought out Hsin, the grandson of the late King Huai of Ch'u, who was living among the common people, herding sheep in the hire of another man, and set him up as King Huai of Ch'u in accordance with the wishes of the people. Ch'en Ying he made prime minister of Ch'u, with a fief of five districts, and sent him with King Huai to establish the capital at Hsü-i. Hsiang Liang himself took the title of lord of Wu-hsin.

After several months he led his troops to attack K'ang-fu. Joining with the armies of T'ien Jung of Ch'i and Marshal Lung Ch'ieh, he went to the rescue of Tung-a, which was besieged by Ch'in, and there inflicted a major defeat upon the Ch'in army. T'ien Jung led his troops back to Ch'i and deposed T'ien Chia, the king of Ch'i. T'ien Chia fled to Ch'u and his prime minister, T'ien Chüeh, fled to Chao, where his younger brother, T'ien Chien, a former general of Ch'i, was living, afraid to return to Ch'i. T'ien Jung set up Shih, the son of T'ien Tan, as king of Ch'i. Hsiang Liang, having already defeated the army at Tung-a, was in pursuit of the Ch'in forces, and several times sent envoys to urge the forces of Ch'i to join him in proceeding west. T'ien Jung announced: "If Ch'u will kill T'ien Chia and Chao will kill T'ien Chüeh and T'ien Chien, then I will dispatch my troops." Hsiang Liang replied, "T'ien Chia is the king of an allied state. He has come to me in distress and placed himself under my care. I cannot bring myself to kill him." Chao likewise declared that it would not kill T'ien Chüeh and T'ien Chien for the sake of buying favor with Ch'i. As a result, Ch'i was unwilling to dispatch troops to aid Ch'u.

Hsiang Liang sent the governor of P'ei and Hsiang Yü with a special force to attack the city of Ch'eng-yang and massacre its inhabitants. After accomplishing this they proceeded west and defeated the Ch'in forces east of P'u-yang. When the Ch'in forces withdrew to cover in P'u-yang the governor of P'ei and Hsiang Yü attacked Ting-t'ao. Failing to capture Ting-t'ao, they withdrew and seized the land to the west until they reached Yung-ch'iu, where they inflicted a major defeat on the Ch'in forces and decapitated Li Yu. Then they turned back and attacked Wai-huang. Before Wai-huang had submitted, Hsiang Liang marched out of Tung-a and proceeded west until he reached Ting-t'ao, where he inflicted a second defeat upon the Ch'in army.

Because of this, and because Hsiang Yü and his men in the meantime had succeeded in decapitating Li Yu, Hsiang Liang became increasingly contemptuous of the Ch'in forces and began to grow proud and overbearing. Sung I warned him, saying "If, because of victory in battle, a general becomes proud and his soldiers unwary, defeat is sure to follow. Now your soldiers have begun to grow rather lazy, while the Ch'in forces increase day by day. I am afraid of what may happen to you!" Hsiang Liang, however, refused to listen to Sung I's counsel, but dispatched him as his envoy to Ch'i. On the way there, Sung I happened to meet the envoy from Ch'i, Hsien, the lord of Kao-ling. "Are you on your way to see Hsiang Liang, the lord of Wu-ling?" he inquired, to which the other replied "I am." "I can tell you," said Sung I, "that the lord of Wu-ling is sure to meet with defeat. If you proceed on your way slowly enough, you may escape death. But if you hurry you will only encounter misfortune!"

As Sung I had foreseen, Ch'in gathered together all its forces and sent them to aid Chang Han, who attacked the Ch'u army at Ting-t'ao, inflicted a decisive defeat, and killed Hsiang Liang.

The governor of P'ei and Hsiang Yü withdrew from Wai-huang and attacked Ch'en-liu, but Ch'en-liu was stoutly defended and they could not conquer it. They discussed what their best plan would be and decided that, since Hsiang Liang's army had been defeated and their soldiers were filled with terror, they had better join with the army of Lü Ch'en and withdraw to the east. Accordingly they retreated, and Lü Ch'en camped east of P'eng-ch'eng, Hsiang Yü west of P'eng-ch'eng, and the governor of P'ei at Tang.

Chang Han, the Ch'in commander, having defeated Hsiang Liang's army, considered that the forces of the Ch'u area were no longer worth worrying about. Therefore he crossed the Yellow River and attacked Chao, inflicting a severe defeat. At this time Chao Hsieh was king of Chao, Ch'en Yü was in command of the army, and Chang Erh was prime minister. All fled and took refuge within the walls of Chü-lu. Chang Han ordered Wang Li and She Chien to encircle the city, while he himself camped to the south and constructed a walled road along which to transport supplies of grain. Ch'en Yü, the Chao general, with a force of some twenty or thirty thousand men, camped north of Chü-lu. This was the so-called Army North of the River.

With the forces of Ch'u already defeated at Ting-t'ao, King Huai grew fearful and moved from Hsü-i to P'eng-ch'eng, where he combined the armies of Hsiang Yü and Lü Ch'en and himself took command. He appointed Lü Ch'en as minister of instruction and his father, Lü Ch'ing, as prime minister. The governor of P'ei he made head of Tang Province, enfeoffed him as marquis of Wu-an, and put him in command of the troops of Tang.

Hsien, the lord of Kao-ling, the envoy from Ch'i whom Sung I had formerly chanced to meet on his way, was at this time with the Ch'u army, and went to see the king of Ch'u. "Sung I," he said, "warned me that Hsiang Liang would surely meet defeat, and after a few days he was in fact defeated. He who can read the signs of defeat before the armies have even engaged in battle may indeed be said to understand the art of warfare." The king thereupon summoned Sung I and discussed affairs of strategy with him. He was delighted with Sung I and made him supreme general of the army. Hsiang Yü, with the title of "Duke of Lu," he made second general, and Tseng Fan third general, and sent them to relieve Chao. All of the other special commanders were placed under the command of Sung I, who was given the title of "His Lordship, the Commander of the Armies."

The armies advanced as far as An-yang, where they halted for forty-six days without proceeding further. Hsiang Yü conferred with Sung I, saying, "News has come that the Ch'in army has besieged the king of Chao at Chü-lu. If we lead our troops across the Yellow River at once, we can attack them with our forces from outside, Chao will respond by attacking from the city, and we are sure to defeat the Ch'in army."

"Not so," replied Sung I. "He who merely slaps at the gadfly on the cow's back will never succeed in killing the pesky lice.[2] Ch'in is now attacking Chao. If she is victorious in battle, then her troops will be weary and we can take advantage of their weakness. And if she is defeated, then we may lead our forces openly and without fear to the west, assured of victory over Ch'in. Therefore it is better for us to let Ch'in and Chao fight it out first. In buckling on armor and wielding a weapon I may be no match for you, but in sitting down and working out problems of strategy you are no match for me!" After this Sung I circulated an order throughout the army reading: "Fierce as a tiger, recalcitrant as a ram, greedy as a wolf, so headstrong they will not

[2] I.e., the Ch'in forces, deployed in small groups all over the empire, cannot be defeated by a single local victory, no matter how spectacular.

submit to orders—if there are any such men, let them all be decapitated." [3]

Sung I dispatched his son, Sung Hsiang, to be prime minister of Ch'i, accompanying him along the way as far as Wu-yen, where he held a great drinking party. The day was cold, a heavy rain was falling, and the soldiers were chilled and starving.

"We joined forces for the purpose of attacking Ch'in," Hsiang Yü declared, "but instead we have sat here all this time without advancing. The year is lean, the people are poor, and our men eat nothing but taro root and pulse. We have no provisions for our army, and yet Sung I holds a great drinking party. He will not lead the troops across the river so that we may live off the food of Chao and join forces with Chao in attacking Ch'in, but instead tells us to 'take advantage of Ch'in's weakness.' Now if Ch'in in all her strength attacks the newly founded state of Chao, she is sure to be powerful enough to defeat Chao. And if Chao is defeated and Ch'in is left as strong as ever, what sort of weakness will there be for us to take advantage of? Our troops were only lately defeated and the king sits uneasy on his throne, yet all the men within our borders are swept up together under Sung I's sole command, so that the entire safety of our state depends upon this one move. Now he takes no thought for our soldiers, but attends only to his personal affairs. He is a traitor to the altars of our soil and grain!"

Early the next day Hsiang Yü went to make his morning report to the supreme general, Sung I, and, when he had entered the tent, he cut off Sung I's head. Then he went outside and issued an order to the army, saying: "Sung I was plotting with Ch'i against Ch'u. The king of Ch'u secretly ordered me to execute him." All the other generals submitted in fear, none daring to raise any objection. "It was General Hsiang's family who first set up the royal family of Ch'u," they declared, "and now the general has executed this traitor!" By mutual assent they set up Hsiang Yü as acting supreme general. Someone was sent to pursue Sung I's son and murder him when he reached Ch'i, while Huan Ch'u was dispatched to report what had happened to King Huai, who confirmed Hsiang Yü's title of supreme general. Ch'ing

---

[3] A hint that he would welcome the assassination of Hsiang Yü.

Pu, the lord of Tang-yang, and General P'u both placed their armies under Hsiang Yü's command.

Hsiang Yü had already killed "His Lordship, the Commander of the Armies"; his might now shook the whole land of Ch'u and his fame reached the ears of all the leaders of the other states. He then dispatched Ch'ing Pu and General P'u at the head of a force of twenty thousand soldiers to cross the Yellow River and bring aid to the city of Chü-lu, but they succeeded in winning only slight success. Ch'en Yü, the Chao commander, sent a request for more troops. With this Hsiang Yü led his entire force across the river. Once across, he sank all his boats, smashed the cooking pots and vessels, and set fire to his huts, taking with him only three days' rations, to make clear to his soldiers that they must fight to the death, for he had no intention of returning. This done, he proceeded to surround the Ch'in general Wang Li and engage his army. After nine battles he managed to cut the supply road and inflict a major defeat, killing the Ch'in general, Su Chüeh, and taking Wang Li prisoner. A third Ch'in general, She Chien, refused to surrender to Ch'u and burned himself to death.

At this time the troops of Ch'u took the lead before those of all the other states. The armies of ten or more of the other states who had come to aid Chü-lu were camped in fortifications outside the city, but none of them dared send forth their troops. When the Ch'u army arrived and set upon Ch'in the leaders of the other armies all stood upon the ramparts of their camps and watched. Of the fighting men of Ch'u there was none who was not a match for ten of the enemy; the war cry of Ch'u shook the heavens and the men of the other armies all trembled with fear.

After Hsiang Yü had defeated the Ch'in army he summoned the leaders of the armies of the other states to audience. Entering the "carriage gates," [4] they all crawled forward on their knees and none dared look up. With this, Hsiang Yü for the first time became supreme commander of the leaders of the various states, and all of them were under his jurisdiction.

Chang Han's army was at this time camped at Chi-yüan and Hsiang Yü's army south of the Chang River, both holding their positions with-

---

[4] Formed by Ch'u's war chariots drawn up in array.

out engaging in battle. The Ch'in armies had several times been forced to retreat, and the Second Emperor sent an envoy to reprimand Chang Han for this. Chang Han grew fearful and dispatched his chief secretary, Ssu-ma Hsin, to plead on his behalf. When Ssu-ma Hsin reached the capital, he waited outside the palace gate for three days, but Chao Kao [5] refused to grant him audience on the grounds that he could not be trusted. Ssu-ma Hsin, filled with apprehension, hastened with all speed back to the army, not daring to take the road by which he had come. As he had feared, Chao Kao sent someone to pursue him, but the man failed to overtake him, and Ssu-ma Hsin succeeded in reaching the army and making his report: "Chao Kao is in complete control of the government and the officials under him can do nothing. If we manage to win victory now, Chao Kao is sure to be jealous of our merit, while if we are not victorious we will never escape the death penalty. I beg you to lay plans with the gravest care!"

Ch'en Yü, commander of the Chao forces, also sent a letter to Chang Han, stating:

Po Ch'i was once a general of Ch'in. In the south he conquered Yen and Ying; in the north he annihilated Ma-fu's army. Countless were the cities he attacked and the lands he seized, but at last he was condemned to death. Meng T'ien, too, was a general of Ch'in. In the north he drove out the barbarians and opened up thousands of miles of border land. But in the end his head was cut off at Yang-chou. Why was this? Because these men had won great merit and Ch'in could not reward them sufficiently with fiefs of land. So it invented some legal excuse to condemn and execute them instead.

Now you have been a general of Ch'in for three years, and while you have lost some hundred thousand troops, the leaders of the other states have risen up in ever increasing numbers. This man Chao Kao has for a long time flattered and deceived the Second Emperor, and now that affairs have reached a crisis he is afraid that the emperor will punish him. Therefore he hopes to use the law to punish you, in order to divert responsibility, and to send someone to take your place so that he may avoid disaster to himself.

You have been in the field for a long time, General, and you have many enemies at court. Regardless of whether you win glory or not, you are sure to be executed. The time has come when Heaven will destroy Ch'in and

[5] The eunuch who controlled the Second Emperor of the Ch'in and wielded the real power in the government.

every man, wise or foolish, knows it. Powerless to speak the truth openly to the court, camping in the fields as the leader of a doomed nation, would it not be pitiful if you were to try to drag out your days thus alone and friendless? Why do you not lead your troops and join with the other leaders of the Vertical Alliance? [6] We will take an oath to attack Ch'in together, divide up the land into kingdoms, face south [7] and call ourselves sovereigns. Would this not be better than bowing your body beneath the executioner's axe and seeing your wife and children slaughtered?

Chang Han was deeply perplexed and secretly sent his lieutenant Shih-ch'eng to Hsiang Yü, requesting an alliance. But before the alliance was concluded Hsiang Yü dispatched General P'u who, marching day and night, led his troops across the Chang River at the ford called Three Houses and camped south of the river, where he fought with the Ch'in army and defeated it again. Hsiang Yü then led all his troops in an attack upon the Ch'in army on the banks of the Yü River and inflicted a major defeat.

Chang Han again sent one of his men to see Hsiang Yü. Hsiang Yü summoned his officers into council and announced, "Our provisions are running low. I think we had better listen to his request for an alliance." When his officers all agreed Hsiang Yü set a date for a meeting with Chang Han at the site of the old capital of Yin south of the Yüan River. After the oaths of alliance had been concluded Chang Han came to Hsiang Yü, the tears streaming from his eyes, and informed him of Chao Kao's behavior. Hsiang Yü made Chang Han the king of Yung and quartered him with his own army. The chief secretary Ssu-ma Hsin he made supreme commander of the Ch'in armies with orders to lead them in an advance march as far as Hsin-an.

The officers and soldiers of the armies of the other states had in the past from time to time been sent to work on construction projects or on garrison duty and, when they had passed through the capital area of Ch'in, had often been ruthlessly treated by the officers and men of Ch'in. Now that the Ch'in army had surrendered to the other leaders they and their men took advantage of their victory to treat the Ch'in

[6] The alliance of states along the eastern coast who were traditionally opposed to Ch'in.

[7] The Chinese sovereign when he sits upon his throne faces south; hence, to "face south" means to become an independent ruler.

soldiers like slaves or prisoners and insult and abuse them with impunity. Many of the Ch'in officers and men whispered among themselves in secret, saying, "General Chang and the rest have tricked us into surrendering to the other leaders. Now if we succeed in entering the Pass and defeating Ch'in, all will be well. But if we are not successful, the other leaders will make prisoners of us and take us east with them, and Ch'in will most certainly execute all our parents and wives and children."

The generals of the army, hearing rumors of these plottings, reported them to Hsiang Yü, who summoned Ch'ing Pu and General P'u and announced to them this plan: "The officers and men of Ch'in are still very numerous, and in their hearts they have not surrendered. If, after we reach the land within the Pass, they should prove disloyal, we will be in a very dangerous situation. It would be better to attack and kill them, sparing only Chang Han, the chief secretary Ssu-ma Hsin, and Colonel Tung I to go with us to invade Ch'in." Accordingly the Ch'u army attacked by night and butchered over 200,000 soldiers of Ch'in south of the city of Hsin-an.

Then they proceeded on their way, overrunning and seizing control of the territory of Ch'in, until they reached the Han-ku Pass. But the Pass was guarded by soldiers, and they could not enter. When news came that the governor of P'ei had already conquered the capital city of Hsien-yang, Hsiang Yü was enraged, and sent Ch'ing Pu and others to attack the Pass. Hsiang Yü was finally able to enter, and proceeded as far as the west side of the Hsi River.

The governor of P'ei was camped at Pa-shang and had not yet had an opportunity to meet with Hsiang Yü. Ts'ao Wu-shang, marshal of the left to the governor of P'ei, sent a messenger to report to Hsiang Yü, saying, "The governor of P'ei is planning to become king of the area within the Pass, employ Tzu-ying [8] as his prime minister, and keep possession of all the precious articles and treasures of the capital." Hsiang Yü was in a rage. "Tomorrow," he announced, "I shall feast my soldiers and then we will attack and crush the governor of P'ei."

At this time Hsiang Yü had a force of 400,000 men encamped at Hung-men in Hsin-feng. The governor of P'ei, with a force of 100,000,

[8] The last ruler of Ch'in, who had already surrendered to the governor of P'ei.

was at Pa-shang. Fan Tseng counseled Hsiang Yü, saying, "When the governor of P'ei was living east of the mountains he was greedy for possessions and delighted in beautiful girls. But now that he has entered the Pass he has not taken a single thing, nor has he dallied with any of the wives or maidens. This proves that his mind is not set upon minor joys. I have sent men to observe the sky over the place where he is encamped, and they all found it full of shapes like dragons and tigers and colored with five colors. These are the signs of a Son of Heaven. You must attack him at once and not lose this chance!"

Hsiang Po, the Ch'u commander of the left, was an uncle of Hsiang Yü and for a long time had been good friends with Chang Liang, the marquis of Liu. Chang Liang was at this time serving under the governor of P'ei. That night Hsiang Po galloped on horse to the camp of the governor of P'ei and visited Chang Liang in secret, telling him of Hsiang Yü's plans and begging Chang Liang to come away with him. "Do not throw your life away along with all the others!" he urged.

"I have been sent by the king of Hann to accompany the governor of P'ei," Chang Liang replied. "Now when he is faced with these difficulties, it would not be right for me to run away and leave him. I must report to him what you have told me."

Chang Liang then went and reported the situation in full to the governor of P'ei. "What shall we do?" exclaimed the governor in great consternation.

"Who was it who thought up this plan of action for you?" asked Chang Liang.

"Some fool advised me that if I guarded the Pass and did not let the other leaders enter, I could rule the entire region of Ch'in, and so I followed his plan," he replied.

"Do you believe that you have enough soldiers to stand up against Hsiang Yü?" Chang Liang asked.

The governor was silent for a while, and then said, "No, certainly not. But what should we do now?"

"You must let me go and explain to Hsiang Po," said Chang Liang, "and tell him that you would not dare to be disloyal to Hsiang Yü."

"How do you happen to be friends with Hsiang Po?" asked the governor.

"We knew each other in the time of Ch'in," replied Chang Liang, "and once when Hsiang Po killed a man I saved his life. Now that we are in trouble, he has for that reason been good enough to come and report to me."

"Is he older or younger than you?" asked the governor.

"He is older than I," replied Chang Liang.

"Call him in for me," said the governor, "and I will treat him as I would an elder brother."

Chang Liang went out and urged Hsiang Po to enter. Hsiang Po came in to see the governor of P'ei, who offered him a cup of wine and drank to his long life, swearing an oath of friendship. "Since I entered the Pass," he said, "I have not dared to lay a finger on a single thing. I have preserved the registers of the officials and people and sealed up the storehouses, awaiting the arrival of General Hsiang Yü. The reason I sent officers to guard the Pass was to prevent thieves from getting in and to prepare for any emergency. Day and night I have looked forward to the arrival of the general. How would I dare be disloyal to him? I beg you to report to him in full and tell him that I would not think of turning my back upon his kindness!"

Hsiang Po agreed to do so, adding, "You must come early tomorrow and apologize in person to General Hsiang." "I shall," promised the governor, and with this Hsiang Po went back out into the night.

When he reached his own camp, he reported to Hsiang Yü all that the governor had said. "If the governor of P'ei had not first conquered the land within the Pass how would you have dared to enter?" he said. "When a man has done you a great service it would not be right to attack him. It is better to treat him as a friend." Hsiang Yü agreed to this.

The next day the governor of P'ei, accompanied by a hundred some horsemen, came to visit Hsiang Yü. When he reached Hsiang Yü's camp at Hung-men, he made his apologies, saying, "You and I have joined forces to attack Ch'in, you fighting north of the Yellow River, I fighting south. Quite beyond my expectation it happened that I was able to enter the Pass first, conquer Ch'in, and meet with you again here. Now it seems that some worthless person has been spreading talk and trying to cause dissension between us."

"It is your own marshal of the left, Ts'ao Wu-shang, who has been doing the talking," replied Hsiang Yü. "If it were not for him, how would I ever have doubted you?"

On the same day Hsiang Yü invited the governor of P'ei to remain and drink with him. Hsiang Yü and Hsiang Po as hosts sat facing east. Fan Tseng (whose other name was Ya-fu) took the place of honor facing south, while the governor of P'ei sat facing north with Chang Liang, as his attendant, facing west. Fan Tseng from time to time eyed Hsiang Yü and three times lifted up the jade pendant in the form of a broken ring which he wore and showed it to Yü, hinting that he should "break" once and for all with the governor, but Hsiang Yü sat silent and did not respond. Fan Tseng then rose and left the tent and, summoning Hsiang Yü's cousin, Hsiang Chuang, said to him, "Our lord is too kind-heated a man. Go back in and ask to propose a toast, and when the toast is finished, request to be allowed to perform a sword dance. Then attack the governor of P'ei and kill him where he sits. If you don't, you and all of us will end up as his prisoners!"

Hsiang Chuang entered and proposed a toast. When the toast was finished he said, "Our lord and the governor of P'ei are pleased to drink together but I fear that, this being an army camp, we have nothing to offer by way of entertainment. I beg therefore to be allowed to present a sword dance." "Proceed," said Hsiang Yü, whereupon Hsiang Chuang drew his sword and began to dance. But Hsiang Po also rose and danced, constantly shielding and protecting the governor of P'ei with his own body so that Hsiang Chuang could not attack him.

With this, Chang Liang left and went to the gate of the camp to see Fan K'uai. "How are things proceeding today?" asked Fan K'uai.

"The situation is very grave," replied Chang Liang. "Now Hsiang Chuang has drawn his sword and is dancing, always with his eyes set on the governor of P'ei!"

"This is serious indeed!" said Fan K'uai. "I beg you to let me go in and share the fate of the rest!" Fan K'uai buckled on his sword, grasped his shield, and entered the gate of the camp. The sentries standing with crossed spears tried to stop him from entering but, tipping his shield to either side, he knocked the men to the ground. Entering the camp, he went and pulled back the curtain of the tent and stood facing west, glaring fixedly at Hsiang Yü. His hair stood on end and his eyes blazed with fire.

Hsiang Yü put his hand on his sword and raised himself up on one knee.[9] "Who is our guest?" he asked.

"Fan K'uai, the carriage attendant of the governor of P'ei," announced Chang Liang.

"He is a stouthearted fellow," said Hsiang Yü. "Give him a cup of wine!" A large cup of wine was passed to Fan K'uai, who knelt and accepted it, and then rose again and drank it standing up. "Give him a shoulder of pork," ordered Hsiang Yü, and he was given a piece of parboiled pork shoulder. Fan K'uai placed his shield upside down on the ground, put the pork shoulder on top of it, drew his sword, and began to cut and eat the meat.

"You are a brave man," said Hsiang Yü. "Can you drink some more?"

"I would not hesitate if you offered me death! Why should I refuse a cup of wine?" he replied. "The king of Ch'in [10] had the heart of a tiger and a wolf. He killed men as though he thought he could never finish, he punished men as though he were afraid he would never get around to them all, and the whole world revolted against him. King Huai of Ch'u made a promise with all the leaders that whoever defeated Ch'in first and entered the capital of Hsien-yang should become its king. Now the governor of P'ei has defeated Ch'in and entered Hsien-yang ahead of all others. He has not dared to lay a finger on the slightest thing, but has closed up and sealed the palace rooms and returned to Pa-shang to encamp and await your arrival. The reason he sent officers to guard the Pass was to prevent thieves from getting in and to prepare for an emergency. After suffering great hardship and winning such merit, he has not been rewarded by the grant of a fief and title. Instead you have listened to some worthless talk and are

---

[9] The Chinese of this age had no chairs, but sat on mats on the floor.
[10] I.e., the First Emperor of Ch'in.

about to punish a man of merit. This is no more than a repetition of the fated Ch'in. If I may be so bold, I advise you not to go through with it!"

Hsiang Yü, having no answer to this, said "Sit down!" Fan K'uai took a seat next to Chang Liang. After they had been seated for a while, the governor of P'ei got up and went to the toilet, summoning Fan K'uai to go with him. When they had been outside for a while, Hsiang Yü sent Colonel Ch'en P'ing to call the governor back in. "When I left just now," said the governor, "I failed to say good-by. What should I do?"

"Great deeds do not wait on petty caution; great courtesy does not need little niceties," replied Fan K'uai. "This fellow is about to get out his carving knife and platter and make mincemeat of us! Why should you say good-by to him?"

With this, the governor of P'ei left, ordering Chang Liang to stay behind and make some excuse for him. "What did you bring as gifts?" asked Chang Liang.

"I have a pair of white jade discs which I intended to give to Hsiang Yü," replied the governor, "and a pair of jade wine dippers for Fan Tseng, but when I found that they were angry I did not dare to present them. You must present them for me." "I will do my best," said Chang Liang.

At this time Hsiang Yü's camp was at Hung-men, and the governor of P'ei's camp at Pa-shang some forty *li* away. The governor of P'ei left his carriages and horsemen where they were and slipped away from the camp on horseback, accompanied by only four men, Fan K'uai, Lord T'eng, Chin Ch'iang, and Chi Hsin, who bore swords and shields and hastened on foot. Following the foot of Mount Li, they returned by a secret way through Chih-yang.

When the governor left the camp he told Chang Liang, "By the road I will take it is no more than twenty *li* back to our camp. When you think I have had time to reach the camp, then go back and join the party." After the governor of P'ei had left and enough time had elapsed for him to reach camp, Chang Liang went in and made apologies. "The governor of P'ei was regrettably rather far gone in his cups and was unable to say good-by. He has respectfully requested me on his behalf to present this pair of white jade discs to Your Lord-ship with his humblest salutation, and to General Fan Tseng this pair of jade wine dippers."

"Where is the governor of P'ei?" asked Hsiang Yü.

"He perceived that Your Lordship was likely to reprove him for his shortcomings," replied Chang Liang, "and so he slipped away alone and returned to his camp."

Hsiang Yü accepted the jade discs and placed them beside him on his mat, but Fan Tseng put the dippers on the ground, drew his sword and smashed them to pieces. "Ah!" he said, "it does not do to lay plans with an idiot! It is the governor of P'ei who will snatch the world out of our hands, and on that day all of us will become his prisoners."

When the governor of P'ei got back to his camp he immediately had Ts'ao Wu-shang seized and executed.

A few days later Hsiang Yü led his troops west and massacred the inhabitants of Hsien-yang, the capital city, killing Tzu-ying, the king of Ch'in, who had already surrendered, and setting fire to the palaces of Ch'in; the fire burned for three months before it went out. Then he gathered up all the goods, treasures, and waiting women, and started east.

Someone advised Hsiang Yü, saying, "The area within the Pass is protected on all four sides by barriers of mountains and rivers, and the land is rich and fertile. This is the place to make your capital and rule as a dictator." But Hsiang Yü saw that the palaces of Ch'in had all been burned and destroyed, and he remembered his native land and longed only to return east. "To become rich and famous and then not go back to your old home is like putting on an embroidered coat and going out walking in the night," he said. "Who is to know about it?"

Later the man who had advised him remarked, "People say that the men of Ch'u are nothing but monkeys with hats on, and now I know what they mean!" Hsiang Yü heard about the remark and had the adviser boiled alive.

Hsiang Yü sent an envoy to report to King Huai of Ch'u. "Let all be done according to the agreement," the king replied. Hsiang Yü then honored King Huai with the title of "Righteous Emperor." Wishing to make himself a king, he first conferred titles on his generals and ministers, telling them, "When the rebellion broke out in the empire, I temporarily set up the heirs of the former feudal rulers, so that they would attack Ch'in. But it was you, my generals, and I who actually donned armor, took up our weapons, and led the undertaking, camping for three years in the open fields, until our might at last destroyed Ch'in and brought peace to the world. As for the Righteous Emperor, though he has done nothing to win merit, it is for various reasons fitting that we assign him a portion of the territory to rule." The generals all expressing agreement, Hsiang Yü accordingly divided the empire and set up the generals as marquises and kings.

Hsiang Yü and Fan Tseng suspected that the governor of P'ei had ambitions to seize the whole empire. But since they had already made their peace with him, and hesitated to go back on the agreement to make him ruler of the land within the Pass, for fear that the other leaders would revolt, they plotted together in secret, saying, "The area of Pa and Shu is cut off by mountains and inhabited largely by settlers sent by Ch'in. Thus we can say that it too is a 'land within the pass.'" With this as an excuse they set up the governor of P'ei as king of Han, ruling over the area of Pa, Shu, and Han,[11] with his capital at Nan-cheng. The real land within the Pass they divided into three parts, and they made kings of the Ch'in generals who had surrendered, so that the latter could block any advance of the king of Han. Thus Hsiang Yü made Chang Han the king of Yung, ruling over the land west of the city of Hsien-yang, with his capital at Fei-ch'iu. The chief secretary Ssu-ma Hsin had formerly been prison warden of Yüeh-yang and had done a great kindness for Hsiang Liang, while Colonel Tung I was the one who had originally urged Chang Han to surrender to the Ch'u army. Therefore Hsiang Yü made Ssu-ma Hsin the king of Sai, ruling the area from Hsien-yang east to the Yellow River, with his capital at Yüeh-yang, and made Tung I the king of Ti, ruling the province of Shang, with his capital at Kao-nu. Pao, the king of Wei, he transferred to the position of king of Western Wei, ruling Ho-tung, with his capital at P'ing-yang. Shen Yang, governor of Hsia-ch'iu, a

---

[11] The area southwest of the Ch'in capital, on the far western border of China.

favorite minister of Chang Erh, had formerly conquered the province of Ho-nan and gone to welcome the Ch'u army on the banks of the Yellow River. Therefore Hsiang Yü set up Shen Yang as king of Ho-nan, with his capital at Lo-yang. Ch'eng, the king of Hann, remained at his former capital, Yang-ti. Ssu-ma Ang, general of Chao, had pacified the area of Ho-nei and several times distinguished himself, so he was set up as king of Yin, ruling Ho-nei, with his capital at Chao-ko. Hsieh, the king of Chao, was removed and made king of Tai. The prime minister of Chao, Chang Erh, was a man of worthy character and had, moreover, followed Hsiang Yü in his march through the Pass. Therefore he was made king of Ch'ang-shan, ruling the land of Chao, with his capital at Hsiang-kuo. The lord of Tang-yang, Ch'ing Pu, as a general of Ch'u had repeatedly won the highest distinction in battle and therefore was made king of Chiu-chiang, his capital at Liu. Wu Jui, the lord of P'o, had led the forces of the hundred Yüeh to aid the other leaders and had also followed Hsiang Yü within the Pass. Therefore he was made king of Heng-shan, his capital at Chu. Kung Ao, chief minister to the Righteous Emperor, had led troops in attacking the Nan district and had won great merit; accordingly he was made king of Lin-chiang, his capital at Chiang-ling. Han Kuang, the king of Yen, was moved to the position of king of Liao-tung. Tsang Tu, general of Yen, had joined the Ch'u forces in rescuing Chao and afterwards had accompanied Hsiang Yü through the Pass, so Hsiang Yü made him king of Yen, his capital at Chi. T'ien Shih, the king of Ch'i, was moved to the position of king of Chiao-tung. T'ien Tu, general of Ch'i, because he had joined Ch'u in rescuing Chao and entering the Pass, was made king of Ch'i, with his capital at Lin-tzu. T'ien An was the grandson of King Chien of Ch'i whom Ch'in had deposed. At the time when Hsiang Yü crossed the Yellow River and went to the aid of Chao, T'ien An had captured several cities of Chi-pei and had led his troops and surrendered to Hsiang Yü. Therefore he was made king of Chi-pei, his capital at Po-yang. T'ien Jung, because he had several times betrayed Hsiang Liang and refused to send troops to join Ch'u in its attack on Ch'in, was not enfeoffed. Ch'en Yü, the lord of Ch'eng-an, had discarded his seals of authority as a general and fled, refusing to follow Hsiang Yü through the Pass.

But Hsiang Yü learned of his reputation as a man of worth and of his services to Chao and, hearing that he was living in Nan-p'i, enfeoffed him with the three surrounding districts. Mei Hsüan, general of Wu Jui, the lord of P'o, because of his many services, was enfeoffed as a marquis with a hundred thousand households. Hsiang Yü made himself "Dictator King of Western Ch'u," ruling nine provinces, with his capital at P'eng-ch'eng.

In the first year of Han [206 B.C.],[12] the fourth month, the various leaders left the command of Hsiang Yü and proceeded to their own countries. Hsiang Yü also departed and went to his kingdom. He then sent an envoy to transfer the residence of the Righteous Emperor, announcing that "the emperors of ancient times, who ruled over an area a thousand miles on each side, invariably resided on the upper reaches of a river." The envoy accordingly moved the Righteous Emperor to the district of Ch'en in Ch'ang-sha, pressing him to hurry on his way. The emperor's ministers became increasingly disillusioned and turned their backs on him. Hsiang Yü then secretly ordered the kings of Heng-shan and Lin-chiang to attack and murder the Righteous Emperor in the region of the Yangtze.

Ch'eng, the king of Hann, had won no merit in battle, so Hsiang Yü did not send him to his kingdom but instead took him with him to P'eng-ch'eng. There he deprived him of his title, made him a marquis, and later murdered him. Tsang Tu, the new king of Yen, proceeded to his realm and attempted to drive out the former king, Han Kuang, and send him to Liao-tung, the territory newly assigned to him. But Han Kuang refused to obey, so Tsang Tu attacked and killed him at Wu-chung and made himself king of Liao-tung as well. When T'ien Jung heard that Hsiang Yü had moved Shih, the king of Ch'i, to Chiao-tung, and set up T'ien Tu, a general of Ch'i, as the new king of Ch'i, he was very angry and refused to send Shih to Chiao-tung. Instead he declared Ch'i to be in revolt, and marched forth to attack T'ien Tu. T'ien Tu fled to Ch'u. T'ien Shih, king of Ch'i, fearful of Hsiang Yü, fled to Chiao-tung, thus reaching his new realm.

[12] The Han dynasty counted its years from the time when its founder, Liu Chi, first became king of Han, though it was not until 202 B.C. that he actually gained control of the whole empire.

T'ien Jung, in a rage, pursued and attacked him, killing him at Chi-mo. T'ien Jung then set himself up as king of Ch'i, marched west, and attacked and killed T'ien An, the new king of Chi-pei. Thus he became ruler of the three areas of Ch'i, Chi-pei, and Chiao-tung. He then presented P'eng Yüeh with the seals of office of a general and sent him to lead a revolt in the region of Liang.

Ch'en Yü, the former general of Chao, secretly sent Chang T'ung and Hsia Yüeh to advise T'ien Jung, saying, "Hsiang Yü's actions as ruler of the empire have been completely unjust. All the former kings he has made rulers of poor territories, giving the best lands to his own ministers and generals to rule. He has expelled the king of Chao, my former lord, and sent him north to live in Tai. I consider such actions inexcusable. I have heard that, as king of Ch'i, you have taken up arms and refused to bow to such unrighteousness. I beg that you will send troops to aid me so that I may attack Chang Erh, the new king of Ch'ang-shan, who is now ruling the land of Chao, and restore the former king of Chao. Then his kingdom may act as a protective barrier for you."

The king of Ch'i approved this suggestion, and dispatched troops to Chao. Ch'en Yü called up all the troops from the three districts under his command and, joining forces with Ch'i, attacked Chang Erh, the king of Ch'ang-shan, inflicting a severe defeat. Chang Erh fled and joined the king of Han. Ch'en Yü proceeded to Tai and escorted Hsieh, the former king of Chao, back to Chao. In turn, the king of Chao set up Ch'en Yü as king of Tai.

It was at this time that the king of Han returned from his fief and reconquered the three new territories of Ch'in. When Hsiang Yü received word that the king of Han had united all the area within the Pass under his rule and was about to proceed east, and that Ch'i and Liang were in revolt against him, he was enraged. He made Cheng Ch'ang, the former district magistrate of Wu, the king of Hann in order to block the advance of the Han armies, and dispatched Chüeh, the lord of Hsiao, and others, with orders to attack P'eng Yüeh, but P'eng Yüeh defeated them.

The king of Han sent Chang Liang to seize the region of Hann. Chang Liang sent a letter to Hsiang Yü, saying, "The king of Han has been deprived of the position which was rightly his. He desires to be given the territory within the Pass according to the original agreement. If this is done he will halt and proceed no farther east." He also sent to Hsiang Yü rebellious letters from Ch'i and Liang, proving that Ch'i intended to join with Liang in destroying Ch'u. As a result, Hsiang Yü for the moment gave up the idea of marching west and instead proceeded north to attack Ch'i. He sent an order for troops to Ch'ing Pu, the king of Chiu-chiang. Ch'ing Pu, pleading illness, refused to go in person, but instead sent his general with a force of several thousand men. Because of this incident, Hsiang Yü came to hate Ch'ing Pu.

In the winter of the second year of Han [205 B.C.] Hsiang Yü proceeded north as far as Ch'eng-yang. T'ien Jung led his troops to meet him there in battle, but failed to win a victory and fled to P'ing-yüan. Hsiang Yü marched north, firing and leveling the fortifications and dwellings of Ch'i, butchering all the soldiers of T'ien Jung who surrendered to him, and binding and taking prisoner the old people, women, and children. Thus he seized control of Ch'i as far as the northern sea, inflicting great damage and destruction. The people of Ch'i once more banded together in revolt. With this, T'ien Jung's younger brother, T'ien Heng, gathered a force of twenty or thirty thousand men from among the soldiers of Ch'i who had fled into hiding, and raised a revolt in Ch'eng-yang. Hsiang Yü was thus forced to remain in the area and continue fighting, but he was not able to put down the rebels.

In the spring the king of Han, with the forces of five of the other feudal leaders numbering 560,000 men under his command, marched east and attacked Ch'u. When Hsiang Yü received word of this, he ordered his subordinate generals to continue the assault on Ch'i, while he himself led a force of thirty thousand picked men south through Lu to Hu-ling.

In the fourth month the king of Han had already entered P'eng-ch'eng, the capital of Ch'u, had seized possession of its treasures and beautiful women, and was spending his days in feasting and revelry. Hsiang Yü marched west through Hsiao and at dawn attacked the Han army, fighting his way back east as far as P'eng-ch'eng, and in the course of the day inflicted a major defeat. When the Han army fled, he pursued it to the Ssu and Ku Rivers, killing over a hundred thousand Han soldiers. The remainder all fled south to the mountains, where Hsiang Yü once more pursued and attacked them on the Sui River east of Ling-pi. Thus in its retreat the Han army was constantly pressed by the Ch'u forces and many of its men killed. Some hundred thousand Han soldiers were driven into the Sui River, so that the flow of the river was blocked. Hsiang Yü had surrounded the king of Han with a threefold line of troops, when a great wind arose and began to blow from the northwest, breaking down trees, toppling roofs, and raising clouds of sand, so that the sky grew dark and the day turned to night. As the storm advanced and bore down upon the forces of Ch'u, they were thrown into great confusion and their lines crumbled. The king of Han was thus able to slip through with twenty or thirty horsemen and escape.

The king of Han hoped to pass through his old home of P'ei and gather up his family before proceeding west. But Hsiang Yü had in the meantime sent men to pursue him to P'ei and seize the members of his family, so that they had all fled into hiding and he could not find them. Along the road, however, he happened to encounter his son (later Emperor Hui) and daughter (later Princess Yüan of Lu). Putting them in the carriage, he hastened on his way.

The horsemen of Ch'u were in close pursuit, and the king of Han in desperation several times pushed his little son and daughter out of the carriage, but each time Lord T'eng, who was with him, got out, picked them up, and put them back in the carriage.[13] This had happened three times when Lord T'eng said, "No matter how sorely we are pressed in chase it will not do to abandon the children!"

The king of Han at last managed to elude his pursuers and went in search of his father and wife, but could find them nowhere. They, in the meantime, accompanied by Shen I-chi, had fled by a secret route and were searching for the king, but instead of finding him they stumbled into the Ch'u army and were seized and led back to the

---

[13] According to the much more plausible account of this incident in the biography of Lord T'eng (*Shih chi* 95) the king did not actually push the children out of the carriage, but only attempted to do so by kicking them with his foot, whereupon Lord T'eng each time pulled them back to safety.

camp. When their capture was reported to Hsiang Yü, he ordered them to be kept under guard in the midst of his army.

At this time Lü Tse, the marquis of Chou-lü, elder brother of the king of Han's wife, was in Hsia-i with a force of troops loyal to the king. The king secretly made his way there and joined him. Gathering his soldiers together bit by bit, he proceeded to Jung-yang, where he held a rendezvous of all his defeated divisions. In addition, Hsiao Ho dispatched all the old men and underaged youths from the area within the Pass to Jung-yang, so that the Han army again reached sizable strength.

Hsiang Yü, after his initial victory at P'eng-ch'eng, had taken advantage of his supremacy to pursue the Han forces north. Now, however, he fought with the Han army once more in the area of So in Ching, south of Jung-yang, and was defeated. Thus Hsiang Yü was unable to proceed west of Jung-yang. While Hsiang Yü was recapturing P'eng-ch'eng from the king of Han and pursuing him to Jung-yang, T'ien Heng managed to gain control of Ch'i and set up T'ien Jung's son Kuang as king of Ch'i. When the king of Han was defeated at P'eng-ch'eng, the other feudal lords all deserted him and went over to the side of Ch'u. The king camped at Jung-yang and constructed a walled supply road along the banks of the Yellow River in order to transport grain from the Ao Granary.

In the third year of Han [204 B.C.] Hsiang Yü several times attacked and cut off the Han supply road so that the king of Han grew short of provisions. Afraid of what might happen, he made a bid for peace, asking that he be allowed to retain all the territory west of Jung-yang as part of Han. Hsiang Yü was in favor of listening to the suggestion, but Fan Tseng (now marquis of Li-yang) advised him against it. "It is easy enough to make concessions to Han, but if you let him go this time and do not seize him, you are bound to regret it later!" Hsiang Yü and Fan Tseng then joined in pressing the siege of Jung-yang.

The king of Han was in great distress but, employing a strategy suggested by Ch'en P'ing, he managed to cause dissension between his two enemies. An envoy having arrived from Hsiang Yü, the king ordered a great feast prepared and brought in to be served to him. When the king saw the envoy, however, he pretended to be thoroughly startled and said, "Oh, I supposed you were the envoy from Fan Tseng, but I see on the contrary you have come from Hsiang Yü!" He then had the feast taken away and a poor meal brought and served to the man. When the envoy returned and reported this, Hsiang Yü began to suspect that Fan Tseng had made some secret alliance with Han and was trying gradually to usurp his own authority. Fan Tseng, deeply angered, announced, "The affairs of the world have been largely settled. My lord must now manage things for himself. For my part, I beg to be relieved of my duties and returned to the ranks of a common soldier." Hsiang Yü granted his request and Fan Tseng departed, but before he had got as far as P'eng-ch'eng an ulcerous sore broke out on his back and he died.

The Han general Chi Hsin advised the king, saying, "The situation is very grave. I beg you to let me deceive Ch'u for you by taking your place as king. In this way you will be able to slip away in secret." Accordingly, the king of Han dressed two thousand women of Jung-yang in armor and, when night fell, sent them out by the eastern gate of the city. The soldiers of Ch'u rushed to attack them from all sides. Chi Hsin then rode forth in the yellow-canopied royal carriage with its plumes attached to the left side and announced, "The food in the city is exhausted. The king of Han surrenders!" While the army of Ch'u joined in cheers of victory, the king of Han with twenty or thirty horsemen slipped out by the western gate and fled to Ch'eng-kao.

When Hsiang Yü saw Chi Hsin he demanded to know where the king of Han was. "The king of Han," replied Chi Hsin, "has already left the city!" Hsiang Yü had Chi Hsin burned alive.

The king of Han left the grand secretary Chou K'o, Lord Ts'ung, and Wei Pao, the former king of Wei, to guard Jung-yang. But Chou K'o and Lord Ts'ung plotted together, saying, "It is hard to guard a city with the king of a country that has once revolted," [14] and so together they murdered Wei Pao.

Hsiang Yü captured Jung-yang and took Chou K'o alive. "If you will be my general, I will make you supreme commander and enfeoff you with thirty thousand households," said Hsiang Yü, but Chou K'o

[14] Wei Pao had formerly revolted against the king of Han and had been taken prisoner.

only cursed him, saying, "If you do not hurry and surrender to the king of Han, you will be taken prisoner! You are no match for him!" Hsiang Yü, enraged, boiled Chou K'o alive and at the same time executed Lord Ts'ung.

After the king of Han escaped from Jung-yang, he fled south to Yüan and She, and joined Ch'ing Pu, the king of Chiu-chiang. Gathering soldiers as he went, he returned and guarded Ch'eng-kao.

In the fourth year of Han [203 B.C.] Hsiang Yü advanced with his forces and surrounded Ch'eng-kao. The king of Han escaped alone from the northern gate of Ch'eng-kao, accompanied only by Lord T'eng, crossed the Yellow River, and fled to Hsiu-wu, where he joined the armies of Chang Erh and Han Hsin. His subordinate generals one by one managed to escape from Ch'eng-kao and join him there. Hsiang Yü finally captured Ch'eng-kao and was about to proceed west, but Han sent troops to block him at Kung so he could go no further west. At the same time P'eng Yüeh crossed the Yellow River and attacked part of the Ch'u army at Tung-a, killing the Ch'u general Lord Hsieh. Hsiang Yü then marched east in person and attacked P'eng Yüeh.

The king of Han, having obtained command of the soldiers of Han Hsin, wished to cross the Yellow River and proceed south. On the advice of Cheng Chung, however, he abandoned this idea and instead stopped at Ho-nei and built a walled camp, sending Liu Chia to lead a band of men to aid P'eng Yüeh and to burn Ch'u's stores and provisions. Hsiang Yü proceeded east and attacked them, forcing P'eng Yüeh to flee.

The king of Han then led his troops back across the Yellow River and retook Ch'eng-kao, camped at Kuang-wu, and again began to draw provisions from the Ao Granary. Hsiang Yü, having pacified the eastern seaboard, returned west and camped opposite the Han forces at Kuang-wu, and thus the two armies remained, each in its own camp, for several months.

Meanwhile P'eng Yüeh continued to foment rebellion in the region of Liang, and from time to time cut off Ch'u's supply lines. Hsiang Yü, much troubled by this, constructed a sacrificial altar and, placing the "Venerable Sire," the king of Han's father, on it, he announced to the king, "If you do not surrender to me at once, I shall boil your 'Venerable Sire' alive!"

"When you and I bowed together before King Huai and acknowledged our allegiance to him, we took a vow to be brothers," replied the king of Han. "Therefore my father is your father, too. If you insist now upon boiling your own father, I hope you will be good enough to send me a cup of the soup!"

Hsiang Yü, in a rage, was about to kill the old man, but Hsiang Po intervened: "No one knows yet how the affairs of the world will turn out. A man like the king of Han who has his eyes set upon the rulership of the world will hardly bother about a member of his family. Even if you kill his father, it will bring you no advantage, but only increase your misfortunes." Following his advice, Hsiang Yü desisted.

For a long time Ch'u and Han held their respective positions without making a decisive move, while their fighting men suffered the hardships of camp life and their old men and boys wore themselves out transporting provisions by land and water. Hsiang Yü sent word to the king of Han, saying, "The world has been in strife and confusion for several years now, solely because of the two of us. I would like to invite the king of Han to a personal combat to decide who is the better man. Let us bring no more needless suffering to the fathers and sons of the rest of the world." The king of Han scorned the offer with a laugh, saying, "Since I am no match for you in strength, I prefer to fight you with brains!"

Hsiang Yü then sent out one of his bravest men to challenge Han to combat. In the Han army there was a man who was very skillful at shooting from horseback, a so-called *lou-fan*.[15] Ch'u three times sent out men to challenge Han to combat, and each time this man shot and killed them on the spot. Hsiang Yü, enraged, buckled on his armor, took up a lance, and went out himself to deliver the challenge. The *lou-fan* was about to shoot when Hsiang Yü shouted and glared so fiercely at him that the man had not the courage to raise his eyes or lift a hand, but finally fled back within the walls and did not dare venture

[15] The men of the barbarian tribe of Lou-fan being famous for their skill in archery, the word *lou-fan* came to mean an expert bowman.

forth again. The king of Han secretly sent someone to find out who the new challenger was, and when he learned that it was Hsiang Yü himself he was greatly astonished. Hsiang Yü approached the place where the king of Han was standing, and the two of them talked back and forth across the ravine of Kuang-wu. The king berated Hsiang Yü for his crimes, while Hsiang Yü angrily demanded a single combat. When the king of Han refused to agree, Hsiang Yü shot him with a crossbow which he had concealed, and the king, wounded, fled into the city of Ch'eng-kao.

Hsiang Yü, receiving word that Han Hsin had already conquered the area north of the Yellow River, defeating Ch'i and Chao, and was about to attack Ch'u, sent Lung Chü to attack him. Han Hsin, joined by the cavalry general Kuan Ying, met his attack and defeated the Ch'u army, killing Lung Chü. Han Hsin then proceeded to set himself up as king of Ch'i. When Hsiang Yü heard that Lung Chü's army had been defeated, he was fearful and sent Wu She, a man of Hsü-i, to attempt to bargain with Han Hsin, but Han Hsin refused to listen.

At this time P'eng Yüeh had once more raised a revolt in the region of Liang, conquered it, and cut off Ch'u's sources of supply. Hsiang Yü summoned the marquis of Hai-ch'un, the grand marshal Ts'ao Chiu, and others and said to them, "Hold fast to the city of Ch'eng-kao. Even if the king of Han challenges you to a battle, take care and do not fight with him! You must not let him advance eastward! In fifteen days I can surely do away with P'eng Yüeh and bring the region of Liang under control once again. Then I will return and join you."

Hsiang Yü marched east and attacked Ch'en-liu and Wai-huang. Wai-huang held out for several days before it finally surrendered. Enraged, Hsiang Yü ordered all the men over the age of fifteen to be brought to a place east of the city, where he planned to butcher them. One of the retainers of the head of the district, a lad of thirteen, went and spoke to Hsiang Yü. "Wai-huang, oppressed by the might of P'eng Yüeh, was fearful and surrendered to him, hopeful that Your Majesty would come to the rescue," he said. "But now that you have arrived, if you butcher all the men, how can you hope to win the hearts of the common people? East of here there are still a dozen cities of Liang, but all will be filled with terror and will not dare to surrender."

Hsiang Yü, acknowledging the reason of his words, pardoned all the men of Wai-huang who were marked for execution and proceeded east to Sui-yang. Hearing what had happened, the other cities made all haste to submit to him.

The king of Han meanwhile several times challenged the Ch'u army to a battle, but the Ch'u generals refused to send out their forces. Then he sent men to taunt and insult them for five or six days, until at last the grand marshal Ts'ao Chiu, in a rage, led his soldiers across the Ssu River. When the troops were halfway across the river, the Han force fell upon them and inflicted a severe defeat on the Ch'u army, seizing all the wealth of the country of Ch'u. Grand marshal Ts'ao Chiu, the chief secretary Tung I, and Ssu-ma Hsin, the king of Sai, all cut their throats on the banks of the Ssu. (Ts'ao Chiu, former prison warden of Chi, and Ssu-ma Hsin, former prison warden of Yüeh-yang, had both done favors for Hsiang Liang, and so had been trusted and employed by Hsiang Yü.)

Hsiang Yü was at this time in Sui-yang but, hearing of the defeat of the grand marshal's army, he led his troops back. The Han army had at the moment surrounded Chung-li Mo at Jung-yang, but when Hsiang Yü arrived, the Han forces, fearful of Ch'u, all fled to positions of safety in the mountains. At this time the Han troops were strong and had plenty of food, but Hsiang Yü's men were worn out and their provisions were exhausted.

The king of Han dispatched Lu Chia to bargain with Hsiang Yü for the return of his father, but Hsiang Yü refused to listen. The king then sent Lord Hou to bargain. This time Hsiang Yü agreed to make an alliance with Han to divide the empire between them, Han to have all the land west of the Hung Canal and Ch'u all the land to the east. In addition, upon Hsiang Yü's consent, the king of Han's father, mother, and wife were returned to him amid cheers of "Long life!" from the Han army. The king of Han enfeoffed Lord Hou as "Lord Who Pacifies the Nation." (Lord Hou retired and was unwilling to show himself again. Someone remarked, "This man is the most eloquent pleader in the world. Wherever he goes he turns the whole nation on its head. Perhaps that is why he has been given the title 'Lord Who Pacifies the Nation.' ") [16]

After concluding the alliance, Hsiang Yü led his troops away to the east and the king of Han prepared to return west, but Chang Liang and Ch'en P'ing advised him, saying, "Han now possesses over half the empire, and all the feudal lords are on our side, while the soldiers of Ch'u are weary and out of food. The time has come when Heaven will destroy Ch'u. It would be best to take advantage of Hsiang Yü's lack of food and seize him once for all. If we were to let him get away now without attacking him, it would be like nursing a tiger that will return to vex us later!"

The king of Han, approving their advice, in the fifth year of Han [202 B.C.] pursued Hsiang Yü as far as the south of Yang-hsia, where he halted and made camp. There he set a date for Han Hsin and P'eng Yüeh to meet him and join in attacking the Ch'u army. But when he reached Ku-ling, the troops of Han Hsin and P'eng Yüeh failed to appear for the rendezvous, and Hsiang Yü attacked him and inflicted a severe defeat. The king of Han withdrew behind his walls, deepened his moats, and guarded his position.

"The other leaders have not kept their promise. What shall I do?" he asked Chang Liang.

"The Ch'u army is on the point of being destroyed," Chang Liang replied, "but Han Hsin and P'eng Yüeh have not yet been granted any territory.[17] It is not surprising that they do not come when summoned. If you will consent to share a part of the empire with them, they will surely come without a moment's hesitation. If this is impossible, I do not know what will happen. If you could assign to Han Hsin all the land from Ch'en east to the sea, and to P'eng Yüeh the land from Sui-yang north to Ku-ch'eng, so that each would feel he

---

[16] The passage in parentheses, the meaning of which is far from certain, does not appear in the parallel passage in *Han shu* 31, and may well be a later addition.

[17] Although they had received impressive titles—Han Hsin was "king of Ch'i," P'eng Yüeh was "prime minister of Wei"—no specific grants of territory had as yet been awarded them.

was actually fighting for his own good, then Ch'u could easily be defeated."

The king of Han, approving this suggestion, sent envoys to Han Hsin and P'eng Yüeh, saying, "Let us join our forces in attacking Ch'u. When Ch'u has been defeated, I will give the land from Ch'en east to the sea to the king of Ch'i, and that from Sui-yang north to Ku-ch'eng to Prime Minister P'eng." When the envoys arrived and reported this to Han Hsin and P'eng Yüeh, both replied, "We beg leave to proceed with our troops." Han Hsin then marched out of Ch'i. Liu Chia led his army from Shou-ch'un to join in attacking and massacring the men of Ch'eng-fu; from there he proceeded to Kai-hsia. The grand marshal Chou Yin revolted against Ch'u, using the men of Shu to massacre the inhabitants of Liu, gained control of the army of Chiu-chiang, and followed after Liu Chia and P'eng Yüeh. All met at Kai-hsia and made their way toward Hsiang Yü.

Hsiang Yü's army had built a walled camp at Kai-hsia, but his soldiers were few and his supplies exhausted. The Han army, joined by the forces of the other leaders, surrounded them with several lines of troops. In the night Hsiang Yü heard the Han armies all about him singing the songs of Ch'u. "Has Han already conquered Ch'u?" he exclaimed in astonishment. "How many men of Ch'u they have with them!" Then he rose in the night and drank within the curtains of his tent. With him were the beautiful lady Yü, who enjoyed his favor and followed wherever he went, and his famous steed Dapple, which he always rode. Hsiang Yü, filled with passionate sorrow, began to sing sadly, composing this song:

> My strength plucked up the hills,
> My might shadowed the world;
> But the times were against me,
> And Dapple runs no more.
> When Dapple runs no more,
> What then can I do?
> Ah, Yü, my Yü,
> What will your fate be?

He sang the song several times through, and Lady Yü joined her voice with his. Tears streamed down his face, while all those about him wept and were unable to lift their eyes from the ground. Then he mounted his horse and, with some eight hundred brave horsemen under his banner, rode into the night, burst through the encirclement to the south, and galloped away.

Next morning, when the king of Han became aware of what had happened, he ordered his cavalry general Kuan Ying to lead a force of five thousand horsemen in pursuit. Hsiang Yü crossed the Huai River, though by now he had only a hundred or so horsemen still with him. Reaching Yin-ling, he lost his way, and stopped to ask an old farmer for directions. But the farmer deceived him, saying, "Go left!", and when he rode to the left he stumbled into a great swamp, so that the Han troops were able to pursue and overtake him.

Hsiang Yü once more led his men east until they reached Tung-ch'eng. By this time he had only twenty-eight horsemen, while the Han cavalry pursuing him numbered several thousand.

Hsiang Yü, realizing that he could not escape, addressed his horsemen, saying, "It has been eight years since I first led my army forth. In that time I have fought over seventy battles. Every enemy I faced was destroyed, everyone I attacked submitted. Never once did I suffer defeat, until at last I became dictator of the world. But now suddenly I am driven to this desperate position! It is because Heaven would destroy me, not because I have committed any fault in battle. I have resolved to die today. But before I die, I beg to fight bravely and win for you three victories. For your sake I shall break through the enemy's encirclements, cut down their leaders, and sever their banners, that you may know it is Heaven which has destroyed me and no fault of mine in arms!" Then he divided his horsemen into four bands and faced them in four directions.

When the Han army had surrounded them several layers deep, Hsiang Yü said to his horsemen, "I will get one of those generals for you!" He ordered his men to gallop in all four directions down the hill on which they were standing, with instructions to meet again on the east side of the hill and divide into three groups. He himself gave a great shout and galloped down the hill. The Han troops scattered before him and he succeeded in cutting down one of their generals. At this time Yang Hsi was leader of the cavalry pursuing Hsiang Yü, but Hsiang Yü roared and glared so fiercely at him that all his men and horses fled in terror some distance to the rear.

Hsiang Yü rejoined his men, who had formed into three groups. The Han army, uncertain which group Hsiang Yü was with, likewise divided into three groups and again surrounded them. Hsiang Yü once more galloped forth and cut down a Han colonel, killing some fifty to a hundred men. When he had gathered his horsemen together a second time, he found that he had lost only two of them. "Did I tell you the truth?" he asked. His men all bowed and replied, "You have done all you said."

Hsiang Yü, who by this time had reached Wu-chiang, was considering whether to cross over to the east side of the Yangtze. The village head of Wu-chiang, who was waiting with a boat on the bank of the river, said to him, "Although the area east of the Yellow River is small, it is some thousand miles in breadth and has a population of thirty or forty thousand. It would still be worth ruling. I beg you to make haste and cross over. I am the only one who has a boat, so that when the Han army arrives they will have no way to get across!"

Hsiang Yü laughed and replied, "It is Heaven that is destroying me. What good would it do me to cross the river? Once, with eight thousand sons from the land east of the river, I crossed over and marched west, but today not a single man of them returns. Although their fathers and brothers east of the river should take pity on me and make me their king, how could I bear to face them again? Though they said nothing of it, could I help but feel shame in my heart?" Then he added, "I can see that you are a worthy man. For five years I have ridden this horse, and I have never seen his equal. Again and again he has borne me hundreds of miles in a single day. Since I cannot bear to kill him, I give him to you."

Hsiang Yü then ordered all his men to dismount and proceed on foot, and with their short swords to close in hand-to-hand combat with the enemy. Hsiang Yü alone killed several hundred of the Han men, until he had suffered a dozen wounds. Looking about him, he spied the Han cavalry marshal Lü Ma-t'ung. "We are old friends, are we not?" he asked. Lü Ma-t'ung eyed him carefully and then, pointing him out to Wang I, said, "This is Hsiang Yü!"

"I have heard that Han has offered a reward of a thousand catties of gold and a fief of ten thousand households for my head," said Hsiang Yü. "I will do you the favor!" And with this he cut his own throat and died.

Wang I seized his head, while the other horsemen trampled over each other in a struggle to get at Hsiang Yü's body, so that twenty or thirty of them were killed. In the end the cavalry attendant Yang Hsi, the cavalry marshal Lü Ma-t'ung, and the attendants Lü Sheng and Yang Wu each succeeded in seizing a limb. When the five of them fitted together the limbs and head, it was found that they were indeed those of Hsiang Yü. Therefore the fief was divided five ways, Lü Ma-t'ung being enfeoffed as marquis of Chung-shui, Wang I as marquis of Tu-yen, Yang Hsi as marquis of Ch'ih-ch'üan, Yang Wu as marquis of Wu-fang, and Lü Sheng as marquis of Nieh-yang.

With the death of Hsiang Yü, the entire region of Ch'u surrendered to Han, only Lu refusing to submit. The king of Han set out with the troops of the empire and was about to massacre the inhabitants of Lu. But because Lu had so strictly obeyed the code of honor and had shown its willingness to fight to the death for its acknowledged sovereign, he bore with him the head of Hsiang Yü and, when he showed it to the men of Lu, they forthwith surrendered.

King Huai of Ch'u had first enfeoffed Hsiang Yü as duke of Lu, and Lu was the last place to surrender. Therefore, the king of Han buried Hsiang Yü at Ku-ch'eng with the ceremony appropriate to a duke of Lu. The king proclaimed a period of mourning for him, wept, and then departed. All the various branches of the Hsiang family he spared from execution, and he enfeoffed Hsiang Po as marquis of She-yang. The marquises of T'ao, P'ing-kao, and Hsüan-wu were all members of the Hsiang family who were granted the imperial surname Liu.

The Grand Historian remarks: I have heard Master Chou say that Emperor Shun had eyes with double pupils. I have also heard that Hsiang Yü, too, had eyes with double pupils. Could it be that Hsiang Yü was a descendant of Emperor Shun? How sudden was his rise to power! When the rule of Ch'in floundered and Ch'en She led his revolt, local heroes and leaders arose like bees, struggling with each other for power in numbers too great to be counted. Hsiang Yü did not have so much as an inch of territory to begin with, but by taking advantage of the times he raised himself in the space of three years from a commoner in the fields to the position of commander of five armies of feudal lords. He overthrew Ch'in, divided up the empire, and parceled it out in fiefs to the various kings and marquises; but all power of government proceeded from Hsiang Yü and he was hailed as a dictator king. Though he was not able to hold this position to his death, yet from ancient times to the present there has never before been such a thing!

But when he went so far as to turn his back on the Pass and return to his native Ch'u, banishing the Righteous Emperor and setting himself up in his place, it was hardly surprising that the feudal lords revolted against him. He boasted and made a show of his own achievements. He was obstinate in his own opinions and did not abide by established ways. He thought to make himself a dictator, hoping to attack and rule the empire by force. Yet within five years he was dead and his kingdom lost. He met death at Tung-ch'eng, but even at that time he did not wake to or accept responsibility for his errors. "It is Heaven," he declared, "which has destroyed me, and no fault of mine in the use of arms!" Was he not indeed deluded?

Shih chi 8: The Basic Annals of Emperor Kao-tsu

Hsiang Yü was violent and tyrannical, while the king of Han practiced goodness and virtue. In anger he marched forth from Shu and Han, returning to conquer the three kingdoms of Ch'in. He executed Hsiang Yü and became an emperor, and all the world was brought to peace. He changed the statutes and reformed the ways of the people. Thus I made The Basic Annals of Emperor Kao-tsu.

Kao-tsu [1] was a native of the community of Chung-yang in the city of Feng, the district of P'ei. His family name was Liu and his polite name Chi. His father was known as the "Venerable Sire" and his mother as "Dame Liu."

Before he was born, Dame Liu was one day resting on the bank of a large pond when she dreamed that she encountered a god. At this time the sky grew dark and was filled with thunder and lightning. When Kao-tsu's father went to look for her, he saw a scaly dragon over the place where she was lying. After this she became pregnant and gave birth to Kao-tsu.

Kao-tsu had a prominent nose and a dragonlike face, with beautiful whiskers on his chin and cheeks; on his left thigh he had seventy-two black moles.[2] He was kind and affectionate with others, liked to help people, and was very understanding. He always had great ideas and paid little attention to the business the rest of his family was engaged in.

When he grew up he took the examination to become an official

[1] Kao-tsu, meaning "Exalted Ancestor," is the posthumous title of Liu Chi, founder of the Han dynasty. Liu Chi's familiar name, Pang, was tabooed during the Han and is never mentioned in the *Shih chi*. Since Ssu-ma Ch'ien was writing during the Han, he often refers to members of the imperial family by the titles they later acquired. Hence Kao-tsu's wife is called Empress Lü, though this is often anachronistic from the point of view of the narrative.

[2] Seventy-two, the multiple of eight and nine, is a mystic number in Chinese thought.

and was made village head of Ssu River. He treated all the other officials in the office with familiarity and disdain. He was fond of wine and women and often used to go to Dame Wang's or old lady Wu's and drink on credit. When he got drunk and lay down to sleep, the old women, to their great wonder, would always see something like a dragon over the place where he was sleeping. Also, whenever he would drink and stay at their shops, they would sell several times as much wine as usual. Because of these strange happenings, when the end of the year came around the old women would always destroy Kao-tsu's credit slips and clear his account.

Kao-tsu was once sent on *corvée* labor to the capital city of Hsien-yang and happened to have an opportunity to see the First Emperor of Ch'in. When he saw him he sighed and said, "Ah, this is the way a great man should be."

There was a man of Shan-fu, one Master Lü, who was a friend of the magistrate of P'ei. In order to avoid the consequences of a feud, he accepted the hospitality of the magistrate and made his home in P'ei. When the officials and the wealthy and influential people of P'ei heard that the magistrate had a distinguished guest, they all came to pay their respects. Hsiao Ho, being the director of officials, was in charge of gifts and informed those who came to call that anyone bringing a gift of less than one thousand cash would be seated below the main hall. Kao-tsu, who as a village head was in the habit of treating the other officials with contempt, falsely wrote on his calling card: "With respects—ten thousand cash," though in fact he did not have a single cash. When his card was sent in, Master Lü was very surprised and got up and came to the gate to greet him. Master Lü was very good at reading people's faces and when he saw Kao-tsu's features he treated him with great honor and respect and led him in to a seat. "Liu Chi," remarked Hsiao Ho, "does a good deal of fine talking, but so far has accomplished very little." But Kao-tsu, disdaining the other guests, proceeded to take a seat of honor without further ado.

When the drinking was nearly over, Master Lü glanced at Kao-tsu in such a way as to indicate that he should stay a while longer, and so Kao-tsu dawdled over his wine. "Since my youth," said Master Lü, "I have been fond of reading faces. I have read many faces, but none with signs like yours. You must take good care of yourself, I beg you. I have a daughter whom I hope you will do me the honor of accepting as your wife."

When the party was over, Dame Lü was very angry with her husband. "You have always idolized this girl and planned to marry her to some person of distinction," she said. "The magistrate of P'ei is a friend of yours and has asked for her, but you would not give your consent. How can you be so insane as to give her to Liu Chi?"

"This is not the sort of thing women and children can understand!" replied Master Lü. Eventually he married the girl to Kao-tsu, and it was this daughter of Master Lü who became Empress Lü and gave birth to Emperor Hui and Princess Yüan of Lu.

When Kao-tsu was acting as village head he once asked for leave to go home and visit his fields. Empress Lü at the time was in the fields weeding with her two children. When an old man passed by and asked for something to drink, Empress Lü accordingly gave him some food. The old man examined her face and said, "Madam will become the most honored woman in the world." She asked him to examine her children. Looking at her son, he said, "It is because of this boy that madam will obtain honor," and when he examined the girl, he said that she too would be honored.

After the old man had gone on, Kao-tsu happened to appear from an outhouse nearby. Empress Lü told him all about how the traveler had passed by and, examining her and her children, had predicted great honor for all of them. When Kao-tsu inquired where the man was, she replied, "He cannot have gone very far away!"

Kao-tsu ran after the old man and, overtaking him, questioned him. "The lady and the little children I examined a while ago," he replied, "all resemble you. But when I examine your face, I find such worth that I cannot express it in words!"

Kao-tsu thanked him, saying "If it is really as you say, I will surely not forget your kindness!" But when Kao-tsu finally became honored he could never find out where the old man had gone.

When Kao-tsu was acting as village head, he fashioned a kind of hat out of sheaths of bamboo and sent his "thief-seeker"[3] to the district of Hsieh to have some made up for him, which he wore from time to time. Even after he became famous he continued to wear these hats. These are the so-called Liu family hats.

As village head Kao-tsu was ordered to escort a group of forced laborers from the district of P'ei to Mount Li.[4] On the way, however, so many of the laborers ran away that Kao-tsu began to suspect that by the time he reached his destination they would all have disappeared. When they had reached a place in the midst of a swamp west of Feng, Kao-tsu halted and began to drink. That night he loosened the bonds of the laborers he was escorting and freed them, saying, "Go, all of you! I too shall go my own way from here."

Among the laborers were ten or so brave men who asked to go with him. Kao-tsu, full of wine, led the men in the night along a path through the swamp, sending one of them to walk ahead. The man who had gone ahead returned and reported, "There is a great snake lying across the path ahead. I beg you to turn back!"

"Where a brave man marches what is there to fear?" replied Kao-tsu drunkenly and, advancing, drew his sword and slashed at the snake. After he had cut the snake in two and cleared the path, he walked on a mile or so and then lay down to sleep off his drunkenness.

When one of the men who had lagged behind came to the place where the snake lay, he found an old woman crying in the night. He asked her why she was crying and she answered, "I am crying because someone has killed my son."

"How did your son come to be killed?" he asked.

"My son was the son of the White Emperor," said the old woman. "He had changed himself into a snake and was lying across the road. Now he has been cut in two by the son of the Red Emperor, and therefore I weep."

The man did not believe the old woman and was about to accuse her of lying, when suddenly she disappeared. When the man caught up with Kao-tsu, he found him already awake and reported what

---

[3] A subordinate official in the local administration.
[4] Where the First Emperor of Ch'in was building his mausoleum.

had happened. Kao-tsu was very pleased in his heart and set great store by the incident, while his followers day by day regarded him with greater awe.

The First Emperor of Ch'in, repeatedly declaring that there were signs in the southeastern sky indicating the presence of a "Son of Heaven," decided to journey east to suppress the threat to his power. Kao-tsu, suspecting that he himself was the cause of the visit, fled into hiding among the rocky wastes of the mountains and swamps between Mang and Tang. Empress Lü and others who went with her to look for him, however, were always able to find him. Kao-tsu, wondering how she could do this, asked her and she replied, "There are always signs in the clouds over the place where you are. By following these we manage to find you every time." Kao-tsu was very pleased in his heart. When word of this circulated among the young men of the district of P'ei, many of them sought to become his followers.

In the autumn of the first year of the reign of the Second Emperor of Ch'in [209] Ch'en She and his band arose in Chi. When Ch'en She had reached the area of Ch'en and made himself a king with the title of "Magnifier of Ch'u," many of the provinces and districts murdered their head officials and joined in the rebellion.

The magistrate of P'ei, fearful of what might happen, wished to declare P'ei a party to the rebellion, but his chief officials Hsiao Ho and Ts'ao Ts'an said, "You are an official of Ch'in. Now, though you hope to turn your back on Ch'in and lead the men of P'ei, we fear they will not listen to you. We would suggest that you summon all the various men who have fled and are in hiding elsewhere. You should be able to obtain several hundred men, and with these you can threaten the rest of the people and force them to obey you."

Accordingly the magistrate sent Fan K'uai to summon Kao-tsu, who by this time had almost a hundred followers. Kao-tsu came with Fan K'uai, but the magistrate, repenting his action and fearing a move against himself, closed the gates and guarded the city, preparing to execute Hsiao Ho and Ts'ao Ts'an. Hsiao Ho and Ts'ao Ts'an in fear climbed over the wall and fled to Kao-tsu's protection. Kao-tsu then wrote a message on a piece of silk and shot it over the city walls saying, "The world has long suffered beneath Ch'in. Now, though you men of P'ei should guard the city for the sake of the magistrate, the other nobles who have risen in rebellion will join in massacring the inhabitants of the city. If you will unite and do away with the magistrate, select from among your sons a worthy man to be your leader, and declare yourselves with the other nobles, then your homes and families shall all be spared. But if you do not, you will all be massacred without further ado!"

The elders then led the young men and together they murdered the magistrate of P'ei, opened the city gates, and welcomed Kao-tsu. They wished to make him magistrate, but Kao-tsu announced, "The world today is in chaos with the nobles rising up everywhere. If you do not make a wise choice of a leader now, you will be cut down in one stroke and your blood will drench the earth. It is not that I care for my own safety, but only that I fear my abilities are not sufficient to insure your welfare. This is a most serious business. I beg you to consult once more among yourselves and select someone who is truly worthy."

Hsiao Ho, Ts'ao Ts'an, and the other civil officials were concerned for their own safety and, fearful that if they assumed leadership and the undertaking proved unsuccessful, Ch'in would exterminate their families, they all yielded in favor of Kao-tsu. Then all the elders announced. "For a long time we have heard of the strange and wonderful happenings and the predictions of greatness concerning Liu Chi. Moreover, when we divine by the tortoise and milfoil, we find that no one receives such responses as Liu Chi!" With this, Kao-tsu declined several times but, since no one else dared to accept the position, he allowed himself to be made governor of P'ei. He then performed sacrifices to the Yellow Emperor and to the ancient warrior Ch'ih Yu in the district office of P'ei and anointed his drums with the blood of the sacrifice. All his flags and banners he had made of red. Because the old woman had said that it was the son of the Red Emperor who had killed the snake, the son of the White Emperor, he decided to honor the color red in this fashion.

The young men and distinguished officials such as Hsiao Ho, Ts'ao Ts'an, Fan K'uai, and others gathered together for him a band of two or three thousand men of P'ei and attacked Hu-ling and Fang-yü. They then returned and guarded the city of Feng.

In the second year of the Second Emperor [208 B.C.] Ch'en She's general Chou Wen marched west with his army as far as Hsi and then returned. Yen, Chao, Ch'i, and Wei all set up their own kings and Hsiang Liang and Hsiang Yü began their uprising in Wu.

Ch'in's overseer in the province of Ssu River, a man named P'ing, led a force of troops and surrounded Feng for two days. The governor of P'ei marched out of the city and fought and defeated him. Then, ordering Yung Ch'ih to guard Feng, he led his troops to Hsieh. The magistrate of Ssu River, Chuang, was defeated at Hsieh and fled to Ch'i, where the governor P'ei's marshal of the left captured and killed him. The governor of P'ei returned and camped in the district of K'ang-fu, proceeding as far as Fang-yü. Chou Shih had arrived to attack Fang-yü, but had not yet engaged in battle. (Chou Shih was a man of Wei who had been sent by Ch'en She to seize the area.)

Chou Shih sent an envoy to Yung Ch'ih, who was guarding Feng, saying, "Feng was originally a colony of Liang, which was part of Wei. Now we have captured more than ten cities of Wei. If you will submit to Wei, Wei will make you a marquis. But if you persist in holding Feng and refuse to surrender, we will massacre the inhabitants."

Yung Ch'ih had originally had no desire to ally himself with the governor of P'ei and, when he was thus invited by Wei, he revolted and held the city of Feng in Wei's name. The governor of P'ei led his troops in an attack on Feng, but was unable to take it. Falling ill, he returned to P'ei.

The governor of P'ei was bitter because Yung Ch'ih and the men of Feng had turned against him. When he heard that Lord Ning of Tung-yang and Ch'in Chia had set up Ching Chü as acting king of Ch'u in Liu, he made his way there and joined them, requesting that they give him soldiers to attack Feng. At this time the Ch'in general Chang Han, pursuing Ch'en She's special general Ssu-ma I, led his troops north to pacify the region of Ch'u, massacring the inhabitants of Hsiang and marching as far as Tang. Lord Ning of Tung-yang and the governor of P'ei led their troops west and fought with him west of Hsiao, but they could win no advantage. Returning, they gathered together their troops in Liu and led them in an attack on Tang. After three days they seized Tang and, adding to their forces some five or six thousand men captured at Tang, attacked and overcame Hsia-i. Then they returned and camped near Feng.

Hearing that Hsiang Liang was in Hsieh, the governor of P'ei, accompanied by some hundred horsemen, went to see him. Hsiang Liang gave him five thousand foot soldiers and ten generals of the rank of fifth lord. The governor of P'ei then returned and led his troops in an attack on Feng.

A month or so after the governor of P'ei had allied himself with Hsiang Liang, Hsiang Yü captured the city of Hsiang-ch'eng and returned. Hsiang Liang then summoned all his various generals to come to Hsieh. Here, having received positive news that Ch'en She was dead, he set up Hsin, grandson of the former King Huai of Ch'u, as king of Ch'u, with his capital at Hsü-i. Hsiang Liang himself took the title of lord of Wu-hsin. After several months he marched north to attack K'ang-fu, rescued the city of Tung-a, and defeated the Ch'in army. Then, while Ch'i led its troops back to its own territory, Hsiang Liang alone pursued the defeated Ch'in army north, dispatching the governor of P'ei and Hsiang Yü with a special force to attack Ch'eng-yang. After massacring the inhabitants of Ch'eng-yang, they camped east of P'u-yang, where they fought with the Ch'in forces and defeated them.

The Ch'in army, recovering from this blow, defended its position at P'u-yang by encircling it with water. The Ch'u army then withdrew and attacked Ting-t'ao, but was unable to conquer it. The governor of P'ei and Hsiang Yü seized the area to the west. Arriving before the walls of Yung-ch'iu, they again engaged the Ch'in forces and gravely defeated them, cutting down the Ch'in general Li Yu. They returned and attacked Wai-huang, but were unable to conquer it. Hsiang Liang in the meantime had inflicted another defeat on Ch'in and began to grow proud and boastful. Sung I cautioned him about this, but he would not listen. Ch'in then sent reinforcements to aid Chang Han. Putting gags in the mouths of his men,[5] Chang Han made a night

---

[5] To prevent them from talking or shouting during the surprise attack.

attack on Hsiang Liang and inflicted a crushing defeat. Hsiang Liang was killed in the battle.

The governor of P'ei and Hsiang Yü were at the time attacking Ch'en-liu but, hearing of Hsiang Liang's death, they joined forces with General Lü Ch'en and marched east. Lü Ch'en camped east of P'eng-ch'eng, Hsiang Yü to the west, and the governor of P'ei at Tang.

Chang Han, having defeated Hsiang Liang, felt that he had nothing more to worry about from the soldiers of the region of Ch'u. Therefore he crossed the Yellow River and marched north to attack Chao, inflicting a severe defeat. At this time the Ch'in general Wang Li surrounded Chao Hsieh, the king of Chao, in the city of Chü-lu. This was the so-called Army North of the River.

In the third year of the Second Emperor [207 B.C.], when King Huai of Ch'u saw that Hsiang Liang's army had been defeated, he grew fearful and moved his capital from Hsü-i to P'eng-ch'eng, where he combined the armies of Lü Ch'en and Hsiang Yü, and himself took command of the troops. He made the governor of P'ei head of Tang Province, enfeoffed him as marquis of Wu-an, and put him in command of the troops of Tang. Hsiang Yü he enfeoffed as marquis of Ch'ang-an with the title of "Duke of Lu." Lü Ch'en was appointed minister of instruction and his father, Lü Ch'ing, was made prime minister.

Since Chao had several times sent pleas for aid, King Huai made Sung I supreme general, Hsiang Yü second general, and Fan Tseng third general, and sent them north to rescue Chao. The governor of P'ei he ordered to seize the region to the west and enter the Pass, making a promise with the various leaders that whoever should enter the Pass first and conquer the area within should become king of the region.

At this time the Ch'in forces were still very strong and took advantage of their supremacy to pursue those they had defeated, so that none of the leaders of the rebellion was anxious to be the first to enter the Pass. But Hsiang Yü, embittered over the defeat of Hsiang Liang's army by Ch'in, angrily demanded to be allowed to go west with the governor of P'ei and attempt to enter the Pass.

King Huai's elder generals all advised him, saying, "Hsiang Yü is by nature extremely impetuous and cruel. When he attacked and conquered the city of Hsiang-ch'eng, he butchered every one of the inhabitants without mercy. Wherever he has passed he has left behind him destruction and death. The armies of Ch'u have several times in the past advanced and won gains, but Ch'en She and Hsiang Liang were both in the end defeated. This time it would be better to send a man of true moral worth who, relying upon righteousness, will proceed west and make a proclamation to the elders of Ch'in. The men of Ch'in have long suffered under their rulers. Now if we can send a truly worthy man who will not come to them with rapine and violence in his heart, we can surely persuade them to submit. Hsiang Yü is far too impetuous to be sent. Only the governor of P'ei, who from the first has shown himself to be a man of tolerance and moral stature, is worthy to go."

In the end King Huai refused to grant Hsiang Yü's request, but dispatched only the governor of P'ei who, gathering up the scattered remnants of Ch'en She's and Hsiang Liang's armies, marched out of Tang to seize the region to the west. Proceeding to Ch'eng-yang and Chiang-li, he threw his weight against the Ch'in fortifications there and defeated both garrisons. (In the meantime the Ch'u forces under Hsiang Yü had attacked the Ch'in general Wang Li at Chü-lu and severely defeated him.)

The governor of P'ei led his forces west and joined P'eng Yüeh at Ch'ang-i. Together they attacked the Ch'in forces but, failing to achieve a victory, retreated to Li. Here they met the marquis of Kang-wu, seized the troops under his command amounting to about four thousand men, and added them to their own forces. Then, joining the armies of the Wei general Huang Hsin and the Wei minister of works Wu P'u, they attacked Ch'ang-i again but, being unable to capture it, proceeded west past Kao-yang.

Li I-chi, the village gatekeeper,[6] remarked, "Many generals have passed through this region, but I can see that the governor of P'ei is the most magnanimous and worthy of them all." Then he requested to be allowed to meet the governor of P'ei and speak with him. At the

---

[6] Following the *Han shu* reading.

time the governor was sitting sprawled upon a couch with two servant girls washing his feet. When Master Li [7] entered, he did not make the customary prostration but instead gave a very deep bow and said, "If you truly desire to punish the evil rulers of Ch'in, it is hardly proper to receive one who is your elder in this slovenly fashion!"

With this the governor arose, straightened his clothes, and apologized, showing Master Li to a seat of honor. Master Li then explained to him how to assault Ch'en-liu and capture the stores of grain which Ch'in had there. The governor of P'ei gave Li I-chi the title of "Lord of Kuang-yeh" and made his brother Li Shang a general, putting him in command of the troops of Ch'en-liu. Together they attacked K'ai-feng but, failing to capture it, proceeded west and engaged the Ch'in general Yang Hsiung in battle at Po-ma and again east of Ch'ü-yung, severely defeating him. Yang Hsiung fled to Jung-yang where, in order to serve as a warning to the rest of the army, he was executed by an envoy sent from the Second Emperor.

The governor of P'ei attacked Ying-yang, massacring its defenders, and then, relying upon the guidance of Chang Liang, proceeded to seize the area of Huan-yüan in the region of Hann. At this time Ssu-ma Ang, a general dispatched by Chao, was about to cross the Yellow River in hopes of entering the Pass. In order to prevent him, the governor of P'ei marched north to attack P'ing-yin, destroyed the fording place across the Yellow River, and then continued south to battle with the Ch'in forces east of Lo-yang. Being unsuccessful here, he withdrew to Yang-ch'eng, gathered together all his horsemen, and attacked and defeated I, the governor of Nan-yang Province, east of Ch'ou. He seized the province of Nan-yang while the governor, I, fled to the city of Yüan for protection.

The governor of P'ei was about to lead his troops on to the west, but Chang Liang cautioned him, saying, "Although you wish to enter the Pass as soon as possible, there are a great many soldiers of Ch'in holding the strong points. Now if you march on without seizing the city of Yüan, Yüan will attack you from behind. With the power of Ch'in awaiting you ahead, your way will be fraught with danger!" Accordingly the governor of P'ei led his troops back by another road

[7] So called because he was a Confucian scholar.

at night, changed his flags and pennants, and just before dawn encircled the city of Yüan with several bands of troops. The governor of Nan-yang was about to cut his throat when one of his followers, Ch'en Hui, stopped him, saying, "There is still plenty of time to die." Then he climbed over the city wall and appeared before the governor of P'ei. "I have heard," he said, "that Your Lordship has made an agreement that whoever shall enter the capital city of Hsien-yang first will become its king. But now you have stayed your march in order to invest the city of Yüan. Yüan is the capital of a great province, with twenty or thirty cities under its control. Its people are numerous and its stores of provisions plentiful. Our officers believe that if they surrender they will certainly be put to death and therefore they have all mounted the walls and are firmly guarding their city. Now if you wear out your days remaining here attacking the city, many of your men are bound to suffer injury and death, while if you lead your troops away from Yüan, Yüan will surely pursue you from behind. Should you choose the former course you will never reach Hsien-yang in time to take advantage of the agreement, while should you choose the latter you will be bedeviled by the power of Yüan. If I were to suggest a plan for you, I would say it is best to promise to enfeoff the governor if he surrenders. Then you may leave him behind to guard the city for you while you lead his troops with you to the west. When the other cities that have not submitted hear of your action, they will hasten to open their gates and await your coming, so that your passage will be freed from all hindrance."

The governor of P'ei approved this idea and accordingly made the governor of Yüan marquis of Yin and enfeoffed Ch'en Hui with a thousand households. Then he led his troops west, and all the cities without exception submitted to him. When he reached the Tan River, Sai, the marquis of Kao-wu, and Wang Ling, the marquis of Hsiang, surrendered the area of Hsi-ling to him. Then he turned back and attacked Hu-yang where he met Mei Hsüan, special general of Wu Jui, the lord of P'o, and together they conquered Hsi and Li.

The governor of P'ei dispatched Ning Ch'ang, a man of Wei, as his envoy to the court of Ch'in. But he had not yet returned when Chang Han surrendered his army to Hsiang Yü at Chao. (Earlier, Hsiang Yü and Sung I had marched north to rescue Chao from the Ch'in attack. Later, when Hsiang Yü murdered Sung I and took his place as supreme general, Ch'ing Pu and the other leaders joined with him. He then defeated the army of the Ch'in general Wang Li, received the surrender of Chang Han, and secured command over all the other leaders.)

After Chao Kao had murdered the Second Emperor, the governor of P'ei's envoy returned with a promise from Ch'in to divide the area within the Pass and make the governor a king over part of it. Believing this to be a trick, however, the governor followed the strategy suggested by Chang Liang and sent Master Li and Lu Chia to go and bargain with the Ch'in generals and tempt them to treason with offers of profit, while he himself proceeded to attack the Wu Pass and capture it. He also fought with the Ch'in armies at Lan-t'ien, disposing his soldiers and increasing the number of his flags and pennants in such a way as to make his forces appear greater than they actually were. Wherever he passed, he forbade his men to plunder or seize prisoners. The people of Ch'in were delighted at this mildness and the Ch'in armies grew unwary so that they suffered great defeat. He also fought to the north of Lan-t'ien and inflicted a major defeat. Taking advantage of these victories, he was able at last to destroy the Ch'in armies.

In the tenth month of the first year of Han [November–December, 207 B.C.] the governor of P'ei finally succeeded in reaching Pa-shang ahead of the other leaders. Tzu-ying, the king of Ch'in, came in a plain carriage drawn by a white horse, wearing a rope about his neck,[8] and surrendered the imperial seals and credentials by the side of Chih Road. Some of the generals asked that the king of Ch'in be executed, but the governor of P'ei replied, "The reason King Huai first sent me upon this mission was that he sincerely believed I was capable of showing tolerance and mercy. Now to kill a man who has already surrendered would only bring bad luck!" With this he turned the king of Ch'in over to the care of his officials. Then he proceeded west

[8] White is the color of mourning, while the rope indicated total submission. Tzu-ying had succeeded the Second Emperor as ruler of Ch'in, but because of the wobbly state of his empire had ventured only to call himself "king."

and entered Hsien-yang. He hoped to stay and rest for a while in the palaces of Ch'in, but Fan K'uai and Chang Liang advised him against this. Therefore he sealed up the storehouses containing Ch'in's treasures and wealth and returned to camp at Pa-shang. There he summoned all the distinguished and powerful men of the districts and addressed them, saying:

"Gentlemen, for a long time you have suffered beneath the harsh laws of Ch'in. Those who criticized the government were wiped out along with their families; those who gathered to talk in private were executed in the public market. I and the other nobles have made an agreement that he who first enters the Pass shall rule over the area within. Accordingly I am now king of this territory within the Pass. I hereby promise you a code of laws consisting of three articles only: He who kills anyone shall suffer death; he who wounds another or steals shall be punished according to the gravity of the offense; for the rest I hereby abolish all the laws of Ch'in. Let the officials and people remain undisturbed as before. I have come only to save you from further harm, not to exploit or tyrannize over you. Therefore do not be afraid! The reason I have returned to Pa-shang is simply to wait for the other leaders so that when they arrive we may settle the agreement."

He sent men to go with the Ch'in officials and publish this proclamation in the district towns and villages. The people of Ch'in were overjoyed and hastened with cattle, sheep, wine, and food to present to the soldiers. But the governor of P'ei declined all such gifts, saying, "There is plenty of grain in the granaries. I do not wish to be a burden to the people." With this the people were more joyful than ever and their only fear was that the governor of P'ei would not become king of Ch'in.

Someone advised the governor of P'ei, saying, "The area of Ch'in is ten times richer than the rest of the empire and the land is protected by strong natural barriers. Now word has come that Chang Han has surrendered to Hsiang Yü and that Hsiang Yü therefore has granted him the title of king of Yung, intending to make him ruler of the area within the Pass. If he arrives, I fear that you will not be able to maintain your present claim. It would be best to send soldiers at once to guard the Han-ku Pass and prevent any of the armies of the other leaders from entering. In the meantime you can little by little gather up soldiers from the area within the Pass and lead them yourself to reinforce those blocking the Pass." The governor of P'ei approved this plan and set about putting it into effect.

During the eleventh month Hsiang Yü led the troops of the various armies west, as the governor had expected, and attempted to enter the Pass. Finding the Pass blocked and hearing that the governor of P'ei had already conquered the land within the Pass, he was greatly enraged and sent Ch'ing Pu and others to attack and break through the Han-ku Pass. In the twelfth month he finally reached Hsi.

Ts'ao Wu-shang, marshal of the left to the governor of P'ei, hearing that Hsiang Yü was angry and wished to attack the governor of P'ei, sent a messenger to speak to Hsiang Yü, saying, "The governor of P'ei hopes to become king of the area within the Pass, employing Tzu-ying as his prime minister and keeping possession of all the precious articles and treasures of the capital." (He thought that by reporting thus he would be rewarded by Hsiang Yü with a fief.)

Fan Tseng strongly urged Hsiang Yü to attack the governor of P'ei. Accordingly Hsiang Yü feasted his soldiers and prepared to join in battle the following day. At this time Hsiang Yü claimed to have a force of 1,000,000 men, though the actual number was 400,000, while the governor of P'ei claimed a force of 200,000, which was actually only 100,000. Thus they were no match for each other in strength.

As it happened, Hsiang Po, hoping to save the life of his friend Chang Liang, had gone the night before to see Chang Liang and as a result was able to convince Hsiang Yü of the governor of P'ei's loyalty, so that Hsiang Yü abandoned his plan to attack. The governor of P'ei, accompanied by some hundred horsemen, hastened to Hung-men, where he met Hsiang Yü and apologized to him. Hsiang Yü replied, "It is your own marshal of the left, Ts'ao Wu-shang, who informed against you. If it were not for him, how would I ever have doubted you?" The governor of P'ei, through the efforts of Fan K'uai and Chang Liang, was at last able to escape and return to his own camp. Upon his return he immediately executed Ts'ao Wu-shang.

Hsiang Yü then proceeded west and massacred the inhabitants of Hsien-yang, burning the city and the palaces of Ch'in, and leaving destruction everywhere he passed. The people of Ch'in were filled with despair, but they were so terrified they had no courage to resist. Hsiang Yü sent a messenger to return and report to King Huai. "Let all be done according to the agreement," King Huai replied. Hsiang Yü was angry that the king had not allowed him to march west with the governor of P'ei and enter the Pass, but instead had sent him north to rescue Chao, thus causing him to miss out on the agreement concerning the rulership of the area within the Pass. "King Huai," he said, "was set up solely through the efforts of my uncle Hsiang Liang. He has won no merit of his own. Why should he be made arbiter of the agreement? It is the other generals and I who actually conquered the empire!" Then he pretended to honor King Huai by giving him the title of "Righteous Emperor," but in fact paid no attention to his commands.

In the first month Hsiang Yü set himself up as "Dictator King of Western Ch'u," ruling nine provinces of Liang and Ch'u, with his capital at P'eng-ch'eng. In violation of the former agreement he made the governor of P'ei king of Han instead of Ch'in, giving him the lands of Pa, Shu, and Han to rule, with his capital at Nan-cheng. The area within the Pass he divided into three parts, setting up three former generals of Ch'in: Chang Han as king of Yung with his capital at Fei-ch'iu, Ssu-ma Hsin as king of Sai with his capital at Yüeh-yang, and Tung I as king of Ti with his capital at Kao-nu. The Ch'u general Shen Yang of Hsia-ch'iu was made king of Ho-nan with his capital at Lo-yang, while the Chao general Ssu-ma Ang was made king of Yin, his capital at Chao-ko. Hsieh, the king of Chao, was transferred to the position of king of Tai, while his prime minister, Chang Erh, was made king of Ch'ang-shan with his capital at Hsiang-kuo. The lord of Tang-yang, Ch'ing Pu, was made king of Chiu-chiang, his capital at Liu; Kung Ao, chief minister to King Huai, was made king of Lin-chiang, his capital at Chiang-ling. The lord of P'o, Wu Jui, became king of Heng-shan, his capital at Chu. The Yen general Tsang Tu was made king of Yen, his capital at Chi, after the former king of Yen, Han Kuang, had been ordered to remove to the position of king of Liao-tung. When Han Kuang refused to obey, Tsang Tu attacked and killed him at Wu-chung. Ch'en Yü, the lord of Ch'eng-an, was enfeoffed with three districts in Ho-chien, at his residence at Nan-p'i, while Mei Hsüan was enfeoffed with a hundred thousand households.

In the fourth month the various armies left the command of Hsiang Yü and proceeded with the feudal leaders to their respective territories. When the king of Han departed for his kingdom, Hsiang Yü allowed him to take along thirty thousand soldiers. Gathering a force of twenty or thirty thousand of the soldiers of Ch'u and the other leaders, he accordingly proceeded from Tu-nan and entered the Li Gorge. As he proceeded, he burned and destroyed the wooden roadway [9] behind him in order to prevent bandit troops of the other feudal lords from attacking him and, at the same time, to demonstrate to Hsiang Yü that he had no intention of marching east again.

When he reached Nan-cheng he found that many of his officers and men had deserted along the way and returned home, while those who were left all sang the songs of their homeland and longed to go back east. Han Hsin advised the king of Han, saying, "Hsiang Yü has made kings of all his generals who achieved merit, but you alone he has sent to live in Nan-cheng as though you were being exiled for some crime. The officers and soldiers of your army are all men of the east, and day and night they gaze into the distance longing to return home. If you take up your lance now and use it, you can win great glory. But if you wait until the world is settled and all men are at peace, then you cannot hope to take it up again. You had best lay plans to return east and fight for mastery of the world!"

When Hsiang Yü returned east through the Pass he sent a messenger to transfer the residence of the Righteous Emperor, announcing that "the emperors of ancient times who ruled an area a thousand miles on each side invariably resided on the upper reaches of a river." The envoy accordingly moved the Righteous Emperor to the district of Ch'en in Ch'ang-sha, pressing him to hurry on his way. With this the emperor's ministers became increasingly disillusioned and turned their backs upon him. Hsiang Yü then secretly ordered the kings of

[9] Built out over the steep side of the gorge.

Heng-shan and Lin-chiang to attack and murder the Righteous Emperor at Chiang-nan.

Hsiang Yü, being angry with T'ien Jung, set up T'ien Tu, a general of Ch'i, as king of Ch'i, but T'ien Jung, enraged at this, declared himself king of Ch'i, murdered T'ien Tu, and revolted against Ch'u. Then he presented P'eng Yüeh with the seals of office of a general and sent him to lead a revolt in the region of Liang. Ch'u ordered Chüeh, lord of Hsiao, to attack P'eng Yüeh, but P'eng Yüeh inflicted a severe defeat on him.

Ch'en Yü, angry that Hsiang Yü had not made him a king, dispatched Hsia Yüeh to plead with T'ien Jung and persuade him to send troops to attack Chang Erh, the king of Ch'ang-shan. Ch'i in response sent a body of soldiers to aid Ch'en Yü in attacking Chang Erh. Chang Erh fled from his territory and went to join the king of Han. Ch'en Yü then proceeded to Tai to fetch Hsieh, the former king of Chao, and restore him to his throne in Chao. In return, the king of Chao set up Ch'en Yü as king of Tai. Hsiang Yü, greatly enraged at these moves, marched north to attack Ch'i.

In the eighth month the king of Han, having decided to follow the plan outlined by Han Hsin, marched back by the Old Road and returned east to attack Chang Han, the king of Yung. Chang Han proceeded west to meet the attack, clashing with the Han forces at Ch'en-ts'ang. The soldiers of Yung were defeated and fled back east but halted to fight at Hao-chih. Defeated again, they fled to Fei-ch'iu. Thus the king of Han was able eventually to win control of the region of Yung and proceed east to Hsien-yang. He led his troops and surrounded the king of Yung at Fei-ch'iu, at the same time dispatching his generals to seize control of the provinces of Lung-hsi, Pei-ti, and Shang. He also ordered his generals Hsieh Ou and Wang Hsi to proceed by the Wu Pass, join the forces of Wang Ling at Nan-yang, and go to fetch his father and mother from P'ei.

When Hsiang Yü heard of this, he dispatched troops to block their march at Yang-hsia and prevent them from advancing. At the same time he made the former district magistrate of Wu, Cheng Ch'ang, king of Hann so that he could aid in blocking the Han forces.

In the second year [205 B.C.] the king of Han proceeded east, seizing control of the land. Ssu-ma Hsin, the king of Sai; Tung I, the king of Ti; and Shen Yang, the king of Ho-nan, all surrendered to him, but Cheng Ch'ang, the king of Hann, refused to submit. Therefore he dispatched Han Hsin to attack and defeat him. Out of the land he had conquered he created the provinces of Lung-hsi, Pei-ti, Shang, Wei-nan, Ho-shang, and Chung-ti within the Pass and beyond the Pass the province of Ho-nan. He made his grand commandant Han Hsin the new king of Hann. Among his generals all those who had defeated a force of ten thousand men or captured a province were enfeoffed with ten thousand households. He then ordered the border defenses north of the Yellow River to be repaired and manned, and turned over all of Ch'in's former royal hunting parks, gardens, and lakes to the people to be converted into fields for farming. In the first month he took Chang P'ing, the younger brother of the king of Yung, prisoner. A general amnesty was declared, freeing criminals. The king of Han journeyed beyond the Pass as far as Hsia, looking after the wants of the people beyond the Pass. On his return, Chang Erh came to see him and the king of Han received him with kindness and generosity.

In the second month the king of Han gave orders for Ch'in's altars of the soil and grain to be abolished, and the altars of Han set up in their place.

In the third month the king of Han proceeded through Lin-chin and crossed the Yellow River, where Pao, the king of Wei, led his troops to join him. He conquered Ho-nei and took Ssu-ma Ang, the king of Yin, prisoner, making his territory into the province of Ho-nei. Proceeding south, he crossed the Yellow River at the P'ing-yin Ford and reached Lo-yang. Here Lord Tung, the elder of Hsin-ch'eng,[10] intercepted him and informed him of the death of the Righteous Emperor. When he heard this the king of Han bared his arms and lamented loudly. He then proclaimed a period of mourning for the sake of the emperor, with three days of lamentation, and dispatched envoys to report to the other nobles, saying, "The people of the world have joined together in setting up the Righteous Emperor and serving him as their sovereign. But now Hsiang Yü has banished him from

[10] The "elders" or *san-lao* were distinguished men over fifty chosen from among the common people to act as consultants to government officials.

his throne and murdered him at Chiang-nan. This is a most treasonable and heinous offense! I myself have proclaimed mourning on his behalf, and I trust the other lords will join me in donning the plain white garments of sorrow. Then I shall lead forth all the troops of the area within the Pass, gather together the forces of the three lands along the river, and in the south descend by the Han and Yangtze rivers, begging to join with the other lords and kings in attacking him of Ch'u who is the murderer of the Righteous Emperor!"

At this time Hsiang Yü had marched north to attack Ch'i, fighting with T'ien Jung at Ch'eng-yang. T'ien Jung was defeated and fled to P'ing-yüan, where the people of P'ing-yüan killed him, and with this all of Ch'i surrendered to the forces of Ch'u. But Hsiang Yü burned its cities and fortifications and enslaved its women and children until the men of Ch'i once more rose up in revolt. T'ien Jung's younger brother, T'ien Heng, set up T'ien Jung's son Kuang as king of Ch'i, holding the area of Ch'eng-yang in revolt against Ch'u.

Although Hsiang Yü had received word of the king of Han's march to the east, he was already engaged in a struggle with the forces of Ch'i and hoped to accomplish their defeat before proceeding to attack Han. For this reason the king of Han was able to commandeer the troops of five of the feudal lords and eventually enter the city of P'eng-ch'eng. When Hsiang Yü received news of this, he led his forces back from Ch'i, marching from Lu through Hu-ling as far as Hsiao, where he engaged the king of Han in a great battle at P'eng-ch'eng and east of Ling-pi on the Sui River, inflicting a severe defeat. So many of the Han officers and men were killed that the Sui River was blocked and ceased to flow. Then Hsiang Yü seized the parents, wife, and children of the king of Han at P'ei and placed them under guard in the midst of his army as hostages.

At this time, when the other nobles saw that the Ch'u forces were very strong and the Han forces were retreating in defeat, they all deserted Han and went over again to the side of Ch'u. Ssu-ma Hsin, the king of Sai, fled to Ch'u. The older brother of the king of Han's wife, Lü Tse, the marquis of Chou-lü, commanded a force of Han soldiers at Hsia-i, and the king of Han, joining him, gradually managed to gather together his soldiers and form an army at Tang. He

then marched west through the territory of Liang as far as Yü. There
he dispatched Sui Ho, his master of guests, as an envoy to go to the
residence of Ch'ing Pu, the king of Chiu-chiang, telling him, "If you
can persuade Ch'ing Pu to raise an army and revolt against Ch'u,
Hsiang Yü will be bound to halt his advance and attack him. If I can
get Hsiang Yü to delay for a few months, I will surely be able to
seize control of the empire!" Sui Ho went and pleaded with Ch'ing
Pu, who as a result revolted against Ch'u. With this, Hsiang Yü dispatched Lung Chü to go and attack him.

When the king of Han was marching west after his defeat at P'eng-
ch'eng, he sent someone to look for the members of his family, but
they had in the meantime all fled and he could not find them. After
his defeat he was able to locate only his son (later Emperor Hui). In
the sixth month he set up his son as heir apparent, proclaiming a general amnesty, and left him to guard the city of Yüeh-yang. All the
relatives of the feudal lords in the area within the Pass gathered in
Yüeh-yang to act as the heir apparent's bodyguards. Then the king of
Han dug canals and flooded the city of Fei-ch'iu. Fei-ch'iu surrendered
and its king, Chang Han, committed suicide. The king of Han
changed the name of the city to Huai-li. At this time he ordered the
officials in charge of religious ceremonies to perform sacrifices to
heaven and earth, the four directions, the Lord on High, and the
various mountains and rivers, all to be celebrated at the due seasons. He
raised a force of soldiers from the area within the Pass to man the various fortifications.

At this time Ch'ing Pu, the king of Chiu-chiang, was fighting with
Lung Chü but, failing to gain a victory, he proceeded with Sui Ho by
a secret route and joined the forces of Han. The king of Han gradually
recruited more soldiers and, with the other generals and the troops
from within the Pass, little by little advanced. Thus he was able to
muster a great force at Jung-yang and defeat the Ch'u army in the
area of So in Ching.

In the third year [204 B.C.] Wei Pao, the king of Wei, begged leave
to return to his home and look after his ailing parents but, when he
had reached his destination, he cut off the ford across the Yellow
River, revolted against Han, and declared himself in alliance with

Ch'u. The king of Han sent Master Li I-chi to persuade him to reconsider, but Wei Pao refused to listen. The king then dispatched his general Han Hsin, who inflicted a decisive defeat and took Wei Pao prisoner. Thus the king of Han managed to conquer the region of Wei, which he made into three provinces, Ho-tung, T'ai-yüan, and Shang-tang. He ordered Chang Erh and Han Hsin to proceed east down the Ching Gorge and attack Chao, where they executed Ch'en Yü and Hsieh, the king of Chao. The following year Chang Erh was made king of Chao.

The king of Han camped south of Jung-yang and constructed a walled supply road following along the banks of the Yellow River in order to transport grain from the Ao Granary. Here he and Hsiang Yü remained at an impasse for well over a year.

Hsiang Yü had several times attacked and cut off the Han supply road, and the Han army was growing very short of provisions. Finally Hsiang Yü succeeded in surrounding the king of Han, who made a bid for peace, suggesting that they divide the empire in two, he himself to retain all the land west of Jung-yang as part of Han. When Hsiang Yü refused to consent to this, the king of Han was much distressed but, following a plan suggested by Ch'en P'ing, he gave Ch'en P'ing a sum of forty thousand catties of gold to use as bribes in causing dissension between the leaders of Ch'u. As a result Hsiang Yü began to doubt his aide, Fan Tseng. Fan Tseng at the time was urging Hsiang Yü to carry through the assault on Jung-yang but, when he found that his loyalty was doubted, he grew angry and begged leave to retire, requesting that he be relieved of his duties and returned to the ranks of a common soldier. His request was granted and he departed, but died before he reached P'eng-ch'eng.

The Han army had by this time run completely out of food. The king of Han dressed some two thousand women in armor and sent them out at night from the eastern gate of Jung-yang. When the Ch'u forces flocked from all directions to attack them, the Han general Chi Hsin, in order to deceive Ch'u, rode forth in the royal chariot, pretending to be the king of Han. With shouts of victory, the men of Ch'u all rushed to the eastern side of the city walls to see him. In this way the king of Han, accompanied by twenty or thirty horsemen, was able to slip out by the western gate and flee, leaving the grand secretary Chou K'o, Wei Pao, the former king of Wei, and Lord Ts'ung to guard Jung-yang. The other generals and their men who had been unable to accompany the king all remained within the city. Chou K'o and Lord Ts'ung, agreeing with each other that it would be difficult to guard the city with the king of a country that had once revolted, proceeded to murder Wei Pao.

After the king of Han escaped from Jung-yang he retired within the Pass and gathered together more troops, hoping once more to march east. Master Yüan advised the king, saying, "While Han and Ch'u remained in stalemate at Jung-yang for several years, our men were in constant difficulty. I beg you this time to go out by the Wu Pass. Hsiang Yü will surely hasten south with his troops to meet you, and you may then take refuge behind heavy fortifications. In this way you can relieve the pressure on the men at Jung-yang and Ch'eng-kao, in the meantime sending Han Hsin and others to gather forces in Ho-pei and the region of Chao and to form an alliance with Yen and Ch'i. Then, if you should again march upon Jung-yang, it would still not be too late. Thus Ch'u will be obliged to guard a number of points and its strength will be divided, while the Han forces, having had time to rest before engaging in battle again, will certainly defeat Ch'u."

The king of Han, adopting this plan, proceeded with his army to the area between Yüan and She, he and Ch'ing Pu gathering troops as they went along. When Hsiang Yü heard that the king of Han was in Yüan, he led his forces south as had been expected, but the king of Han remained within his fortifications and would not engage in battle. At this time P'eng Yüeh crossed the Sui River and fought with the Ch'u general Hsiang Sheng and the lord of Hsieh at Hsia-p'ei, defeating their army. Hsiang Yü then led his troops east to attack P'eng Yüeh, while the king of Han in the meantime marched north and camped at Ch'eng-kao.

After Hsiang Yü had defeated P'eng Yüeh and put him to flight, he received news that the king of Han had moved his camp to Ch'eng-kao. He accordingly led his troops back west and seized Jung-yang, executing Chou K'o and Lord Ts'ung and taking Hsin, the king of Hann, prisoner, and then proceeded to surround Ch'eng-kao. The king of Han fled, accompanied only by Lord T'eng in a single carriage, escaping by the Jade Gate of the city of Ch'eng-kao.

Hastening north across the Yellow River, he stopped for a night at Little Hsiu-wu and at dawn the next day, pretending to be an envoy from the king of Han, hurriedly entered the fortifications of Chang Erh and Han Hsin and seized command of their armies. He at once dispatched Chang Erh to proceed north and gather more troops in the region of Chao and sent Han Hsin east to attack Ch'i.

Having gained command of Han Hsin's army and recovered his strength, the king of Han led his troops to the edge of the Yellow River and camped south of Little Hsiu-wu, facing south across the river. He intended to proceed once more to battle, but his attendant Cheng Chung advised him not to fight but instead to fortify his position with high walls and deep moats. The king followed this advice, sending Lu Wan and Liu Chia to lead a force of twenty thousand infantry and several hundred horsemen across the Yellow River at the White Horse Ford to invade Ch'u. They joined P'eng Yüeh in attacking and defeating the Ch'u army west of Yen-kuo, and then proceeded to seize control of ten or more cities in the region of Liang.

Han Hsin had already been ordered to march east but had not yet crossed the P'ing-yüan Ford when the king of Han dispatched Master Li I-chi to go to Ch'i and plead for him with T'ien Kuang, the king of Ch'i. As a result T'ien Kuang revolted against Ch'u and joined in alliance with Han, agreeing to participate in an attack on Hsiang Yü. But Han Hsin, following the advice of K'uai T'ung, proceeded to attack Ch'i in spite of this, inflicting a defeat. The king of Ch'i boiled Master Li I-chi alive for his supposed treachery and marched east to Kao-mi.

When Hsiang Yü heard that Han Hsin had already raised a force of troops north of the river, defeated Ch'i and Chao, and was about to attack Ch'u, he dispatched Lung Chü and Chou Lan to attack him. Han Hsin, aided in battle by the cavalry general Kuan Ying, attacked them and defeated the Ch'u army, killing Lung Chü. T'ien Kuang, the king of Ch'i, fled to join P'eng Yüeh. At this time P'eng Yüeh was in the region of Liang, leading his troops back and forth, harassing the Ch'u forces and cutting off their supplies of food.

In the fourth year [203 B.C.] Hsiang Yü said to the marquis of Hai-ch'un, the grand marshal Ts'ao Chiu, "Hold fast to the city of Ch'eng-kao. Even if the king of Han challenges you to a battle, take care and do not fight with him. By no means let him advance to the east. In fifteen days I will be able to bring the region of Liang under control, and then I will join you again." He then proceeded to attack and subdue Ch'en-liu, Wai-huang, and Sui-yang.

As Hsiang Yü had foreseen, the king of Han several times challenged the Ch'u armies to battle, but they refused to take up the challenge. Then the king of Han sent men to insult and revile them for five or six days, until the grand marshal in anger led his troops across the Ssu River. When the soldiers were halfway across the river the Han forces fell upon them, inflicting a crushing defeat on Ch'u and seizing all the gold, treasures, and wealth of the kingdom of Ch'u. The grand marshal Ts'ao Chiu and Ssu-ma Hsin, the king of Sai,[11] both committed suicide by cutting their throats on the banks of the Ssu.

When Hsiang Yü reached Sui-yang he received word of Ts'ao Chiu's defeat and led his forces back. The Han forces had at the time encircled Chung-li Mo at Jung-yang, but on Hsiang Yü's arrival they all fled to the safety of the mountains.

After Han Hsin had defeated Ch'i he sent someone to report to the king of Han, saying, "Ch'i lies directly upon the border of Ch'u and my grip upon it is still unsure. I fear that unless I am given the title of acting king I will not be able to hold the area."

The king of Han was in favor of attacking Han Hsin, but Chang Liang said, "It is better to comply with his request and make him a king so that he will guard the area in his own interest." The king of Han accordingly dispatched Chang Liang to present the seals and cords of authority, setting up Han Hsin as king of Ch'i. When Hsiang Yü heard that Han Hsin had defeated Lung Chü's army, he was very much afraid and sent Wu She, a man of Hsü-i, to attempt to bargain with Han Hsin, but Han Hsin would not listen to his arguments.

For a long while Ch'u and Han held their respective positions and

[11] Both here and in the corresponding passage in "The Annals of Hsiang Yü" there seems to be considerable confusion of names and titles. I have translated in accordance with suggested emendations.

made no decisive move, while their fighting men suffered the hardships of camp life and their old men and boys wore themselves out
transporting provisions. The king of Han and Hsiang Yü faced each
other across the ravine of Kuang-wu and talked back and forth. Hsiang
Yü challenged the king of Han to meet him in single combat, but the
king berated Hsiang Yü, saying, "When you and I bowed together
before the command of King Huai, we agreed that whoever should
enter the Pass first and conquer the land within should become its king.
But you went back on this agreement, making me king of Shu and
Han instead. This was your first crime. Feigning orders from King
Huai, you murdered his lordship Sung I, the commander of the army,
and elevated yourself to his position. This was your second crime.
After you had gone to rescue Chao, it was proper that you should have
returned and made your report to King Huai, but instead you wantonly
seized the troops of the other leaders and entered the Pass. This was
your third crime. King Huai had promised that whoever entered the
Pass would commit no violence or theft. Yet you fired the palaces of
Ch'in, desecrated the grave of the First Emperor, and appropriated
the wealth and goods of Ch'in for your private use. This was your
fourth crime. You inflicted violent death upon Tzu-ying, the king of
Ch'in, who had already surrendered; this was your fifth crime. At
Hsin-an you butchered two hundred thousand of the sons of Ch'in
whom you had tricked into surrender and made their general, Chang
Han, a king; this was your sixth crime. You enfeoffed all your generals
as kings in the best lands and transferred or exiled the former kings,
setting their subjects to strife and rebellion; this was your seventh
crime. You drove the Righteous Emperor from P'eng-ch'eng and set
up your own capital there, seized the territory of the king of Hann
and made yourself ruler of the combined areas of Liang and Ch'u,
appropriating all for yourself. This was your eighth crime. You sent
a man in secret to assassinate the Righteous Emperor at Chiang-nan,
your ninth crime. As a subject you have assassinated your sovereign;
you have murdered those who had already surrendered, administered
your rule unjustly, and broken faith with the agreement that you made.
You are guilty of such heinous treason as the world cannot forgive.
This is your tenth crime. I and my soldiers of righteousness have

joined with the other nobles to punish tyranny and rebellion. I have plenty of criminals and exconvicts that I can send to attack and kill you. Why should I go to the trouble of engaging in combat with you myself?"

Hsiang Yü was enraged and, with a crossbow that he had concealed, shot and hit the king of Han. The king was wounded in the breast, but he seized his foot and cried, "The scoundrel has hit me in the toe!" [12]

The king lay ill of his wound, but Chang Liang begged him to get up and walk about the camp in order to comfort and reassure his officers and men so that Ch'u would not be able to profit from its advantage. The king of Han went out and walked about his camp, but when the pain became too great he hurried into the city of Ch'eng-kao. After his wound had healed, he retired west through the Pass until he reached Yüeh-yang, where he held a feast for the elders of the city and set out wine for them. Then he had the head of the former king of Sai, Ssu-ma Hsin, exposed in the market place of his old capital, Yüeh-yang. After staying for four days the king returned to his army, which was still camped at Wu-kuang. A number of reinforcements of troops arrived from within the Pass.

At this time P'eng Yüeh was in the region of Liang, leading his troops back and forth, harassing the Ch'u forces and cutting off their supplies of food. T'ien Heng fled and joined him there. Hsiang Yü had several times attacked P'eng Yüeh and the others when Han Hsin, the new king of Ch'i, appeared and began to attack Ch'u as well. Hsiang Yü became fearful and made an agreement with the king of Han to divide the empire, all the territory west of the Hung Canal to belong to Han and all that east of the canal to belong to Ch'u. Hsiang Yü returned the king of Han's parents, wife, and children to him, amid cheers of welcome from the whole army of Han. Then the two leaders parted, and Hsiang Yü broke camp and started back east.

The king of Han was about to lead his forces west but, on the advice of Chang Liang and Ch'en P'ing, instead marched forward, sending his troops to pursue Hsiang Yü. When he reached the south of Yang-hsia, he stopped and made camp. He arranged with Han Hsin

[12] So that his men would not perceive the seriousness of his wound.

and P'eng Yüeh to meet on a certain date and join in an attack on Ch'u. But when he reached Ku-ling, they failed to appear for the meeting and Ch'u attacked Han, inflicting a grave defeat. The king of Han again withdrew behind his fortifications, deepened his moats, and guarded his position. Using a plan suggested by Chang Liang, he was finally able to induce Han Hsin and P'eng Yüeh to join him. Liu Chia also invaded Ch'u and surrounded Shou-ch'un. When the king of Han was defeated at Ku-ling, he sent an envoy to invite the grand marshal of Ch'u, Chou Yin, to revolt. Accordingly Chou Yin raised the forces of Chiu-chiang and marched to join Liu Chia and Ch'ing Pu, the king of Wu, in massacring the inhabitants of Ch'eng-fu. Following Liu Chia, he and the leaders of Ch'i and Liang all joined in a general meeting at Kai-hsia, at which Ch'ing Pu was made king of Huai-nan.

In the fifth year [202 B.C.] the king of Han with the forces of the other leaders joined in an attack on the army of Ch'u, fighting with Hsiang Yü for a decisive victory at Kai-hsia. Han Hsin led a force of three hundred thousand to attack in the center, with General K'ung leading the left flank and General Pi leading the right flank, while the king of Han followed behind. Chou P'o, the marquis of Chiang, and General Ch'ai followed behind the king. Hsiang Yü's troops numbered some one hundred thousand. Han Hsin advanced and joined in combat but, failing to gain the advantage, retired and allowed General K'ung and General Pi to close in from the sides. When the Ch'u forces began to falter, Han Hsin took advantage of their weakness to inflict a great defeat at Kai-hsia. The soldiers of Hsiang Yü, hearing the Han armies singing the songs of Ch'u, concluded that Han had already conquered the whole land of Ch'u. With this, Hsiang Yü fled in despair, leaving his soldiers to suffer total defeat. The king of Han dispatched his cavalry general Kuan Ying to pursue and kill Hsiang Yü at Tung-ch'eng. After cutting off the heads of eighty thousand of the enemy, he overran and conquered the land of Ch'u.

Lu held out on behalf of Hsiang Yü and refused to surrender but, when the king of Han led the forces of the various nobles north and displayed the head of Hsiang Yü before the elders of Lu, they finally capitulated. The king of Han buried Hsiang Yü at Ku-ch'eng with the title of "Duke of Lu." He then returned to Ting-t'ao, hastily entered the fortifications of Han Hsin, the king of Ch'i, and seized control of his army.

In the first month the various nobles and generals all joined in begging the king of Han to take the title of emperor, but he replied, "I have heard that the position of emperor may go only to a worthy man. It cannot be claimed by empty words and vain talk. I do not dare to accept the position of emperor."

His followers all replied, "Our great king has risen from the humblest beginnings to punish the wicked and violent and bring peace to all within the four seas. To those who have achieved merit he has accordingly parceled out land and enfeoffed them as kings and marquises. If our king does not assume the supreme title, then all our titles as well will be called into doubt. On pain of death we urge our request!"

The king of Han three times declined and then, seeing that he could do no more, said, "If you, my lords, consider it a good thing, then it must be to the good of the country." On the day *chia-wu* [13] [Feb. 28, 202 B.C.] he assumed the position of Supreme Emperor on the north banks of the Ssu River.

The Supreme Emperor declared, "The Righteous Emperor of Ch'u was without an heir, but Han Hsin, king of Ch'i, is well acquainted with the customs and ways of Ch'u." Accordingly he transferred Han Hsin to the position of king of Ch'u with his capital at Hsia-p'ei. Hsin, the former king of Hann, was confirmed in his title, with his capital at Yang-ti. P'eng Yüeh, the marquis of Chien-ch'eng, was made king of Liang, with his capital at Ting-t'ao; Wu Jui, the king of Heng-shan, was transferred to the position of king of Ch'ang-sha, his capital at Lin-hsiang. (Wu Jui's general, Mei Hsüan, had won merit in battle, while he himself had joined in the march through the Wu Pass, and therefore he was rewarded in this fashion.) Ch'ing Pu, the king of Huai-nan; Tsang Tu, the king of Yen; and Chang Ao,[14] the king of Chao, remained in their former positions. With the entire empire now

[13] To indicate days the Chinese employ a series of signs, the so-called ten stems and twelve branches, which combine to form sixty designations used to name the days (and in some cases the years) of a sixty-day or -year cycle.

[14] Chang Ao succeeded his father, Chang Erh, who had died this year.

at peace, Kao-tsu [15] made his capital at Lo-yang, where all the nobles acknowledged his sovereignty. Huan,[16] the former king of Lin-chiang, had in the name of Hsiang Yü revolted against Han, but Lu Wan and Liu Chia were sent to surround him and, though he held out for several months, he was eventually forced to surrender and was killed at Lo-yang.

In the fifth month the armies were disbanded and the soldiers returned to their homes. The relatives of the feudal lords who remained in the area within the Pass were exempted from all taxes and services for twelve years, while those who returned to their territories were exempted for six years and granted stipends of food for a year. Kao-tsu gave a banquet for the nobles in the Southern Palace of Lo-yang and announced, "My lords and generals, I ask you all to speak your minds quite frankly without daring to hide anything from me. Why is it that I won possession of the world and Hsiang Yü lost?"

Kao Ch'i and Wang Ling replied, "Your Majesty is arrogant and insulting to others, while Hsiang Yü was kind and loving. But when you send someone to attack a city or seize a region, you award him the spoils of the victory, sharing your gains with the whole world. Hsiang Yü was jealous of worth and ability, hating those who had achieved merit and suspecting anyone who displayed his wisdom. No matter what victories were achieved in battle, he gave his men no reward; no matter what lands they won, he never shared with them the spoils. This is why he lost possession of the world."

Kao-tsu said, "You have understood the first reason, but you do not know the second. When it comes to sitting within the tents of command and devising strategies that will assure us victory a thousand miles away, I am no match for Chang Liang. In ordering the state and caring for the people, in providing rations for the troops and seeing to it that the lines of supply are not cut off, I cannot compare to Hsiao Ho. In leading an army of a million men, achieving success with every battle and victory with every attack, I cannot come up to Han Hsin. These three are all men of extraordinary ability, and it

[15] From now on Liu Chi is called by his posthumous title, Kao-tsu, or "Exalted Ancestor."

[16] Probably a mistake for Kung Wei, who succeeded his father, Kung Ao, as king of Lin-chiang.

is because I was able to make use of them that I gained possession of the world. Hsiang Yü had his one Fan Tseng, but he did not know how to use him and thus he ended as my prisoner."

Kao-tsu wished to continue to make his capital at Lo-yang, but Liu Ching, a man of Ch'i, advised him against this and Chang Liang likewise urged him to establish his capital within the Pass. Accordingly on the same day Kao-tsu mounted his carriage and entered the Pass to take up residence there. In the sixth month he proclaimed a general amnesty for the empire.

In the seventh month Tsang Tu, the king of Yen, revolted, invading and seizing control of the land of Tai. Kao-tsu himself led a force to attack and capture him. He proceeded to set up the grand commandant Lu Wan as the new king of Yen, sending Fan K'uai with a force of troops to attack Tai.

In the autumn Li Chi revolted. Kao-tsu again led the troops in person to attack him, whereupon Li Chi fled. (Li Chi had originally been a general of the Hsiang family. When the Hsiangs were defeated, Li Chi, then the governor of the district of Ch'en, revoked his allegiance to the Hsiangs and fled and surrendered to Kao-tsu. Kao-tsu made him marquis of Ying-ch'uan. When Kao-tsu arrived in Lo-yang, he summoned to court all the marquises whose titles had thus far been registered, but Li Chi, misinterpreting the summons and fearing punishment for his former connection with the Hsiangs, revolted.)

The sixth year [201 B.C.]: Every five days Kao-tsu would go to visit his father, the "Venerable Sire," observing the etiquette proper for an ordinary son towards his father. The steward of his father's household spoke to the Venerable Sire, saying, "As heaven is without two suns, so the earth has not two lords. Now although the emperor is your son, he is the ruler of men, and although you are his father, you are his subject as well. How does it happen then that the ruler of men is doing obeisance to one of his subjects? If this is allowed to continue, the emperor's majesty will never prevail upon the world!"

The next time Kao-tsu came to visit, his father, bearing a broom in his hands as a sign of servitude, went to the gate to greet him and stood respectfully to one side. Kao-tsu in great astonishment descended from his carriage and hastened to his father's side. "The emperor is the ruler of men," his father said. "How should he on my account violate the laws of the empire?" With this Kao-tsu honored his father with the title of "Grand Supreme Emperor" and, because he was secretly pleased with the advice of his father's steward, he awarded the man five hundred catties of gold.

In the twelfth month someone reported a case of disaffection to the emperor, announcing that Han Hsin, the king of Ch'u, was plotting a revolt. When the emperor consulted his advisers, they all urged him to attack but, rejecting this advice, he instead employed a strategy suggested by Ch'en P'ing whereby, pretending to embark upon a pleasure visit to Yün-meng, he summoned the various feudal lords to a meeting at Ch'en. When Han Hsin appeared at the meeting, Kao-tsu immediately seized him. The same day he proclaimed a general amnesty to the empire.

T'ien K'en congratulated the emperor upon his success, saying, "Your Majesty has succeeded in seizing Han Hsin, and also fixed the capital in the area of Ch'in within the Pass. The land of Ch'in is of superlative configuration, surrounded by natural barriers of rivers and mountains and stretching a thousand miles. He who commands an army of a million lances commands a hundred times that number if he holds the land of Ch'in. From such an advantageous stronghold, sending forth troops to subdue the feudal lords is as easy as standing on a roof and pouring down water from a jug. But the land of Ch'i too has its rich fields of Lang-ya and Chi-mo in the east, the fastnesses of Mount T'ai to the south, in the west the banks of the muddy Yellow River, and in the north the resources of the Gulf of Pohai. Its land stretches for two thousand miles. He who commands an army of a million lances in this vast area commands ten times that number when he holds the land of Ch'i. Therefore there is a Ch'in in the east as well as in the west. Only one of the emperor's sons or brothers is fit to be made king of Ch'i."

Kao-tsu approved his words and rewarded him with five hundred catties of yellow gold. Ten or so days later he enfeoffed Han Hsin as marquis of Huai-yin. Han Hsin's original fief he divided into two kingdoms. Because General Liu Chia had several times achieved merit, he enfeoffed him as king of Ching ruling over one of them, the area of Huai-tung; he made his younger brother Liu Chiao king of Ch'u ruling over the other, the area of Huai-hsi. His own son Liu Fei he made king of Ch'i, ruling over more than seventy cities of Ch'i; all the people who spoke the dialect of Ch'i were to belong to the fief of Ch'i. The emperor held debates upon the merits of his followers and presented to the various feudal lords the split tallies, symbols of their formal enfeoffment. He transferred Hsin, the king of Hann, to the region of T'ai-yüan.

In the seventh year [200 B.C.] the Hsiung-nu [17] attacked Hsin, the king of Hann, at Ma-i. Hsin joined with them in plotting a revolt in T'ai-yüan. His generals, Man-ch'iu Ch'en of Po-t'u and Wang Huang, set up Chao Li, a descendant of the royal family of Chao,[18] as king of Chao in revolt against the emperor. Kao-tsu in person led a force to attack them, but he encountered such severe cold that two or three out of every ten of his soldiers lost their fingers from frostbite. At last he reached P'ing-ch'eng, where the Hsiung-nu surrounded him. After seven days of siege they finally withdrew. Kao-tsu ordered Fan K'uai to remain behind and subdue the region of Tai, and set up his older brother Liu Chung as king of Tai.

In the second month Kao-tsu passed through Chao and Lo-yang and returned to the capital at Ch'ang-an. With the completion of the Palace of Lasting Joy, the prime minister and subordinate officials all moved and took up residence in Ch'ang-an.

Eighth year [199 B.C.]: Kao-tsu marched east and attacked the remnants of the king of Hann's revolutionaries at Tung-yüan. The prime minister Hsiao Ho had been put in charge of the building of the Eternal Palace, constructing eastern and western gate towers, a front hall, an arsenal, and a great storehouse. When Kao-tsu returned from his expedition and saw the magnificence of the palace and its towers, he was extremely angry. "The empire is still in great turmoil," he said to Hsiao Ho, "and though we have toiled in battle these several years, we cannot tell yet whether we will achieve final success. What do you mean by constructing palaces like this on such an extravagant scale?"

[17] See note 11, "The Hereditary House of Ch'en She."
[18] Following the *Han shu* reading.

Hsiao Ho replied, "It is precisely because the fate of the empire is still uncertain that we must build such palaces and halls. A true Son of Heaven takes the whole world within the four seas to be his family. If he does not dwell in magnificence and beauty, he will have no way to manifest his authority, nor will he leave any foundation for his heirs to build upon." With these words, Kao-tsu's anger turned to delight.

When Kao-tsu was on his way to Tung-yüan he passed through a place called Po-jen. The prime minister of Chao, Kuan Kao, and others were at this time plotting to assassinate Kao-tsu, but when Kao-tsu heard the name of the place he grew uneasy in his heart and proceeded on without stopping.[19]

Liu Chung, the king of Tai, fled from his kingdom and returned to Lo-yang. Accordingly he was deprived of his title and made marquis of Ho-yang.

Ninth year [198 B.C.]: The plot of Kuan Kao and others to assassinate the emperor came to light, and they were executed along with their three sets of relatives.[20] Chang Ao, the king of Chao, was removed from his position and made marquis of Hsüan-p'ing. In this year the Chao, Ch'ü, Ching, and Huai families of Ch'u and the T'ien family of Ch'i, all powerful noble clans, were moved to the area within the Pass.[21]

When the Eternal Palace was completed, Kao-tsu summoned the nobles and officials to a great reception, setting forth wine for them in the front hall of the palace. Kao-tsu rose and, lifting his jade cup, proposed a toast to his father, the Grand Supreme Emperor. "You, my father, always used to consider me a worthless fellow who could never look after the family fortunes and had not half the industry of my older brother Chung," he said. "Now that my labors are com-

---

[19] Because the name "Po-jen" suggested to him the phrase "po yü jen" (to be pursued by someone).

[20] There is disagreement on the exact meaning of the term "three sets of relatives," but it is certain that, because of the principle of corporate responsibility recognized in Chinese law, the parents and the other members of a criminal's immediate family were executed along with him. One reason was to prevent the possibility of blood revenge.

[21] So that the emperor could keep a closer watch on them.

Feng from its taxes in the same manner as P'ei. He then transferr[ed] the marquis of P'ei, Liu P'i, to the position of king of Wu.

The Han generals made separate attacks upon Ch'ing Pu's armi[es] north and south of the T'ao River, defeating them all, and pursue[d] and executed Ch'ing Pu at P'o-yang. Fan K'uai in the meantime le[d] the troops under his command in pacifying the region of Tai an[d] executed Ch'en Hsi at Tang-ch'eng. In the eleventh month Kao-ts[u] returned from his campaign against Ch'ing Pu to the capital a[t] Ch'ang-an.

In the twelfth month Kao-tsu announced: "The First Emperor o[f] Ch'in, King Yin of Ch'u [Ch'en She], King An-li of Wei, King Mi[n] of Ch'i, and King Tao-hsiang of Chao are all without surviving heirs. I hereby establish ten families for each to act as guardians of thei[r] graves, except that the First Emperor of Ch'in shall be granted twenty families. In addition the nobleman Wu-chi of Wei shall be granted five families." [25] He also granted pardon to the region of Tai and to all the people and officials who had been robbed and plundered by Ch'en Hsi and Chao Li.

One of Ch'en Hsi's generals who had surrendered reported to Kao-tsu that, at the time when Ch'en Hsi revolted, Lu Wan, the king of Yen, had sent an envoy to Ch'en Hsi to join in plotting with him. The emperor sent Shen I-chi, the marquis of Pi-yang, to fetch Lu Wan, but Lu Wan pleaded illness and declined to go with him. Shen I-chi returned and reported on his mission, declaring that there seemed to be some basis for the report of Lu Wan's disaffection.

In the second month the emperor dispatched Fan K'uai and Chou P'o to lead a force of soldiers and attack Lu Wan. He issued a proclamation freeing all the officials and people of Yen from responsibility for the revolt, and set up his son Liu Chien as the new king of Yen.

When Kao-tsu was fighting against Ch'ing Pu, he was wounded by a stray arrow and on the way back he fell ill. When his illness con-

[25] Since these men had no descendants of their own to look after their graves and perform sacrifices to them, the state undertook to provide families for this purpose, even in the case of the hated First Emperor of Ch'in. For one's grave to go entirely untended was in Chinese eyes the cruelest of fates.

---

pleted, which of us has accomplished more, Chung or I?" All the officials in the hall shouted "Long life!" and roared with merriment.

In the tenth month of the tenth year [197 B.C.] Ch'ing Pu, the king of Huai-nan; P'eng Yüeh, the king of Liang; Lu Wan, the king of Yen; Liu Chia, the king of Ching; Liu Chiao, the king of Ch'u; Liu Fei, the king of Ch'i; and Wu Jui, the king of Ch'ang-sha, all came to pay homage at the Palace of Lasting Joy. The spring and summer passed without incident. In the seventh month [22] the Grand Supreme Emperor, father of Kao-tsu, passed away in the palace of Yüeh-yang. The kings of Ch'u and Liang came to attend the funeral. All prisoners in the district of Yüeh-yang were freed and the name of the city of Li-i was changed to "New Feng."

In the eighth month Ch'en Hsi, prime minister of the kingdom of Tai, started a revolt in the region of Tai.[23] "Ch'en Hsi," said the emperor, "formerly acted as my envoy, and I had the deepest faith in him. Tai is a region of crucial importance to me, and therefore I enfeoffed Ch'en Hsi as a marquis and made him prime minister of the kingdom so that he could guard Tai for me. But now he has joined with Wang Huang and the rest in plundering the land of Tai. The officials and people of Tai, however, are not to blame for this and therefore I absolve them of all guilt."

In the ninth month the emperor marched east to attack the rebels. When he reached Han-tan he announced with joy, "Since Ch'en Hsi has not come south to occupy Han-tan and guard the frontier of the Chang River, I am confident he will never be able to do me much harm." When he heard that all of Ch'en Hsi's generals had formerly been merchants he remarked, "I know how to take care of them." Then he offered large sums of money to tempt them to desert, so that most of Ch'en Hsi's generals surrendered to him.

Eleventh year [196 B.C.]: While Kao-tsu was still in Han-tan engaged in putting down the revolt of Ch'en Hsi and his followers, one of Ch'en's generals, Hou Ch'ang, with a band of some ten thousand men roamed from place to place, while Wang Huang camped at Ch'ü-ni

[22] The Han year at this time began with the tenth month and ended with the ninth.

[23] The text erroneously reads "prime minister of Chao."

and Chang Ch'un crossed the Yellow River and attacked Liao-ch'eng. Kao-tsu dispatched his general Kuo Meng to join with the general of Ch'i in attacking them, inflicting a decisive defeat. The grand commandant Chou P'o marched by way of T'ai-yüan into the region of Tai, conquering the area as far as Ma-i. When Ma-i refused to surrender, he attacked it and massacred its defenders. Kao-tsu attacked Tung-yüan, which was being held by Ch'en Hsi's general Chao Li. The city held out for over a month, while its men cursed the emperor. When the city finally capitulated, Kao-tsu had all those who had cursed him dragged forth and beheaded, while those who had not joined in cursing him he pardoned. With this, he took from Chao the land north of the Ch'ang Mountains and assigned it to Tai, setting up his son Liu Heng as king of Tai with his capital at Chin-yang.

In the spring Han Hsin, the marquis of Huai-yin, plotted a revolt in the area within the Pass. He was executed with his three sets of relatives.

In the summer P'eng Yüeh, the king of Liang, plotted a revolt. He was removed from his position and exiled to Shu but, when it was found that he was once more scheming to revolt, he was executed with his three sets of relatives. Kao-tsu set up his son Liu Hui as king of Liang and his son Liu Yu as king of Huai-yang.

In autumn, the seventh month, Ch'ing Pu, the king of Huai-nan, revolted, seized the land of Liu Chia, the king of Ching, to the east, and marched north across the Huai River. Liu Chiao, the king of Ch'u, fled to Hsieh. Kao-tsu in person led a force to attack Ch'ing Pu, setting up his son Liu Ch'ang as king of Huai-nan.

In the tenth month of the twelfth year [195 B.C.] Kao-tsu had already attacked Ch'ing Pu's army at Kuei-chui, and Ch'ing Pu was in flight. Kao-tsu dispatched a special general to pursue him, while he himself started back to the capital, passing through his old home of P'ei on his way. Here he stopped and held a feast at the palace of P'ei, summoning all his old friends and the elders and young men to drink to their hearts' content. He gathered together a group of some hundred and twenty children of P'ei and taught them to sing and, when the feast was at its height, Kao-tsu struck the lute and sang a song which he had composed:

A great wind came forth;
The clouds rose on high.
Now that my might rules all within the seas,
I have returned to my old village.
Where shall I find brave men
To guard the four corners of my land?

He made the children join in and repeat the song, while he rose and danced. Deeply moved with grief and nostalgia, and with tears streaming down his face, he said to the elders of P'ei, "The traveler sighs for his old home. Though I have made my capital within the Pass, after I have departed this life my spirit will still think with joy of P'ei. From the time when I was governor of P'ei, I went forth to punish the wicked and violent until at last the whole world is mine. It is my wish that P'ei become my bath-town.[24] I hereby exempt its people from all taxes. For generation after generation, nothing more shall be required of you." Then for over ten days the old men and women and Kao-tsu's former friends of P'ei spent each day drinking and rejoicing, reminiscing and joking about old times.

When Kao-tsu made ready to leave, the men of P'ei all begged him to stay a little longer. Kao-tsu replied, "My retinue is very large and I fear it would be too much for you to supply them with food any longer," and with this he departed. The entire district of P'ei became deserted as everyone flocked to the western edge of the city to present parting gifts. Kao-tsu again halted his progress, set up tents, and drank for three days more. The elders of P'ei all bowed their heads and said, "P'ei has been fortunate enough to have its taxes revoked, but the city of Feng has not been so blessed. We beg that Your Majesty will take pity upon it as well."

"Feng is the place where I was born and grew up," replied Kao-tsu. "It least of all could I ever forget. It is only that I remember how under Yung Ch'ih it turned against me and joined Wei." But the elders of P'ei continued to plead with him until he finally agreed to absolve

[24] A mark of special honor. Such estates were not required to pay taxes to the government, their revenues going instead to provide "bath-water," i.e., private funds for the holder. In later chapters we shall often find "bath-towns" being assigned to princesses.

tinued to grow worse, Empress Lü sent for a skilled doctor. The doctor examined Kao-tsu and, in answer to his question, replied, "This illness can be cured." With this, Kao-tsu began to berate and curse him, saying, "I began as a commoner and with my three-foot sword conquered the world. Was this not the will of Heaven? My fate lies with Heaven. Even P'ien Ch'üeh, the most famous doctor of antiquity, could do nothing for me!" In the end he would not let the doctor treat his illness, but gave him fifty catties of gold and sent him away.

When the doctor had gone, Empress Lü asked, "After my lord's allotted years have run out, if Prime Minister Hsiao Ho should die, who could be appointed to fill his place?"

"Ts'ao Ts'an will do," replied the emperor.

"And after him?" the empress asked.

"Wang Ling will do," he replied. "But Wang Ling is rather stupid. He will need Ch'en P'ing to help him. Ch'en P'ing has more than enough brains but he could hardly be entrusted with the position alone. Chou P'o has dignity and generosity, though he lacks learning. Yet it will be Chou P'o who will look out for the welfare of the Liu family. He deserves to be made grand commandant."

"And who after him?" the empress asked again.

"After all these men are gone," he replied, "you will no longer be here to know about it."

Lu Wan, with a force of several thousand cavalry, proceeded to a spot along the border, sending to inquire whether the emperor's condition had improved so that he might be allowed to come to the capital and apologize for his disaffection.

In the fourth month, the day *chia-ch'en* [June 1, 195 B.C.], Kao-tsu passed away in the Palace of Lasting Joy. Four days went by, but no mourning was announced. Empress Lü consulted with Shen I-chi, saying, "The other leaders, like the emperor himself, all made their way up from the ranks of the common people. At present they face north and acknowledge themselves his subjects, but in their hearts they nurse a constant discontent. Now they will be called upon to serve a young master. I fear that, if they and their families are not completely done away with, there will be no peace for the empire!"

Someone overheard these words and reported them to General Li Shang. The general went to visit Shen I-chi and said, "I have heard that the emperor passed away four days ago, but no mourning has yet been announced. I also understand that there are plans for executing all the present leaders. If this is actually carried out, I fear the empire will be in grave peril. Ch'en P'ing and Kuan Ying with a force of a hundred thousand are guarding Jung-yang, while Fan K'uai and Chou P'o with two hundred thousand men are engaged in pacifying Yen and Tai. If they hear that the emperor has passed away and that all the leaders in the capital have been executed, they will surely lead their troops back in this direction and attack the area within the Pass. With the major officials in the capital in revolt and the feudal lords beyond up in arms, we may look for total defeat in a matter of days."

Shen I-chi returned to the palace and reported these words to the empress. Accordingly, on the day *ting-wei* [June 4, 195 B.C.] mourning was proclaimed for the emperor and a general amnesty granted to the empire. When Lu Wan received word of the emperor's passing, he fled from the country and joined the Hsiung-nu.

On the day *ping-yin* [June 23] of the fifth month the emperor was buried at Ch'ang-ling.[26] On the day *chi-ssu* [June 26] the heir apparent was set up. He proceeded to the funerary temple of his grandfather, the Grand Supreme Emperor, where the assembled officials announced: "Kao-tsu rose from the humblest beginnings to correct a discordant age and turn it back to the right. He brought peace and order to the world and became the founder of the Han. His merit was of the most exalted order, and it is therefore appropriate that we should honor him with the title of 'Exalted Supreme Emperor.'" The heir apparent succeeded to the title of Supreme Emperor; he is known posthumously as Emperor Hui the Filial. He gave orders that the feudal lords in each province and kingdom should set up funerary temples to Kao-tsu and perform sacrifices in them at the appropriate seasons of the year. In the fifth year of his reign Emperor Hui, recalling how Kao-tsu had rejoiced and sorrowed on his last visit to P'ei, had the palace of

---

[26] The end of this sentence has been misplaced and appears in present texts at the very close of the chapter.

P'ei made into a funerary temple for Kao-tsu, ranking second only to the main temple in the capital. The hundred and twenty children whom Kao-tsu had taught to sing he ordered to perform the song to the accompaniment of wind instruments, and when any of the group later dropped out he had them immediately replaced.

Kao-tsu had eight sons. The oldest, a son by a concubine, was Fei, the king of Ch'i, posthumously titled King Tao-hui. The second, a son by Empress Lü, became Emperor Hui. The third, son of Lady Ch'i, was Ju-i, the king of Chao, posthumously titled King Yin. The fourth was Heng, the king of Tai, who later became Emperor Wen the Filial; he was a son of Empress Dowager Po. The fifth was Hui, the king of Liang, who in the reign of Empress Lü was transferred to the position of king of Chao; he was given the posthumous title of King Kung. The sixth was Yu, the king of Huai-yang, whom Empress Lü made the king of Chao; his posthumous title was King Yu. The seventh was Ch'ang, who became King Li of Huai-nan, and the eighth was Chien, the king of Yen.

The Grand Historian remarks: The government of the Hsia dynasty was marked by good faith, which in time deteriorated until mean men had turned it into rusticity. Therefore the men of Shang who succeeded to the Hsia reformed this defect through the virtue of piety. But piety degenerated until mean men had made it a superstitious concern for the spirits. Therefore the men of Chou who followed corrected this fault through refinement and order. But refinement again deteriorated until it became in the hands of the mean a mere hollow show. Therefore what was needed to reform this hollow show was a return to good faith, for the way of the Three Dynasties of old is like a cycle which, when it ends, must begin over again.

It is obvious that in late Chou and Ch'in times the earlier refinement and order had deteriorated. But the government of Ch'in failed to correct this fault, instead adding its own harsh punishments and laws. Was this not a grave error?

Thus when the Han rose to power it took over the faults of its predecessors and worked to change and reform them, causing men to be unflagging in their efforts and following the order properly ordained by Heaven. It held its court in the tenth month,[27] and its vestments and carriage tops were yellow, with plumes on the left sides of the carriages.

[27] I.e., this was the time each year when the feudal lords were required to attend the court in person and pay their respects for the new year, which in the early Han began in this month.

pleted, which of us has accomplished more, Chung or I?" All the officials in the hall shouted "Long life!" and roared with merriment.

In the tenth month of the tenth year [197 B.C.] Ch'ing Pu, the king of Huai-nan; P'eng Yüeh, the king of Liang; Lu Wan, the king of Yen; Liu Chia, the king of Ching; Liu Chiao, the king of Ch'u; Liu Fei, the king of Ch'i; and Wu Jui, the king of Ch'ang-sha, all came to pay homage at the Palace of Lasting Joy. The spring and summer passed without incident. In the seventh month [22] the Grand Supreme Emperor, father of Kao-tsu, passed away in the palace of Yüeh-yang. The kings of Ch'u and Liang came to attend the funeral. All prisoners in the district of Yüeh-yang were freed and the name of the city of Li-i was changed to "New Feng."

In the eighth month Ch'en Hsi, prime minister of the kingdom of Tai, started a revolt in the region of Tai.[23] "Ch'en Hsi," said the emperor, "formerly acted as my envoy, and I had the deepest faith in him. Tai is a region of crucial importance to me, and therefore I enfeoffed Ch'en Hsi as a marquis and made him prime minister of the kingdom so that he could guard Tai for me. But now he has joined with Wang Huang and the rest in plundering the land of Tai. The officials and people of Tai, however, are not to blame for this and therefore I absolve them of all guilt."

In the ninth month the emperor marched east to attack the rebels. When he reached Han-tan he announced with joy, "Since Ch'en Hsi has not come south to occupy Han-tan and guard the frontier of the Chang River, I am confident he will never be able to do me much harm." When he heard that all of Ch'en Hsi's generals had formerly been merchants he remarked, "I know how to take care of them." Then he offered large sums of money to tempt them to desert, so that most of Ch'en Hsi's generals surrendered to him.

Eleventh year [196 B.C.]: While Kao-tsu was still in Han-tan engaged in putting down the revolt of Ch'en Hsi and his followers, one of Ch'en's generals, Hou Ch'ang, with a band of some ten thousand men roamed from place to place, while Wang Huang camped at Ch'ü-ni

---

[22] The Han year at this time began with the tenth month and ended with the ninth.

[23] The text erroneously reads "prime minister of Chao."

and Chang Ch'un crossed the Yellow River and attacked Liao-ch'eng. Kao-tsu dispatched his general Kuo Meng to join with the general of Ch'i in attacking them, inflicting a decisive defeat. The grand commandant Chou P'o marched by way of T'ai-yüan into the region of Tai, conquering the area as far as Ma-i. When Ma-i refused to surrender, he attacked it and massacred its defenders. Kao-tsu attacked Tung-yüan, which was being held by Ch'en Hsi's general Chao Li. The city held out for over a month, while its men cursed the emperor. When the city finally capitulated, Kao-tsu had all those who had cursed him dragged forth and beheaded, while those who had not joined in cursing him he pardoned. With this, he took from Chao the land north of the Ch'ang Mountains and assigned it to Tai, setting up his son Liu Heng as king of Tai with his capital at Chin-yang.

In the spring Han Hsin, the marquis of Huai-yin, plotted a revolt in the area within the Pass. He was executed with his three sets of relatives.

In the summer P'eng Yüeh, the king of Liang, plotted a revolt. He was removed from his position and exiled to Shu but, when it was found that he was once more scheming to revolt, he was executed with his three sets of relatives. Kao-tsu set up his son Liu Hui as king of Liang and his son Liu Yu as king of Huai-yang.

In autumn, the seventh month, Ch'ing Pu, the king of Huai-nan, revolted, seized the land of Liu Chia, the king of Ching, to the east, and marched north across the Huai River. Liu Chiao, the king of Ch'u, fled to Hsieh. Kao-tsu in person led a force to attack Ch'ing Pu, setting up his son Liu Ch'ang as king of Huai-nan.

In the tenth month of the twelfth year [195 B.C.] Kao-tsu had already attacked Ch'ing Pu's army at Kuei-chui, and Ch'ing Pu was in flight. Kao-tsu dispatched a special general to pursue him, while he himself started back to the capital, passing through his old home of P'ei on his way. Here he stopped and held a feast at the palace of P'ei, summoning all his old friends and the elders and young men to drink to their hearts' content. He gathered together a group of some hundred and twenty children of P'ei and taught them to sing and, when the feast was at its height, Kao-tsu struck the lute and sang a song which he had composed:

A great wind came forth;
The clouds rose on high.
Now that my might rules all within the seas,
I have returned to my old village.
Where shall I find brave men
To guard the four corners of my land?

He made the children join in and repeat the song, while he rose and danced. Deeply moved with grief and nostalgia, and with tears streaming down his face, he said to the elders of P'ei, "The traveler sighs for his old home. Though I have made my capital within the Pass, after I have departed this life my spirit will still think with joy of P'ei. From the time when I was governor of P'ei, I went forth to punish the wicked and violent until at last the whole world is mine. It is my wish that P'ei become my bath-town.[24] I hereby exempt its people from all taxes. For generation after generation, nothing more shall be required of you." Then for over ten days the old men and women and Kao-tsu's former friends of P'ei spent each day drinking and rejoicing, reminiscing and joking about old times.

When Kao-tsu made ready to leave, the men of P'ei all begged him to stay a little longer. Kao-tsu replied, "My retinue is very large and I fear it would be too much for you to supply them with food any longer," and with this he departed. The entire district of P'ei became deserted as everyone flocked to the western edge of the city to present parting gifts. Kao-tsu again halted his progress, set up tents, and drank for three days more. The elders of P'ei all bowed their heads and said, "P'ei has been fortunate enough to have its taxes revoked, but the city of Feng has not been so blessed. We beg that Your Majesty will take pity upon it as well."

"Feng is the place where I was born and grew up," replied Kao-tsu. "It least of all could I ever forget. It is only that I remember how under Yung Ch'ih it turned against me and joined Wei." But the elders of P'ei continued to plead with him until he finally agreed to absolve

[24] A mark of special honor. Such estates were not required to pay taxes to the government, their revenues going instead to provide "bath-water," i.e., private funds for the holder. In later chapters we shall often find "bath-towns" being assigned to princesses.

Feng from its taxes in the same manner as P'ei. He then transferred the marquis of P'ei, Liu P'i, to the position of king of Wu.

The Han generals made separate attacks upon Ch'ing Pu's armies north and south of the T'ao River, defeating them all, and pursued and executed Ch'ing Pu at P'o-yang. Fan K'uai in the meantime led the troops under his command in pacifying the region of Tai and executed Ch'en Hsi at Tang-ch'eng. In the eleventh month Kao-tsu returned from his campaign against Ch'ing Pu to the capital at Ch'ang-an.

In the twelfth month Kao-tsu announced: "The First Emperor of Ch'in, King Yin of Ch'u [Ch'en She], King An-li of Wei, King Min of Ch'i, and King Tao-hsiang of Chao are all without surviving heirs. I hereby establish ten families for each to act as guardians of their graves, except that the First Emperor of Ch'in shall be granted twenty families. In addition the nobleman Wu-chi of Wei shall be granted five families." [25] He also granted pardon to the region of Tai and to all the people and officials who had been robbed and plundered by Ch'en Hsi and Chao Li.

One of Ch'en Hsi's generals who had surrendered reported to Kao-tsu that, at the time when Ch'en Hsi revolted, Lu Wan, the king of Yen, had sent an envoy to Ch'en Hsi to join in plotting with him. The emperor sent Shen I-chi, the marquis of Pi-yang, to fetch Lu Wan, but Lu Wan pleaded illness and declined to go with him. Shen I-chi returned and reported on his mission, declaring that there seemed to be some basis for the report of Lu Wan's disaffection.

In the second month the emperor dispatched Fan K'uai and Chou P'o to lead a force of soldiers and attack Lu Wan. He issued a proclamation freeing all the officials and people of Yen from responsibility for the revolt, and set up his son Liu Chien as the new king of Yen.

When Kao-tsu was fighting against Ch'ing Pu, he was wounded by a stray arrow and on the way back he fell ill. When his illness con-

---

[25] Since these men had no descendants of their own to look after their graves and perform sacrifices to them, the state undertook to provide families for this purpose, even in the case of the hated First Emperor of Ch'in. For one's grave to go entirely untended was in Chinese eyes the cruelest of fates.

tinued to grow worse, Empress Lü sent for a skilled doctor. The doctor examined Kao-tsu and, in answer to his question, replied, "This illness can be cured." With this, Kao-tsu began to berate and curse him, saying, "I began as a commoner and with my three-foot sword conquered the world. Was this not the will of Heaven? My fate lies with Heaven. Even P'ien Ch'üeh, the most famous doctor of antiquity, could do nothing for me!" In the end he would not let the doctor treat his illness, but gave him fifty catties of gold and sent him away.

When the doctor had gone, Empress Lü asked, "After my lord's allotted years have run out, if Prime Minister Hsiao Ho should die, who could be appointed to fill his place?"

"Ts'ao Ts'an will do," replied the emperor.

"And after him?" the empress asked.

"Wang Ling will do," he replied. "But Wang Ling is rather stupid. He will need Ch'en P'ing to help him. Ch'en P'ing has more than enough brains but he could hardly be entrusted with the position alone. Chou P'o has dignity and generosity, though he lacks learning. Yet it will be Chou P'o who will look out for the welfare of the Liu family. He deserves to be made grand commandant."

"And who after him?" the empress asked again.

"After all these men are gone," he replied, "you will no longer be here to know about it."

Lu Wan, with a force of several thousand cavalry, proceeded to a spot along the border, sending to inquire whether the emperor's condition had improved so that he might be allowed to come to the capital and apologize for his disaffection.

In the fourth month, the day *chia-ch'en* [June 1, 195 B.C.], Kao-tsu passed away in the Palace of Lasting Joy. Four days went by, but no mourning was announced. Empress Lü consulted with Shen I-chi, saying, "The other leaders, like the emperor himself, all made their way up from the ranks of the common people. At present they face north and acknowledge themselves his subjects, but in their hearts they nurse a constant discontent. Now they will be called upon to serve a young master. I fear that, if they and their families are not completely done away with, there will be no peace for the empire!"

Someone overheard these words and reported them to General Li Shang. The general went to visit Shen I-chi and said, "I have heard that the emperor passed away four days ago, but no mourning has yet been announced. I also understand that there are plans for executing all the present leaders. If this is actually carried out, I fear the empire will be in grave peril. Ch'en P'ing and Kuan Ying with a force of a hundred thousand are guarding Jung-yang, while Fan K'uai and Chou P'o with two hundred thousand men are engaged in pacifying Yen and Tai. If they hear that the emperor has passed away and that all the leaders in the capital have been executed, they will surely lead their troops back in this direction and attack the area within the Pass. With the major officials in the capital in revolt and the feudal lords beyond up in arms, we may look for total defeat in a matter of days."

Shen I-chi returned to the palace and reported these words to the empress. Accordingly, on the day *ting-wei* [June 4, 195 b.c.] mourning was proclaimed for the emperor and a general amnesty granted to the empire. When Lu Wan received word of the emperor's passing, he fled from the country and joined the Hsiung-nu.

On the day *ping-yin* [June 23] of the fifth month the emperor was buried at Ch'ang-ling.[26] On the day *chi-ssu* [June 26] the heir apparent was set up. He proceeded to the funerary temple of his grandfather, the Grand Supreme Emperor, where the assembled officials announced: "Kao-tsu rose from the humblest beginnings to correct a discordant age and turn it back to the right. He brought peace and order to the world and became the founder of the Han. His merit was of the most exalted order, and it is therefore appropriate that we should honor him with the title of 'Exalted Supreme Emperor.'" The heir apparent succeeded to the title of Supreme Emperor; he is known posthumously as Emperor Hui the Filial. He gave orders that the feudal lords in each province and kingdom should set up funerary temples to Kao-tsu and perform sacrifices in them at the appropriate seasons of the year. In the fifth year of his reign Emperor Hui, recalling how Kao-tsu had rejoiced and sorrowed on his last visit to P'ei, had the palace of

[26] The end of this sentence has been misplaced and appears in present texts at the very close of the chapter.

P'ei made into a funerary temple for Kao-tsu, ranking second only to the main temple in the capital. The hundred and twenty children whom Kao-tsu had taught to sing he ordered to perform the song to the accompaniment of wind instruments, and when any of the group later dropped out he had them immediately replaced.

Kao-tsu had eight sons. The oldest, a son by a concubine, was Fei, the king of Ch'i, posthumously titled King Tao-hui. The second, a son by Empress Lü, became Emperor Hui. The third, son of Lady Ch'i, was Ju-i, the king of Chao, posthumously titled King Yin. The fourth was Heng, the king of Tai, who later became Emperor Wen the Filial; he was a son of Empress Dowager Po. The fifth was Hui, the king of Liang, who in the reign of Empress Lü was transferred to the position of king of Chao; he was given the posthumous title of King Kung. The sixth was Yu, the king of Huai-yang, whom Empress Lü made the king of Chao; his posthumous title was King Yu. The seventh was Ch'ang, who became King Li of Huai-nan, and the eighth was Chien, the king of Yen.

The Grand Historian remarks: The government of the Hsia dynasty was marked by good faith, which in time deteriorated until mean men had turned it into rusticity. Therefore the men of Shang who succeeded to the Hsia reformed this defect through the virtue of piety. But piety degenerated until mean men had made it a superstitious concern for the spirits. Therefore the men of Chou who followed corrected this fault through refinement and order. But refinement again deteriorated until it became in the hands of the mean a mere hollow show. Therefore what was needed to reform this hollow show was a return to good faith, for the way of the Three Dynasties of old is like a cycle which, when it ends, must begin over again.

It is obvious that in late Chou and Ch'in times the earlier refinement and order had deteriorated. But the government of Ch'in failed to correct this fault, instead adding its own harsh punishments and laws. Was this not a grave error?

Thus when the Han rose to power it took over the faults of its predecessors and worked to change and reform them, causing men to be unflagging in their efforts and following the order properly ordained by Heaven. It held its court in the tenth month,[27] and its vestments and carriage tops were yellow, with plumes on the left sides of the carriages.

[27] I.e., this was the time each year when the feudal lords were required to attend the court in person and pay their respects for the new year, which in the early Han began in this month.

Shih chi 16 (excerpt): Reflections on the Rise of Emperor Kao-tsu

[This introduction to the "Table by Months of the Times of Ch'in and Ch'u," *Shih chi* 16, is given with a title supplied by the translator.]

Against the tyranny and oppression of the Ch'in the men of Ch'u began their revolt, but Hsiang Yü in turn betrayed his ruler, until the king of Han came to the aid of right and conquered him. Thus in the course of eight years the rulership changed hands three times.[1] Since the period was so crowded with events and the shifts of power were so frequent, I have chosen to outline it in detail in this Table by Months of the Times of Ch'in and Ch'u.

On reading the accounts of the struggle between Ch'in and Ch'u, the Grand Historian remarks: It was Ch'en She who first began the uprising, the Hsiang family who with cruelty and treason destroyed the Ch'in, and the founder of the house of Han who dispersed the rebellion, punished the evildoers, brought peace to all within the seas, and in the end ascended the imperial throne. Within the space of eight years the command of the empire changed hands three times. Since the birth of mankind there have never before been such rapid changes of rulership!

In ancient times, when Shun and Yü became rulers, they had first to accumulate goodness and merit for twenty or thirty years, impress the people with their virtue, prove that they could in practice handle the affairs of government, and meet the approval of Heaven before they were able to ascend the throne. Again, when Kings T'ang and Wu founded the Shang and Chou dynasties, they had behind them over ten generations of ancestors, stretching back to Hsieh and Hou Chi respectively, who had been distinguished for their just and virtuous conduct. Yet, though eight hundred nobles appeared unsummoned to

[1] I.e., from the Ch'in to Hsiang Yü to Han Kao-tsu.

aid King Wu at the Meng Ford, he still did not venture to move; it was only later that he assassinated the tyrant Chou, and only after similar cautious delay that King T'ang banished the tyrant Chieh. Ch'in first rose to prominence under Duke Hsiang and achieved eminence under Dukes Wen and Mu. From the reigns of Dukes Hsieh and Hsiao on, it gradually swallowed up the Six States until, after a hundred years or so, the First Emperor was able to bring all the noblemen under his power. Thus, even with the virtue of Shun, Yü, T'ang, and Wu, or the might of the First Emperor, it is, as one can see, an extremely difficult task to unite the empire in one rule!

After the Ch'in ruler had assumed the title of emperor, he was fearful lest warfare should continue because of the presence of feudal lords. Therefore he refused to grant so much as a foot of land in fief, but instead destroyed the fortifications of the principal cities, melted down the lance and arrow points, and ruthlessly wiped out the brave men of the world, hoping thus to ensure the safety of his dynasty for countless generations to come. Yet from the lanes of the common people there arose a man with the deeds of a king whose alliances and campaigns of attack surpassed those of the three dynasties of Hsia, Shang, and Chou. Ch'in's earlier prohibitions against feudalism and the possession of arms, as it turned out, served only to aid worthy men and remove from their path obstacles they would otherwise have encountered. Therefore Kao-tsu had but to roar forth his indignation to become a leader of the world. Why should people say that one cannot become a king unless he possesses land? Was this man not what the old books term a "great sage"? Surely this was the work of Heaven! Who but a great sage would be worthy to receive the mandate of Heaven and become emperor?

Shih chi 53: The Hereditary House of Prime Minister Hsiao

When the armies of Ch'u surrounded us at Jung-yang and we were locked in stalemate for three years, Hsiao Ho governed the land west of the mountains, plotting our welfare, sending a constant stream of reinforcements, and supplying rations and provisions without end. He caused the people to rejoice in Han and hate the alliance of Ch'u. Thus I made The Hereditary House of Prime Minister Hsiao.

Prime Minister Hsiao Ho was a native of Feng in the district of P'ei. Because of his thorough understanding of law and letters he was made a director of officials in P'ei. While Kao-tsu was still a commoner, Hsiao Ho on numerous occasions took advantage of his official capacity to help Kao-tsu out. After Kao-tsu became a village head he in turn did all he could to assist Hsiao Ho. When Kao-tsu was sent with a band of *corvée* laborers to Hsien-yang, each of the other officials presented him with three hundred cash as a parting gift, but Hsiao Ho alone gave five hundred.

As an official of P'ei, Hsiao Ho worked with the secretary of Ch'in who was in charge of overseeing the province. Because he conducted his affairs with consistent discretion and understanding, he was given the position of a provincial secretary of Ssu River, where his record was also of the highest order. The secretary of Ch'in planned on his return to the capital to make a report of Hsiao Ho's good record and have him appointed to a position in the central government, but Hsiao Ho begged not to be transferred.

When Kao-tsu rose to the position of governor of P'ei, Hsiao Ho always served as his aide and looked after official business for him. At the time when Kao-tsu marched into the capital of Hsien-yang, all the generals rushed to the storehouses and fought with each other over Ch'in's goods and treasures. But Hsiao Ho entered ahead of them and gathered up all the maps and official records that had belonged to Ch'in's ministers and secretaries and stored them away. When Kao-tsu became king of Han, Hsiao Ho served as his prime minister. Hsiang Yü arrived later with the other nobles, massacred the inhabitants of Hsien-yang, burned the city, and then marched away. But because of the maps and registries of Ch'in which Hsiao Ho had in his possession, the king of Han was able to inform himself of all the strategic defense points of the empire, the population and relative strength of the various districts, and the ills and grievances of the people.

On the recommendation of Hsiao Ho, the king of Han took Han Hsin into his service and made him a major general. (A discussion of this will be found in the chapter on Han Hsin, the marquis of Huai-yin.)

When the king of Han led his forces east again to conquer the three kingdoms of Ch'in, he left Hsiao Ho behind as his prime minister to govern Pa and Shu, with instructions to ensure their well-being and loyalty, propagandize for his cause, and see that provisions were sent to feed his army.

In the second year of Han [205 B.C.], while the king of Han and the other feudal leaders were attacking Ch'u, Hsiao Ho remained behind to guard the area within the Pass and look after the heir apparent. Establishing the seat of government in Yüeh-yang, he worked to simplify the laws and statutes and set up dynastic temples and altars, palaces and district offices. All affairs he reported immediately to the king of Han, and acted only upon his permission and approval. If it was impossible to report to the king at the time, he disposed of the matter as he thought best and asked the king's opinion on his return. He had charge of all affairs within the Pass, drawing up registers of the population and sending supplies by land and water to provision the army. The king of Han several times lost large parts of his army and was forced to retreat in flight, but each time Hsiao Ho raised more troops from the area within the Pass and immediately brought the army back up to strength. For this reason the king entrusted sole charge of the land within the Pass to him.

In the third year of Han [204 B.C.], the king of Han and Hsiang Yü were locked in stalemate in the area So in Ching. The king several times sent envoys to reward and encourage Hsiao Ho for his labors. Master Po spoke to Hsiao Ho, saying, "While His Majesty is forced to camp in the fields and suffer the hardships of exposure, he sends envoys to reward and encourage you. It must be that he doubts your loyalty. I think it would be best for you to summon all your sons and brothers who are fit to take up arms and send them to join the army. Then the king will surely have greater confidence in you." Hsiao Ho followed his suggestion and the king was greatly pleased.

In the fifth year of Han [202 B.C.], after Hsiang Yü had been killed and the empire brought to peace, discussions were begun as to who had won merit and who should be enfeoffed but, because there was a great deal of contention among the officials over their respective achievements, the year passed before the matter could be settled.

The king of Han, now emperor, considered that Hsiao Ho had achieved the highest merit, and hence enfeoffed him as marquis of Tsuan with the revenue from a large number of towns. But the other distinguished officials objected, saying, "We have all buckled on armor and taken up our weapons, some of us fighting as many as a hundred or more engagements, the least of us fighting twenty or thirty. Each, to a greater or lesser degree, has engaged in attacks upon cities or seizures of territory. And yet Hsiao Ho, who has never campaigned on the sweaty steeds of battle, but only sat here with brush and ink deliberating on questions of state instead of fighting, is awarded a position above us. How can this be?"

"Gentlemen," the emperor asked, "do you know anything about hunting?"

"We do," they replied.

"And do you know anything about hunting dogs?"

"We do."

"Now in a hunt," the emperor said, "it is the dog who is sent to pursue and kill the beast. But the one who unleashes the dog and points out the place where the beast is hiding is the huntsman. You, gentlemen, have only succeeded in capturing the beast, and so your achievement is that of hunting dogs. But it is Hsiao Ho who unleashed you and pointed out the place, and his achievement is that of the huntsman. Also in your case only you yourselves, or at most two or three of your family, joined in following me. But Hsiao Ho dispatched his whole family numbering twenty or thirty members to accompany me. This is a service I can hardly forget."

None of the officials dared say anything further. The various marquises having been granted their fiefs, the question of what order of precedence they should take was brought before the emperor. "Ts'ao Ts'an, the marquis of P'ing-yang," the officials stated, "bears on his body the scars of seventy wounds. In attacking cities and seizing territory he has achieved the greatest merit. It is proper that he should be given first place."

The emperor had already contravened the will of his ministers by granting Hsiao Ho such a generous fief, and when it came to the question of precedence he did not feel that he could dispute their judgment a second time, though personally he wanted Hsiao Ho to be given first place. At this point Lord E, a marquis of the area within the Pass, came forward. "The opinion of the other ministers," he said, "is in my estimation a mistake. Although Ts'ao Ts'an has won merit by fighting in the field and seizing territory, this was an accomplishment of the moment. While the emperor was locked in battle with Hsiang Yü for five years, he several times lost the major part of his army, and was on occasion forced to flee for his life in retreat. But each time Hsiao Ho sent reinforcements from the area within the Pass to bring the army back to strength. The emperor sent no orders for men and yet, just when his forces were weakest and most in danger of annihilation, a new contingent of some ten thousand recruits would arrive. Again, when Han and Ch'u were stalemated for several years at Jung-yang, our army ran completely out of provisions, but Hsiao Ho sent supplies by land and water from the area within the Pass and saved our men from starvation. Though His Majesty several times lost control of the land east of the mountains, Hsiao Ho kept firm hold on the area within the Pass and awaited His Majesty's final return. His achievements were not a matter of a moment, but deserve everlasting honor. Han could have done without a hundred men like Ts'ao Ts'an and never felt the loss, nor would their presence have assured inevitable victory by any means. How then can one suggest that the achievements of a moment take precedence over those of all time? Hsiao Ho should clearly be granted first place, and Ts'ao Ts'an ranked second."

The emperor approved this suggestion; in addition he granted Hsiao Ho the privilege of wearing his sword and shoes when he ascended to the audience chamber, and absolved him from the duty of hurrying when he entered court.[1]

The emperor announced, "I have heard that he who works for the advancement of worthy men deserves the highest reward. Although Hsiao Ho achieved the most outstanding merit, it was Lord E who made this fact clear." With this he granted Lord E the title of marquis of P'ing-an, awarding him the cities from which he already received the revenue as a marquis within the Pass.[2] On the same day he enfeoffed all of Hsiao Ho's male relatives, some ten or more, with the revenue of various towns, and increased Hsiao Ho's original fief by two thousand households. This last, according to the emperor, was done because when he had once been sent on labor service to Hsien-yang Hsiao Ho had presented him with two hundred cash more than any of the other officials as a parting gift.

In the eleventh year of Han [196 B.C.] Ch'en Hsi revolted. Kao-tsu marched to Han-tan to attack him, but before the campaign was completed Han Hsin, the marquis of Huai-yin, began to plot a rebellion in the area within the Pass. Empress Lü followed Hsiao Ho's advice and executed Han Hsin. (A discussion will be found in the chapter on Han Hsin.) When the emperor received word of Han Hsin's execution, he sent a messenger to honor Hsiao Ho with the position of prime minister and increase his fief by five thousand households, granting him at the same time a private retinue of five hundred soldiers headed by a colonel to act as his bodyguard.

All the other ministers went to congratulate Hsiao Ho on his good fortune, but Shao P'ing alone presented condolences as though upon

---

[1] Chinese etiquette forbade ministers to wear their swords or shoes when they entered the emperor's presence. In addition they were required to scurry into court instead of walking at a normal pace. By excepting him from these requirements the emperor was conferring upon Hsiao Ho the marks of extreme honor.

[2] The "marquises within the Pass" ordinarily did not hold possession of any lands, but only received the revenues from the cities in their fiefs.

a death. (Shao P'ing had been the marquis of Tung-ling under Ch'in, but when Ch'in was defeated he was made a commoner. Being very poor, he used to raise melons east of the city of Ch'ang-an. His melons were known for their excellent flavor and everyone called them "Tung-ling melons" after the title that Shao P'ing had once held.) Shao P'ing said to him, "Some misfortune will come from this. The emperor is away in battle and has left you to guard the capital area, and yet, though you suffer none of the perils of war, he suddenly increases your fief and grants you a bodyguard. It must be that, because of the recent revolt of Han Hsin in the capital area, he doubts your loyalty. He has granted you a bodyguard not for your own protection but because he does not trust you. I beg you to decline the new enfeoffment and not accept it, but instead to make a contribution to the expenses of the campaign from your own private wealth. Then the emperor's mind will be set at ease." Hsiao Ho followed his advice, to the great pleasure of the emperor.

In the autumn of the twelfth year of Han [195 B.C.] Ch'ing Pu revolted. The emperor in person led a force to attack him, from time to time sending envoys back to the capital to ask what Hsiao Ho was doing. While the emperor was away in battle Hsiao Ho continued to look after the wants of the people and encourage them in their labors, sending all the assistance he could to the army as he had done at the time of Ch'en Hsi's revolt. But one of his retainers advised him, saying, "It will not be long before your family is wiped out. You have been made prime minister and given the highest rank in the empire. There is no further honor that can be added to this. Now it has been over ten years since you first entered the Pass and won the hearts of the people. They are all unswervingly loyal to you, for you have ceaselessly and with the greatest diligence worked for their peace and well-being. The reason the emperor keeps sending to ask what you are doing is that he is afraid you will betray him and start an uprising within the Pass. Why don't you buy up a lot of farm land on credit and start speculating in goods at a cheap price so that you will create a reputation for being corrupt? Then the emperor's mind will be set somewhat at ease." [3]

[3] This would seem an odd way to set the emperor's mind at ease, but all the

Hsiao Ho followed this suggestion and the emperor was very pleased. When his campaign against Ch'ing Pu was completed and he led his army back to the capital, the people crowded along the roadside presenting petitions to the emperor accusing the prime minister of forcing them to sell their land and houses at an unfair price and accumulating a fortune of twenty or thirty million cash. After the emperor reached the capital, Hsiao Ho appeared before him. "I see that you have been making a profit from the people," said the emperor laughing. He then handed over to Hsiao Ho the petitions that had been presented, adding, "You must do something to make amends to them!"

Hsiao Ho accordingly made this request on behalf of the people: "The region of Ch'ang-an is very narrow and constricted, and yet there is a great deal of idle land going to waste in the Shang-ling Park.[4] I beg that the people be allowed to use the park for farm land, leaving the straw and other remains of their crops as fodder for beasts."

The emperor flew into a rage. "You have succeeded in getting a lot of money and bribes from the merchants and now for their sake you want to take my park away from me!" He turned Hsiao Ho over to the law officials to be put into chains.

A few days later one of the palace guards named Wang who was in attendance advanced and inquired, "What terrible crime has the prime minister committed that Your Majesty has so suddenly thrown him into prison?"

"I have heard," replied the emperor, "that when Li Ssu was prime minister to the emperor of Ch'in if anything good came about he attributed it to his sovereign, but for anything bad he accepted responsibility himself. But now my prime minister has been accepting money from a lot of dirty merchants and in return asks for my park so that he can ingratiate himself with the people. Therefore I have had him put in chains and punished."

"But if in the course of his duties the prime minister becomes aware of something that will benefit the people," objected Wang, "it is his

---

suggestion means is that Hsiao Ho should do something to decrease his popularity, which had reached dangerous proportions.

[4] The emperor's private hunting park.

duty to request it. Why should Your Majesty suppose that he has been accepting money from the merchants? During the years when Your Majesty was battling Ch'u, and later, when Ch'en Hsi and Ch'ing Pu revolted, Your Majesty was away leading the armies, while the prime minister the whole time guarded the area within the Pass. At that time he had no more than to nod his head and Your Majesty would have lost possession of the whole area west of the Pass. But since he did not take that opportunity to scheme for his own profit, why should he now try to profit from the money of the merchants? As for the ruler of Ch'in, the reason he did not become aware of his own faults and eventually lost the empire was that Li Ssu kept accepting the blame for things himself. Ch'in can therefore hardly be taken as a model. Is it not very shortsighted of Your Majesty to suspect the prime minister in this fashion?"

The emperor was deeply perplexed, but before the day was over he dispatched a messenger bearing the imperial seals with orders to pardon Hsiao Ho and release him. Hsiao Ho was by this time well on in years and, being by nature extremely respectful and circumspect in his manner, came before the emperor barefooted and begged for forgiveness. "You may go!" said the emperor. "You asked for the park for the sake of the people. In denying your request I have acted no better than the tyrants Chieh and Chou of old, while you have shown yourself a worthy minister. The reason I had you bound was so that the people might all hear of my fault."

Hsiao Ho had never been on good terms with Ts'ao Ts'an. When Hsiao Ho fell ill Emperor Hui, who had succeeded his father, Kao-tsu, on the throne, came in person to inquire about his illness. "When your hundred years are ended," the emperor asked, "who can fill your place?"

"No one knows his ministers better than their lord," Hsiao Ho replied.

"What about Ts'ao Ts'an?"

Hsiao Ho bowed his head and answered, "As long as my lord has him, I may die without regret."

In selecting his lands and residence, Hsiao Ho always chose to live in an out-of-the-way place with no elaborate walls or roofs to his house.

"This way, if my descendants are worthy men," he used to say, "they will follow my example of frugal living. And if they turn out to be unworthy, they will at least have nothing that the more powerful families can take away from them."

In the second year of Emperor Hui [193 B.C.] Prime Minister Hsiao Ho died. He was granted the posthumous title of Wen-chung or "Civil Fulfillment Marquis." In the fourth generation his heirs, because of some offense, were deprived of the marquisate, but shortly afterwards the emperor sought out Hsiao Ho's descendant and enfeoffed him as marquis of Tsuan to carry on the line. None of the other distinguished ministers received such honor.

The Grand Historian remarks: Prime Minister Hsiao Ho in the time of Ch'in was a petty official, wielding his brush and scraper [5] and going about his business without distinction or honor. But when the Han, like a great sun or moon, rose in the sky, he caught a little of its brilliance. With the gravest care he guarded what was charged to him as though under lock and key and, because the people groaned under the laws of Ch'in, he gratified their wishes by making a new beginning for the empire. When Han Hsin, Ch'ing Pu, and the others had all been wiped out, his glory alone grew ever brighter. First among the ranks of officials, renowned in later ages, his fame rivals that of the ancient ministers Hung Yao and San I!

[5] Writing at this time was done on strips of wood. When the clerk made a mistake, he would scrape the surface of the wood clean and write on it again.

Shih chi 55: The Hereditary House of the Marquis of Liu (Chang Liang)

Plotted within the tents of command, shaping victory out of chaos, these were the schemes and strategies of Chang Liang. Though he lacked fame or the renown of valor, he foresaw the difficult while it was still easy and brought forth great things from small. Thus I made The Hereditary House of the Marquis of Liu.

The ancestors of Chang Liang,[1] the marquis of Liu, were men of the state of Hann. His grandfather Chang K'ai-ti served as prime minister to Marquis Chao and Kings Hsüan-hui and Hsiang-ai of Hann. His father, Chang P'ing, was prime minister to Kings Li and Tao-hui and died in the twenty-third year of King Tao-hui's reign. Twenty years after Chang P'ing's death Ch'in destroyed the state of Hann. Because of his youth, Chang Liang never had an opportunity to serve as a minister of Hann. When the state was destroyed, Chang Liang was left with a retinue of three hundred male servants. On his younger brother's death, he conducted no elaborate funeral but instead used all his family's wealth to search for someone who would undertake to assassinate the king of Ch'in for him, hoping thus to avenge the rulers of Hann, five generations of whom his father and grandfather had served.

Chang Liang once journeyed to Huai-yang to study ritual and there met the lord of Ts'ang-hai. Through him he obtained the services of a man renowned for his great strength. Chang Liang had an iron bludgeon made which weighed a hundred and twenty catties and, when the Ch'in emperor came east on a tour, he and the assassin lay in wait for him. When the emperor reached the area of Po-lang-sha they made their attack, but mistakenly struck the carriage of his attendants. The emperor was enraged and ordered an immediate search throughout the

[1] His polite name was Tzu-fang.

empire for the rebels, hoping to seize Chang Liang. Chang Liang assumed a false name and fled into hiding in Hsia-p'ei.

Chang Liang was once strolling idly along an embankment in Hsia-p'ei when an old man wearing a coarse gown appeared. Reaching the place where Chang Liang was, he deliberately dropped his shoe down the embankment and, turning to Chang Liang, said, "Fetch me my shoe, young man!"

Chang Liang, completely taken aback, was about to hit him, but because the man was old he swallowed his resentment and climbed down and got the shoe. "Put it on for me!" ordered the old man, and Chang Liang, since he had already gone to the trouble of fetching it, knelt respectfully and prepared to put on the shoe. The old man held out his foot and, when the shoe was on, laughed and went on his way. Chang Liang, more startled than ever, stood looking after him. When the old man had gone some distance, he turned and came back. "You could be taught, young man," he said. "Meet me here at dawn five days from now!" Chang Liang, thinking this all very strange, knelt and replied, "I will do as you say."

At dawn five days later he went to the place, but found the man already there. "When you have an appointment with an old man, how is it that you come late?" he asked angrily. "Go away, and meet me at dawn five days from now, only come earlier!"

Five days later Chang Liang got up at the crow of the cock and went to the place, but once more the old man had gotten there before him. "Why are you late again?" the old man asked in anger. "Go away, and five days from now come earlier!"

Five days later Chang Liang went to the place before half the night was through. After a while the old man came along. "This is the way it should be!" he said. Then, producing a book, he said, "If you read this you may become the teacher of kings. Ten years from now your fortune will rise. Thirteen years from now you will see me again. A yellow stone at the foot of Mount Ku-ch'eng in northern Ch'i—that will be I." Without another word he left and Chang Liang never saw him again.

When dawn came Chang Liang examined the book which the old man had given him and found it to be *The Grand Duke's Art of*

War. He set great store by it and was to be found constantly poring over it.

Chang Liang lived the life of a wandering knight in Hsia-p'ei, where he was joined in hiding by Hsiang Po, who had killed a man. Ten years later Ch'en She and his men started their uprising. Chang Liang also gathered a band of some hundred young men and, when Ching Chü set himself up as acting king of Ch'u in Liu, started out to join him there. Along the way, however, he met the governor of P'ei, who was leading a force of a thousand soldiers and attempting to seize control of the region from Hsia-p'ei west. Chang Liang joined the governor of P'ei, who honored him with the position of cavalry general. From time to time Chang Liang expounded *The Grand Duke's Art of War* to the governor of P'ei. The latter greatly admired it and always followed the strategies which it outlined, but when Chang Liang discussed the book with other men they refused to pay him any heed. "The governor of P'ei will soon be chosen by Heaven," he said, and for this reason he followed him and did not go to join Ching Chü.

The governor of P'ei went to Hsieh to meet Hsiang Liang, who at this time set up King Huai of Ch'u. Chang Liang took this opportunity to speak to Hsiang Liang. "You have already set up the descendants of Ch'u," he said, "but Ch'eng, the lord of Heng-yang, who is a descendant of the royal house of Hann, is also a worthy man. If you were to set him up as a king you would greatly increase the strength of your party."

Hsiang Liang accordingly sent Chang Liang to seek out Hann Ch'eng and make him king of Hann, with Chang Liang as his minister of instruction. Chang Liang joined the king in leading a band of a thousand men west to seize the region of Hann but, though they captured several cities, the Ch'in forces immediately retook them. Chang Liang then roamed with his troops back and forth in the region of Ying-ch'uan.

When the governor of P'ei marched south from Lo-yang to Huan-yüan, Chang Liang led his men to join him; together they captured more than ten cities of Hann and defeated the Ch'in general, Yang Hsiung. The governor of P'ei ordered Ch'eng, the king of Hann, to stay behind and guard the city of Yang-ti while he and Chang Liang marched south, attacking and capturing Yüan. From there they marched west and entered the Wu Pass. The governor of P'ei wanted to take a force of twenty thousand men and attack the Ch'in army encamped at the foot of Mount Yao, but Chang Liang advised against this. "Ch'in's forces are still strong and cannot be lightly dismissed. I have heard that their general is the son of a butcher. Such paltry tradespeople are easily moved by the prospect of gain. I would advise you to remain here and build defense walls, sending someone ahead with a force of fifty thousand men and the necessary provisions, and set up pennants and flags on the surrounding hills so that they will think we have more soldiers than we do. Then you may dispatch Li I-chi with rich presents to tempt the Ch'in general."

As they had hoped, the Ch'in general succumbed to the temptation and turned traitor, asking to join the governor of P'ei in marching west to attack Hsien-yang. The governor of P'ei was about to grant his request, but Chang Liang once more intervened. "It is only the general who has expressed his willingness to revolt. I fear that his soldiers will not follow him. If his men do not follow his example, it will be most dangerous for us. It would be better to take advantage of their present laxity and attack."

The governor of P'ei accordingly led his troops in an attack on the Ch'in army, inflicting a great defeat. Pursuing them northward, he once more engaged them in battle at Lan-t'ien until the Ch'in army agreed to a final surrender. The governor of P'ei then marched to Hsien-yang where Tzu-ying, the king of Ch'in, surrendered to him.

When the governor of P'ei entered the palace of Ch'in, he found halls and pavilions, dogs, horses, treasures, and waiting women by the thousand. He wanted to remain in the palace, but Fan K'uai advised him to leave the capital and camp in the field. When the governor refused to listen, Chang Liang spoke up. "It is because of Ch'in's violent and unprincipled ways that you have come this far. Now that you have freed the world of these tyrannical bandits it is proper that you should don the plain white garments of mourning as a pledge of your sympathy for the sufferings of the people. Having just entered the capital of Ch'in, if you were now to indulge yourself in its pleasures, this would be 'helping the tyrant Chieh to work his violence.' Good advice is hard on the ears, but it profits the conduct just as good medicine, though bitter in the mouth, cures the sickness. I beg you to listen to Fan K'uai's counsel!"

The governor of P'ei accordingly returned and camped at Pa-shang. When Hsiang Yü reached Hung-men, he made preparations to attack the governor. Hsiang Po hastened in the night to the governor's camp and visited Chang Liang in secret, urging him to run away with him, but Chang Liang replied, "I have been sent by the king of Hann to follow the governor of P'ei. Now when he is in grave difficulty it would not be right for me to run away."

Chang Liang then went and reported to the governor all that Hsiang Po had told him. "What shall we do?" asked the governor in great astonishment.

"Do you really intend to defy Hsiang Yü?" Chang Liang asked in reply.

"Some fool advised me that if I blocked the Pass and did not allow the other leaders to enter, I could become king of the whole region of Ch'in," said the governor. "Therefore I followed his suggestion."

"And do you yourself actually believe that you can defeat Hsiang Yü?"

The governor of P'ei was silent for a long time and then said, "No, of course not. But what should we do now?"

Chang Liang went outside and urged Hsiang Po to come in and join them. When Hsiang Po had entered, the governor drank a toast with him and they swore to be friends. The governor requested Hsiang Po to explain to Hsiang Yü that he had no intention of betraying him, but had closed the Pass only to prevent bandits from getting in. On his return, Hsiang Po went to see Hsiang Yü and explained the situation so that the governor was cleared of suspicion. (A full account will be found in the chapter on Hsiang Yü.)

In the first month of the first year of Han [206 B.C.] the governor of P'ei became king of Han ruling the area of Pa and Shu. He presented Chang Liang with a gift of a hundred weights of gold and two pecks of pearls, which Chang Liang in turn presented to Hsiang Po. The king of Han also instructed Chang Liang to give Hsiang Po a generous farewell and request him on behalf of the king of Han to ask

Hsiang Yü for the territory of Han. Hsiang Yü granted the request, and as a result the region of Han was added to the territories of Pa and Shu as part of the king of Han's fief.

When the king of Han proceeded to his territory, Chang Liang accompanied him as far as Hsiu. The king then ordered Chang Liang to return to his own land of Hann. "Would it not be well," Chang Liang advised, "to burn and destroy the wooden roadway which you have passed over? This would prove to the world that you have no intention of marching east again and thus set Hsiang Yü's mind at ease." The king ordered Chang Liang to destroy the roadway on his way back.

When Chang Liang reached Hann, he discovered that Hsiang Yü had not allowed Ch'eng, the king of Hann, to proceed to his own territory, but instead had taken Ch'eng with him in his march to the east. This he had done because Ch'eng had sent Chang Liang to serve the governor of P'ei. Chang Liang reported to Hsiang Yü that the king of Han had destroyed the wooden roadway and had no intention of returning east; he also revealed to him that T'ien Jung, the king of Ch'i, was planning a revolt. Because of this Hsiang Yü considered that he had nothing to worry about from Han in the west and instead sent his troops north to attack Ch'i. But he would never allow the king of Hann to proceed to his kingdom; instead he changed his title to that of marquis and later murdered him at P'eng-ch'eng.

Chang Liang fled and secretly made his way to join the king of Han, who in the meantime had already marched back from his territory and conquered the three kingdoms of Ch'in. Chang Liang was made marquis of Ch'eng-hsin, and accompanied the king of Han east to attack Hsiang Yü at P'eng-ch'eng, but they were defeated and forced to retreat to Hsia-i. The king of Han dismounted, threw his saddle on the ground and, squatting on it, said, "I wish to give away the lands east of the Pass! [2] But if I am in any case to abandon them, it would be best to assign them to someone who is likely to be of service to me. Who would be suitable?"

[2] The king's wish was rather premature, since he by no means possessed control of the area east of the Pass at this time. What he means is that he is willing to abandon any direct claim to the lands in an effort to win allies to his side.

Chang Liang came forward and said, "Ch'ing Pu, the king of Chiu-chiang, has fought courageously as a general for Ch'u but is now at odds with Hsiang Yü, while P'eng Yüeh has joined with T'ien Jung, the king of Ch'i, in raising a revolt in the region of Liang. It would be well to dispatch envoys to consult with these two men as soon as possible. Among your own generals Han Hsin alone could be entrusted with a fourth of our great undertaking. If you wish to give away your lands, you had best give them to these three. Then Hsiang Yü can surely be defeated."

The king of Han accordingly dispatched Sui Ho to bargain with Ch'ing Pu, and another envoy to conclude an agreement with P'eng Yüeh. When Pao, the king of Wei, revolted, he sent Han Hsin with a force to attack him. Thus he was able to win the lands of Yen, Tai, Ch'i, and Chao over to his side. It was due to the efforts of these three men—Ch'ing Pu, P'eng Yüeh, and Han Hsin—that he eventually destroyed Hsiang Yü. Chang Liang himself suffered from frequent illness and could not take part in any expeditions. Instead he plotted the course of the various campaigns for the king of Han and accompanied him from time to time.

In the third year of Han [204 B.C.] Hsiang Yü suddenly surrounded the king of Han at Jung-yang. Alarmed at the situation, the king consulted with Li I-chi to see if there were not some way to weaken Hsiang Yü's grip on the empire. "In ancient times," Li I-chi replied, "when T'ang overthrew Chieh, he enfeoffed Chieh's descendants in Chi, and later when King Wu attacked Chou, he enfeoffed Chou's heirs in Sung. Now Ch'in, abandoning virtue and disregarding righteousness, has overthrown the sacred altars of the feudal lords and wiped out the descendants of the Six States, leaving them not enough territory to stick the point of an awl into. If you could only reestablish the descendants of the former kingdoms and present them with the seals of enfeoffment, then they, their ministers, and their people, being every one indebted to your virtue, would one and all turn in longing toward your righteousness and beg to become your subjects. With virtue and righteousness made manifest, you might face south and name yourself a dictator, and Hsiang Yü, gathering his sleeves together in respectful salute, would most certainly come to pay you homage." [3]

"Excellent!" exclaimed the king. "I shall have the seals of enfeoffment carved at once and you, sir, shall bear them to the lords for me."

Li I-chi had not yet departed on his mission when Chang Liang entered the presence of the king, who was at his meal. "Come in," said the king. "One of my followers has just been explaining to me how I can break the power of Ch'u," and he repeated all that Li I-chi had said. "What do you think?" he asked.

"Who has thought up this plan for you?" said Chang Liang. "It will destroy you!"

"How so?" asked the king.

"Let me borrow this pair of chopsticks and I will explain my ideas to you," he said. [4] "Now in ancient times when T'ang attacked Chieh and enfeoffed his descendants in Chi he did so only because he knew that he had the power to put Chieh to death. But do you have the power to inflict death on Hsiang Yü?"

"No, not yet," said the king.

"That is the first reason this plan will not succeed. Again, when King Wu attacked Emperor Chou and enfeoffed his descendant in Sung, he knew that he could have Chou's head whenever he wanted it. But could you have Hsiang Yü's head?"

"Not yet."

"This is the second reason. When King Wu entered the capital of the Shang dynasty, he honored the village where Shang Yung lived, freed Chi Tzu from prison, and enlarged the grave of Pi Kan. Are you in a position to enlarge the graves of the sages, honor the villages of the virtuous, and bow before the gates of the wise?"

"No."

---

[3] The typical idealistic Confucian argument that virtue alone will conquer all obstacles.

[4] In the following discourse we must imagine Chang Liang marking off the points of his argument in some way with the chopsticks. He deliberately uses the same historical precedents which Li I-chi has used, but shows that they are not relevant to the present case.

"This is the third reason. In addition King Wu distributed grain from the Chü-ch'iao granary, and scattered among the poor and starving the riches of the Deer Terrace. Can you too open the storehouses and granaries to relieve the needy?"

"No," replied the king.

"The fourth reason," said Chang Liang. "When King Wu had completed the conquest of Shang, he converted his war chariots into carriages, cast aside his shields and spears, and covered them with tiger skins to show the world that he did not intend again to take up arms. But can you put away your weapons and apply yourself to the arts of peace, never again taking up arms?"

"No," replied the king.

"The fifth reason," said Chang Liang. "He loosed his war horses on the sunny side of Mount Hua to show he had no further use for them. Can you?"

"No."

"The sixth reason. He turned his oxen to pasture in the shade of the T'ao forest to show he would transport no more supplies. Can you do without oxen to haul supplies?"

Once more, "No."

"The seventh reason. At present all the brave men throughout the empire have taken leave of their families, left the graves of their ancestors, and flocked from their old homes to join in following you, only because day and night they dream of winning a bit of land for themselves. Now if you restore the Six States and set up the descendants of Hann, Wei, Yen, Chao, Ch'i and Ch'u, these followers of yours will go back to serve their own lords, return to their old homes and the graves of their ancestors, and look after their own families. And who will be left to fight with you? This is the eighth reason! As long as Hsiang Yü is as strong as he is, the descendants of the Six States will simply bow to his power and follow him. How could you possibly make him submit to you? Therefore I say that if you follow this plan, it will destroy you!"

The king of Han stopped eating, spat out a mouthful of food, and began to curse. "That idiot Confucianist came near to spoiling the whole business for his father!"⁵ he cried, and sent orders at once to have the seals destroyed.

In the fourth year of Han [203 B.C.] Han Hsin conquered Ch'i and announced that he wished to set himself up as king of Ch'i. The king of Han was angry but, on the advice of Chang Liang, sent Chang to present Han Hsin with the seals making him king of Ch'i. (A full account will be found in the chapter on Han Hsin.)

In the autumn the king of Han pursued Hsiang Yü as far as the south of Yang-hsia but, failing to win a victory, fortified his position at Ku-ling. The other leaders did not appear for the meeting which had been arranged but Chang Liang suggested a plan for the king whereby they were induced to come. (Full account in the chapter on Hsiang Yü.)

In the first month of the sixth year [201 B.C.] the king of Han, now emperor, enfeoffed his followers who had won distinction. Though Chang Liang had achieved no glory on the field of battle, the emperor said to him, "Your merit was won by sitting within the tents of command and plotting strategies that assured us victories a thousand miles away. You must select for yourself thirty thousand households of Ch'i."

"When I first began an uprising at Hsia-p'ei," Chang Liang replied, "I met Your Majesty at Liu. It was as though Heaven had sent me to serve you. You listened to my suggestions, and fortunately they turned out to be apt for the times. I shall be content if I may be enfeoffed with Liu alone. I dare not accept thirty thousand households." The emperor made him marquis of Liu and enfeoffed him at the same time as Hsiao Ho and the others.

The sixth year: The emperor had already enfeoffed over twenty of his ministers who had achieved signal distinction, but the rest of his followers argued day and night over who had won greater merit so that no further enfeoffments could be carried out. When the emperor was residing at the Southern Palace in Lo-yang, he looked down one

⁵ The use of the phrase "his father" or "your father" to denote oneself is highly insulting, because it employs the familiar pronouns *nai* or *erh,* and perhaps also because it implies that one has made free with the mother of the person referred to or addressed.

day from a covered walk [6] and saw his followers walking restlessly about the courtyard and sitting on the ground talking together. "What are they talking about?" he asked Chang Liang.

"Your Majesty does not know?" said Chang Liang. "They are plotting a revolt."

"But peace and order have only just been restored to the empire. Why should they be planning a revolt?"

"When Your Majesty rose from among the common people, it was through these men that you seized control of the empire. You have become the Son of Heaven, but those whom you have enfeoffed have all been close friends from old days, such as Hsiao Ho and Ts'ao Ts'an, while all your enemies of former times you have had executed. Now these, the officers of your army, reckoning up the merits they have won, believe that there is not sufficient land in the whole empire to enfeoff them all. So some of them fear they will not receive a just allotment, while others tremble lest, falling under suspicion for some error of their past, they be condemned to execution. Therefore they gather together in this way and plot rebellion."

"What should I do?" asked the emperor in consternation.

"Among the men you dislike, and all your followers know you dislike, whom do you hate the most?"

"Yung Ch'ih and I are ancient enemies," replied the emperor. "Many times in the past he has brought me trouble and shame. I would like to have killed him, but because his merit is great I have not had the heart."

"You must hurry and enfeoff Yung Ch'ih before anyone else, and make known what you have done to your other followers. When they see that Yung Ch'ih has been enfeoffed, they will all feel assured of their own rewards," said Chang Liang.

The emperor thereupon held a feast and enfeoffed Yung Ch'ih as marquis of Shih-fang, ordering the prime minister and imperial secretary to settle the question of rewards and carry out the remainder of the enfeoffments with all dispatch. When the other ministers left

---

[6] These elevated walks were built to connect various buildings in the palace grounds and allowed the emperor to pass over the upper level undisturbed while lesser officials and lackeys went about their business in the courtyard below, thus saving time and bother for all concerned.

the banquet, they said to each other happily, "If even Yung Ch'ih can become a marquis, the rest of us have nothing to worry about!"

Liu Ching had advised the emperor to make his capital in the area within the Pass, but the emperor still hesitated. Since most of his followers came from east of the mountains, they urged him to establish the capital at Lo-yang, pointing out that it was protected by Ch'eng-kao on the east and Mount Yao and the Min Lake on the west, with its back to the Yellow River and the I and Lo rivers flowing before it, and could therefore be easily fortified and held. But Chang Liang objected, saying, "Although Lo-yang has these natural defenses, the area within is so small it does not exceed a few hundred *li*. The land is poor and open to attack from four sides, so that from a military point of view it is quite unsuitable. The area within the Pass, on the other hand, is protected by Mount Yao and the Han-ku Pass on the left and by Lung and Shu to the right,[7] comprising some thousand *li* of fertile plain, with the rich fields of Pa and Shu to the south and the advantages of the pasture lands of the barbarians to the north. With three sides protected by natural barriers, one has only to worry about controlling the feudal lords to the east. So long as the feudal lords are at peace, tribute can be transported up the Yellow and Wei Rivers to supply the capital area in the west, and if the lords should revolt one can descend these same rivers and attack them, assured of an adequate supply of provisions. The area within the Pass is in fact one vast fortress of iron, a veritable storehouse created by nature. Therefore Liu Ching's advice is correct."

The same day the emperor mounted his carriage and began the journey west to make his capital within the Pass, Chang Liang accompanying him through the Pass. Because he suffered from frequent illness, Chang Liang practiced various austerities, eating no grain and not venturing out of his house for a year or more.

The emperor wished to remove the heir apparent[8] and set up Ju-i, the king of Chao, his son by Lady Ch'i, in his place. Many of the high ministers had strongly advised him against this, but they could not get

---

[7] I.e., to the left and right of the emperor if he were imagined as seated in his capital within the Pass and facing south.

[8] The emperor's son by Empress Lü. He later became Emperor Hui.

him once and for all to give up the idea. Empress Lü, fearful for the position of her son, was at a loss what to do, when someone reminded her that Chang Liang was very skillful at devising schemes and enjoyed the confidence of the emperor. She therefore sent Lü Tse,[9] the marquis of Chien-ch'eng, to threaten Chang Liang, saying, "You have always advised the emperor on matters of policy. Now the emperor is planning to change the heir apparent. How can you sit calmly by and let this happen?"

"In the past," replied Chang Liang, "when the emperor on a number of occasions found himself in difficulty, he was good enough to follow certain plans which I suggested. Now, however, the world is at peace. If, because of his love for Lady Ch'i, the emperor wishes to change his choice of heir apparent, this is a family matter. Nothing I or all the other ministers might say could have any effect."

But Lü Tse persisted. "You must think of some plan for us!"

"In this sort of affair mere arguments and reproaches are of little use," Chang Liang replied. "I recall, however, that there are four men in the world whom the emperor has not succeeded in attracting to his court. These four men are very old and, because they believe that the emperor is haughty and rude to others, they have hidden themselves away in the mountains and refused on principle to acknowledge any allegiance to the house of Han. Yet I know that the emperor admires them greatly. Now if you are willing to spare no expense in gold and precious gifts, you might have the heir apparent write them a letter offering in the humblest possible terms to send carriages to fetch them, and at the same time dispatch some artful talker to press the invitation. In that case I think they would come. If they came, you could entertain them as your guests and from time to time take them with you to court. The emperor will be sure to wonder who they are and ask about them. When he discovers that they are worthy men, this will help somewhat to strengthen the position of the heir apparent."

Empress Lü, adopting this plan, had Lü Tse send someone to fetch the four old men, bearing a letter from the heir apparent couched in terms of humility and according them the highest respect and courtesy.

---

[9] Lü Tse's name is apparently used here in error for that of his younger brother, Lü Shih-chih.

When the four arrived, they were entertained as guests at the home of Lü Tse.

In the eleventh year [196 B.C.] Ch'ing Pu revolted. Since the emperor himself was ill, he planned to send the heir apparent to lead the attack against him. The four old men said to one another, "We have come all this way simply to help protect the heir apparent. But if he is sent to lead the troops, the whole plan will be imperiled." Accordingly they advised Lü Tse, saying, "We hear that the heir apparent is to be sent to lead the troops. But even if he is victorious he cannot be given any position higher than that which he already holds, while if he returns without merit he will henceforth face grave misfortune. The other generals who will go with him on the expedition are all veteran commanders who fought with the emperor in the past to win possession of the empire. To put the heir apparent in command of a group of men such as this is like sending a lamb to lead a pack of wolves. None of them will be willing to do his best for such a leader, and the failure of the expedition will be assured. The saying goes, 'If the mother is loved, the child will be embraced.' Now Lady Ch'i day and night attends the emperor, and her son Ju-i is always with him in his arms. The emperor himself, they say, has sworn that 'no unworthy son shall ever hold a place above this beloved child.' Is this not clear proof that he intends to replace the heir apparent? You must hasten to Empress Lü and beg her to take advantage of some moment of leisure to appear before the emperor and plead with him in tears. She must tell him that Ch'ing Pu is known throughout the world as a fierce fighter and a master at arms, while the other generals who will go to fight against him are all comrades of the emperor from former days. To send the heir apparent to lead such a group would be no different from setting a lamb to lead wolves. They would never consent to obey his orders, and Ch'ing Pu, learning of the situation, would march fearlessly west to attack us. Although the emperor is ill, he must make an effort to rise and accompany the expedition in a transport carriage. Even though he is bedridden, so long as he is directing them the other generals will not dare to shirk their duties. She must beg him, at whatever pain, to do this much for his wife and child."

Lü Tse went at night to see the empress, who did as he advised, appearing before the emperor in tears and repeating the words of the four old men. "It appears to me," the emperor replied, "that this worthless boy is not fit to be sent. Very well, then, I will go myself."

The emperor made preparations to lead the troops east himself; all the ministers who were to stay behind to guard the capital accompanied him as far as Pa-shang to see him off. Though Chang Liang was ill, he forced himself to get up and go to visit the emperor at Ch'ü-yu. "I should by right be accompanying you," he said, "but I am too sick. The men of Ch'u are very swift and nimble. I beg Your Majesty not to cross swords with them in person." Then before parting he advised the emperor, "It would be well to make the heir apparent a general of the army and put him in charge of the troops within the Pass."

"Although you are ill," replied the emperor, "I would like you to do as much as you can to instruct the heir apparent." Shu-sun T'ung was at this time grand tutor to the heir apparent, but because of the emperor's request Chang Liang undertook the duties of secondary tutor.

In the twelfth year of Han [195 B.C.] the emperor, having crushed Ch'ing Pu's army, returned to the capital. His illness had grown worse, and he was more than ever determined to change the heir apparent. Chang Liang counseled him against this, but he refused to listen and, because of his grave condition, ceased to attend to matters of state. Shu-sun T'ung also, as grand tutor, pleaded and argued, citing examples from ancient and recent history and begging that the present heir apparent be retained, though he knew that his stand might cost him his life. The emperor, although he had not altered his intention, finally pretended to give in.

It happened that a banquet was held and wine set out in the palace; the heir apparent waited upon the emperor and the four old men accompanied him. All of them were over eighty, with snow-white beards and eyebrows and arrayed in the most imposing caps and gowns. The emperor, struck with curiosity, asked who they were, whereupon each of them came forward and announced his name: "Master Tung-yüan," "Scholar Lu-li," "Ch'i Li-chi," "Master Hsia-huang."

"Gentlemen," the emperor replied in astonishment, "I have sought you for many years, but you have always hidden from me. How is it that you deign to come now and wait upon my son?"

"Your Majesty is contemptuous of others and given to cursing people," the four replied. "We did not consider it right to subject ourselves to insult, and therefore we were afraid and fled into hiding. But it came to our ears that the heir apparent was a man of kindness and reverence who loved others. The whole world, we heard, looked to him with yearning, and not a man but would give his life for him. Therefore we have come."

"If it is not too much trouble," said the emperor. "I hope you will be kind enough to look after the heir apparent and assist him."

The four men proposed a toast to the emperor's health and, when this was finished, rose and departed. The emperor stared after them and then, calling Lady Ch'i to his side, pointed to them and said, "I had hoped to change the heir apparent, but these four men have come to his aid. Like a pair of great wings they have borne him aloft where we cannot reach him. Empress Lü is your real master now!" Lady Ch'i wept.

"If you will do a dance of Ch'u for me," said the emperor, "I will make you a song of Ch'u," and he sang:

> The great swan soars aloft,
> In one swoop a thousand miles.
> He has spread his giant wings
> And spans the four seas.
> He who spans the four seas—
> Ah, what can we do?
> Though we bear stringed arrows to down him,
> Whereto should we aim them?

While Lady Ch'i sobbed and wept, the emperor sang the song through several times; then he rose and left the banquet. The fact that in the end the emperor did not change the heir apparent was due to the influence of these four men whom Chang Liang had originally summoned.

Chang Liang accompanied the emperor in his attack on Tai and devised the unusual plan by which the city of Ma-i was captured; later he was instrumental in having Hsiao Ho appointed prime minister. Chang Liang often freely discussed matters of state with the emperor, but since none of these were questions which vitally affected the existence of the empire I shall not go into them here.

"My family for generations served as ministers to the state of Hann," Chang Liang announced. "When Hann was destroyed, we spared no expense in rousing the world to revolt and avenging its fate upon the rapacious Ch'in. Now with the wagging of my meager tongue I have become teacher to an emperor, enfeoffed with ten thousand households and set among the ranks of the nobility. A common man can reach no greater heights; here I am content to rest. I wish now to lay aside the affairs of this world, and join the Master of the Red Pine [10] in immortal sport." He set about practicing dietary restrictions and breathing and stretching exercises to achieve levitation.

At the time of Kao-tsu's demise, Empress Lü, who was greatly indebted to Chang Liang, urged him to eat, saying, "Man's life in this world is as brief as the passing of a white colt glimpsed through a crack in the wall. Why should you punish yourself like this?" Chang Liang had no other recourse but to listen to her advice and begin eating again. Eight years later he died and was given the posthumous title of "Wen-ch'eng" or "Civil Accomplishment Marquis." His son Pu-i succeeded to the marquisate.

Thirteen years after Chang Liang had first met the old man on the embankment at Hsia-p'ei and had been given *The Book of the Grand Duke,* he was accompanying Kao-tsu through Chi-pei. There, at the foot of Mount Ku-ch'eng, just as the old man had said, he found a yellow stone, which he took away with him, treating it with the utmost reverence and worshiping it. When he died the stone was placed with him in the grave mound and in the sixth and twelfth months, when his descendants ascended the mound to pay their respects, they worshiped it. In the fifth year of Emperor Wen, Chang Liang's son Pu-i was accused of lese majesty and his territory taken away.

The Grand Historian remarks: Most scholars agree that there are no such things as ghosts and spirits, though they concede the existence of weird beings. What, I wonder, are we to make of the old man whom Chang Liang met and the book he gave him? Kao-tsu on a number of occasions found himself in grave difficulty, and yet Chang

[10] A legendary sage of ancient times who achieved immortality.

Liang always had a way out. Was this not the work of Heaven? The emperor himself admitted that "when it comes to sitting within the tents of command and devising strategies that will assure victory a thousand miles away, I am no match for Chang Liang." I had always imagined, therefore, that Chang Liang must have been a man of majestic stature and imposing appearance. And yet when I saw a picture of him, his face looked like that of a woman or a pretty young girl. Confucius once remarked, "If I had judged by looks alone I would have sadly mistaken Tzu-yü." The same might be said of Chang Liang.

Shih chi 92: The Biography of the Marquis of Huai-yin (Han Hsin)

The men of Ch'u harried us between Ching and So, but Han Hsin captured Wei and Chao, won over Yen and Ch'i, and made it posible for Han to control two thirds of the empire and thereby destroy Hsiang Yü. Thus I made The Biography of the Marquis of Huai-yin.

Han Hsin, the marquis of Huai-yin, was a native of Huai-yin. In his young days when he was still a commoner, being poor and without any noteworthy deeds, he was not able to get himself recommended for a position as an official. He was likewise unable to make a living as a merchant and so was constantly dependent upon others for his meals, which made many people dislike him. One of the persons whose hospitality he often imposed upon was the head of his village of Nan-ch'ang in Hsia County. After he had stayed for several months on end, the wife of the village head became much annoyed. One morning she got up very early, cooked her own breakfast, and ate it in bed. When breakfast time came, Han Hsin appeared as usual, but found that she had prepared nothing for him. Hsin perceived what she had in mind and was incensed and in the end he broke off the friendship and went away.

Han Hsin went fishing in the Huai River at the foot of the city wall, where some old women were washing coarse silk to bleach it. One of the old women noticed that Han Hsin was nearly starved and she fed him, and continued to do so for the twenty or thirty days until the bleaching was finished. Han Hsin was very grateful and said to the old woman, "Some day I will pay you back handsomely without fail!"

But the old woman was offended and replied, "I could tell you had no way of getting food for yourself, young gentleman, and so I felt sorry for you and gave you something to eat. What makes you think I was looking for any reward?"

Among the butchers of Huai-yin was a young man who jeered at Han Hsin and said, "You are big and tall and love to carry a sword, but at heart you're nothing but a coward!" In front of a crowd of people he insulted Han Hsin, and then said, "If you feel like dying, come on and attack me! If not, then crawl between my legs!"

Han Hsin looked him over carefully, and then bent down and crawled between the man's legs. The people in the market place all roared with laughter at Han Hsin's cowardice.

When Hsiang Liang crossed the Huai River, Han Hsin took up his sword and went to join the band under his command, but he did nothing to distinguish himself. After Hsiang Liang was defeated he joined Hsiang Yü, who made him one of his attendants. Han Hsin several times offered suggestions on strategy, but Hsiang Yü made no use of them.

After the king of Han had retired to his territory in Shu, Han Hsin fled from Ch'u and joined the forces of Han. Being still a man of no particular renown, he was given a minor position as attendant to guests.

Han Hsin became involved in an offense and was condemned to die. Thirteen other men in the group had already been beheaded and it was Han Hsin's turn next. He raised his head and looked about, when his eye fell upon Lord T'eng. "Has our sovereign no desire to win the world?" he asked. "Why does he deliberately cut off the head of a brave man?"

Lord T'eng was struck by his words and saw that he had a brave appearance, and so he did not execute him but set him free. After talking to Han Hsin, and finding him much to his liking, Lord T'eng mentioned him to the king of Han, who made him a commissary colonel, though the king saw nothing unusual in him. Han Hsin several times talked to Hsiao Ho, who regarded him with peculiar respect.

By the time the Han army reached Nan-cheng, it was found that twenty or thirty of the generals had deserted along the way. "Hsiao Ho and others have several times spoken about me to the king," Han Hsin considered to himself, "but the king has no use for me," and with this he too deserted. When Hsiao Ho heard that Han Hsin had run away, he did not wait to ask the king but started after him in person.

Someone reported to the king that Prime Minister Hsiao Ho had deserted. The king flew into a rage and was as distressed as if he had lost his right or left hand. After a day or so Hsiao Ho returned and appeared before the king. The king, half in anger and half in joy, began to curse him. "You deserted, didn't you!" he said. "Why?"

"How would I dare to desert?" replied Hsiao Ho. "I went after a deserter!"

"Who is it you went after?"

"Han Hsin."

The king cursed again. "When my generals were deserting me by the tens you did not pursue one of them. This going after Han Hsin is a lie!"

"Generals are easy enough to get," replied Hsiao Ho, "but men like Han Hsin are the best in the nation. If Your Majesty's ambition is to rule the area of Han for as long as possible, then you have no use for Han Hsin's services. But if you hope to contend for mastery of the world, then Han Hsin is the only man to lay plans with. It is entirely a matter of which course you choose to take."

"My whole ambition is to march east," the king replied. "How could I bear to stay pent up in a place like this forever?"

"Since your plans are aimed at moving east again, if you can make good use of Han Hsin, then he will stay with you. But if you cannot use him properly, then he will eventually desert!"

"For your sake I will make him a general," said the king.

"If you make him no more than a general, he will never stay."

"Then I will make him a major general!"

"That would be most gracious of you," Hsiao Ho replied. The king was about to summon Han Hsin and invest him with the position at once, but Hsiao Ho said, "Your Majesty is inclined to be rather brusque and lacking in ceremony. If you were to call him in and make him a general at once, it would be like ordering a little boy about. This is precisely the reason Han Hsin deserted. If you wish to confer a title on him, you must select an auspicious day, fast and purify yourself, erect an altar and go through the whole ceremony. This is the only way."

The king gave his consent to this. All of the generals were filled with joy, each considering that it was himself who was about to be made a major general. But when the title was conferred, to the astonishment of the entire army, it was upon Han Hsin. After the ceremony of investiture was concluded and Han Hsin had returned to his seat, the king said, "Prime Minister Hsiao Ho has often spoken to me about you, general. What sort of strategy is it that you would teach me?"

Han Hsin expressed his gratitude for the honor and took advantage of the king's inquiry to ask a question of his own. "Anyone who marched east to contend for the empire would have to face Hsiang Yü, would he not?"

"He would," replied the king.

"In Your Majesty's estimation, which of you, Hsiang Yü or yourself, excels in fierceness of courage and depth of kindness?"

The king of Han was silent for a while and then he said, "I am inferior to Hsiang Yü."

Han Hsin bowed once more and commended the king, saying, "Yes, I too believe that you are inferior. But I once served Hsiang Yü, and I would like to tell you what sort of person he is. When Hsiang Yü rages and bellows it is enough to make a thousand men fall down in terror. But since he is incapable of employing wise generals, all of it amounts to no more than the daring of an ordinary man.

"When Hsiang Yü meets people he is courteous and thoughtful, his manner of speaking is gentle and, if someone is ill or in distress, he will weep over him and give him his own food and drink. But when someone he has sent upon a mission has achieved merit and deserves to be honored and enfeoffed he will fiddle with the seal of investiture until it crumbles in his hand before he can bring himself to present it to the man. This sort of kindness deserves to be called merely womanish!

"Now although Hsiang Yü has made himself dictator of the world and subjugated the other nobles to his rule, he has not taken up residence in the area within the Pass, but has made his capital at P'eng-ch'eng. He has gone against the agreement made with the Righteous Emperor and instead given out kingdoms to the nobles on the basis of his own likes and preferences, which has resulted in much injustice. The nobles, seeing that Hsiang Yü has banished the Righteous Emperor and sent him to reside in Chiang-nan, when they return to their own territories in like manner drive out their sovereigns and make themselves rulers of the choicest lands. Hsiang Yü has left death and destruction everywhere he has passed. Much of the world hates him. The common people do not submit to him out of affection, but are awed by his might alone. In name he is a dictator, but in truth he has lost the hearts of the world. Therefore I say that his might can be easily weakened!

"Now if you could only pursue the opposite policy and make use of the brave men of the world, what enemy would not fall before you? If you were to enfeoff your worthy followers with the territories of the empire, who would not submit? If you were to take your soldiers of righteousness and lead them back east where they long to return, who would not flee from your path?

"The three kings of the region of Ch'in were formerly generals of Ch'in and led the sons of Ch'in for several years. The number of men who were killed under their command exceeds estimation. In addition they deceived their men into surrendering to the other nobles and, when they reached Hsin-an, Hsiang Yü treacherously butchered over two hundred thousand soldiers of the Ch'in army who had surrendered, sparing only the three generals Chang Han, Ssu-ma Hsin, and Tung I. Therefore the fathers of Ch'in loath these three men with a passion that eats into their very bones. Now Hsiang Yü has managed by sheer force to make kings of these men, but the people of Ch'in have no love for them. When you entered the Wu Pass, you inflicted not a particle of harm, but repealed the harsh laws of Ch'in and gave to the people a simple code of laws in three articles only, and there were none of the people of Ch'in who did not wish to make you their king. According to the agreement concluded among all the nobles, you ought to have been made king of the area within the Pass, and the people of the area all knew this. And when you were deprived of your rightful position and retired to the region of Han, the people of Ch'in were all filled with resentment. Now if you will raise your army and march east, you can win over the three kingdoms of Ch'in simply by proclamation!"

The king of Han was overjoyed and only regretted that he had been so long in discovering Han Hsin. He proceeded to follow the strategy

Han Hsin had outlined and assigned to his generals the areas which each was to attack. In the eighth month the king of Han raised his army, marched east out of Ch'en-ts'ang, and subjugated the three kingdoms of Ch'in.

In the second year of Han the king marched out of the Pass and seized control of Wei and Ho-nan. The kings of Hann and Yin both surrendered to him. Joining the forces of Ch'i and Chao, he attacked Ch'u. In the fourth month he reached P'eng-ch'eng, where his forces were defeated and compelled to retreat in disorder. Han Hsin gathered a second force of troops and joined the king of Han at Jung-yang and once more they attacked Ch'u in the region of Ching and So. As a result of this attack the armies of Ch'u were unable to proceed any further west.

When the Han army was defeated at P'eng-ch'eng and driven back, Ssu-ma Hsin, the king of Sai, and Tung I, the king of Ti, fled from Han and surrendered to Ch'u. Ch'i and Chao also revolted against Han and made peace with Ch'u.

In the sixth month Pao, king of Wei, asked to be allowed to go home and look after his ailing parents but, when he reached his kingdom, he cut off the fords over the Yellow River, revolted against Han, and concluded an alliance with Ch'u. The king of Han dispatched Master Li I-chi in an attempt to dissuade him, but he refused to listen. In the eighth month of this year Han Hsin was made prime minister of the left and sent to attack Wei. The king of Wei concentrated his forces at P'u-fan and blockaded Lin-chin. Han Hsin thereupon planted a dummy army and lined up a number of boats as though he were about to attempt to cross the river at Lin-chin. In the meantime he secretly led another force of men by way of Hsia-yang, where he ferried them across the river on floats and attacked An-i. Pao, the king of Wei, taken completely by surprise, led his troops to oppose Han Hsin but was taken prisoner. Han Hsin subjugated Wei and made it into the province of Ho-tung.

The king of Han dispatched Chang Erh to join Han Hsin and with him lead a force of troops to the northeast to attack Chao and Tai. In the intercalary ninth month they defeated the troops of Tai and took Hsia Yüeh prisoner at Yen-yü. As soon as Han Hsin had conquered

Wei and defeated Tai the king of Han hastily sent someone to take command of Han Hsin's best troops and bring them to Jung-yang to help in the blockade against Ch'u.

Han Hsin and Chang Erh with their force of twenty or thirty thousand men prepared to march east through the Ching Gorge to attack Chao. The king of Chao and Ch'en Yü, lord of Ch'eng-an, hearing that the Han forces were about to attack them, gathered an army, ostensibly numbering two hundred thousand, at the mouth of the gorge. Li Tso-ch'e, lord of Kuang-wu, advised Ch'en Yü, saying, "I have heard that the Han general Han Hsin has forded the Yellow River to the west, made the king of Wei and Hsia Yüeh his prisoners, and spilled blood anew at Yen-yü. Now with the help of Chang Erh he has laid his plans and intends to conquer Chao. An army such as his, riding the crest of victory and fighting far from its homeland, cannot be opposed.

"I have heard it said that, when provisions must be transported a thousand miles, the soldiers have a hungry look and, when fuel must be gathered before the mess is prepared, the army seldom sleeps with a full stomach. Now the road through the Ching Gorge is such that two carts cannot drive side by side, nor two horsemen ride abreast. On a march of several hundred miles under such circumstances, their provisions are sure to be in the rear. I beg you to lend me a force of thirty thousand surprise troops which I can lead by a secret route to cut off their supply wagons. In the meantime, if you deepen your moats, heighten your ramparts, strengthen your camp, and refuse to engage in battle, they will be unable either to advance and fight, or to retreat and go back home. With my surprise force I will cut off their rear and see to it that they get no plunder from the countryside, and before ten days are out I will bring the heads of their two commanders and lay them beneath your banners! I beg you to give heed to my plan for, if you do not, you will most certainly find yourself their prisoner!"

But Ch'en Yü was a Confucianist who always spoke of his "soldiers of righteousness" and had no use for tricky schemes or unusual strategies. "I have always heard that in the art of warfare," he said, "if you outnumber the enemy ten to one, you surround him, but if you outnumber him two to one, you engage him in battle. Now al-

"They say," answered the lord of Kuang-wu, "that among the schemes of the wisest man one in a thousand will end in error, while among those of the greatest fool one in a thousand will succeed. Therefore it is said that a sage will find something to choose even from the words of a madman. I am doubtful whether any plan I might suggest would be worthy of consideration, but I beg to exercise the limits of my poor ability.

"Ch'en Yü had a plan which seemed to insure a hundred victories in as many battles, and yet in one morning it proved a failure, his army was defeated before the walls of Ho, and he himself met death on the banks of the Ch'ih. Now you have crossed the Yellow River to the west, made a prisoner of the king of Wei, captured Hsia Yüeh at Yen-yü, in one stroke descended the Ching Gorge and, before the morning was out, defeated Chao's great army of two hundred thousand and executed Ch'en Yü. Your fame resounds throughout the land and your might fills the world with awe. The farmers have left their plowing and cast aside their hoes and, anticipating that your armies will soon be upon them, have donned their finest clothes and are feasting while they may, inclining their ears in wait for your command. Such is the strength of your position.

"On the other hand, your troops are tired and worn out, and in point of fact are not of much use. Now you plan to lead this force of weary and exhausted men and further exhaust them before the stout walls of Yen. Yet, no matter how long you battle, your strength will be sufficient to overcome them. The hopelessness of your situation become apparent as your might declines, the days will pass fruit- while your supplies grow scarce, and still Yen, weak though it not submit. Ch'i in the meantime will certainly man its fron- strengthen its defense and, with Yen and Ch'i supporting and refusing to capitulate, the king of Han and Hsiang Yü ue at a stalemate and their fate will never be decided. This side of your position. In my humble opinion such a move mistake, for one who is skilled in the use of arms never th with weakness, but only weakness with strength."

course should I follow?" asked Han Hsin.

suggest a plan for you," replied the lord of Kuang-wu,

though Han Hsin's forces are reputed to be twenty or thirty thousand, they do not in fact exceed three or four thousand. Furthermore, he has marched a thousand miles to attack me, so he must already be thoroughly exhausted. If I were to flee and decline to fight under such circumstances, what would I do in the future when faced with a larger number? The other nobles would call me coward and think nothing of coming to attack me!"

Thus he refused to listen to the lord of Kuang-wu's plan, and the suggestion went unheeded. Han Hsin sent men to spy in secret and when they learned that the lord of Kuang-wu's plan was not being followed, they returned and reported to Han Hsin. He was overjoyed and proceeded without fear to lead his troops down the gorge. When they were still thirty *li* from the mouth of the gorge, he halted and made camp. During the night he sent an order through the camp to dispatch a force of two thousand light cavalry. Each man was to carry a red flag and, proceeding along a secret route, to conceal himself in the mountains and observe the Chao army. "When the Chao forces see me marching out, they are sure to abandon their fortifications and come in pursuit. Then you must enter their walls with all speed, tear down the Chao flags, and set up the red flags of Han in their place," he instructed them. Then he ordered his lieutenant generals to distribute a light meal to the army, saying, "This day we shall defeat Chao and feast together!" None of his generals believed that the plan would work, but they feigned agreement and answered "Very well."

Han Hsin addressed his officers, saying, "The Chao forces have already constructed their fortifications in an advantageous position. Moreover, until they see the flags and drums of our commanding general, they will be unwilling to attack our advance column for fear that I will see the difficulty of the position and retreat back up the gorge." Han Hsin therefore sent ten thousand men to march ahead out of the gorge and draw up in ranks with their backs to the river that ran through the gorge. The Chao army, observing this from afar, roared with laughter.[1]

At dawn Han Hsin raised the flags of the commanding general, set

[1] It was an axiom of Chinese military art that one should never fight with his back to a river.

his drums to sounding, and marched out of the mouth of the Ching Gorge. The Chao army opened their gates and poured out to attack, and for a long time the two armies fought together fiercely. At this point Han Hsin and Chang Erh deceptively abandoned their flags and drums and fled to the forces drawn up along the river. The columns along the river opened to receive them, and the battle continued to rage. As Han Hsin had anticipated, the Chao forces finally abandoned their fortifications completely in their eagerness to contend for the Han flags and pursue Han Hsin and Chang Erh. With Han Hsin and Chang Erh in their ranks, however, the army along the river determined to fight to the death and could not be defeated.

In the meantime the surprise force of two thousand cavalry which Han Hsin had sent out, waiting until the Chao forces had abandoned their camp in order to follow up their advantage, rushed into the Chao fortifications, tore down the Chao flags, and set up two thousand red flags of Han in their place. The Chao forces, unable to achieve a victory and capture Han Hsin and the others, were about to return to their fortifications when they discovered that the walls were lined with the red flags of Han. The soldiers were filled with alarm and, concluding that the Han army had already captured the generals of the king of Chao, fled in panic in all directions. Though the Chao generals cut them down on the spot, they could not stop the rout. With this the Han forces closed in from both sides, defeated and captured the Chao army, executed Ch'en Yü on the banks of the Ch'ih River, and took Hsieh, the king of Chao, prisoner.

Han Hsin issued orders to his army that the lord of Kuang-wu was not to be killed, and offered a reward of a thousand catties of gold to the man who could capture him alive. As a result the lord of Kuang-wu was bound by one of the men and led before the commanding general. Han Hsin loosed his bonds, placed him in the seat of honor facing east, and himself took a seat facing west, treating him with the respect due a teacher. The subordinate generals arrived to present their captives and the heads of their victims, and then rested from their labors and joined in congratulating Han Hsin on the victory.

Taking advantage of the opportunity, they began to question Han Hsin. "According to *The Art of War,* when one fights he should

keep the hills to his right or rear, and bodies of water in front of him or to the left," they said. "Yet today you ordered us on the contrary to draw up ranks with our backs to the river, saying 'We shall defeat Chao and feast together!' We were opposed to the idea, and yet it has ended in victory. What sort of strategy is this?"

"This is in *The Art of War* too," replied Han Hsin. "It is just that you have failed to notice it! Does it not say in *The Art of War*: 'Drive them into a fatal position and they will come out alive; place them in a hopeless spot and they will survive'? Moreover, I did not have at my disposal troops that I had trained and led from past times, but was forced, as the saying goes, to round up men from the market place and use them to fight with. Under such circumstances, if I had not placed them in a desperate situation where each man was obliged to fight for his own life, but had allowed them to remain in a safe place, they would have all run away. Then what good would they have been to me?"

"Indeed!" his generals exclaimed in admiration. "We would never have thought of that."

Then Han Hsin questioned the lord of Kuang-wu. "I am plan to march north and attack Yen, and from there proceed east t at Ch'i. What would be the most effective way to go about

The lord of Kuang-wu, however, declined to answer, s general of a defeated army, they say, is not qualified to t nor the minister of a lost nation to invent schemes fo that I am a prisoner taken in defeat, how could I b such great undertakings?

Hans Hsin replied, "I have heard it said that in Yü, Yü was destroyed, but when he lived a great power. This was not because he was and wise when in Ch'in. It was only bec and in the other he was not; in one he ignored. As a matter of fact, if Ch'en I would have become your prisoner use of you that I have the honor continued to press him for an a aside and do whatever you suggest.

"I would say the best thing to do would be to halt your army and rest your soldiers. Patrol the land of Chao and comfort the orphans made in today's battle. From the surrounding area have oxen and wine brought each day to feast your officers and banquet your men, and face them north towards the roads of Yen. After that you may dispatch your rhetoricians bearing documents to prove how superior your strength is to that of Yen, and Yen will not dare to turn a deaf ear. When Yen has submitted, you may send your propagandists to the east to talk to Ch'i, and Ch'i too will be obliged by the trend of events to submit, for even her wisest councilors will be able to think of no alternative. In this way you can have your will with the whole empire. In warfare the important thing is to publicize yourself first, and act afterward. Therefore I have suggested this plan."

Han Hsin approved of his plan and set about putting it into action, dispatching an envoy to Yen. Yen bowed before the report of Han Hsin's power and submitted. Han Hsin sent an envoy to report this to the king of Han, at the same time requesting that Chang Erh be made king of Chao to bring peace and order to the land. The king of Han gave his permission and set up Chang Erh as king of Chao.

Ch'u from time to time sent surprise forces across the Yellow River to attack Chao, but Chang Erh and Han Hsin, by moving back and forth through the area, were able to save Chao, step by step gain control of its cities, and eventually dispatch a force of troops to aid the king of Han, who at this time was in Jung-yang surrounded and sorely pressed by the armies of Ch'u. The king of Han escaped south to the area of Yüan and She, where he obtained the aid of Ch'ing Pu, and then fled to safety in Ch'eng-kao. The Ch'u forces once more surrounded and pressed him. In the sixth month the king of Han fled from Ch'eng-kao, crossed to the east side of the Yellow River and, accompanied only by Lord T'eng, went to join the army of Chang Erh at Hsiu-wu. When he arrived he stopped for a night at the posthouse and at dawn the next day, representing himself as an envoy from the king of Han, hastened into the Chao camp. Chang Erh and Han Hsin being still in bed, he went to their chambers, seized their seals of command, and with these summoned all the subordinate generals and began assigning them to new posts. When Han Hsin and

Chang Erh woke up and found that the king of Han had arrived, they were astounded. Thus the king of Han seized the armies of both men, ordering Chang Erh to man and guard the region of Chao, and making Han Hsin his prime minister with orders to form an army from the men of Chao who had not yet been pressed into service and proceed to attack Ch'i.

Han Hsin led his troops east but, before he had crossed the Yellow River at the P'ing-yüan Ford, he received word that the king of Han had sent Li I-chi to bargain with Ch'i and that Ch'i had already submitted. Han Hsin wanted to halt his march, but K'uai T'ung, a rhetorician from Fan-yang, counseled him against this. "You have received a royal order to attack Ch'i. In the meantime the king of Han has independently dispatched a secret envoy to talk Ch'i into submission. But there has been no royal order instructing you to halt, has there? How can you fail to proceed on your mission? Furthermore, this one man, Master Li I-chi, by bowing graciously from his carriage and wagging his meager tongue, has conquered the seventy-odd cities of Ch'i, while you, with your army of thousands, needed a year and over before you could gain control of the fifty-odd cities of Chao. Could it be that what you have done in your several years as a general is not equal to the accomplishments of one wretched Confucianist?"

Persuaded by his arguments, Han Hsin followed his advice and proceeded to cross the Yellow River. Ch'i in the meantime, having heeded Master Li's persuasions, was detaining him with wine and feasts and had at the same time dispersed the defenses which it had prepared against the Han armies. Han Hsin was thus able to attack the Ch'i army at Li-hsia and proceed as far as Lin-tzu. T'ien Kuang, the king of Ch'i, concluding that Master Li had betrayed him, had Master Li boiled alive and then fled to Kao-mi, where he sent an envoy to Ch'u to beg for aid.

After conquering Lin-tzu, Han Hsin proceeded east in pursuit of T'ien Kuang as far as the west of Kao-mi. Ch'u also sent its general Lung Chü with a reputed force of two hundred thousand to aid Ch'i. The king of Ch'i and Lung Chü with their combined armies fought with Han Hsin but, before the armies had closed in battle, someone advised Lung Chü, saying, "The soldiers of Han, battling far from their homeland, will fight to the death. They cannot be opposed in combat. Ch'i and Ch'u, however, are fighting on their own ground and their soldiers may easily run away in defeat. It would be better to strengthen your fortifications and have the king of Ch'i send his trusted ministers to rally the lost cities of Ch'i. If the lost cities hear that their king is still alive and that aid has come from Ch'u, they will certainly revolt against the Han army. The Han soldiers have marched a thousand miles into a strange land. If the cities of Ch'i all turn against them, they will find themselves with no way to get food for their forces, and they can be overcome without a fight."

Lung Chü replied, "I have long known what sort of man Han Hsin is. He is easy enough to deal with. Furthermore, now that I have come to rescue Ch'i, if I were to overcome him without a battle, what merit would I gain from the expedition? But if I fight and beat him, half of Ch'i can be mine. Why should I stop now?"

In the end he engaged Han Hsin in battle, the two armies drawing up on opposite sides of the Wei River. In the night Han Hsin ordered his men to make more than ten thousand bags, fill them with sand, and block the flow of the river upstream. Then he led his army halfway across the river to attack Lung Chü but, pretending to be defeated, fled back to the shore. As Han Hsin had expected, Lung Chü announced delightedly, "I always knew that Han Hsin was a coward!" and forthwith pursued Han Hsin across the river. Han Hsin then ordered his men to break open the dam of sandbags. The water came rushing down so that the large part of Lung Chü's army could not get across the river. With all speed Han Hsin closed in and killed Lung Chü, while the men of Lung Chü's army who had crossed to the east side of the river fled in disorder. T'ien Kuang, the king of Ch'i, fled at the same time. Han Hsin pursued the defeated army as far as Ch'eng-yang, where he captured all the soldiers of Ch'u.

In the fourth year of Han, having completed the conquest and pacification of Ch'i, Han Hsin dispatched an envoy to report to the king of Han, saying, "Ch'i is full of deceit and shifty loyalties, a land fickle in its faith. Moreover, it borders Ch'u on the south. Unless I am made an acting king with power to bring it to order, the situation cannot be stabilized. For the sake of convenience I ask to be made an acting king."

Han Hsin's envoy arrived just at the time when the king of Han was being pressed in siege at Jung-yang. When Han Hsin's letter was handed to him the king began to curse. "Here I am in a critical position, hoping day and night that he will come to aid me, and now he wants to make himself a king!" Chang Liang and Ch'en P'ing stepped on the king's foot and, drawing close to his ear, whispered, "We are at a disadvantage at the moment. How can we stop Han Hsin from becoming a king? It would be better to go along with his request, make him a king, and treat him well so that he will guard Ch'i for his own sake. Otherwise he may desert us altogether!"

The king realized his error and began to curse again. "When one of my men overcomes a feudal lord I make him nothing less than a real king. Why should I make him only an 'acting' king?" Then he dispatched Chang Liang to go and install Han Hsin as king of Ch'i, and levy his troops to fight against Ch'u.

Ch'u had already lost Lung Chü, and Hsiang Yü, growing fearful, sent Wu She, a man of Hsü-i, to go and talk to the new king of Ch'i. "The world suffered a long time under the tyranny of Ch'in," he said, "until we joined our strength and attacked it. When Ch'in was defeated we calculated the merit each had won, divided up the land, gave each his portion to rule, and set our soldiers to rest. Now the king of Han has called up his army again and marched east, invading the territories of other men and seizing their lands. He has already destroyed the three kingdoms of Ch'in, led his men out of the Pass, drafted the soldiers of the other nobles, and marched east to attack Ch'u. It is his intention not to rest until he has swallowed up the whole empire, so insatiable are his desires!

"Moreover, the king of Han cannot be trusted. Several times Hsiang Yü, the king of Ch'u, has had him in his grasp, but always he has taken pity on him and let him live. And yet no sooner had the king of Han escaped than he went back on his agreement and once more attacked King Hsiang. This shows how untrustworthy he is. Now you consider yourself his fast friend and are doing your best to fight for him, but in the end you will find yourself his prisoner. The only reason you have been able to go your way so far is that King Hsiang is still alive.

"Today the fate of these two kings lies with you. If you throw your weight one way, the king of Han will win; if you throw it the other way, King Hsiang of Ch'u will win. But if King Hsiang should perish today, it would be your turn to be seized next. You and King Hsiang are old friends. Why do you not turn against Han, make your peace with Ch'u, and rule a third of the empire? Now you are going to throw this opportunity away, put your faith in Han, and attack Ch'u. Is this in truth the policy of a wise man?"

Han Hsin, however, declined his advice. "When I served under King Hsiang," he replied, "my office was no more than that of an attendant, and my position only that of spear bearer. He did not listen to my counsels nor make use of my plans. Therefore I turned my back on Ch'u and gave my allegiance to Han. The king of Han presented me with the seals of a commanding general and granted me a force of twenty or thirty thousand men. He doffed his own garments to clothe me, gave me food from his own plate, listened to my words, and used my counsels. Therefore I have been able to come this far. When a man has treated me with such deep kindness and faith, I could never be disloyal to him. I beg you to convey my regrets to King Hsiang."

When Wu She departed, K'uai T'ung, a man of Ch'i, realizing that Han Hsin held the balance of power in the empire, thought to sway his resolution by means of a curious scheme. Mentioning the art of physiognomy to Han Hsin, he said, "I once studied this art of reading people's faces."

"Just how do you go about reading faces?" asked Han Hsin.

"High or low position are revealed in the bone structure, sorrow or joy in the countenance, and success or failure in the power of decision. If one considers these three factors, he will make no mistake in a thousand cases!"

"Indeed! And what would you say of me?"

"May I speak to you a moment in private?" said K'uai T'ung.

"Let those about me retire!" Han Hsin ordered.

"Examining your face," K'uai T'ung continued, "I see that you will never be more than a feudal lord. And I see danger and unrest. But if you turn your back,[2] I see such honor as cannot be expressed in words!"

"How so?" asked Han Hsin.

"When revolt first broke out in the world the great warriors and brave heroes proclaimed their titles and shouted as with one voice, and the soldiers of all the world massed about them like thickening clouds, meshed their forces like the scales of a fish, flamed forth, and rose before the wind. At that time the thought of each was only to destroy Ch'in. But now Ch'u and Han rend the empire with their contention so that countless innocent men of the world spill their bowels upon the soaking earth and the bones of father and son are left to bleach in the open field. The men of Ch'u rose up from P'eng-ch'eng, and in battle after battle pursued the fleeing Han forces as far as Jung-yang, riding upon the crest of victory and rolling up the empire like a mat before them, until the whole world trembled at their might. But for three years now their soldiers have suffered reverses in the area between Ching and So, blocked by the western mountains and unable to advance. The king of Han with a host of two or three hundred thousand men has blocked their advance at Kung and Lo-yang, relying upon the defenses of mountains and rivers. But though he fights several engagements a day, he is powerless to win an inch of territory, nor can he break away and flee without perishing. He was defeated at Jung-yang, wounded at Ch'eng-kao, and finally forced to flee into the area of Yüan and She. This is a case in which both the wise and the brave are at a stalemate. The keen spirits of the one are dashed against impregnable barriers; the provisions of the other grow scarce in his storehouses, while the common people, exhausted and worn with hatred and resentment, reel and stagger without means of support. It is my judgment that under such conditions none but the wisest of men can ever bring surcease to the ills of the world!

"Now the fate of these two rulers lies with you. If you declare for Han, Han will win; if for Ch'u, then Ch'u will win. I would open my heart and mind to you, exhaust my poor energies, and devise for you a plan, but I fear that you will not heed it. If, however, you were truly

---

[2] A *double-entendre*, i.e., "if you turn against Han."

to give ear to my scheme, I would say that it would be best to take advantage of these two rivals and preserve them both. Divide the empire into three shares and let each of you stand like the legs of a tripod. Under such circumstances neither of the others will dare to make the first move.

"With your great wisdom and your host of soldiers, you could make your base in powerful Ch'i, command Yen and Chao and, moving out into the unoccupied lands, seize control of the areas to the rear of Han and Ch'u. Then you could gratify the desires of the people by facing the powers of the west and demanding that they spare the lives of the masses. The whole world will respond to your call and hasten to you as though upon the wind. Who would dare to turn a deaf ear? You could divide the great states, weaken the powerful, and set up feudal rulers and, when the lords were established, all the world would harken to your words and bow before the beneficence of Ch'i. You may base your power upon the old land of Ch'i, occupy the regions of Chiao and Ssu, win over the nobles through your favors, retire within your palace, fold your hands and bow in humble deprecation, and the rulers of the earth will lead each other on to pay homage to Ch'i. Yet I have heard that 'he who does not take when Heaven offers, receives misfortune instead; he who does not act when the time comes, suffers disaster instead.' I beg you to consider most carefully!"

Han Hsin replied, "The king of Han has treated me most generously, placing me in his own carriage, clothing me with his own garments, and giving me to eat from his own plate. I have heard it said that he who rides in another man's carriage must share his woes, he who puts on another man's clothes dons his sorrows as well, and he who eats another man's food must serve him to the death. How could I turn my back on what is right merely for the hope of gain?"

"You consider yourself a close friend of the king of Han," said K'uai T'ung, "and hope thereby to create a position for yourself and your family for all time to come. But if I may be so bold, I believe you are mistaken. When Chang Erh, the king of Ch'ang-shan, and Ch'en Yü, the lord of Ch'eng-an, were still commoners, they swore to be friends until death, and yet after they had quarreled over the affair of Chang Yen and Ch'en Shih, they grew to hate each other.

Chang Erh turned his back upon Hsiang Yü and, cowering with his head between his hands, crept off to join the king of Han. There he borrowed soldiers from the king of Han, marched east again, and, south of the Ch'ih River, slaughtered Ch'en Yü who, his head and feet torn asunder, ended as a laughingstock of the world. These two had been the fastest friends in the world. Why then did one end as the prisoner of the other? Because evil arises from excess of desires, and the heart of man is hard to fathom!

"Now though you hope to conduct your dealings with the king of Han in loyalty and good faith, you can never be closer to him than these two men, Chang Erh and Ch'en Yü, were to each other, while there are many things to stand between you more serious than the affair of Chang Yen and Ch'en Shih. Therefore I believe that you are mistaken in thinking that there is no danger in trusting the king of Han.

"Ta-fu Chung and Fan Li once saved the doomed state of Yüeh, made its ruler, Kou-chien, a dictator, and won fame and glory, and yet they themselves perished. 'When the wild beasts have all been captured,' says the old proverb, 'the hunting dog is put into the pot to boil.' You talk of friendship, but yours is nothing like that of Chang Erh and Ch'en Yü; you speak of loyalty, but you cannot do more than Ta-fu Chung and Fan Li did for Kou-chien. These two cases are well worth noting. I beg you to consider them deeply.

"They say that bravery and cunning which make even one's own ruler tremble only endanger one's self, while the merit which overshadows the world is never rewarded. Let me for a moment recount your own merit and cunning. You crossed the western reaches of the Yellow River, made a prisoner of the king of Wei, and captured Hsia Yüeh; you led your troops down the Ching Gorge, executed Ch'en Yü, subdued Chao, terrified Yen into submission, and subjugated Ch'i. In the south you crushed the Ch'u army of two hundred thousand men; in the east you killed Lung Chü, and now you have turned west to report your deeds to the king of Han. One may say that you have won merit unparalleled in the world, and shown a cunning unmatched in generations. Now that you wield power enough to make a sovereign tremble and have won more merit than can be rewarded, should you choose to follow Ch'u, the men of Ch'u would never trust you, and should you follow Han, the men of Han would quake with fear. With gifts such as these, whom should you follow? Your position is that of a subject, and yet you possess power enough to make a sovereign tremble and a name which resounds throughout the world. This is why I consider that you are in danger!"

Han Hsin thanked him and said, "Stop a while, I beg you. I will think over what you have said."

After several days K'uai T'ung began to lecture him again. "Listening to advice is the basis of an undertaking, and planning is the key to success. Where there is bad listening or faulty planning, the undertaking seldom prospers for long. But if one listens with a sense of logic, he will not be confused by mere words; if he plans with a sense of relative importance, he cannot be distracted by mere talk. One who contents himself with the labors of a menial will never wield the power of a great lord; one who clings to a post that pays only a bushel or two of grain will never occupy the position of prime minister.

"Therefore to be wise is to be resolute in decision, but to doubt is to destroy one's undertaking. The petty schemes which take account of every detail miss the greater destinies of the world. To be wise only in knowledge but lack the resoluteness to act is to meet disaster in every undertaking. Thus it is said, 'Better a wasp bent on stinging than a hesitant tiger; better an old nag plodding safely along than a hobbling thoroughbred; better a common man determined to act than the bravest hero vacillating! You may be as wise as Shun and Yü, but if you mumble and do not speak out, you are less use than a deaf mute making gestures!' These sayings prove the worth of being able to act. Merit is difficult to achieve and easy to lose. The right time is hard to find and easy to let slip. The time, my lord, the time! It will not come twice! I beg you to consider carefully!"

But Han Hsin hesitated and could not bear to turn against Han. Also he considered that he had won such merit that the king of Han would never take Ch'i away from him. So in the end he refused K'uai T'ung's advice. When K'uai T'ung realized that his advice would not be followed, he desisted and, feigning madness, became a shaman.

The king of Han was in considerable difficulty at Ku-ling but, employing a scheme suggested by Chang Liang, he summoned Han Hsin, the king of Ch'i, who led his army to join the Han forces at Kai-hsia. After Hsiang Yü had been defeated, the king of Han, now emperor, surprised Han Hsin and seized his army.

In the first month of the fifth year of Han the emperor moved Han Hsin from Ch'i to the position of king of Ch'u with his capital at Hsia-p'ei. When Han Hsin reached his state he summoned the old washerwoman who had given him food long ago and presented her with a thousand catties of gold. To the village head of Nan-ch'ang in Hsia he gave a hundred cash, remarking, "You are a small-minded man! When you do favors for people, you are not willing to see them through to the end!" Then he sent for the young man who had humiliated him and made him crawl between his legs, and made him a military commander. "He is a brave man," Han Hsin told his generals and ministers. "At the time when he humiliated me, I could of course have killed him. But killing him would have won me no fame. So I put up with it and got where I am today."

Chung-li Mo, a fugitive general of Hsiang Yü whose home was at Yin-lu, had long been a friend of Han Hsin and, after the death of Hsiang Yü, he fled to join Han Hsin. The king of Han hated Chung-li Mo and, hearing that he was in Ch'u, sent an order to Ch'u to have him seized. When Han Hsin first arrived in Ch'u, he made a tour of the various district towns, leading his soldiers in formation here and there about the state. In the sixth year of Han someone sent a report to the emperor stating that Han Hsin, king of Ch'u, was about to revolt. Kao-tsu, at the suggestion of Ch'en P'ing, decided to make an imperial tour and summon a meeting of the nobles. In the south there is a lake called Yün-meng, and so the emperor dispatched envoys to the nobles saying, "Meet me at Ch'en, since I am going to visit Yün-meng." His real intention was to make a surprise attack on Han Hsin, though Han Hsin was unaware of this.

With the emperor about to arrive in Ch'u, Han Hsin began to consider whether he should not dispatch his troops in revolt but, since he believed himself guilty of no crime, he decided to visit the emperor. He was afraid of being taken prisoner, however. Someone advised him, saying, "If you execute Chung-li Mo before you go to visit the emperor, His Majesty is sure to be pleased and there will be no trouble." Han Hsin went to see Chung-li Mo to discuss what he ought to do. "The only reason the Han forces do not attack and take Ch'u away from you is that I am with you!" said Chung-li Mo. "Now if you wish to seize me in order to ingratiate yourself with the emperor, I am prepared to die today, but you yourself will follow close behind!" Then he cursed Han Hsin, saying, "You are no man of honor!" and in the end cut his own throat.

Han Hsin, bearing Chung-li Mo's head, went to visit Kao-tsu at Ch'en. The emperor ordered his guards to bind Han Hsin and place him in one of the rear carriages. "It is just as men say," sighed Han Hsin. "When the cunning hares are dead, the good dog is boiled; when the soaring birds are gone, men put away the good bow; when the enemy states have been defeated, the ministers who plotted their downfall are doomed. The world is now at peace, and so it is fitting that I be boiled!"

"Someone told me that you were about to revolt," said the emperor, and had Han Hsin put into fetters, but when they reached Lo-yang he absolved him of guilt and made him marquis of Huai-yin.

Han Hsin, knowing that the emperor feared and hated his ability, always pleaded illness and failed to attend court or join the imperial processions. He brooded day and night on his discontent and was ashamed to be ranked equal with Chou P'o and Kuan Ying. Once, when he visited General Fan K'uai, Fan K'uai knelt in deep respect to greet him and see him off and, employing terms of the greatest humility, said, "Your Highness has condescended to look upon his servant." "I am still alive," laughed Han Hsin as he went out the gate, "but I am now the same rank as you and the rest!"

The emperor was once casually discussing with Han Hsin the relative abilities of his generals and ranking them in order.

"About how many soldiers could a person like myself command?" asked the emperor.

"Your Majesty would not exceed the hundred thousand class," replied Han Hsin.

"And what about yourself?"

"As for me, the more the better!"

"If the more the better," laughed the emperor, "how is it that you became my prisoner?"

"Your Majesty cannot command soldiers," replied Han Hsin, "but you are good at commanding generals. That is why I became your prisoner. Moreover you are one of those who are 'chosen of Heaven.' Your power is not human!"

When Ch'en Hsi was appointed governor of Chü-lu, he went to take his leave of Han Hsin. Han Hsin grasped his hand and, dismissing his attendants, walked with him into the courtyard. Gazing up at the sky and sighing, he said, "I wonder if you are the sort I can talk with. . . . I have something I would like to say to you."

"You have only to mention it," replied Ch'en Hsi.

"The place where you live has the finest troops in the empire. And you, of course, are a trusted and favored minister of the emperor. If someone were to report that you were about to revolt, the emperor would certainly not believe it. If it were reported a second time, the emperor might begin to doubt, and if a third time he would surely become angry and lead an expedition in person. In that case I might contrive to raise an army for you and we could scheme for the empire!"

Ch'en Hsi had long known of Han Hsin's ability and trusted him. "I shall honor your instructions with the greatest care!" replied Ch'en Hsi.

In the tenth year of Han, Ch'en Hsi did in fact revolt. The emperor marched against him in person, but Han Hsin, ill as usual, did not join the expedition. He sent a man in secret to the place where Ch'en Hsi was, saying, "Just raise your troops! I will help you from here." Han Hsin then plotted with his ministers and in the middle of the night forged an edict pardoning all the convict laborers attached to the government offices, intending to dispatch them in an attack on Empress Lü and the heir apparent. After he had assigned them their various places he waited for a report from Ch'en Hsi. It happened that one of Han Hsin's retainers had committed some fault against Han Hsin, who had him imprisoned and was about to execute him. The retainer's younger brother reported Han Hsin's disaffection to the capital, sending a letter to inform Empress Lü that he was planning to revolt. The empress thought of summoning him, but she was afraid that he would not come, so together with Hsiao Ho, the prime minister, she devised a scheme whereby they had a man pretend to come from the emperor with news that Ch'en Hsi had already been captured and killed. When the nobles and ministers all appeared to offer their congratulations Hsiao Ho sent word to trick Han Hsin, saying, "Although you are ill, you must make an effort to come to the capital and present your congratulations." Han Hsin came.

Empress Lü ordered the guards to bind Han Hsin and execute him in the bell-room of the Palace of Lasting Joy. When he was about to be beheaded, he said, "To my regret I did not listen to K'uai T'ung's scheme. And now I have been tricked by this bitch and her lackey! Is it not fate?" Han Hsin's family, to the third degree of kinship, was exterminated.

Kao-tsu had completed his campaign against Ch'en Hsi's army and returned to the capital when he learned of Han Hsin's death. He was both pleased and saddened by the news, and asked whether Han Hsin had said anything before he died. "He said he regretted not having listened to the scheme of K'uai T'ung," said Empress Lü.

"He is a rhetorician of Ch'i," said Kao-tsu and sent an order to Ch'i to have K'uai T'ung arrested.

When K'uai T'ung was brought before him, the emperor asked, "Did you advise Han Hsin to revolt?"

"I did," he replied. "I advised him most strongly. But the idiot did not listen to my scheme and so brought destruction upon himself and his family. Idiot though he was, if he had used my plan, how would Your Majesty ever have been able to destroy him?"

"Boil him alive!" ordered the emperor in a rage.

"But, Your Majesty, how unjust! To have me boiled . . . !" cried K'uai T'ung.

"You advised Han Hsin to revolt! What do you mean, unjust?"

"The web of Ch'in's government had rotted away and the strands of its rule grew slack. East of the mountains all was in chaos, as men of the other clans raised their armies and brave men flocked about them. The empire slipped from the house of Ch'in like a fleeing deer and all the world joined in its pursuit. As it happened, he with the tallest stature and the swiftest feet seized it first. Now the bandit

Chih's dog would bark even at a sage like Yao, but that is not because Yao is evil, but because it is a dog's nature to bark at anyone who is not his master. At that time I knew only Han Hsin. I did not know Your Majesty. There are countless men in the empire who plucked up their spirits and seized their swords in hopes of doing what you did. It is only that their strength was not equal to the task. And do you think you can boil all of them alive as well?"

"Free him!" said the emperor, and he absolved K'uai T'ung of his guilt.

The Grand Historian remarks: When I visited Huai-yin one of the men of the place told me that even when Han Hsin was still a commoner his ambitions were different from those of ordinary men. At the time of his mother's death he was so poor that he could not give her a proper burial, and yet he had her buried on a high, broad expanse of earth with room enough around to set up ten thousand households,[3] this man said. I went to visit Han Hsin's mother's grave, and it was quite true.

If Han Hsin had given thought to the Way and been more humble instead of boasting of his achievements and priding himself on his own ability, how fine a man he might have been! For his services to the house of Han he might have ranked with the dukes of Chou and Shao and Grand Duke Wang of old, and for ages after have enjoyed the blood and flesh of sacrifices. Yet he did not strive for such things but, when the world was already gathered under one rule, plotted treason instead. Was it not right that he and his family should be wiped out?

[3] As grave tenders, in the manner of the most exalted ruler.

With artful words they carried out their missions, and won over the nobles so that, united in goodwill, the nobles gave their allegiance to the Han and became its protectors and guardians. Thus I made The Biographies of Li I-chi and Lu Chia.

Li I-chi

Li I-chi was a native of Kao-yang in Ch'en-liu. He loved to read books. His family was poor and had fallen on such hard times that they had no means of procuring food and clothing, so Li I-chi became keeper of the village gate, but the worthy and influential people of the district would not venture to employ him at anything else. Throughout the district everyone called him "the Mad Scholar."

After Ch'en She, Hsiang Liang, and others had begun their uprisings several dozen of their generals, sent to subdue various regions, passed through Kao-yang. Li I-chi made inquiries about each of these generals, but found them all to be petty-minded and given to empty ceremony, vain men quite incapable of listening to plans for greater and nobler deeds. Therefore Li I-chi withdrew deep within himself.

Later, word came that the governor of P'ei was leading his troops to seize the region about the outskirts of Ch'en-liu. It happened that one of the cavalrymen under the governor's command was from the same village as Li I-chi, and the governor several times inquired of this man who were the wise and important people of the city. When the cavalryman paid a visit to his old home Li I-chi went to see him and said, "I have heard that the governor of P'ei is arrogant and treats others with contempt, but that he has many great plans. This is truly the sort of man I would like to follow after, but I have no one to recommend me. If you should see him, you must tell him, 'In my village there is a man named Master Li who is over sixty years old and eight feet tall. People all call him the Mad Scholar, but he himself insists that he is not mad.'"

"The governor of P'ei does not care for Confucian scholars," replied the cavalryman. "Whenever a visitor wearing a Confucian hat comes to see him, he immediately snatches the hat from the visitor's head and pisses in it, and when he talks to other people he always curses them up and down. He will never consent to be lectured to by a Confucian scholar!"

"Just tell him what I said, anyway," answered Li I-chi. The cavalryman took advantage of a propitious moment to speak to the governor as Li I-chi had instructed him and, when the governor reached the official lodge in Kao-yang, he sent for Li I-chi. Li I-chi arrived and went in for the interview. It happened that the governor was sprawled upon a couch with two servant girls washing his feet when he received Li I-chi. On entering, Li I-chi did not make the customary prostration, but instead gave a deep bow and said, "Do you intend to assist Ch'in in attacking the nobles, or do you intend to lead the nobles in overthrowing Ch'in?"

"Stupid pedant!" cursed the governor. "It is because the whole world has suffered so long together under the Ch'in that the nobles have joined in leading forth their troops to attack it! What do you mean by asking if I intend to 'assist Ch'in in attacking the nobles'?"

"If you really mean to gather a band of followers and create a righteous army to punish the unprincipled Ch'in, it is hardly proper for you to receive your elder sprawled about in this fashion!"

With this the governor stopped the foot washing, rose, straightened his clothes and, apologizing, led Li I-chi to a seat of honor. Li I-chi proceeded to talk to him about the horizontal and vertical alliances of the period of the Six States. The governor was pleased and ordered a meal brought for him, asking, "What strategy do you consider best for me to adopt?"

"You have taken up arms with this motley band, gathered together this disordered army, which does not number a full ten thousand men, and with this you plan to march straight into the powerful Ch'in. Such action is what men call 'seeking out the tiger's jaws.' Now the city of Ch'en-liu is a thoroughfare of the world. From its suburbs roads lead in every direction, while within its walls are many stores of grain. Since I am friendly with its magistrate, I beg to be sent as your emissary so that I can bring the city over to your side. If it should happen that the magistrate will not listen to me, then you may raise your troops and attack, and I will aid you from within the city."

Accordingly the governor of P'ei sent Master Li ahead, while he led his troops after him, and eventually they seized control of Ch'en-liu. He awarded Li I-chi the title of lord of Kuang-yeh. Master Li mentioned his younger brother Li Shang to the governor and managed to have him put in command of several thousand men and sent with the governor to seize the land to the southwest. Li I-chi himself constantly acted as spokesman for the governor's cause, hastening on diplomatic missions from one feudal lord to another.

In the autumn of the third year of Han, Hsiang Yü attacked the Han forces and captured the city of Jung-yang. The Han troops fled and took up a defensive position in the area of Kung and Lo-yang. In the meantime Hsiang Yü, receiving word that Han Hsin had defeated Chao and that P'eng Yüeh was inciting frequent rebellions in the region of Liang, divided his forces and sent troops to the aid of these two areas. Han Hsin was at the time marching east to attack Ch'i.

The king of Han had several times found himself sorely pressed in the area of Jung-yang and Ch'eng-kao and had decided that the best plan would be to abandon any attempt to hold the territory east of Ch'eng-kao, garrisoning Kung and Lo-yang instead, in order to block the advance of the Ch'u forces. It was at this point that Master Li said to the king, "There is a saying that 'he who knows the "heaven" of Heaven may make himself a king, but he who has not this knowledge may not. To a king the people are "heaven," and to the people food is "heaven".' [1] For a long time now grain from all over the empire has been transported to the Ao Granary and I have heard that huge quantities are stored in its vaults. After Hsiang Yü captured Jung-yang, however, he did not remain to guard the Ao Granary, but instead led his men east, leaving only a party of convict soldiers to hold

[1] In this rather curious expression the word "heaven" is being used in the sense of a *sine qua non*.

"Now the king of Han has led his men forth from Shu and Han, and recaptured the three kingdoms of Ch'in. His forces have crossed the western reaches of the Yellow River to the northern side, gathered up the troops of Shang-tang, descended the Ching Gorge, overthrown Ch'en Yü, the lord of Ch'eng-an, defeated the Northern Wei, and captured thirty-two cities. Such an army is like that of the great Ch'ih Yu of ancient times, winning its victories not by human strength but by the blessing of Heaven. Now the king of Han has acquired the grain supplies of the Ao Granary, blockaded the strategic points of Ch'eng-kao, guarded the White Horse Ford, blocked the slopes of Mount T'ai-hsing, and closed the pass at Flying Fox. Therefore those who are slow to submit to him will be the first to perish. If you will hasten to bow before the king of Han, then you may keep possession of Ch'i's altars of the soil and grain. But if you do not bow to him, you may expect danger and destruction in a matter of days!"

T'ien Kuang, the king of Ch'i, considered that Master Li spoke the truth. He therefore heeded his advice, dispersed the troops which he had sent to defend Li-hsia, and spent the days drinking to his heart's content with Master Li.

When Han Hsin got word that Master Li, by no more than nodding a diplomatic greeting from his carriage, had won over Ch'i with its seventy-odd cities, he led his troops across the Yellow River at P'ing-yüan and made a surprise attack on Ch'i. T'ien Kuang, hearing that the Han soldiers had arrived, supposed that Master Li had betrayed him. "If you can halt the Han armies," he told Li I-chi, "I will let you live. But if not, I will boil you alive!"

"Great deeds do not wait upon petty caution," replied Master Li, "nor shining virtue upon niceties of etiquette. Your father [2] has no intention of going back on what he has said for the sake of the likes of you!"

With this the king of Ch'i boiled Master Li alive and fled east with his army.

In the twelfth year of Han, Li I-chi's brother Li Shang, the marquis of Ch'ü-chou, acting as chancellor of the right, led a force of troops

[2] For the use of this insulting phrase, see note 5, "The Hereditary House of the Marquis of Liu."

in an attack on Ch'ing Pu, winning distinction in battle. When Kao-tsu was rewarding the various nobles and great ministers he remembered Li I-chi, whose son Chieh had from time to time led bands of troops, though his achievements had not qualified him for the rank of marquis. For his father's sake the emperor enfeoffed Li Chieh as marquis of Kao-liang, and later changed the territory which he was awarded to Wu-sui. The marquisate was handed down for three generations. During the first year of the era *yüan-shou* [122 B.C.] Li P'ing, then the marquis of Wu-sui, was tried on charges of forging an imperial edict and extorting from the king of Heng-shan a sum of a hundred catties of gold. He was condemned to be executed in the public market, but before the sentence could be carried out he died of illness and his territory was abolished.

Lu Chia

Lu Chia was a native of Ch'u who became a follower of Kao-tsu and joined him in conquering the world. He was renowned as a skillful speaker and rhetorician and was one of Kao-tsu's trusted advisers, serving time and again as envoy to the various nobles.

When Kao-tsu became emperor, and peace was first restored to China, the military commander Chao T'o conquered the region of Southern Yüeh and proceeded to make himself its ruler. Kao-tsu dispatched Lu Chia to present Chao T'o with the imperial seal making him king of Southern Yüeh. When Master Lu[3] arrived Chao T'o received him in audience with his hair done up in the mallet-shaped fashion of the natives of Southern Yüeh, and sprawled on his mat. Master Lu advanced and addressed Chao T'o. "You are a Chinese, and your forefathers and kin lie buried in Chen-ting in the land of Chao. Yet now you turn against that nature which Heaven has given you at birth, cast aside the dress of your native land and, with this tiny, far-off land of Yüeh, think to set yourself up as a rival of the Son of Heaven and an enemy state. Disaster will surely fall upon you!

"When Ch'in lost control of the empire the nobles and heroes rose on all sides, yet it was the king of Han alone who entered the Pass

---

[3] Because he was a scholar and a writer, Ssu-ma Ch'ien refers to him as "Master," as in the case of Li I-chi above.

ahead of the others and took possession of Hsien-yang. Hsiang Yü broke the promise which he had made to the nobles and set himself up as 'Dictator King of Western Ch'u,' and all the other nobles became subject to his command, for his strength was the greatest. Yet the king of Han rose up from Pa and Shu, chastised the world as with a great whip, drove the nobles before him, and in the end punished and destroyed Hsiang Yü until, in the space of five years, he had brought all within the four seas to peace and unity. Such deeds were not done by human strength, but were ordained by Heaven!

"Now it has come to the ears of the Son of Heaven that, although you lent no aid in punishing the traitors who plagued the world, you have made yourself ruler of Southern Yüeh. The generals and high ministers wish to send out an army to punish you. But because the Son of Heaven is unwilling in his compassion to inflict new suffering and hardship upon the common people, he has set aside their proposals and sent me instead to confer upon you the seals of a king, splitting the tallies of enfeoffment and opening diplomatic intercourse. It is proper under such circumstances that you should advance as far as the suburbs to greet me and bow to the north and refer to yourself as a 'subject.' Yet with this newly created state of Yüeh, which is not even firmly established, you behave with such effrontery! If the Han emperor should actually hear of this, he would dig up and desecrate the graves of your ancestors, wipe out your family, and dispatch one of his subordinate generals with a force of a hundred thousand men to march to the borders of Yüeh. At that point the people of Yüeh would murder you and surrender to the Han forces faster than I can turn my hand!"

With this, Chao T'o scrambled up off his mat in the greatest alarm and apologized to Master Lu, saying, "I have lived among these barbarians for so long that I have lost all sense of manners and propriety!"

In the course of their conversations Chao T'o asked Master Lu, "Who is worthier, I or the great ministers Hsiao Ho, Ts'ao Ts'an, and Han Hsin?"

"You would appear to be the worthier man," replied Master Lu.

"And of the emperor and myself, who is worthier?" he asked again.

"The emperor rose up from the city of Feng in P'ei, overthrew the violent Ch'in, and punished the powerful leaders of Ch'u, driving out harm and bringing benefit to the whole world. He succeeded to the labors of the Five Emperors and the Three Dynasties of the past, uniting all China under a single rule. The population of China numbers in the millions, while its land area measures thousands of square miles. It occupies the richest and most fertile region of the world, with an abundance of people, carriages, and every other thing imaginable. And yet its government proceeds from a single family. Since the creation of heaven and earth there has never before been such a thing!

"Now Your Majesty's people do not number over a few hundred thousand, and all of them are barbarians, crowded awkwardly between the mountains and the sea. Such a kingdom would amount to no more than a single province of the Han empire! How can you compare yourself with the emperor of Han?"

Chao T'o laughed loudly and replied, "It is only because I did not begin my uprising in China that I have become king of this region. If I had been in China, would I not have done just as well as the Han emperor?"

Chao T'o took great delight in Master Lu and detained him with feasts and drinking parties for several months. "There is no one in all of Yüeh worth talking to," he said. "Now that you have come, every day I hear something I have never heard before!" He presented Master Lu with a bag of precious objects worth a thousand pieces of gold and in addition gave him a thousand pieces of gold as a going away present. In the end Master Lu awarded him the title of king of Yüeh and persuaded him to acknowledge his allegiance to the Han and enter into relations with it.

When Lu Chia returned and reported on his mission, Kao-tsu was greatly pleased and honored him with the rank of palace counselor.

In his audiences with the emperor, Master Lu on numerous occasions expounded and praised the *Book of Odes* and the *Book of Documents*, until one day Kao-tsu began to rail at him. "All I possess I have won on horseback!" said the emperor. "Why should I bother with the *Odes* and *Documents*?"

"Your Majesty may have won it on horseback, but can you rule it on horseback?" asked Master Lu. "Kings T'ang and Wu in ancient

occur in the empire, there will be no danger of authority slipping from their grasp. Hence the security of the altars of the state lies solely in the hands of these two men. I have always wanted to speak to the grand commandant Chou P'o, the marquis of Chiang, but he and I are only on joking terms and I am afraid he would dismiss my words too lightly. Why do you not establish more friendly relations with him so that you two can cooperate to the fullest in this matter?"

This and several other plans he suggested to Ch'en P'ing concerning the matter of the Lü family. Ch'en P'ing followed his advice and proceeded to spend five hundred pieces of gold on a birthday celebration for Chou P'o at which, amid a lavish array of dishes, they drank and feasted merrily. Chou P'o in turn responded with similar generosity, so that the two men became close friends and the plottings of the Lü clan accordingly met with less and less success.

Ch'en P'ing sent Master Lu a hundred female slaves, fifty carriages and horses, and a sum of five million cash to be used to cover drinking and eating expenses. With this Master Lu began to mingle freely with the highest officials of the Han court, and his fame spread in all directions.

When the Lü family was overthrown and Emperor Wen set up, Master Lu acquired unprecedented power. After Emperor Wen had come to the throne he wished to send an envoy to Southern Yüeh, and Prime Minister Ch'en P'ing and others immediately suggested Master Lu. Master Lu was accordingly made a palace counselor and sent as an envoy to Chao T'o, where he succeeded in persuading Chao T'o to stop riding in a yellow-covered carriage and calling his orders "edicts" in imitation of the Han emperors, and to conduct himself in the same way as the feudal lords of China proper. Chao T'o agreed to do just as the Han court suggested. (A more detailed discussion will be found in the chapter on Southern Yüeh.) Master Lu finally died of old age.

Chu Chien

Chu Chien, lord of P'ing-yüan, was a native of Ch'u. Originally he served as prime minister to Ch'ing Pu, the king of Huai-nan, but because of some offense he was removed from his post. Later he returned to the service of Ch'ing Pu. When Ch'ing Pu was planning to revolt he asked Chu Chien's advice. Chu Chien counseled him to desist. Ch'ing Pu, however, refused to heed him but instead listened to the marquis of Liang-fu and eventually revolted. After the Han forces had executed Ch'ing Pu it was learned that Chu Chien had remonstrated with Ch'ing Pu and refused to take part in the plot, and he was thus allowed to go free without punishment.

Chu Chien was a very eloquent speaker and a man of strict honesty and integrity. In his actions he refused to compromise with expediency, nor would he modify his principles for the sake of appearances. He made his home in Ch'ang-an.

Shen I-chi, the marquis of Pi-yang, who at the time had managed by dubious ways to win great favor with Empress Lü, was desirous of becoming friends with Chu Chien, but the latter refused to receive him. It happened that Chu Chien's mother died and Master Lu, who from early days had been a friend of Chu Chien, went to visit him. Chu Chien's family, he found, was so poor that Chu Chien was forced to delay announcement of the funeral while he looked about for some place to borrow the necessary clothes and accessories. Master Lu instructed Chu Chien to go ahead and announce the funeral, while he himself went to call on Shen I-chi and congratulated him, saying, "The mother of Chu Chien, lord of P'ing-yüan, has died!"

"Why in the world should you congratulate *me* on the death of Chu Chien's mother?" asked Shen I-chi.

"Some time ago," said Master Lu, "you expressed a desire to get to know Chu Chien. At that time, however, he did not consider it proper to become friends with you because his mother was still alive.[5] Now that she is dead, if you are willing to arrange a generous funeral for her, Chu Chien will do anything for you."

Shen I-chi accordingly went to Chu Chien's house and presented a hundred pieces of gold as a funeral gift, and the other nobles and high officials, because Shen I-chi had brought a gift, followed his

[5] The reader should recall that, under the system of corporate responsibility before the law, if Chu Chien's association with Shen I-chi had led to his being implicated in any offense of Shen I-chi's, his mother would be held as guilty and punished as severely as Chu Chien himself. Because Shen I-chi's power was based not on ability but on the personal favoritism of Empress Lü, his position at court was naturally precarious.

example until Chu Chien had received a sum of five hundred pieces of gold in all.

Shen I-chi enjoyed unusual favor with Empress Lü. It happened that someone slandered him to Emperor Hui, who was enraged and had Shen I-chi seized by the law officers in preparation for executing him. Empress Lü was chagrined and could say nothing in his defense, while many of the high officials joined in criticizing his activities and pressing for his execution. Shen I-chi, in a most difficult position, sent someone to ask Chu Chien to come to see him, but Chu Chien declined to go, saying, "Your trial is about to take place. I dare not see you!" Meanwhile, however, he requested an interview with Emperor Hui's favorite, the catamite Hung, and attempted to persuade him to act. "There is no one in the empire who does not know why you enjoy such favor with the emperor," he said. "And yet now Shen I-chi, who enjoys similar favor with Empress Lü, is seized by the law officers. People about town all say that you have slandered him and are trying to have him killed. But if Shen I-chi is executed today, you may be sure that by tomorrow morning Empress Lü in her rage will have you executed, too! Would it not be better to bare your shoulders like a suppliant and plead for Shen I-chi with the emperor? If the emperor listens to you and frees Shen I-chi, Empress Lü will be overjoyed. Then you will enjoy the favor of both sovereigns, and your honor and wealth will be doubled!"

The catamite Hung, thoroughly alarmed, followed his suggestion and spoke to the emperor, who as a result released Shen I-chi. Earlier, when Shen I-chi sent for Chu Chien to come to see him in prison and Chu Chien refused to appear, he had been enraged, believing that Chu Chien had betrayed him, but his rage turned to complete astonishment when Chu Chien's plan succeeded and he was released.

After Empress Lü passed away, the high officials executed the members of the Lü family, but Shen I-chi, who had had the most intimate connections with the family, managed in the end to escape. In all cases the schemes which saved his life were due to the efforts of Master Lu and Chu Chien.

During the reign of Emperor Wen, King Li of Huai-nan killed Shen I-chi on the grounds that he had been an associate of the Lü family. When Emperor Wen heard that one of Shen I-chi's friends, Chu Chien, had planned his affairs for him, he sent a law officer to arrest Chu Chien and bring him to trial. Word being brought to him that the law officer was at his gate, Chu Chien prepared to commit suicide, but his son and the officer both said, "No one knows yet how the affair will end! Why should you make such haste to commit suicide?"

"If I am dead the trouble will come to an end," he replied, "and no harm will fall upon you, my son!" and with this he cut his throat.

When Emperor Wen received the news he was filled with regret. "I had no intention of killing him," he said, and summoned Chu Chien's son and made him a palace counselor. He was sent as an envoy to the Huns. When the *Shan-yü* behaved rudely to him, he proceeded to curse the *Shan-yü,* and eventually died among the Hsiung-nu.[6]

The Grand Historian remarks: Many of the books circulating these days which record the story of Master Li state that it was after the king of Han had captured the three kingdoms of Ch'in, marched east to attack Hsiang Yü, and was encamped with his army in the area between Kung and Lo-yang that Master Li, dressed in the robes of a Confucian, went to advise him. But this is an error. It was actually while the emperor was still governor of P'ei and before he had entered the Pass that, parting from Hsiang Yü and marching to Kao-yang, he obtained the services of Master Li and his brother.

I have read Master Lu's *New Discourses* in twelve sections. He was surely one of the outstanding rhetoricians of his day. In the case of Chu Chien, lord of P'ing-yüan, I was a friend of his son and so have been able to obtain a full account of his life.

[6] At this point in the text there appears a variant account of the meeting of Master Li I-chi and the governor of P'ei. Scholars have long regarded it with suspicion and considered it to be a later interpolation. I have omitted the entire section.

Shih chi 99: The Biographies of Liu Ching and Shu-sun T'ung

They moved the powerful clans, established the capital within the Pass, made a treaty of peace with the Hsiung-nu, and clarified the ritual of the court and the ceremonial laws concerning the ancestral temples. Thus I made The Biographies of Liu Ching and Shu-sun T'ung.

Liu Ching

Liu Ching, whose family name was originally Lou, was a native of Ch'i. In the fifth year of Han, while he was on his way to garrison duty in Lung-hsi, he passed through Lo-yang, where Emperor Kao-tsu was at the time residing. He climbed out of the little, man-drawn cart in which he was riding and, still wearing his lambskin traveling clothes, went to see General Yü, who was also a native of Ch'i, and said, "I wish to see the emperor and talk to him about a matter which will be to his advantage."

General Yü wanted to give him some fresh clothes to wear, but Liu Ching replied, "If I were wearing silk, I would see him wearing silk, and if I were wearing the coarsest haircloth, I would see him in that!" He refused to change his clothes.

General Yü accordingly went in and spoke to the emperor, who summoned Liu Ching to an audience and had a meal brought for him. This done, he asked Liu Ching his business and the latter began his discourse: "Your Majesty, in establishing the capital at Lo-yang, is, I should say, attempting to imitate the glory of the house of Chou."

"That is correct," replied the emperor.

"And yet the way Your Majesty acquired the empire was quite different from the way the house of Chou acquired it. The Chou ancestral line began with Hou Chi, who was enfeoffed in T'ai by Emperor Yao. The family continued to accumulate virtue and goodness for over ten generations until Kung Liu fled from the tyrant Chieh and went to live in Pin. Later, because of the attacks of the Ti barbarians, he left Pin, with only his horsewhip in his hand, and went to live in Ch'i, but the people of his former kingdom hastened to follow after him. When King Wen became chief of the west and settled the dispute between the states of Yü and Jui, he first received the mandate of Heaven, and Lü Wang and Po-i journeyed from the distant borders of the sea to be his followers. Then King Wu set out to attack the Shang tyrant Chou and, at the Meng Ford, though he had not summoned them, eight hundred of the other nobles gathered to join him. All of them cried, 'Let us attack the tyrant Chou!' And in the end they overthrew the Shang dynasty. After King Ch'eng came to the throne he had as his aides and ministers the duke of Chou and others, who at this time established a capital called Ch'eng-chou at the city of Lo because it is the center of the world.[1] The feudal lords were able to present their tribute and journey to the capital for *corvée* services from all four sides, and the distance was equal for all.

"From such a capital it is easy for a king who is virtuous to rule, but it is also easy for a king who is not virtuous to be overthrown. In establishing the capital here, it was the hope of the founders that their descendants would devote themselves wholly to virtue and thereby attract the people to their rule, rather than, by placing the capital in a strong position militarily, to encourage later rulers to become arrogant and wasteful and tyrannize over the people. At the height of the Chou dynasty the whole world was at peace and the barbarians of the four quarters turned in longing and admiration toward its virtuous ways, submitted to its rule, and paid homage to the Son of Heaven. Not one soldier was sent off to garrison duty, not one man marched into battle, and yet the eight barbarian tribes and the people of the other great states all without exception came of their own accord in submission to the Chou to bear tribute and undertake its duties.

"But, when the Chou declined, it split into two parts. The world ceased to attend its court, and the house of Chou could no longer enforce its will. This was not because its virtue had grown ineffective, but rather because its geographical position was too weak.

[1] Lo-yang was reputed to be the geographical center of the world.

"Now Your Majesty, rising up from Feng in P'ei, gathered together a band of three thousand men and proceeded at once to roll up the areas of Shu and Han and conquer the three kingdoms of Ch'in. You fought with Hsiang Yü at Jung-yang, and contended for the pass at Ch'eng-kao, engaging in seventy major battles and forty skirmishes. You have caused the men of the world to spill their blood and bowels upon the earth, and the fathers and sons to bleach their bones in the open fields, in numbers too great to reckon. The sound of weeping has not yet ceased, the wounded have not yet risen from their beds, and still you would attempt to imitate the glorious reigns of Kings Ch'eng and K'ang of the Chou. Yet, if I may be so bold as to say so, there is no resemblance.

"The area of Ch'in, surrounded by mountains and girdled by the Yellow River, is strongly protected on all four sides. In the case of sudden need it is capable of supplying a force of a million soldiers. He who holds the old area of Ch'in and enjoys the advantages of its vast and fertile fields possesses a veritable storehouse created by nature. If Your Majesty will enter the Pass and make your capital there, then, although there should be an uprising east of the mountains, you can still keep complete control of the old land of Ch'in. Now when you fight with a man, you have to grip his throat and strike him in the back before you can be sure of your victory. In the same way, if you will now enter the Pass and make your capital there, basing yourself upon the old land of Ch'in, you will in effect be gripping the throat and striking the back of the empire!"

Emperor Kao-tsu consulted his various officials, but the officials, all being men from east of the mountains, hastened to point out that the house of Chou had lasted several hundred years, while the Ch'in perished with the Second Emperor, and that it was therefore wiser to establish the capital at the site of the Chou capital in Lo-yang. The emperor was in doubt and had not yet made up his mind when Chang Liang, the marquis of Liu, made clear to him the advantages of locating the capital within the Pass, and on the same day he mounted his carriage and began the journey west, determined to establish the capital within the Pass.

"Since it was Lou Ching who first advised me to make my capital in the land of Ch'in," the emperor announced, "let Lou from now on become Liu," and he awarded Lou Ching the imperial surname Liu, made him a palace attendant, and gave him the title of lord of Feng-ch'un.

In the seventh year Hsin, the king of Hann, revolted and Kao-tsu went in person to attack him. When the emperor reached Chin-yang he received word that Hsin was about to join the Hsiung-nu in a joint attack on the Han. In a rage, the emperor dispatched envoys to the Hsiung-nu. The Hsiung-nu took care to conceal all of their fine young men and fat cattle and horses, and let the envoys see only the old men and boys and the leanest of their livestock. As many as ten envoys made the trip but all, when they returned, announced that the Hsiung-nu could be attacked. The emperor then sent Liu Ching to go as his envoy. On his return, Liu Ching reported on his mission. "When two states are about to attack each other, it is customary for each to exaggerate and make a show of its superiority. Now when I journeyed to the Hsiung-nu, I saw only emaciated animals, old men, and boys. It can only be that they deliberately wish to appear inferior and are counting on surprising us with an ambush attack and winning victory. In my opinion the Hsiung-nu cannot be attacked!"

At this time the Han force of two hundred thousand or more had already crossed Chü-chu Mountain and arrived for the assault. The emperor began to curse Liu Ching angrily. "This scoundrel from Ch'i has managed to win himself a position with his wagging tongue, and now he comes with his foolish lies and tries to halt my army!" He had Liu Ching fettered and bound at Kuang-wu, and proceeded on his way as far as P'ing-ch'eng.

As Liu Ching had foreseen, the Hsiung-nu sent out a surprise force and surrounded the emperor on the White Peak for seven days, until they at last withdrew. When the emperor returned to Kuang-wu he pardoned Liu Ching, saying, "Because I did not listen to your advice I encountered great difficulty at P'ing-ch'eng. I have already executed the ten earlier envoys who advised me that the Hsiung-nu could be attacked!" He proceeded to enfeoff Liu Ching as a marquis in the area within the Pass, awarding him two thousand households and the title of marquis of Chien-hsin.

Kao-tsu abandoned the P'ing-ch'eng campaign and returned to the capital, while Hsin, the king of Hann, fled to the Hsiung-nu. Mo-tun, who at this time had just become *Shan-yü,* had a powerful force of troops, including three hundred thousand crossbow-stretchers, and several times attacked the northern frontier. The emperor, troubled about the situation, consulted Liu Ching, who replied, "The empire has only just been brought to peace and the officers and men are worn out by fighting. It is not possible at this time to make the Hsiung-nu submit by force of arms. Moreover, Mo-tun acquired the position of *Shan-yü* by murdering his father. He has taken his father's concubines as wives and relies solely on force to maintain his rule. Such a man can never be swayed by appeals to benevolence and righteousness. Therefore I can only suggest a plan whereby in time Mo-tun's descendants can be made subjects of the Han. But I fear Your Majesty will not be able to carry it out. . . ."

"If it will actually work, why should I not be able to carry it out?" asked the emperor. "Only tell me what I must do!"

"If you could see your way clear to send your eldest daughter by the empress to be the consort of Mo-tun, accompanied by a generous dowry and presents, then Mo-tun, knowing that a daughter of the emperor and empress of the Han must be generously provided for, would with barbarian cunning receive her well and make her his legitimate consort and, if she had a son, he would make him heir apparent. Why would he do this? Because of his greed for Han valuables and gifts. Your Majesty might at various times during the year inquire of his health and send presents of whatever Han has a surplus of, and the Hsiung-nu lack. At the same time you could dispatch rhetoricians to begin expounding to the barbarians in a tactful way the principles of etiquette and moral behavior. As long as Mo-tun is alive he will always be your son-in-law, and when he dies your grandson by your daughter will succeed him as *Shan-yü.* And who ever heard of a grandson trying to treat his grandfather as an equal? Thus your soldiers need fight no battles, and yet the Hsiung-nu will gradually become your subjects. If, however, Your Majesty cannot send the eldest princess, but should attempt to deceive Mo-tun by sending someone else and having the princesses and their ladies in waiting address her as 'Princess,' I fear he would discover the deception and be unwilling to pay her any honor, so that no advantage would be gained."

"Excellent!" agreed the emperor, and prepared to send the eldest princess, but Empress Lü day and night wept and pleaded, saying, "The only children I have are the heir apparent and this one girl! How can you bear to cast her away to the Hsiung-nu?"

In the end the emperor could not bring himself to send the princess, but instead selected the daughter of another family and, calling her the eldest princess, sent her to marry Mo-tun, dispatching Liu Ching to go along at the same time and conclude a peace treaty.

When he returned from his mission to the Hsiung-nu, Liu Ching spoke to the emperor, saying, "The Hsiung-nu in the Ordos region south of the Yellow River who are under the Po-yang and Lou-fan kings are situated no more than seven hundred *li* from Ch'ang-an. With a day and a night of riding their light cavalry can reach the old land of Ch'in within the Pass. This region has only recently suffered conquest, so that its people are rather few in number, but the land is rich and fertile and can support many more. Furthermore, at the time when the nobles began their uprisings against Ch'in, it was said that no one but a member of the T'ien clan of Ch'i or the Chao, Ch'ü, or Ching clans of Ch'u could ever succeed. Now although Your Majesty has established the capital within the Pass, there are in fact few people in the area. Close to the north are the barbarian bandits, while in the east live these powerful clans of the Six States of former times, so that if some day trouble should arise somewhere, I fear you could never rest with an easy mind. I beg therefore that you move the various members of the T'ien clan of Ch'i, the Chao, Ch'ü, and Ching clans of Ch'u, the descendants of the former royal families of Yen, Chao, Hann, and Wei, and the other powerful and renowned families to the area within the Pass. As long as things are going well, they can defend the area against the barbarians, and if there should be disaffection among the feudal lords, they would form an army which could be led east and used in putting down the trouble. This is the type of strategy known as 'strengthening the root and weakening the branches' of the empire."

The emperor approved the plan and sent Liu Ching to see to the moving of the said clans to the area within the Pass, over a hundred thousand persons in all.

Shu-sun T'ung

Shu-sun T'ung was a native of Hsieh. During the Ch'in dynasty he was summoned to court because of his literary ability and served along with the erudits for several years. When Ch'en She began his uprising east of the mountains, messengers came to report the fact to the throne. The Second Emperor summoned the erudits and various Confucian scholars and questioned them. "Some soldiers from a garrison in Ch'u have attacked Chi and made their way into Ch'en," he announced. "What do you make of this, gentlemen?"

One after another some thirty or more erudits and scholars came forward and gave their opinion: "A subject must not harbor so much as the thought of disaffection. If he has even the thought, he is already guilty of rebellion, an unpardonable crime which deserves only death. We beg Your Majesty to dispatch troops at once to attack this fellow!"

At this the emperor's face flushed with rage. Then Shu-sun T'ung advanced and began to speak. "The other scholars are all mistaken," he announced. "The whole world is now united as one family. The walls of the provincial and district cities have been razed and their weapons melted down to make clear to the world that these things of war will never again be used. Moreover, an enlightened lord now reigns above, while laws and ordinances order all below, so that all men attend to their own duties and on every side acknowledge allegiance to the central authority. Under such circumstances who would dare to rebel? These men are clearly no more than a band of petty outlaws—rat thieves, dog bandits, no more! They are not worth wasting breath on. Even now the provincial governor is arresting and sentencing them. What is there to worry about?"

"Why of course!" cried the Second Emperor with delight. Then he questioned the rest of the scholars, and some of them said the uprising was a rebellion and others said it was only the work of bandits. The emperor then ordered the imperial secretary to make a note of all the scholars who had called it a rebellion and have them sent to jail on charges of speaking improperly, while those who had called it the work of bandits were all dismissed without further incident. To Shu-sun T'ung he awarded twenty rolls of silk and a suit of clothes and honored him with the position of erudit.

After Shu-sun T'ung had left the palace and returned to the officials' lodge the other scholars said to him, "Master Shu-sun, what made you speak such flattery?"

"You would not understand," he replied, "but if I had not, I could hardly have escaped from the tiger's jaws!"

After this Shu-sun T'ung ran away from the capital and fled to his old home in Hsieh. When Hsieh surrendered to the Ch'u forces and Hsiang Liang reached there, Shu-sun T'ung became a follower of his but, after Hsiang Liang was defeated at Ting-t'ao, he joined the followers of King Huai of Ch'u in P'eng-ch'eng. Later King Huai was given the title of Righteous Emperor and transferred to Ch'ang-sha, but Shu-sun T'ung remained behind in P'eng-ch'eng to serve Hsiang Yü.

In the second year of Han the king of Han, accompanied by five of the other nobles, entered P'eng-ch'eng, at which time Shu-sun T'ung surrendered to him. When the king of Han was defeated and fled west, Shu-sun T'ung accordingly followed along. Shu-sun T'ung customarily wore the robes of a Confucian scholar but, because the king of Han had such a great dislike for this costume, he changed to a short robe cut in the fashion of Ch'u, which pleased the king.

When Shu-sun T'ung surrendered to the king of Han, he was accompanied by over a hundred Confucian scholars who had been studying under him. However, he did not recommend any of them to the king, but instead spent his time recommending all sorts of men who had originally been outlaws or roughnecks. His disciples began to curse him behind his back, saying, "Here we have served the master for a number of years until at last we are lucky enough to surrender and join the forces of the king of Han. But now, instead of recommending us for positions, he spends all his time recommending a bunch of gangsters! What sort of behavior is this?"

Shu-sun T'ung got word of what they were saying, and told them, "The king of Han is at the moment busy dodging arrows and missiles in a struggle for control of the world. What could a lot of scholars like you do in such a fight? Therefore I have first recommended the sort of men who can cut off the heads of enemy generals and seize their pennants. Wait a while! I won't forget you!"

The king of Han made Shu-sun T'ung an erudite and awarded him the title of lord of Chi-ssu. In the fifth year of Han, after the entire empire had been conquered, the nobles joined in conferring upon the king of Han the title of Supreme Emperor at Ting-t'ao, and Shu-sun T'ung arranged the ceremony and titles to be used. The emperor completely did away with the elaborate and irksome ritual which the Ch'in had followed and greatly simplified the rules of the court. His followers and ministers, however, were given to drinking and wrangling over their respective achievements, some shouting wildly in their drunkenness, others drawing their swords and hacking at the pillars of the palace, so that Emperor Kao-tsu worried about their behavior. Shu-sun T'ung knew that the emperor was becoming increasingly disgusted by the situation, and so he spoke to him about it. "Confucian scholars," he said, "are not much use when one is marching to conquest, but they can be of help in keeping what has already been won. I beg to summon some of the scholars of Lu who can join with my disciples in drawing up a ritual for the court."

"Can you make one that is not too difficult?" asked the emperor.

"The Five Emperors of antiquity all had different types of court ·music and dance; the kings of the Three Dynasties by no means followed the same ritual. Rites should be simplified or made more elaborate according to the state of the times and the people's feelings. Therefore, as Confucius has said, the way in which the Hsia, Shang, and Chou dynasties took from or added to the rites of their predecessors may be known. He meant by this that they did not merely copy their predecessors. It is my desire to select from a number of ancient codes of ritual, as well as from the ceremonies of Ch'in, and make a combination of these."

"You may try and see what you can do," replied the emperor. "But make it easy to learn! Keep in mind that it must be the sort of thing I can perform!"

Shu-sun T'ung accordingly went as an envoy to summon some thirty or more scholars of Lu. Two of the Lu scholars, however, refused to come. "You have served close to ten different masters," they replied, "and with each of them you have gained trust and honor simply by flattering them to their faces. Now the world has just been set at peace, the dead have not been properly buried, and the wounded have not risen from their beds, and yet you wish to set up rites and music for the new dynasty. But rites and music can only be set up after a dynasty has accumulated virtue for a period of a hundred years. We could never bring ourselves to take part in what you are doing, for what you are doing is not in accord with the ways of antiquity. We will never go! Now go away and do not defile us any longer!"

"True pig-headed Confucianists you are, indeed!" said Shu-sun T'ung, laughing. "You do not know that the times have changed!"

Shu-sun T'ung eventually returned west to the capital, accompanied by the thirty or so scholars he had summoned. There, with the learned men who acted as the emperor's advisers and his own disciples, making up a group of over a hundred, he stretched ropes and constructed a pavilion out in the open where for over a month he and the others worked out the ritual. Then he asked the emperor to come and see what he thought of it. "I can do that all right!" said the emperor when he had seen it, and ordered it to be put into effect, instructing all the officials to practice it so that it could be used in the tenth month at the beginning of the year.

In the seventh year, with the completion of the Palace of Lasting Joy, all the nobles and officials came to court to attend the ceremony in the tenth month. Before dawn the master of guests, who was in charge of the ritual, led the participants in order of rank through the gate leading to the hall. Within the courtyard the chariots and cavalry were drawn up. The foot soldiers and palace guards stood with their weapons at attention and their banners and pennants unfurled, passing the order along to the participants to hurry on their way. At the foot of the hall stood the palace attendants, lined up on either side of the stairway, several hundred on each step. The distinguished officials, nobles, generals, and other army officers took their places on the west side of the hall facing east, while the civil officials from the chancellor on down proceeded to the east side of the hall facing west. The master of ceremonies then appointed men to relay instructions to the nine degrees of guests.

At this point the emperor, borne on a litter, appeared from the inner rooms, the hundred officials holding banners and announcing his arrival. Then each of the guests, from the nobles and kings down to the officials of six hundred piculs' salary, was summoned in turn to come forward and present his congratulations, and from the nobles down every one trembled with awe and reverence.

When the ceremony was finished ritual wine was brought out. All those seated in attendance in the hall bowed their heads to the floor and then, in the order of their rank, each rose and drank a toast to the emperor. The grand secretary was charged with seeing that the regulations were followed, and anyone who did not perform the ceremony correctly was promptly pulled out of line and expelled from the hall. During the drinking which followed the formal audience there was no one who dared to quarrel or misbehave in the least. With this, Emperor Kao-tsu announced, "Today for the first time I realize how exalted a thing it is to be an emperor!" He appointed Shu-sun T'ung his master of ritual and awarded him five hundred catties of gold.

Shu-sun T'ung took advantage of the opportunity to speak to the emperor. "My disciples, students of Confucianism, have been with me a long time and worked with me in drawing up the new ceremonial. I beg Your Majesty to make them officials." The emperor accordingly made all of them palace attendants. When Shu-sun T'ung emerged from his audience with the emperor he proceeded to give away the entire five hundred catties of gold to the scholars who had worked with him. "Master Shu-sun is a true sage!" they all exclaimed with delight. "He knows just what is important and appropriate for the times."

In the ninth year of Han, Emperor Kao-tsu transferred Shu-sun T'ung to the position of grand tutor to the heir apparent. Later, in the twelfth year, when Kao-tsu was considering removing the heir apparent and putting Ju-i, the king of Chao, in his place, Shu-sun T'ung remonstrated with him. "In ancient times," he said, "Duke Hsien of Chin, because of his love for Princess Li, removed the heir apparent and set up her son Hsi-ch'i in his place, and as a result the state of Chin was thrown into chaos for several decades and became a laughing-stock before the world. Because the First Emperor of Ch'in did not decide in time to designate Prince Fu-su as his heir, he made it possible for the eunuch Chao Kao, after his death, to set up Hu-hai by trickery and thus bring about the destruction of the dynastic altars. This last is a case Your Majesty witnessed in person. Now the present heir apparent is kind and filial, and all the world has heard of his fame. It was his mother, Empress Lü, who shared your struggles to power and ate with you the insipid fare of poverty! How can you turn your back upon them now? If Your Majesty persists in this desire to cast aside the legitimate heir and set up a junior in his place, I beg that before the deed is done I be granted the executioner's axe, and let the blood from my severed neck drench this ground!"

"That is enough!" said the emperor. "I was only joking, anyway."

"The heir apparent is the foundation of the empire," protested Shu-sun T'ung. "If the foundation once should rock, the whole empire would rock! How can Your Majesty jest about such a matter?"

"I shall do as you say," said the emperor. Later the emperor gave a banquet and, when he saw the venerable guests whom Chang Liang had invited attending the heir apparent and appearing in court, he abandoned once for all his intention of changing the heir.

After Kao-tsu had passed away, and Emperor Hui had come to the throne, he sent for Shu-sun T'ung. "None of the officials know what sort of ceremonies should be performed at the funerary park and temple of the former emperor," he complained, and transferred Shu-sun T'ung back to the position of master of ritual. Shu-sun T'ung established the ceremonial rules for the ancestral temples of the dynasty, and settled the various ceremonial procedures for the Han as a whole, all set down in works which he wrote during his time as master of ritual.

When Emperor Hui went to the eastern side of the palace grounds to pay his formal respects to his mother, Empress Dowager Lü, in the Palace of Lasting Joy, or visited her informally at other times, it was often necessary to stop the passers-by and clear the path for him. For this reason the emperor had an elevated walk built above the path from the main palace to the Palace of Lasting Joy and extending along the south side of the arsenal.

After reporting some other affairs to the throne one day, Shu-sun T'ung asked for a moment of leisure to speak to the emperor in private. "Why has Your Majesty had this elevated walk built?" he asked. "The robes and caps of Emperor Kao-tsu, when they are taken out of his tomb and brought to his funerary temple once a month, must pass beneath this walk. The temple of Kao-tsu is dedicated to the Founding Father of the Han! Surely Your Majesty will not make it necessary for your descendants in later ages to walk *above* the path leading to the temple of the Founder!"

Emperor Hui was horrified and said, "Let the walk be torn down at once!" But Shu-sun T'ung replied, "The ruler of men never makes a mistake! The walk is already built, and the common people all know about it. Now if Your Majesty were to tear it down, it would be admitting that you had made a mistake in the first place. I beg you instead to set up a second funerary temple north of the Wei River to which the late emperor's robes and caps may be taken each month. To enlarge or increase the number of ancestral temples is after all the beginning of true filial piety!"

The emperor accordingly issued an edict to the authorities to set up a second funerary temple to Kao-tsu, the establishment of which was due in fact to this elevated walk.

Emperor Hui one spring was setting out on an excursion to one of the detached palaces to enjoy himself when Shu-sun T'ung said, "In ancient times in spring they used to have something called the 'Presentation of Fruits.' Right now the cherries are ripe and might be used as an offering. While Your Majesty is in the country, I beg you to gather some cherries and offer them in the ancestral temple." The emperor approved the suggestion, and from this arose the custom of making offerings of various kinds of fruit.

The Grand Historian remarks: There is a saying that the pelt of one fox will not make a costly robe of fur, one limb of a tree will not do for the rafters of a tall pavilion, and the wisdom of one man alone cannot bring about the great ages of the Three Dynasties of old. How true! Kao-tsu, who rose from humble beginnings to conquer all within the seas, knew all there was to know, one may say, about strategies and the use of arms. And yet Liu Ching stepped down from his little cart and made a single suggestion which assured the security of the dynasty for countless years to come. Truly, no one has a monopoly on wisdom!

Shu-sun T'ung placed his hopes in the world and calculated what was needed; in planning rites and in all his other actions, he changed with the times, until in the end he became the father of Confucian scholars for the house of Han. The greatest directness seems roundabout, people say. Even the Way itself twists and turns. Is this perhaps what they mean?

Shih chi 29: The Treatise on the Yellow River and Canals

In ancient times Emperor Yü deepened the rivers and saved the empire from flood, bringing relief and security to the nine provinces. Concerning the waterways that were opened or diked, the river courses that were fixed, and the canals that were constructed, I made The Treatise on the Yellow River and Canals.

The documents on the Hsia dynasty tell us that Emperor Yü spent thirteen years controlling and bringing an end to the floods, and during that period, though he passed by the very gate of his own house, he did not take the time to enter. On land he traveled in a cart and on water in a boat; he rode a sledge to cross the mud and wore cleated shoes in climbing the mountains. In this way he marked out the nine provinces, led the rivers along the bases of the mountains, decided what tribute was appropriate for each region in accordance with the quality of its soil, opened up the nine roads, built embankments around the nine marshes, and made a survey of the nine mountains.

Of all the rivers, the Yellow River caused the greatest damage to China by overflowing its banks and inundating the land, and therefore he turned all his attention to controlling it. Thus he led the Yellow River in a course from Chi-shih past Lung-men and south to the northern side of Mount Hua; from there eastward along the foot of Ti-chu Mountain, past the Meng Ford and the confluence of the Lo River to Ta-p'ei. At this point Emperor Yü decided that, since the river was descending from high ground and the flow of the water was rapid and fierce, it would be difficult to guide it over level ground without danger of frequent disastrous break-throughs. He therefore divided the flow into two channels, leading it along the higher ground to the north, past the Chiang River and so to Ta-lu. There he spread it out to form the Nine Rivers, brought it together again to make the

Backward-flowing River [i.e., tidal river], and thence led it into the Gulf of Pohai.¹ When he had thus opened up the rivers of the nine provinces and fixed the outlets of the nine marshes, peace and order were brought to the lands of the Hsia and his achievements continued to benefit the Three Dynasties which followed.

Sometime later the Hung Canal was constructed, leading off from the lower reaches of the Yellow River at Jung-yang, passing through the states of Sung, Cheng, Ch'en, Ts'ai, Ts'ao, and Wei, and joining up with the Chi, Ju, Huai, and Ssu rivers. In Ch'u two canals were built, one in the west from the Han River through the plains of Yün-meng, and one in the east to connect the Yangtze and Huai rivers.² In Wu a canal was dug to connect the three mouths of the Yangtze and the Five Lakes, and in Ch'i one between the Tzu and Chi rivers. In Shu, Li Ping, the governor of Shu, cut back the Li Escarpment to control the ravages of the Mo River and also opened up channels for the Two Rivers through the region of the Ch'eng-tu.

All of these canals were navigable by boat, and whenever there was an overflow of water it was used for irrigation purposes, so that the people gained great benefit from them. In addition there were literally millions of smaller canals which led off from the larger ones at numerous points along their courses and were employed to irrigate an increasingly large area of land, but none of these are worth mentioning here.

Hsi-men Pao built a canal to lead off the waters of the Chang River and irrigate Yeh, and as a result the region of Ho-nei in the state of Wei became rich.

Another time the state of Hann, learning that the state of Ch'in was fond of undertaking large projects, dispatched a water engineer named Cheng Kuo to go to Ch'in and persuade the ruler to construct a canal from a point on the Ching River west of Mount Chung to the pass at Hu-k'ou, and from there along the Northern Mountains east into the the Lo River, a distance of over three hundred *li*. Ostensibly the pur-

---

¹ Needless to say, this is simply a description of the course of the Yellow River in ancient times. The passage, though not a direct quotation, is based upon the "Tribute of Yü" section of the *Book of Documents*.

² Following the reading in *Han shu* 29.

pose of the project was to provide irrigation for the fields, though in fact Cheng Kuo and the rulers of Hann hoped thereby to wear out the energies of the state of Ch'in so that it would not march east to attack Hann. Cheng Kuo succeeded in getting the project started, but halfway through the real nature of his mission came to light. The Ch'in ruler was about to kill him, but Cheng Kuo said, "It is true that I came here originally with underhanded intentions. But if the canal is completed, it will profit the state of Ch'in as well!"

The Ch'in ruler, deciding that this was sensible, in the end allowed him to go ahead with the canal. When it was finished, it was used to spread muddy, silt-laden water over more than forty thousand *ch'ing* of land in the area which up until this time had been very brackish, bringing the yield of the land up to one *chung* per acre [*mou*].[3] As a result the area within the Pass was converted into fertile fields and no longer suffered from lean years; Ch'in became rich and powerful and eventually was able to conquer all the other feudal lords and unite the empire. In honor of its builder the canal was named Cheng Kuo Canal.

Thirty-nine years after the founding of the Han [168 B.C.], in the reign of Emperor Wen, the Yellow River overflowed its banks at Suan-tsao and destroyed the Metal Embankment east of there. Accordingly a large force of laborers was called up in Tung Province to repair the break.

Some forty years later,[4] during the era *yüan-kuang* [134-129 B.C.] of the present emperor, the Yellow River broke its banks at Hu-tzu, flowing southeast into the marsh of Chü-yeh and joining up with the Huai and Ssu rivers. The emperor accordingly ordered Chi An and Cheng Tang-shih to raise a force of laborers and repair the breach, but no sooner had they done so than the river broke through again. At this time T'ien Fen, the marquis of Wu-an, was serving as chancellor and his income came from an estate in Shu. Shu is located north of the Yellow River, and since the break was on the southern side, suffered no damage from floods; on the contrary the revenue from the estate

---

[3] One *ch'ing* was equal to about 57 English acres, and there were 500 *mou* in a *ch'ing*. One *chung* was equal to ten *hu*, or about five and a half bushels.

[4] Ssu-ma Ch'ien's figure is misleading; the break took place in 132 B.C., only thirty-six years after the earlier break.

actually increased. T'ien Fen said to the emperor, "Breaks in the banks of the Yangtze and the Yellow River are all the work of Heaven. It is no easy task to stop up such breaks forcibly by human labor, and indeed to do so would hardly be in accord with the will of Heaven!" The numerologists and those who interpret the emanations in the sky supported him in this view and the emperor therefore hesitated and for a long time made no further attempts to repair the break.

At this time Cheng Tang-shih, who was serving as minister of agriculture, said to the emperor, "Up to now grain from east of the Pass has been brought to the capital by being transported up the Wei River. The operation requires six months to complete and the course is over nine hundred *li* and beset with dangerous places. Now if we were to dig a canal from the Wei River, beginning at Ch'ang-an and following along the Southern Mountains to the Yellow River, the distance could be reduced to something over three hundred *li*. We would have a much easier route for transporting grain, and the trip could be accomplished in three months. Moreover, the people living along the canal could utilize the water to irrigate over ten thousand *ch'ing* of farmland. Thus we could reduce the time and labor required to haul grain and at the same time increase the fertility of the lands within the Pass and obtain a higher yield."

Approving the plan, the emperor ordered Hsü Po, a water engineer from Ch'i, to plot the course of the transport canal and called up a force of twenty or thirty thousand laborers to do the digging. After three years of labor, it was opened for use in hauling grain and proved extremely beneficial. From this time on grain transport to the capital gradually increased, while the people living along the canal were able to make considerable use of the water to irrigate their fields.

After this, P'an Hsi, the governor of Ho-tung, said to the emperor, "Every year over a million piculs of grain are transported to the capital from the area east of the mountains. Since it is brought up the Yellow River, it must be shipped through the dangerous narrows at Ti-chu Mountain, where much of it is lost, and in addition the cost of transportation is very high. Now if we were to dig canals from the Fen River to irrigate the region of P'i-shih and parts of Fen-yin, and other canals from the Yellow River to irrigate P'u-p'o and the rest of Fen-yin,

I believe we could bring five thousand *ch'ing* of land under cultivation. At present this region is nothing more than a strip of uncultivated land along the Yellow River where the people graze their flocks but, if it were turned into irrigated fields, I think it could be made to yield over two million piculs of grain. This could be transported up the Wei River to the capital and would be no more expensive than grain produced in the area within the Pass. It would then no longer be necessary to haul grain from the east past the dangerous part of the river at Ti-chu."

The emperor considered this a sound idea and called up a force of twenty or thirty thousand laborers who worked for several years digging canals and opening up the fields. But the Yellow River changed its course so that the water did not flow into the canals properly and the farmers who worked the newly opened fields were unable to produce enough to repay the cost of planting. After some time, therefore, the newly opened canals and fields in Ho-tung were abandoned and the area was turned over to settlers from the state of Yüeh. What little revenue it produced was allotted to the privy treasury.

Following this, someone sent a letter to the throne proposing that a road be opened up between the Pao and Yeh rivers, and that they be used to transport grain. The emperor referred the proposal to the imperial secretary Chang T'ang who, after conducting an inquiry, reported as follows: "At present anyone wishing to travel to the province of Shu must go over the Old Road, a very long and roundabout route beset with steep places. Now if the Pao and Yeh rivers were dredged and a road opened between them, it would provide a much more level route and the distance could be reduced to four hundred *li*. The Pao River runs into the Mien River and the Yeh River runs into the Wei, both of which can be used to transport grain. Therefore grain could be brought from Nan-yang up the Mien River and into the Pao, and where the Pao ends it could be transported overland by carts for a distance of a hundred *li* or so to where the Yeh begins, and from there down the Wei to Ch'ang-an. Thus grain from Han-chung could be brought to the capital. At the same time, by making use of the Mien River, grain could be transported from east of the mountains in unlimited quantities and the route would be much more convenient than the present one up the Yellow River and through the narrows at Ti-chu. Moreover, the region of the Pao and Yeh is as rich in timber and bamboo as the provinces of Pa and Shu."

The emperor approved the proposal and appointed Chang T'ang's son Chang Ang as governor of Han-chung, calling up a force of twenty or thirty thousand laborers and setting them to work constructing the Pao and Yeh road and waterway which extended more than five hundred *li*. When the road was finished it did in fact prove to be much shorter and more convenient than the old route, but the rivers were too full of rapids and boulders to be used for transporting grain.

Following this, a man named Chuang Hsiung-p'i reported to the emperor that the people of Lin-chin wished to dig a canal from the Lo River to be used to irrigate some ten thousand *ch'ing* of land east of Ch'ung-chüan. The land in this area was brackish, but the people believed that if it could be irrigated with water led in from the Lo River, it could be made to produce ten piculs per acre. The emperor therefore called up a labor force of over ten thousand men and set them to work digging a canal leading off from the Lo River at Cheng and extending to the foot of Mount Shang-yen. There, however, it was found that the banks of the canal kept collapsing, so the men dug wells, some of them over forty *chang* deep, at various points along the course and induced the water to flow from one well to another. Thus the water disappeared from sight at Mount Shang-yen and flowed underground to the eastern side of the mountain, a distance of over ten *li*. This was the beginning of the so-called well-canals. In the course of the digging a dragon bone was discovered and the canal was therefore named Dragon Head Canal. It has been over ten years now since it was constructed but, although the water flows through it fairly well, the land has not yet shown much improvement.

More than twenty years had passed since the Yellow River broke through its banks at Hu-tzu. The break had not been repaired and the harvests were frequently poor, the damage being particularly severe in Liang and Ch'u. The emperor, having gone east to perform the Feng and Shan sacrifices [110 B.C.], made a tour through the empire, sacrificing to various mountains and rivers. The following year [109 B.C.] there was a drought (the purpose of which, it was said, was to dry out the earth of the altar mound constructed for the Feng sacrifice), and very little rain fell. The emperor ordered Chi Jen and Kuo Ch'ang to raise a force of twenty or thirty thousand men and close the break in the banks of the Yellow River at Hu-tzu, while he himself went east to pray for rain at the Altar of the Ten Thousand Mile Sands. On his way back to the capital he stopped to inspect the break in person and cast offerings of jade and a white horse into the river. He ordered all the courtiers and ministers who were accompanying him, from the generals on down, to carry bundles of brushwood and help close the break in the embankment. As it happened, the people of Tung Province had just burned off all their grasslands, so there was very little brushwood to be found in the area. The workmen were therefore obliged to sink lengths of bamboo from the Ch'i Park to form a weir across the opening. As the emperor surveyed the break, he was filled with despair at the difficulty of the task and composed this song:

> The river broke through at Hu-tzu;
> What could we do?
> Beneath its rushing waves,
> Villages all became rivers.
> The villages have all become rivers
> And there is no safety for the land.
> Our labors know no rest,
> Our mountains crumble.
> Our mountains crumble
> And the marsh of Chü-yeh overflows.
> Even the fish lament
> As the winter days press near.
> The river raged from its boundaries,
> It has left its constant course.
> Dragons and water monsters leap forth,
> Free to wander afar.
> Let it return to the old channel
> And we will truly bless the gods.
> But for my journey to the Feng and Shan,
> How would I have known what it was like?
> Ask the Lord of the River for me,
> "Why are you so cruel?

Your surging inundations will not cease;
You grieve my people!
The city of Nieh-sang is awash;
The Huai and Ssu brim over.
So long, and yet you will not return—
You break the laws of nature!"

The river rages on,
Its wild waters tossing.
It swirls back to the north,
A swift and dangerous torrent.
We bring the long stakes
And cast the precious jade.
The Lord of the River hears our plea
But there is not enough brushwood.
There is not enough brushwood—
The fault of the people of Wei.
They have wasted the land with fire—
What can we use to check the waters?
We sink the forest bamboo
And ballast the weir with stones.
We will stem the break at Hsüan-fang
And bring ten thousand blessings!

Thus they finally succeeded in closing the gap at Hu-tzu and built a temple on top of the embankment called the Temple of Hsüan-fang. They led the waters of the river off to the north in two channels so that it returned to the course it had followed in the time of Emperor Yü. Safety was restored to the regions of Liang and Ch'u, and they no longer suffered any damage from flood waters.

After this the men who were concerned with such affairs all rushed to the emperor with proposals for utilizing the rivers to greater advantage. As a result canals were dug in So-fang, Hsi-ho, Ho-hsi, and Chiu-ch'üan to draw off water from the Yellow River or smaller rivers in the valleys and use it to irrigate the fields. Within the Pass the Fu and Ling-chih canals were constructed, making use of the water of various rivers in the region; in Ju-nan and Chiu-chiang water was drawn off from the Huai River; in Tung-hai from the marsh of

Chü-ting; and at the foot of Mount T'ai from the Wen River. In all these places canals were dug to water the fields, providing irrigation for over ten thousand *ch'ing* of land in each area. In addition many other small canals and waterways through the mountains were opened up, but they are too numerous to describe here. Of all these exploits, however, the most outstanding was the closing of the break in the Yellow River at Hsüan-fang.

The Grand Historian remarks: I have climbed Mount Lu in the south to observe the courses which Emperor Yü opened up for the nine tributaries of the Yangtze. From there I journeyed to K'uai-chi and T'ai-huang and, ascending the heights of Ku-su, looked out over the Five Lakes. In the east I have visited the confluence of the Yellow and Lo rivers, Ta-p'ei, and the Backward-flowing River, and have traveled along the waterways of the Huai, Ssu, Chi, T'a, and Lo rivers. In the west I have seen Mount Min and the Li Escarpment in the province of Shu, and I have journeyed through the north from Lung-men to So-fang. How tremendous are the benefits brought by these bodies of water, and how terrible the damages! I was among those who carried bundles of brushwood on their backs to stem the break at Hsüan-fang and, deeply moved by the song of Hu-tzu, I made this treatise on the Yellow River and the canals.

Shih chi 107: The Biographies of the Marquises of Wei-ch'i and Wu-an

When Wu and Ch'u rose in revolt, Tou Ying, the marquis of Wei-ch'i, proved to be the wisest leader among the families related to the imperial house by marriage. He appreciated the worth of other men and as a result they all flocked to him. He led his army to Jung-yang east of the mountains and there blocked the advance of the rebel armies. Thus I made The Biographies of the Marquises of Wei-ch'i and Wu-an.

Tou Ying, the marquis of Wei-ch'i, was the son of a cousin of Empress Tou, the consort of Emperor Wen and mother of Emperor Ching. Up until his father's time, his family had been residents of Kuan-chin.[1] He himself was very fond of supporting guests and retainers in his home.

In the reign of Emperor Wen, Tou Ying was appointed prime minister of Wu, but later retired on grounds of ill health. When Emperor Ching first came to the throne, Tou Ying was made steward of the household of the empress and the heir apparent.

King Hsiao of Liang was the younger brother of Emperor Ching and the favorite son of Empress Dowager Tou. Whenever he came to court Emperor Ching would hold a banquet for him, treating him as a brother rather than a vassal. On one such occasion, before Emperor Ching had formally announced his choice for heir apparent, he remarked casually at the height of the drinking, "After my thousand years of life are over, I shall pass the rule of the empire along to the king of Liang!"

Empress Dowager Tou was delighted at this announcement, but Tou Ying, seizing a goblet of wine and hastening forward to offer it to the emperor, said, "The empire is the empire of the founder, Kao-tsu, and

[1] The old home of Empress Tou. After she became empress, she summoned her relatives to the capital.

it is a law of the Han dynasty that the rule must pass from father to son! How could Your Majesty arbitrarily hand it over to the king of Liang?"

Because of this affair Empress Dowager Tou grew to hate Tou Ying, while he in turn came to despise his post of steward and resigned on grounds of illness. The empress dowager then had his name removed from the roster of officials that was kept at the palace gate so that he could no longer come and go at court as he had in the past.

In the third year of Emperor Ching's reign, when the kings of Wu and Ch'u revolted, the emperor began to cast about among the members of the imperial house and the Tou family for able leaders and found that no one could match the wisdom of Tou Ying. He accordingly summoned Tou Ying to an audience, but when the latter appeared before the emperor he adamantly declined to accept any appointment, insisting that he was unfit because of illness to take on the responsibilities of leadership. Empress Dowager Tou likewise was embarrassed by the emperor's proposal to appoint Tou Ying. But the emperor refused to listen. "At a time when the empire is faced with crisis, how can you think of making polite excuses?" he demanded, and proceeded to appoint Tou Ying as general in chief, presenting him with a gift of a thousand catties of gold. Tou Ying in turn recommended Yüan Ang, Lüan Pu, and other distinguished military men and worthy gentlemen who were not at the time employed in the government and succeeded in having them appointed to various posts. The money presented to him by the emperor he stored along the corridors and in the gatehouse of his home, where his junior officers, if they needed any for military expenditures, could help themselves to it without further ado. Not a cent of it went into his own coffers.

Tou Ying marched east to guard Jung-yang and observe the movements of the troops of Ch'i and Chao. After the armies of the seven rebellious kingdoms had been defeated, he was enfeoffed as marquis of Wei-ch'i, and all sorts of gentlemen with no fixed place of employment, guests and retainers, vied with each other in offering him their services. During the reign of Emperor Ching, whenever there was some important matter to be discussed at court, none of the marquises dared to try to stand on an equal footing with Chou Ya-fu, the marquis of T'iao, and Tou Ying, the marquis of Wei-ch'i.

In the fourth year of his reign, when Emperor Ching set up his son Prince Li as heir apparent, he appointed Tou Ying as the boy's tutor. In the seventh year, however, the emperor decided to dismiss Prince Li from the position of heir apparent, and though Tou Ying several times remonstrated with him, he was unable to prevent the move. Pleading illness once more, he retired to Lan-t'ien in the foothills of the Southern Mountains, where he lived in seclusion for several months. Although a number of his retainers and rhetoricians attempted to make him change his mind, he refused to return to the capital. Among them was a man from Liang named Kao Sui who advised him in these words: "The emperor has the power to make you rich and honored and the empress dowager, your relative, can offer you intimate friendship. Now you have been appointed to tutor the heir apparent and, in spite of your protests, he has been dismissed from his position. Yet, though you were unable to argue your case successfully, you have also proved yourself unable to die for your cause. Instead you have taken yourself off on the excuse of illness and sit here, living a life of ease and retirement, dallying with beautiful women and, with your band of followers, passing judgment on the rest of the world. By such conduct you are deliberately attempting, it would seem, to broadcast to everyone the faults of the ruler! But if you should thereby incur the anger of both the emperor and the empress dowager, I fear, General, it would mean extinction for you and your whole family!"

Tou Ying, realizing that what he said was true, eventually returned to the capital and attended court as before.

At this time Liu She, the marquis of T'ao, retired from the post of chancellor, and Empress Dowager Tou several times suggested to Emperor Ching that Tou Ying be appointed as his successor, but the emperor replied, "I hope you do not think, Mother, that I begrudge him the post. It is only that Tou Ying tends to be somewhat self-righteous and fond of having his own way. On numerous occasions he has acted rather thoughtlessly, and I am afraid that it would be difficult to entrust him with the heavy responsibilities of chancellor." In the end Tou Ying did not get the post; instead Wei Wan, the marquis of Chien-ling, was appointed chancellor.

T'ien Fen, the marquis of Wu-an, was a younger brother of Empress Wang, the consort of Emperor Ching and mother of Emperor Wu; he was born after his mother, Tsang Erh, had remarried into the T'ien family and was living in Ch'ang-ling. When Tou Ying had already become general in chief and was at the height of his power, T'ien Fen still held a rather humble post as palace attendant. He used to go to Tou Ying's house from time to time to wait on him and serve him his wine, bowing politely and treating Tou Ying with great courtesy as though he himself were one of Tou Ying's sons. Toward the end of Emperor Ching's reign T'ien Fen began to enjoy increasing favor at court until he had risen to the post of palace counselor.

T'ien Fen was a very skillful talker and studied the "Cauldron Inscriptions" [2] and similar works on statecraft. His sister, Empress Wang, had great respect for his wisdom. When Emperor Ching passed away and the heir apparent, Empress Wang's son, was proclaimed emperor, the empress for a while issued edicts in her son's name, and many of the measures which she took to insure order and stability in the government during the period of change were suggested to her by T'ien Fen's retainers. In the same year, the third year of the latter part of Emperor Ching's reign [141 b.c.], T'ien Fen and his younger brother T'ien Sheng were both enfeoffed, T'ien Fen as marquis of Wu-an and T'ien Sheng as marquis of Chou-yang. This was done because they were both younger brothers of Empress Dowager Wang.[3]

T'ien Fen found himself in a position of new importance at court and decided that he would like to become chancellor. He therefore conducted himself with great humility before his guests and retainers and worked to advance eminent gentlemen who were living in retirement and secure them honorable positions, hoping thereby to outshine Tou Ying and the elder statesmen of the time.

[2] A work in 26 sections, no longer extant, supposedly compiled by K'ung Chia, the official historian at the court of the Yellow Emperor.

[3] Although the year is designated as the third year of the latter period of Emperor Ching's reign, the enfeoffments took place two months after the death of Emperor Ching when Empress Dowager Wang was managing the government for her son, Emperor Wu.

In the first year of the era *chien-yüan* [140 B.C.] Wei Wan retired from the post of chancellor because of ill health, and the emperor began deliberations with the court to decide who should be appointed to fill this position, as well as that of grand commandant. Chi Fu, one of T'ien Fen's retainers, advised him, saying, "Tou Ying has held a position of great honor for a long time and many of the most worthy men of the empire were originally members of his group. Now, although you have begun to come up in the world, you still cannot rival Tou Ying. If the emperor offers to make you chancellor, you should therefore yield the post to Tou Ying. If Tou Ying is made chancellor, you will surely be made grand commandant, a position which is just as distinguished as that of chancellor. In addition you will thereby gain a reputation for humility and wisdom!"

Impressed by this advice, T'ien Fen mentioned the matter in secret to his sister, Empress Dowager Wang, asking her to drop a hint with the emperor to this effect. As a result the emperor appointed Tou Ying as chancellor and T'ien Fen as grand commandant.

Chi Fu went to congratulate Tou Ying on his new appointment but took the opportunity to deliver a grave warning: "It is Your Lordship's nature, I know, to delight in good men and hate evil ones. At the present time it happens that the good men have joined together in praising you and you have thereby been able to reach the position of chancellor. And yet you hate evil, and evil men are numerous. It will not be long before they too join together—to slander you! If you could find some way to get along with both groups, then I believe you could enjoy your present high position for a long time. But if not, their slanders will drive you right out of office!" Tou Ying paid no attention to this advice.

Tou Ying and T'ien Fen were both admirers of Confucian teachings, and they combined their efforts in boosting Chao Wan into the post of imperial secretary and Wang Tsang into that of chief of palace attendants and in bringing the eminent Confucian scholar Master Shen of Lu to court. They also worked for the establishment of a Bright Hall like the great audience halls of antiquity, ordered the marquises to proceed to their territories, abolished the customs barriers, and changed the funeral ceremonies to conform with correct ritual practice, striving to bring about an era of peace and prosperity. In addition, they conducted an inquiry into the members of the various branches of the imperial family and the Tou family and expunged the names of anyone found guilty of misconduct. At this time many of the male members of the families related to the throne by marriage had become marquises and, since a number of them were married to princesses of the blood, they had no desire to leave the capital and proceed to ·their own territories. They were unanimously opposed to the new order directing them to leave the capital and their criticisms of the law day after day came to the ears of the emperor's grandmother, Empress Dowager Tou.

Empress Dowager Tou was very fond of the teachings of the Yellow Emperor and Lao Tzu, while Tou Ying, T'ien Fen, Chao Wan, Wang Tsang, and the others of their group all did their best to advance the influence of Confucian doctrines and disparage the teachings of the Taoist school. As a result Empress Dowager Tou grew more and more displeased with Tou Ying and his party.

Eventually, in the second year of *chien-yüan* [139 B.C.], when the imperial secretary Chao Wan asked the emperor for permission to dispose of state affairs himself without consulting Empress Dowager Tou, the empress dowager flew into a rage and proceeded to expel Chao Wan, Wang Tsang, and the others from office and to force the resignation of the chancellor Tou Ying and the grand commandant T'ien Fen. She then had Hsü Ch'ang, the marquis of Po-chih, appointed as the new chancellor, and Chuang Ch'ing-ti, the marquis of Wu-ch'iang, as imperial secretary.

As a result of this affair Tou Ying and T'ien Fen were both obliged to retire to their homes to live the life of ordinary marquises. T'ien Fen, however, although holding no position in the government, still enjoyed his usual favor and intimacy with his sister, Empress Dowager Wang, and was therefore able on occasion to express his opinion concerning affairs of state with considerable effect. The officers and gentlemen of the empire and all who sought after profit and position thereupon abandoned Tou Ying and flocked about T'ien Fen, who grew more arrogant in his ways with each passing day.

In the sixth year of the era *chien-yüan* [135 B.C.] Empress Dowager Tou passed away. The chancellor Hsü Ch'ang and the imperial secretary Chuang Ch'ing-ti were accused of delay in arranging the funeral ceremonies and were dismissed from office. T'ien Fen was then appointed chancellor and Han An-kuo, the former minister of agriculture, was made imperial secretary. The gentlemen of the empire, the officials of the provinces, and the other marquises hastened in even greater numbers to ally themselves with T'ien Fen.

T'ien Fen was rather short and unimposing in appearance but, because he was related by birth to the emperor, he conducted himself with a very lordly air. He believed that, since many of the marquises and kings were men of mature years, while the emperor, who had just ascended the throne, was still very young, it was up to him as a close relative of the ruler and chancellor of the central government to force others to submit to his will and treat him with the proper courtesy. Otherwise, he felt, the world would have no respect for the imperial house.

At this time, whenever he would enter the palace to report on some affair connected with his duties as chancellor, he would sit for hours, and sometimes for days, in conference with the emperor, and whatever suggestions he made were always followed. In recommending people for office he succeeded on occasion in having men promoted in one leap from private citizen to official of the two thousand picul rank. His authority in fact outweighed that of the emperor himself, who remarked to him one day, "Have you quite finished making your appointments and dismissals of officials? Because if you have, I think I might like to make a few appointments too!" Another time T'ien Fen asked the emperor for the land used by the government artisans so that he could increase the grounds of his estate, to which the emperor replied angrily, "Why yes! And while you're about it why don't you go ahead and take over the imperial arsenal as well!" After this last remark, T'ien Fen conducted himself with somewhat more discretion in the emperor's presence.

Once when he had invited some guests to his home to drink, he seated his older brother, Wang Hsin, the marquis of Kai, in a place facing south, while he himself took the place of honor facing east. He explained that this arrangement was necessary because of the honor due to himself as chancellor of the Han, which could not be disregarded for the sake of a private family relationship such as that of older and younger brother.

From this time on T'ien Fen lived a life of increasing arrogance and ostentation, building for himself the finest mansions in the capital, laid out with sumptuous grounds and gardens; the merchants with their wares from the distant provinces stood in lines before his door. In his front hall he hung bells and drums, with pennants on curved flagstaffs, while the women's quarters at the back housed wives and maidens in the hundreds. The other nobles flocked about with gifts of gold and jewels, dogs, horses, and trinkets for his amusement, in quantities too great to be reckoned. Tou Ying for his part had grown more and more estranged from the emperor since the death of Empress Dowager Tou. His advice was no longer heeded, his power was gone, and his friends and retainers one by one drifted away, treating him with scorn and indifference. Only General Kuan continued to respect him as before. He spent his days in silent frustration and despair, lavishing his generosity on his one remaining friend, General Kuan.

General Kuan Fu was a native of Ying-yin. His father, whose name was Chang Meng, had originally been a servant of Kuan Ying, the marquis of Ying-yin, and had enjoyed great favor. Eventually, on the strength of the marquis's recommendation he advanced to a post paying two thousand piculs, and out of gratitude he adopted the family name of his patron, being known thereafter as Kuan Meng. At the time of the revolt of Wu and Ch'u, Kuan Ho, who had succeeded to the marquisate after the death of his father, Kuan Ying, was made a general in the command of the grand commandant Chou Ya-fu. He requested that Kuan Meng be made a subordinate commander and his son Kuan Fu be allowed to accompany his father as head of a battalion of a thousand men. Kuan Meng was actually too old for such a post, but the marquis pressed his request until he succeeded in getting permission. Kuan Meng was profoundly embittered by the reluctance with which his appointment had been granted and decided that he would never be allowed to exercise his authority with any freedom; therefore, whenever a battle took place he always plunged into the midst of the enemy's fortifications. Eventually he died a prisoner in the Wu camp.

According to the rules of warfare, when a father and son are both taking part in a campaign and one of them is killed, the other is permitted to accompany the body home for burial. But Kuan Fu refused to take his father's body back home, declaring passionately, "I would far rather seize the head of the king of Wu or one of his generals and thereby avenge my father's death!" Donning his armor and taking up his halberd, he went about the camp, gathering together twenty or thirty stalwart young friends of his who were willing to accompany him. When the group emerged from the gate of the Han camp, however, none of the men dared advance any further. In the end Kuan Fu, with only two companions and ten or twelve mounted attendants, galloped off to the encampment of the Wu army, fighting his way right up to the headquarters of the Wu general and killing or wounding twenty or thirty of the enemy. When he found that he could advance no further, he wheeled about and galloped back to the Han fortifications. His companions had lost almost all of their attendants, only one returning with the party, and Kuan Fu himself bore over ten serious wounds. Fortunately he happened to have some excellent medicine which he applied to his injuries and thus saved his life.

When his wounds had healed a little, he again spoke to his commanding officer, General Kuan Ho. "Now that I know a little more about the ins and outs of the Wu camp, I beg you to let me make another try!" The general admired his bravery and sympathized with his desire, but he was afraid that this time he would surely lose Kuan Fu. He therefore took the matter up with the grand commandant, but the latter absolutely forbade another such foray.

After the armies of Wu had been defeated, the story of Kuan Fu's daring exploit spread all over the empire. General Kuan Ho recommended him to Emperor Ching, who appointed him as a general of palace attendants, but after a few months he was accused of some violation of the law and dismissed. After this he made his home in Ch'ang-an, where he was known and praised by all the gentlemen of the capital. He was later recalled to government service and during the reign of Emperor Ching reached the post of prime minister of the kingdom of Tai.

When Emperor Ching passed away and the present emperor first came to the throne, he was afraid that the province of Huai-yang, being one of the main crossroads of the empire and noted for its military strength, might become a source of trouble and he therefore shifted Kuan Fu to the position of governor of Huai-yang. In the first year of the *chien-yüan* era [140 B.C.] he summoned Kuan Fu to court to take over the post of master of carriage.

In the second year of the same era Kuan Fu was one time drinking with Tou Fu, the colonel of the guard of the Palace of Lasting Joy, when the two men got into an argument over some question of etiquette. Kuan Fu, who was drunk at the time, ended by striking Tou Fu. Tou Fu, it happened, was a close relative of Empress Dowager Tou, and the emperor, fearful that the empress dowager would demand Kuan Fu's life for the insult, hastily transferred him to the post of prime minister of Yen. Several years later Kuan Fu was accused of some violation of the law and removed from office, after which he returned to private life in Ch'ang-an.

Kuan Fu was a very stubborn and outspoken man, especially when he had had something to drink, and despised any kind of flattery. When he was in the company of members of the aristocracy, influential statesmen, or anyone who was socially his superior, he showed great reluctance to treat them with the proper politeness, and indeed was actually insulting; but when it came to men who were socially inferior, the poorer and more humble they were the greater respect he showed them, behaving as though they were his equals. When he was with a large group, he made a point of recommending and showing favor to his inferiors, a trait for which he was much admired by people.

He had no taste for literature but loved feats of honor and daring and was absolutely true to his word. All his friends were rich or influential citizens, local bosses, or gangster leaders. His wealth amounted to almost ten thousand in gold, and every day he had from twenty or thirty to a hundred men eating at his house. He owned a number of lakes and farm lands in Ying-ch'uan Province from which his relatives and the retainers of the family derived great profit, and this permitted the Kuan family to run the affairs of the province in any way they pleased. The children of Ying-ch'uan made up a song about this which went:

> While the waters of the Ying run bright
> It means the Kuans are still all right;
> But when the waters run polluted
> We'll know they've all been executed!

When Kuan Fu returned to private life in Ch'ang-an, although he was still very wealthy, his political influence was gone, and he soon found the ministers and courtiers, the guests and retainers who had frequented his home in the past gradually drifting away. When Tou Ying likewise lost his political power, he was happy to make friends with Kuan Fu and rid himself once and for all of those acquaintances who had avidly sought his company in the old days but later turned their backs upon him. Kuan Fu in turn profited from his friendship with Tou Ying, which allowed him to mingle with the nobles and members of the imperial family and increase his fame. Thus the two men aided and respected each other and their friendship was like that of father and son. They never tired of the pleasures they shared and their only regret was that they had come to know each other so late in life.

Once, while Kuan Fu was in mourning for one of his relatives, he happened to pay a call on the chancellor T'ien Fen. In the course of the visit T'ien Fen remarked casually, "I was thinking that I would like to go with you some time to call on Tou Ying, but of course at the moment you are in mourning." [4]

"If you would really be so kind as to go with me to visit Tou Ying, I would certainly not let the matter of my mourning stand in the way!" replied Kuan Fu. "If I may have your permission, I will speak to Tou Ying about it at once so that he may make preparations to entertain you. I trust he may expect the honor of your presence early tomorrow morning."

T'ien Fen gave his consent, whereupon Kuan Fu went to tell Tou Ying, repeating to him what T'ien Fen had said. Tou Ying and his wife hastily laid in a large supply of beef and wine and spent the night sweeping and cleaning the house, working until dawn to set up the curtains and lay out the dishes. When daybreak came Tou Ying sent

---

[4] And therefore ought not, according to custom, pay social calls.

his servants to escort T'ien Fen to his house, but noon came and the chancellor had still not appeared.

"You don't think the chancellor has forgotten, do you?" Tou Ying asked Kuan Fu, who replied uneasily, "I was the one who invited him to come, in spite of the fact that I am in mourning. I had better go and see what has happened."

Kuan Fu then rode off in his carriage to fetch the chancellor in person. As it turned out, however, T'ien Fen had only been joking the day before when he consented to the visit and had not the slightest intention of going. When Kuan Fu reached T'ien Fen's house, he found that the chancellor was still in bed. He marched straight into the room and confronted T'ien Fen. "Yesterday you were kind enough to agree to visit Tou Ying, and that gentleman and his wife have made all the preparations! They have been waiting from dawn until now without daring to take a bite to eat!"

T'ien Fen was very startled and began to apologize, saying, "I was a little drunk yesterday and I completely forgot about our conversation." He finally got up and set off in his carriage, but on the way he insisted upon driving very slowly, which made Kuan Fu angrier than ever.

When the party finally got started and the drinking had reached its height, Kuan Fu stood up and performed a dance, requesting the chancellor to follow with a dance of his own, but T'ien Fen merely sat where he was and refused to move. Kuan Fu then began to make insulting remarks from his seat until Tou Ying pulled him to his feet and hurried him out of the room, apologizing to the chancellor for his behavior. T'ien Fen stayed and drank until evening when, having enjoyed himself thoroughly, he took his leave.

Some time later, T'ien Fen sent his retainer Chi Fu to ask Tou Ying if he would mind turning over to him some farm land south of the city which Tou Ying owned. Tou Ying was furious when he heard the request. "Though I am only an old man who has been abandoned by his friends and though the chancellor is a high official, he has absolutely no right to try to seize my possessions from me like this! I refuse to give up the land!"

When Kuan Fu heard of the incident he cursed Chi Fu roundly. Chi Fu for his part was sorry to see enmity develop between Tou Ying and

T'ien Fen and so he did his best to smooth over the affair, returning to T'ien Fen with excuses which he himself had invented. "After all, Tou Ying is an old man and will die soon. Surely you can do without the land for a while. You had better wait a bit," he said.

Later on, however, T'ien Fen chanced to hear that Tou Ying and Kuan Fu had in fact been greatly angered at his request and had refused to hand over the land, whereupon he too became incensed. "Once in the past Tou Ying's son killed a man but I managed to save him from punishment. I have always treated Tou Ying with respect and done everything he has asked me to. Why should he begrudge me a few acres of land? As for Kuan Fu, what does he have to say in the matter? If that is the way they act, I will make no further requests for land!" Because of this T'ien Fen came to bear a deep grudge against Kuan Fu and Tou Ying.

In the spring of the fourth year of *yüan-kuang* [131 B.C.] T'ien Fen reported to the emperor that Kuan Fu's family in Ying-ch'uan were behaving with complete disregard for the law and causing great hardship to the common people. He requested that their conduct be investigated. "It is up to you as chancellor to settle such matters," replied the emperor. "Why ask me about it?" Meanwhile Kuan Fu happened to learn about certain secret dealings of the chancellor involving illegal profits, bribes received from the king of Huai-nan, and agreements made between the king and the chancellor. The retainers of T'ien Fen and Kuan Fu undertook to mediate between the two men and eventually persuaded them to cease their attacks and let each other alone.

In the summer of the same year T'ien Fen married the daughter of Liu Chia, the king of Yen. Empress Dowager Wang issued an edict inviting all of the nobles and members of the imperial family to visit T'ien Fen and offer their congratulations. Tou Ying called on Kuan Fu and asked him to go with him to T'ien Fen's house, but Kuan Fu declined. "I have already gotten into trouble with the chancellor on several occasions by trying to drink with him. And anyway at the moment he and I are not on good terms."

"But that matter has been all settled!" said Tou Ying, and kept insisting until Kuan Fu finally agreed to join him. When the drinking had reached its height, T'ien Fen arose and proposed a toast, whereupon all the guests moved off their mats and bowed.[5] This over, Tou Ying proposed a toast, but only his old friends moved off their mats, the rest of the company simply kneeling where they were.

Kuan Fu, highly displeased at the way things were going, got up with a container of wine and went over to pour a drink for T'ien Fen. "I can't drink a whole cup!" T'ien Fen protested, rising to his knees on the mat.

Kuan Fu was angrier than ever, but he gave a forced laugh and said, "Come, sir, surely a man of your eminence. . . . I insist!" But T'ien Fen refused to drink.

Kuan Fu went next with the wine container to the marquis of Lin-ju. The marquis was at the moment busy whispering in the ear of Ch'eng Pu-shih, and he too failed to get off his mat. Kuan Fu, unable to find any other outlet for his rage, began to curse the marquis. "On ordinary days you go around speaking ill of Ch'eng Pu-shih and telling people he isn't worth a cent, and yet today all of a sudden when one of your elders comes and offers you a drink, you start cooing in Ch'eng Pu-shih's ear like a love-sick maiden!"

T'ien Fen called Kuan Fu aside and said, "Ch'eng Pu-shih and Li Kuang are the commanders of the guards at the Eastern and Western Palaces, you know.[6] If you start insulting General Ch'eng in front of everyone, won't you be casting aspersions on your friend General Li as well?"

"Let them cut off my head or rip open my breast right now!" said Kuan Fu. "What do I care about Ch'eng or Li?"

With this the guests began to excuse themselves and go out to the toilet, one by one drifting away from the party. When Tou Ying was about to leave, he motioned to Kuan Fu to go out with him, but T'ien Fen exclaimed angrily, "I was at fault for ever letting Kuan Fu behave in such an arrogant manner!" and ordered his horsemen to detain Kuan Fu. Thus when Kuan Fu tried to leave the house he found he

[5] As in Japan today, the highest degree of courtesy was expressed by sliding all the way off one's mat and kneeling on the floor. A lesser degree of courtesy was expressed by straightening up on the mat and coming to a kneeling position.

[6] The Eastern Palace, of which Ch'eng Pu-shih was the commander of the guard, was the residence of the empress dowager; the Western Palace was another name for the emperor's palace.

could not get out. Chi Fu jumped up and came forward to apologize, pushing Kuan Fu by the neck and trying to make him kneel down and apologize too, but Kuan Fu only grew angrier than ever and refused to offer any apology.

T'ien Fen then signaled to his horsemen to bind Kuan Fu and take him to the post station. After this he sent for his chief secretary and, explaining that he had invited the members of the imperial family to his house in accordance with an edict from the empress dowager, instructed him to draw up charges against Kuan Fu for insulting the guests and failing to show the proper respect, and to have him put into chains in the Inquiry Room. He then proceeded to investigate the earlier rumors of the misconduct of Kuan Fu's relatives and sent his officers out in parties to arrest all the branches of the Kuan family and charge them with crimes punishable by public execution.

Tou Ying was greatly distressed by this turn of events and, laying out funds from his own resources, sent his retainers to plead on Kuan Fu's behalf, but they were unable to obtain his release. T'ien Fen's officers did their best to carry out their orders but the other members of the Kuan family all succeeded in escaping into hiding. Since Kuan Fu was bound and imprisoned, he had no opportunity to report to the emperor what he knew about T'ien Fen's secret dealings.

Tou Ying tried everything he could to save Kuan Fu. His wife warned him, saying, "Kuan Fu has offended the chancellor and gotten into trouble with Empress Dowager Wang and her whole family. How can you possibly save him?" But Tou Ying replied, "I won the title of marquis by my own efforts and if necessary I will give it up of my own accord and have no regrets. In any event I could not think of leaving Kuan Fu to die while I am still alive!"

Then, without informing his family, he slipped out of the house and sent a letter to the emperor. He was immediately summoned to an audience at which he explained in detail that Kuan Fu's misconduct had been due simply to an excess of wine and did not deserve the death penalty. The emperor expressed his agreement and even invited Tou Ying to dine in the palace. "However," he added, "you will have to go to the Eastern Palace and explain things to the empress dowager."

Proceeding to the court of the empress dowager, Tou Ying began to point out with zeal all of Kuan Fu's good points. He explained that Kuan Fu had behaved rudely when he was in his cups, but that the chancellor was trying to use other charges to build a false case against him. The chancellor, however, who was also present, set out with equal zeal to accuse Kuan Fu of arrogant and unlawful conduct, claiming that he was guilty of rebellion and treason. Tou Ying, judging that no other course would be of any avail, finally began to speak ill of the chancellor himself.

T'ien Fen replied to these charges as follows: "Today the world is blessed with peace and harmony, and I have the special fortune to belong to a family which is related to the imperial house by marriage. I am the sort of man who delights in music, in dogs and horses, gardens and houses; I have a fondness for singers, actors, and clever craftsmen. In this respect I am different from Tou Ying and Kuan Fu, who summon to their homes all the powerful bosses and daring young men of the empire and sit day and night talking with them; whose hearts are set on slander and whose minds are full of deceit; who, when they are not searching the heavens for omens of change, are scanning the earth to plot their campaigns, always with a crafty eye fixed upon the relations between the emperor and the empress dowager, praying that the empire may be convulsed by some strife and that they may thereby win great merit for themselves! To what lengths men like. Tou Ying and his party will go, I would not venture to guess!"

The emperor then assembled the ministers of his court and asked them which of the two contestants, Tou Ying or T'ien Fen, they believed was in the right. The imperial secretary Han An-kuo gave his opinion as follows: "As Tou Ying has pointed out, Kuan Fu's father died in the service of the dynasty, while Kuan Fu himself seized his spear and galloped into the midst of the rebel camp of Wu, facing untold danger. He bore on his body a dozen wounds and his fame outshone that of every other soldier in the three armies. Truly he is one of the bravest men of the empire. Now he has committed no serious offense, but only become involved in a petty argument over a cup of wine. There is therefore no reason, as Tou Ying says, to drag in other charges and condemn him to execution. In this respect Tou Ying's opinion is correct.

"On the other hand the chancellor has charged Kuan Fu with associating with evil and lawless men, oppressing the poor, amassing a fortune that runs into millions, running his affairs in Ying-ch'uan in an arbitrary and tyrannical manner, insulting the dignity of the imperial house, and molesting men who are flesh and blood of that family. As the proverb says, 'When the branches grow bigger than the roots, then something must break; when the shins grow mightier than the thighs, then something must give.' Thus the opinion of the chancellor is also correct. It remains only for our enlightened sovereign to decide in the case."

The master of titles chief commandant Chi An expressed himself in agreement with Tou Ying, and the prefect of the capital Cheng Tang-shih also said he thought Tou Ying was right, though in the course of the deliberations he became frightened and did not dare to defend his assertion. (None of the other officials ventured to offer any opinion at all.) The emperor was furious with Cheng Tang-shih and said, "All the time you go around discoursing on the relative merits and faults of Tou Ying and T'ien Fen, and yet today when I summon you to court to give your opinion, you cringe and hang your head like a pony in the shafts! I ought to cut off your head as well!"

With this the emperor dismissed the court and, rising from his seat, retired to the inner palace to wait on his mother, Empress Dowager Wang, while she took her meal. The empress dowager had sent her observers to court and they had already reported to her in detail the discussions which had taken place. She was in a rage and refused to eat. "Even while I am alive, people go about insulting my brother T'ien Fen! After I have passed on, I have no doubt that they will gobble him up like so much fish and flesh! And you—you are no man of stone! You are mortal the same as everyone else! Can't you see that these men are only biding their time and pretending to be docile while you are still alive? After your days are ended, do you think there is one of them who can be trusted?"

The emperor apologized, saying, "It is only because T'ien Fen and Tou Ying are both related to the imperial family by marriage that I brought the matter before the court for discussion. If it were not for that, the affair could be left for any law officer to settle."

At this time the chief of palace attendants Shih Chien drew up for the emperor a list of the opinions presented for and against the two contestants. When the court session was over T'ien Fen left the palace and went to the gate where the carriages were drawn up. Calling to the imperial secretary Han An-kuo to join him in his carriage, he began to berate him angrily. "You and I together are pitted against a single, bald-headed old man, Tou Ying! Why did you have to be so timid in expressing your opinion, like a rat trying to look both ways at once?"

After considering for some time, Han An-kuo replied, "You ought to think a little more highly of yourself. If Tou Ying abuses you, you should remove your cap, undo your seals of office and, handing them over to the emperor, say, 'Because of my family connections I have graciously been permitted to serve Your Majesty, but I am basically unfit for the position. Everything that Tou Ying has said about me is quite correct!' In that case the emperor would be sure to admire your humility and would refuse to accept your resignation. As for Tou Ying, he would be so ashamed of himself that he would retire to his home and, biting his tongue with remorse, take his own life. Instead of that, when someone abuses you, you begin abusing him back until the two of you end up quarreling like a pair of fishwives! This is surely not a very dignified way to behave!"

"I am sorry," said T'ien Fen, acknowledging his fault. "In the heat of the argument I became so carried away that it never occurred to me to do such a thing."

Shortly after, the emperor ordered the imperial secretary Han An-kuo to draw up charges against Tou Ying, accusing him of making statements in Kuan Fu's defense that were wholly false and irresponsible. Tou Ying was impeached and imprisoned in the custody of the head of criminal affairs for the imperial family.

Previously, at the end of Emperor Ching's reign, Tou Ying had received a testamentary edict from the emperor stating, "If you ever find yourself in any difficulty, you should appeal your case directly to the throne." Now Kuan Fu had been arrested and accused of a crime punishable by death for himself and his whole family, and the situation grew more serious each day. Moreover, none of the officials dared make any further attempt to explain Tou Ying's position to the emperor. Tou Ying therefore directed his brother's son to write a letter on his behalf to the emperor requesting that he be granted another audience. The letter was submitted to the throne, but when the master of documents searched the files, he could find no such testamentary edict among the papers dating from the time of Emperor Ching's decease. The only copy of the edict in existence, it appeared, was the one preserved in Tou Ying's house, bearing the seal of Tou Ying's private secretary. Hence Tou Ying was charged with having forged an edict of the former emperor, a crime punishable by execution in the market place.

In the tenth month of the fifth year of *yüan-kuang* [130 B.C.] Kuan Fu and all the members of his family were condemned to execution. After some time, news of this reached Tou Ying in jail. He was deeply embittered and, being afflicted with a swelling in his joints, refused to eat anything in hopes that he would soon die. Someone assured him, however, that the emperor had no intention of executing him, and with this he took heart and began to eat again so that his illness improved. The emperor and his ministers had in fact decided not to sentence Tou Ying to death, but just then rumors began to reach the emperor's ears that Tou Ying was speaking evilly of him, and so on the last day of the twelfth month the emperor ordered the death sentence.[7] Tou Ying was executed in the market place of Wei-ch'eng.

The following spring, T'ien Fen, the marquis of Wu-an, fell ill; he spent all his time crying out "I was at fault!" and begging forgiveness for his crimes. When he summoned sorcerers with the power to discern ghosts and asked them what they saw, they reported that they could see Tou Ying and Kuan Fu standing watch together by his bedside and preparing to kill him. Before long T'ien Fen died and his son T'ien T'ien succeeded to the marquisate. In the third year of the era *yüan-so* [126 B.C.] T'ien T'ien was tried on charges of disrespect for

[7] Since spring is the time when life returns to the earth, it was considered unlucky to perform executions in the spring, and the beginning of spring (the first month) was often accompanied by an amnesty. T'ien Fen therefore had to work quickly to spread his rumors in order to dispose of his enemy before the end of the twelfth month.

the throne because he came to the palace dressed in short robes, and was deprived of his territory.

Sometime afterwards it was discovered that Liu An, the king of Huai-nan, had been plotting a revolt. Liu An and his conspirators were brought to justice, and in the course of the investigations it was found that once in the past, when the king paid a visit to court, T'ien Fen, then grand commandant, had driven out as far as Pa-shang to greet him. "The emperor has not yet designated an heir apparent," T'ien Fen was reported to have said, "while Your Highness is the most worthy among the kings, being a grandson of the founder of the dynasty, Kao-tsu. If there should be a funeral in the imperial palace, I cannot think of anyone but you who would be suitable to succeed to the throne!" The king of Huai-nan, it was said, was greatly pleased with these words and presented T'ien Fen with generous gifts of money and goods.

From the time of the Tou Ying affair the emperor no longer put any trust in T'ien Fen, but merely tolerated him because he was a brother of the empress dowager. When he heard these reports of money presented to T'ien Fen by the king of Huai-nan, he declared, "If T'ien Fen were still around today I would have him and his whole family executed!"

The Grand Historian remarks: Tou Ying and T'ien Fen both commanded great respect because they belonged to families related to the throne by marriage. Kuan Fu became famous as a result of a daring exploit of the moment; Tou Ying won promotion in the Wu and Ch'u rebellion; but T'ien Fen's position of honor was more a matter of time and fortunate circumstance.[8]

Tou Ying, however, did not know how to change with the times, and Kuan Fu, though a man of no learning, refused to be humble. Both men tried to help each other, but they succeeded only in bringing disaster upon themselves.

T'ien Fen enjoyed great honor and loved the feel of power, but because of the resentment occasioned by a single cup of wine, he set

---

[8] I.e., that Emperor Ching died young and T'ien.Fen's sister, Empress Dowager Wang, was able to exercise great power.

about to destroy two men. How pitiful! Those who attempt to vent their anger on innocent persons can never hope to live for long. Those who fail to win the commendation of the mass of lesser men will end by suffering their slanders. Alas, alas! No misfortune ever comes without due cause!

Valorous in the face of the enemy, good to his men, he gave no petty or vexatious orders, and for this reason his subordinates looked up to him with admiration. Thus I made The Biography of General Li.

General Li Kuang was a native of Ch'eng-chi in Lung-hsi Province. Among his ancestors was Li Hsin, a general of the state of Ch'in, who pursued and captured Tan, the crown prince of Yen.[1] The family originally lived in Huai-li but later moved to Ch'eng-chi. The art of archery had been handed down in the family for generations.

In the fourteenth year of Emperor Wen's reign [166 B.C.] the Hsiung-nu entered the Hsiao Pass in great numbers. Li Kuang, as the son of a distinguished family, was allowed to join the army in the attack on the barbarians. He proved himself a skillful horseman and archer, killing and capturing a number of the enemy, and was rewarded with the position of palace attendant at the Han court. His cousin Li Ts'ai was also made a palace attendant. Both men served as mounted guards to the emperor and received a stipend of eight hundred piculs of grain. Li Kuang always accompanied Emperor Wen on his hunting expeditions. The emperor, observing how he charged up to the animal pits, broke through the palisades, and struck down the most ferocious beasts, remarked, "What a pity you were not born at a better time! Had you lived in the age of Emperor Kao-tsu, you would have had no trouble in winning a marquisate of at least ten thousand households!"

When Emperor Ching came to the throne, Li Kuang was made chief commandant of Lung-hsi; later he was transferred to the post of general of palace horsemen. At the time of the revolt of Wu and Ch'u, he served as a cavalry commander under the grand commandant Chou Ya-fu, joining in the attack on the armies of Wu and Ch'u, capturing the enemy pennants, and distinguishing himself at the battle of

---

[1] He had sent a man to the Ch'in court in an unsuccessful attempt to assassinate the king who later became the First Emperor of the Ch'in.

Ch'ang-i. But because he had accepted the seals of a general from the king of Liang without authorization from the Han government, he was not rewarded for his achievements when he returned to the capital.

Following this he was transferred to the post of governor of Shang-ku Province, where he engaged in almost daily skirmishes with the Hsiung-nu. The director of dependent states Kung-sun K'un-yeh went to the emperor and, with tears in his eyes, said, "There is no one in the empire to match Li Kuang for skill and spirit and yet, trusting to his own ability, he repeatedly engages the enemy in battle. I am afraid one day we will lose him!" The emperor therefore transferred him to the post of governor of Shang Province.[2]

At this time the Hsiung-nu invaded Shang Province in great force. Emperor Ching sent one of his trusted eunuchs to join Li Kuang, ordering him to train the troops and lead them in an attack on the Hsiung-nu. The eunuch, leading a group of twenty or thirty horsemen, was casually riding about the countryside one day when he caught sight of three Hsiung-nu riders and engaged them in a fight. The three Hsiung-nu, however, began circling the party and shooting as they went until they had wounded the eunuch and were near to killing all of his horsemen. The eunuch barely managed to flee back to the place where Li Kuang was. "They must be out hunting eagles!" said Li Kuang, and galloped off with a hundred horsemen in pursuit of the three Hsiung-nu. The Hsiung-nu, having lost their horses, fled on foot. After they had journeyed twenty or thirty *li,* Li Kuang caught up with them and, ordering his horsemen to fan out to the left and right of them, began to shoot at them. He killed two with his arrows and took the third one alive. As he had guessed, they were eagle hunters.

Li Kuang had bound his prisoner and remounted his horse, when he spied several thousand Hsiung-nu horsemen in the distance. The Hsiung-nu, catching sight of Li Kuang and his men, supposed that they were a decoy sent out from the main body of the Han forces to lure them into combat. They made for a nearby hill in alarm and drew up their ranks on its crest.

[2] The thirty-one characters which follow at this point in the text have been shifted in the translation to a point farther along in the narrative, following the reading in the parallel passage in *Han shu* 54.

Li Kuang's horsemen were thoroughly terrified and begged him to flee back to camp as quickly as possible, but he replied, "We are twenty or thirty *li* away from the main army. With only a hundred of us, if we were to try to make a dash for it, the Hsiung-nu would be after us in no time and would shoot down every one of us. But if we stay where we are, they are bound to think we are a decoy from the main army and will not dare to attack!"

Instead of retreating, therefore, Li Kuang gave the order to his men to advance. When they had reached a point some two *li* from the Hsiung-nu ranks, he told his men, "Dismount and undo your saddles!"

"But there are too many of them and they are almost on top of us!" his men protested. "What will we do if they attack?"

"They expect us to run away," said Li Kuang. "But now if we all undo our saddles and show them we have no intention of fleeing, they will be more convinced than ever that there is something afoot."

The Hsiung-nu in fact did not venture to attack, but sent out one of their leaders on a white horse to reconnoitre. Li Kuang mounted again and, with ten or so of his horsemen, galloped after the barbarian leader and shot him down. Then he returned to his group and, undoing his saddle, ordered his men to turn loose their horses and lie down on the ground. By this time night was falling and the Hsiung-nu, thoroughly suspicious of what they had seen, still had not ventured to attack. They concluded that the Han leaders must have concealed soldiers in the area and be planning to fall upon them in the dark, and so during the night the Hsiung-nu chiefs and their men all withdrew. When dawn came Li Kuang finally managed to return with his group to the main army, which, having no idea where he had gone, had been unable to follow him.

After this Li Kuang was assigned to the governorship of several other border provinces in succession, returning finally to Shang Province. In the course of these moves he served as governor of Lung-hsi, Pei-ti, Tai, and Yün-chung Provinces and in each won fame for his fighting.

After some time, Emperor Ching passed away and the present emperor came to the throne. The emperor's advisers informed him of Li Kuang's fame as a general, and he made Li Kuang the colonel of the guard of the Eternal Palace, while allowing him to retain the governorship of Shang Province.

At this time Ch'eng Pu-chih was the colonel of the guard of the Palace of Lasting Joy. Ch'eng Pu-chih had been a governor in the border provinces and a garrison general at the same time as Li Kuang. When Li Kuang went out on expeditions to attack the Hsiung-nu, he never bothered to form his men into battalions and companies. He would make camp wherever he found water and grass, leaving his men to set up their quarters in any way they thought convenient. He never had sentries circling the camp at night and beating on cooking pots, as was the custom, and in his headquarters he kept records and other clerical work down to a minimum. He always sent out scouts some distance around the camp, however, and he had never met with any particular mishap.

Ch'eng Pu-chih, on the other hand, always kept his men in strict battalion and company formation. The sentries banged on the cooking pots, his officers worked over their records and reports until dawn, and no one in his army got any rest. He likewise had never had any mishaps. Ch'eng Pu-chih once expressed the opinion, "Although Li Kuang runs his army in a very simple fashion, if the enemy should ever swoop down on him suddenly he would have no way to hold them off. His men enjoy plenty of idleness and pleasure, and for that reason they are all eager to fight to the death for him. Life in my army may be a good deal more irksome, but at least I know that the enemy will never catch me napping!"

Li Kuang and Ch'eng Pu-chih were both famous generals at this time, but the Hsiung-nu were more afraid of Li Kuang's strategies, while the Han soldiers for the most part preferred to serve under him and disliked being under Ch'eng Pu-chih's command. Ch'eng Pu-chih advanced to the position of palace counselor under Emperor Ching because of the outspoken advice he gave the emperor on several occasions. He was a man of great integrity and very conscientious in matters of form and law.

Sometime later, the Han leaders attempted to entice the *Shan-yü* into entering the city of Ma-i, concealing a large force of men in the valley around the city to ambush the Hsiung-nu. At this time Li Kuang was appointed as cavalry general under the command of Han An-kuo, the leader of the supporting army. As it happened, however, the *Shan-yü* discovered the plot and escaped in time, so that neither Li Kuang nor any of the other generals connected with the plot achieved any merit.

Four years later [129 B.C.] Li Kuang, because of his services as colonel of the guard, was made a general and sent north from Yen-men to attack the Hsiung-nu. But the Hsiung-nu force he was pitted against turned out to be too numerous and succeeded in defeating Li Kuang's army and capturing him alive.

The *Shan-yü* had for a long time heard of Li Kuang's excellence as a fighter and had given orders, "If you get hold of Li Kuang, take him alive and bring him to me!" As it turned out, the barbarian horsemen did manage to capture Li Kuang and, since he was badly wounded, they strung a litter between two horses and, laying him on it, proceeded on their way about ten *li*. Li Kuang pretended to be dead but managed to peer around him and noticed that close by his side was a young Hsiung-nu boy mounted on a fine horse. Suddenly he leaped out of the litter and onto the boy's horse, seizing his bow and pushing him off the horse. Then, whipping the horse to full gallop, he dashed off to the south. After traveling twenty or thirty *li* he succeeded in catching up with what was left of his army and led the men back across the border into Han territory. While he was making his escape, several hundred horsemen from the party that had captured him came in pursuit, but he turned and shot at them with the bow he had snatched from the boy, killing several of his pursuers, and was thus able to escape.

When he got back to the capital, he was turned over to the law officials, who recommended that he be executed for losing so many of his men and being captured alive. He was allowed to ransom his life and was reduced to the status of commoner.

Following this, Li Kuang lived in retirement for several years, spending his time hunting. His home was in Lan-t'ien, among the Southern Mountains, adjoining the estate of Kuan Ch'iang, the grandson of Kuan Ying, the former marquis of Ying-yin.

One evening Li Kuang, having spent the afternoon drinking with some people out in the fields, was on his way back home, accompanied by a rider attendant, when he passed the watch station at Pa-ling. The watchman, who was drunk at the time, yelled at Li Kuang to halt.

"This is the former General Li," said Li Kuang's man.

"Even present generals are not allowed to go wandering around at night, much less former ones!" the watchman retorted, and made Li Kuang halt and spend the night in the watch station.

Shortly after this, the Hsiung-nu invaded Liao-hsi, murdered its governor, and defeated General Han An-kuo. Han An-kuo was transferred to Yu-pei-p'ing, where he died, and the emperor forthwith summoned Li Kuang to be the new governor of Yu-pei-p'ing. When he accepted the post, Li Kuang asked that the watchman of Pa-ling be ordered to accompany him, and as soon as the man reported for duty Li Kuang had him executed.[3]

After Li Kuang took over in Yu-pei-p'ing, the Hsiung-nu, who were familiar with his reputation and called him "The Flying General," stayed away from the region for several years and did not dare to invade Yu-pei-p'ing.

Li Kuang was out hunting one time when he spied a rock in the grass which he mistook for a tiger. He shot an arrow at the rock and hit it with such force that the tip of the arrow embedded itself in the rock. Later, when he discovered that it was a rock, he tried shooting at it again, but he was unable to pierce it a second time.

Whatever province Li Kuang had been in in the past, whenever he heard that there was a tiger in the vicinity he always went out to shoot it in person. When he got to Yu-pei-p'ing he likewise went out one time to hunt a tiger. The beast sprang at him and wounded him, but he finally managed to shoot it dead.

Li Kuang was completely free of avarice. Whenever he received a reward of some kind, he at once divided it among those in his command, and he was content to eat and drink the same things as his men. For over forty years he received a salary of two thousand piculs, but when he died he left no fortune behind. He never discussed matters of

---

[3] The parallel text in *Han shu* 54 records that Li Kuang wrote a letter to the emperor apologizing for this act of personal vengeance, but the emperor replied that he expected his generals to be merciless so that they would inspire awe in their men and terrify the enemy.

family wealth. He was a tall man with long, apelike arms. His skill at
archery seems to have been an inborn talent, for none of his descendants or others who studied under him were ever able to equal his
prowess. He was a very clumsy speaker and never had much to say.
When he was with others he would draw diagrams on the ground to
explain his military tactics or set up targets of various widths and
shoot at them with his friends, the loser being forced to drink. In fact,
archery remained to the end of his life his chief source of amusement.

When he was leading his troops through a barren region and they
came upon some water, he would not go near it until all his men had
finished drinking. Similarly he would not eat until every one of his
men had been fed. He was very lenient with his men and did nothing
to vex them, so that they all loved him and were happy to serve under
him. Even when the enemy was attacking, it was his custom never to
discharge his arrows unless his opponent was within twenty or thirty
paces and he believed he could score a hit. When he did discharge an
arrow, however, the bowstring had no sooner sounded than his victim
would fall to the ground. Because of this peculiar habit he often found
himself in considerable difficulty when he was leading his troops against
an enemy, and this is also the reason, it is said, that he was occasionally
wounded when he went out hunting wild beasts.

Sometime after Li Kuang was made governor of Yu-pei-p'ing, Shih
Chien died, and Li Kuang was summoned to take his place as chief of
palace attendants.

In the sixth year of *yüan-so* [123 B.C.] Li Kuang was again made a
general and sent with the general in chief Wei Ch'ing to proceed
north from Ting-hsiang and attack the Hsiung-nu. Most of the other
generals who took part in the expedition killed or captured a sufficient
number of the enemy to be rewarded for their achievements by being
made marquises, but Li Kuang's army won no distinction.

Three years later Li Kuang, as chief of palace attendants, was sent
to lead a force of four thousand cavalry north from Yu-pei-p'ing.
Chang Ch'ien, the Po-wang marquis, leading ten thousand cavalry,
rode out with Li Kuang but took a somewhat different route. When
Li Kuang had advanced several hundred *li* into enemy territory, the
Hsiung-nu leader known as the Wise King of the Left appeared with

forty thousand cavalry and surrounded Li Kuang's army. His men were all terrified, but Li Kuang ordered his son Li Kan to gallop out to meet the enemy. Li Kan, accompanied by only twenty or thirty riders, dashed straight through the Hsiung-nu horsemen, scattering them to left and right, and then returned to his father's side, saying, "These barbarians are easy enough to deal with!" After this Li Kuang's men were somewhat reassured.

Li Kuang ordered his men to draw up in a circle with their ranks facing outward. The enemy charged furiously down on them and the arrows fell like rain. Over half the Han soldiers were killed, and their arrows were almost gone. Li Kuang then ordered the men to load their bows and hold them in readiness, but not to discharge them, while he himself, with his huge yellow crossbow, shot at the sub-commander of the enemy force and killed several of the barbarians. After this the enemy began to fall back a little.

By this time night had begun to fall. Every one of Li Kuang's officers and men had turned white with fear, but Li Kuang, as calm and confident as though nothing had happened, worked to get his ranks into better formation. After this the men knew that they could never match his bravery.

The following day Li Kuang once more fought off the enemy, and in the meantime Chang Ch'ien at last arrived with his army. The Hsiung-nu forces withdrew and the Han armies likewise retreated, being in no condition to pursue them. By this time Li Kuang's army had been practically wiped out. When the two leaders returned to the capital, they were called to account before the law. Chang Ch'ien was condemned to death for failing to keep his rendezvous with Li Kuang at the appointed time, but on payment of a fine he was allowed to become a commoner. In the case of Li Kuang it was decided that his achievements and his failures canceled each other out and he was given no reward.

Li Kuang's cousin Li Ts'ai had begun his career along with Li Kuang as an attendant at the court of Emperor Wen. During the reign of Emperor Ching, Li Ts'ai managed to accumulate sufficient merit to advance to the position of a two thousand picul official, and under the present emperor he became prime minister of Tai. In the fifth year of *yüan-so* [124 B.C.] he was appointed a general of light carriage and accompanied the general in chief Wei Ch'ing in an attack on the Hsiung-nu Wise King of the Right. His achievements in this campaign placed him in the middle group of those who were to receive rewards and he was accordingly enfeoffed as marquis of Lo-an. In the second year of *yüan-shou* [121 B.C.] he replaced Kung-sun Hung as chancellor of the central court. In ability one would be obliged to rank Li Ts'ai very close to the bottom, and his reputation came nowhere near to equaling that of Li Kuang. And yet, although Li Kuang never managed to obtain a fief and never rose higher than one of the nine lower offices of the government, that of colonel of the guard, his cousin Li Ts'ai was enfeoffed as a marquis and eventually reached the position of chancellor, one of the three highest posts. Even some of Li Kuang's own officers and men succeeded in becoming marquises.

Li Kuang was once chatting with Wang So, a diviner who told men's fortunes by the configurations of the sky, and remarked on this fact. "Ever since the Han started attacking the Hsiung-nu, I have never failed to be in the fight. I've had men in my command who were company commanders or even lower and who didn't even have the ability of average men, and yet twenty or thirty of them have won marquisates on the strength of their achievements in attacking the barbarian armies. I have never been behind anyone else in doing my duty. Why is it I have never won an ounce of distinction so that I could be enfeoffed like the others? Is it that I just don't have the kind of face to become a marquis? Or is it all a matter of fate?"

"Think carefully, general," replied Wang So. "Isn't there something in the past that you regret having done?"

"Once, when I was governor of Lung-hsi, the Ch'iang tribes in the west started a revolt. I tried to talk them into surrendering, and in fact persuaded over eight hundred of them to give themselves up. But then I went back on my word and killed them all the very same day. I have never ceased to regret what I did. But that's the only thing I can think of."

"Nothing brings greater misfortune than killing those who have already surrendered to you," said Wang So. "This is the reason, general, that you have never gotten to be a marquis!"

Two years later the general in chief Wei Ch'ing and the general of swift cavalry Ho Ch'ü-ping set off with a large force to attack the Hsiung-nu. Li Kuang several times asked to be allowed to join them, but the emperor considered that he was too old and would not permit him to go. After some time, however, the emperor changed his mind and gave his consent, appointing him as general of the vanguard. The time was the fourth year of *yüan-shou* [119 B.C.].

Li Kuang accordingly joined the general in chief Wei Ch'ing and set off to attack the Hsiung-nu. After the group had crossed the border, Wei Ch'ing captured one of the enemy and learned the whereabouts of the *Shan-yü*. He therefore decided to take his own best troops and make a dash for the spot, ordering Li Kuang to join forces with the general of the right Chao I-chi and ride around by the eastern road. The eastern road was rather long and roundabout and, since there was little water or grass in the region, it presented a difficult route for a large army to pass over. Li Kuang therefore asked Wei Ch'ing to change the order. "I have been appointed as general of the vanguard," he said, "and yet now you have shifted my position and ordered me to go around by the east. I have been fighting the Hsiung-nu ever since I was old enough to wear my hair bound up, and now I would like to have just one chance to get at the *Shan-yü*. I beg you to let me stay in the vanguard and advance and fight to the death with him!"

Wei Ch'ing had been warned in private by the emperor that Li Kuang was an old man and had already had a lot of bad luck in the past. "Don't let him try to get at the *Shan-yü,* or he will probably make a mess of things!" the emperor had said. Also, at this time Kung-sun Ao, who had recently been deprived of his marquisate, was serving as a general under Wei Ch'ing, and Wei Ch'ing wanted to take him along with him in his attack on the *Shan-yü* so that Kung-sun Ao would have a chance to win some distinction. For these reasons he removed Li Kuang from his post of general of the vanguard.

Li Kuang was aware of all this and tried his best to get out of obeying the order, but Wei Ch'ing refused to listen to his arguments. Instead he sent one of his clerks with a sealed letter to Li Kuang's tent and orders to "proceed to your division at once in accordance with the instructions herein!" Li Kuang did not even bother to take leave of Wei Ch'ing but got up and went straight to his division, burning with rage and indignation and, leading his troops to join those of the general of the right Chao I-chi, set out by the eastern road. Lacking proper guides, however, they lost their way and failed to meet up with Wei Ch'ing at the appointed time. Wei Ch'ing in the meantime engaged the *Shan-yü* in battle, but the latter fled and Wei Ch'ing, being unable to capture him, was forced to turn back south again. After crossing the desert, he joined up with the forces of Li Kuang and Chao I-chi.

When Li Kuang had finished making his report to Wei Ch'ing and returned to his own camp, Wei Ch'ing sent over his clerk with the customary gifts of dried rice and thick wine for Li Kuang. While the clerk was there, he began to inquire how it happened that Li Kuang and Chao I-chi had lost their way, since Wei Ch'ing had to make a detailed report to the emperor on what had happened to the armies. Li Kuang, however, refused to answer his questions.

Wei Ch'ing sent his clerk again to reprimand Li Kuang in the strongest terms and order him to report to general headquarters at once and answer a list of charges that had been drawn up against him. Li Kuang replied, "None of my commanders was at fault. I was the one who caused us to lose our way. I will send in a report myself."

Then he went in person to headquarters and, when he got there, said to his officers, "Since I was old enough to wear my hair bound up, I have fought over seventy engagements, large and small, with the Hsiung-nu. This time I was fortunate enough to join the general in chief in a campaign against the soldiers of the *Shan-yü* himself, but he shifted me to another division and sent me riding around by the long way. On top of that, I lost my way. Heaven must have planned it this way! Now I am over sixty—much too old to stand up to a bunch of petty clerks and their list of charges!" Then he drew his sword and cut his throat.

All the officers and men in his army wept at the news of his death, and when word reached the common people, those who had known him and those who had not, old men and young boys alike, were all moved to tears by his fate. Chao I-chi was handed over to the law officials and sentenced to death, but on payment of a fine he was allowed to become a commoner.

Li Kuang had three sons, Tang-hu, Chiao, and Kan, all of whom were palace attendants. One day when the present emperor was amusing himself with his young favorite, Han Yen, the boy behaved so impertinently that Li Tang-hu struck him and drove him from the room. The emperor was much impressed with Tang-hu's courage. Li Tang-hu died young. Li Chiao was made governor of Tai Province. He and Tang-hu both died before their father. Tang-hu had a son named Li Ling who was born shortly after Tang-hu died. Li Kan was serving in the army under the general of light cavalry Ho Ch'ü-ping when Li Kuang committed suicide.

The year after Li Kuang's death his cousin Li Ts'ai, who was serving as chancellor at the time, was accused of appropriating land that belonged to the funerary park of Emperor Ching. He was to be handed over to the law officials for trial, but he too committed suicide rather than face being sent to prison, and his fief was abolished.

Li Kan served as a commander under Ho Ch'ü-ping, taking part in an attack on the Hsiung-nu Wise King of the Left. He fought bravely in the attack, seizing the pennants of the barbarian king and cutting off many heads. He was rewarded by being enfeoffed as a marquis in the area within the Pass, receiving the revenue from a city of two hundred households. In addition he was appointed to replace his father, Li Kuang, as chief of palace attendants.

Sometime afterwards, deeply resentful at the general in chief Wei Ch'ing for having brought about his father's disgrace, he struck and wounded Wei Ch'ing. Wei Ch'ing, however, hushed up the incident and said nothing about it. Shortly afterwards, Li Kan accompanied the emperor on a trip to Yung. When the party reached the Palace of Sweet Springs, an imperial hunt was held. Ho Ch'ü-ping, who was on very close terms with Wei Ch'ing, took the opportunity to shoot and kill Li Kan. At this time Ho Ch'ü-ping enjoyed great favor with the emperor, and the emperor therefore covered up for him, giving out the story that Li Kan had been gored and killed by a stag. A year or so later, Ho Ch'ü-ping died.

Li Kan had a daughter who became a lady in waiting to the heir apparent and was much loved and favored by him. Li Kan's son Li Yü also enjoyed favor with the heir apparent, but he was somewhat too fond of profit. So the fortunes of the Li family gradually waned.

(When Tang-hu's son Li Ling grew up, he was appointed as supervisor of the Chien-chang Palace, being in charge of the cavalry. He was skillful at archery and took good care of his soldiers. The emperor, considering that the Li family had been generals for generations, put Li Ling in charge of a force of eight hundred cavalry. Once he led an expedition that penetrated over two thousand *li* into Hsiung-nu territory, passing Chü-yen and observing the lay of the land, but he returned without having caught sight of the enemy. On his return he was appointed a chief commandant of cavalry and put in command of five thousand men from Tan-yang in the region of Ch'u, and for several years he taught archery and garrisoned the provinces of Chiuch'üan and Chang-i to protect them from the Hsiung-nu.

In the autumn of the second year of *t'ien-han* [99 B.C.] the Sutrishna General Li Kuang-li led a force of thirty thousand cavalry in an attack on the Hsiung-nu Wise King of the Right at the Ch'i-lien or Heavenly Mountains. He ordered Li Ling to lead a force of five thousand infantry and archers north from Chü-yen and advance about a thousand *li* into enemy territory. In this way he hoped to split the Hsiung-nu forces so that they would not all race in his direction.

Li Ling had already reached the point he was ordered to proceed to and had begun the march back, when the *Shan-yü* with a force of eighty thousand men surrounded his army and began to attack. Li Ling and his army of five thousand fought a running battle for eight days, retreating as they fought, until all their weapons and arrows were gone and half the men had been killed. In the course of the fighting they managed to kill or wound over ten thousand of the enemy.

When they reached a point only a hundred *li* or so from Chü-yen, the Hsiung-nu cornered them in a narrow valley and cut off their avenue of escape. Li Ling's food supplies were exhausted and no rescue troops were in sight, while the enemy pressed their attack and called on Li Ling to surrender. "I could never face the emperor and report such a disaster," Li Ling told his men, and finally surrendered to the Hsiung-nu. Practically all his soldiers perished in the fight; only some four hundred managed to escape and straggle back to Han territory. The *Shan-yü* had already heard of the fame of Li Ling's family and observed his bravery in battle, and as a result he gave him his own daughter as a wife and treated him with honor. When the emperor received news of this, he executed Li Ling's mother and his wife and children. From this time on the name of the Li family was disgraced and all the retainers of the family in Lung-hsi were ashamed to be associated with it.) [4]

The Grand Historian remarks: One of the old books says, "If he is an upright person, he will act whether he is ordered to or not; if he is not upright, he will not obey even when ordered." [5] It refers, no doubt, to men like General Li.

I myself have seen General Li—a man so plain and unassuming that you would take him for a peasant, and almost incapable of speaking a word. And yet the day he died all the people of the empire, whether they had known him or not, were moved to the profoundest grief, so deeply did men trust his sincerity of purpose. There is a proverb which says, "Though the peach tree does not speak, the world wears a path beneath it." It is a small saying, but one which is capable of conveying a great meaning.

[4] This last section in parentheses is most likely not by Ssu-ma Ch'ien, but a later addition. It differs from the account of Li Ling's life in *Han shu* 54 and deals with events that are later than those described elsewhere in the *Shih chi*. It may be recalled that Ssu-ma Ch'ien was condemned to castration for speaking out in defense of Li Ling to the emperor when the news of Li Ling's surrender reached the court. Ssu-ma Ch'ien's own account of Li Ling's battle and surrender is found in his letter to Jen Shao-ch'ing, translated in *Ssu-ma Ch'ien: Grand Historian of China*, pp. 57–67.

[5] *Analects* XIII, 6.

Shih chi 123: The Account of Ta-yüan

After the Han had sent its envoy to open up communications with the state of Ta-hsia [Bactria], all the barbarians of the distant west craned their necks to the east and longed to catch a glimpse of China. Thus I made The Account of Ta-yüan.

Chang Ch'ien was the first person to bring back a clear account of Ta-yüan [Ferghana].[1] He was a native of Han-chung and served as a palace attendant during the *chien-yüan* era [140–135 B.C.]. At this time the emperor questioned various Hsiung-nu who had surrendered to the Han and they all reported that the Hsiung-nu had defeated the king of the Yüeh-chih people [Indo-scythians] and made his skull into a drinking vessel. As a result the Yüeh-chih had fled and bore a constant grudge against the Hsiung-nu, though as yet they had been unable to find anyone to join them in an attack on their enemy.

The Han at this time was engaged in a concerted effort to destroy the Hsiung-nu, and therefore, when the emperor heard this, he decided to try to send an envoy to establish relations with the Yüeh-chih. To reach them, however, an envoy would inevitably have to pass through Hsiung-nu territory. The emperor accordingly sent out a summons for men capable of undertaking such a mission. Chang Ch'ien, who was a palace attendant at the time, answered the summons and was appointed as envoy.

He set out from Lung-hsi, accompanied by Kan-fu, a Hsiung-nu slave who belonged to a family in T'ang-i. They traveled west through the territory of the Hsiung-nu and were captured by the Hsiung-nu and taken before the *Shan-yü*. The *Shan-yü* detained them and refused to let them proceed. "The Yüeh-chih people live north of me," he said. "What does the Han mean by trying to send an envoy to them! Do you

---

[1] The better-known western equivalents of Chinese geographical names have been added in brackets where possible. Some of these identifications, however, are still a matter of dispute among scholars.

suppose that if I tried to send an embassy to the kingdom of Yüeh in the southeast the Han would let my men pass through China?"

The Hsiung-nu detained Chang Ch'ien for over ten years and gave him a wife from their own people, by whom he had a son. Chang Ch'ien never once relinquished the imperial credentials that marked him as an envoy of the Han, however, and after he had lived in Hsiung-nu territory for some time and was less closely watched than at first, he and his party finally managed to escape and resume their journey toward the Yüeh-chih.

After hastening west for twenty or thirty days, they reached the kingdom of Ta-yüan. The king of Ta-yüan had heard of the wealth of the Han empire and wished to establish communication with it, though as yet he had been unable to do so. When he met Chang Ch'ien he was overjoyed and asked where Chang Ch'ien wished to go.

"I was dispatched as envoy of the Han to the Yüeh-chih, but the Hsiung-nu blocked my way and I have only just now managed to escape," he replied. "I beg Your Highness to give me some guides to show me the way. If I can reach my destination and return to the Han to make my report, the Han will reward you with countless gifts!"

The king of Ta-yüan trusted his words and sent him on his way, giving him guides and interpreters to take him to the state of K'ang-chü [Trans-Oxiana]. From there he was able to make his way to the land of the Great Yüeh-chih.

Since the king of the Great Yüeh-chih had been killed by the Hsiung-nu, his son had succeeded him as ruler and had forced the kingdom of Ta-hsia [Bactria] to recognize his sovereignty. The region he ruled was rich and fertile and seldom troubled by invaders, and the king thought only of his own enjoyment. He considered the Han too far away to bother with and had no particular intention of avenging his father's death by attacking the Hsiung-nu. From the court of the Yüeh-chih, Chang Ch'ien traveled on to the state of Ta-hsia, but in the end he was never able to interest the Yüeh-chih in his proposals.

After spending a year or so in the area, he began to journey back along the Nan-shan or Southern Mountains, intending to reenter China through the territory of the Ch'iang barbarians, but he was once more captured by the Hsiung-nu and detained for over a year.

Just at this time the *Shan-yü* died and the Lu-li King of the Left attacked the *Shan-yü*'s heir and set himself up as the new *Shan-yü* [126 B.C.]. As a result of this the whole Hsiung-nu nation was in turmoil and Chang Ch'ien, along with his Hsiung-nu wife and the former slave Kan-fu, was able to escape and return to China. The emperor honored Chang Ch'ien with the post of palace counselor and awarded Kan-fu the title of "Lord Who Carries Out His Mission."

Chang Ch'ien was a man of great strength, determination, and generosity. He trusted others and in turn was liked by the barbarians. Kan-fu, who was a Hsiung-nu by birth, was good at archery, and whenever he and Chang Ch'ien were short of food he would shoot birds and beasts to keep them supplied. When Chang Ch'ien first set out on his mission, he was accompanied by over a hundred men, but after thirteen years abroad, only he and Kan-fu managed to make their way back to China.

Chang Ch'ien in person visited the lands of Ta-yüan, the Great Yüeh-chih, Ta-hsia, and K'ang-chü, and in addition he gathered reports on five or six other large states in the neighborhood. All of this information he related to the emperor on his return. The substance of his report was as follows:

Ta-yüan lies southwest of the territory of the Hsiung-nu, some ten thousand *li* directly west of China. The people are settled on the land, plowing the fields and growing rice and wheat. They also make wine out of grapes. The region has many fine horses which sweat blood;[2] their forebears are supposed to have been foaled from heavenly horses. The people live in houses in fortified cities, there being some seventy or more cities of various sizes in the region. The population numbers several hundred thousand. The people fight with bows and spears and can shoot from horseback.

Ta-yüan is bordered on the north by K'ang-chü, on the west by the kingdom of the Great Yüeh-chih, on the southwest by Ta-hsia, on the northeast by the land of the Wu-sun, and on the east by Yü-mi and Yü-t'ien [Khotan].

West of Yü-t'ien, all the rivers flow west and empty into the Western Sea, but east of there they flow eastward into the Salt Swamp [Lob

---

[2] The "bloody sweat" was apparently the result of parasites which caused small running sores in the hides of the horses.

Nor]. The waters of the Salt Swamp flow underground and on the south form the source from which the Yellow River rises. There are many precious stones in the region and the rivers flow into China. The Lou-lan and Ku-shih peoples live in fortified cities along the Salt Swamp. The Salt Swamp is some five thousand *li* from Ch'ang-an. The western branch of the Hsiung-nu occupies the region from the Salt Swamp east to a point south of the Great Wall at Lung-hsi, where its territory adjoins that of the Ch'iang barbarians, thus cutting off the road from China to the west.

The Wu-sun live some two thousand *li* northeast of Ta-yüan, moving from place to place in the region with their herds of animals. Their customs are much like those of the Hsiung-nu. They have twenty or thirty thousand skilled archers and are very daring in battle. They were originally subjects of the Hsiung-nu, but later, becoming more powerful, they refused any longer to attend the gatherings of the Hsiung-nu court, though still acknowledging themselves part of the Hsiung-nu nation.

K'ang-chü is situated some two thousand *li* northwest of Ta-yüan. Its people likewise are nomads and resemble the Yüeh-chih in their customs. They have eighty or ninety thousand skilled archer fighters. The country is small, and borders Ta-yüan. It acknowledges nominal sovereignty to the Yüeh-chih people in the south and the Hsiung-nu in the east.

Yen-ts'ai lies some two thousand *li* northwest of K'ang-chü. The people are nomads and their customs are generally similar to those of the people of K'ang-chü. The country has over a hundred thousand archer warriors, and borders a great shoreless lake, perhaps what is known as the Northern Sea [Caspian Sea?].

The Great Yüeh-chih live some two or three thousand *li* west of Ta-yüan, north of the Kuei [Oxus] River. They are bordered on the south by Ta-hsia, on the west by An-hsi [Parthia], and on the north by K'ang-chü. They are a nation of nomads, moving from place to place with their herds, and their customs are like those of the Hsiung-nu. They have some one or two hundred thousand archer warriors. Formerly they were very powerful and despised the Hsiung-nu, but later, when Mo-tun became leader of the Hsiung-nu nation, he attacked and defeated the Yüeh-chih. Some time afterwards his son, the Old *Shan-yü,* killed the king of the Yüeh-chih and made his skull into a drinking cup.

The Yüeh-chih originally lived in the area between the Ch'i-lien or Heavenly Mountains and Tun-huang, but after they were defeated by the Hsiung-nu they moved far away to the west, beyond Ta-yüan, where they attacked and conquered the people of Ta-hsia and set up the court of their king on the northern bank of the Kuei River. A small number of their people who were unable to make the journey west sought refuge among the Ch'iang barbarians in the Southern Mountains, where they are known as the Lesser Yüeh-chih.

An-hsi is situated several thousand *li* west of the region of the Great Yüeh-chih. The people are settled on the land, cultivating the fields and growing rice and wheat. They also make wine out of grapes. They have walled cities like the people of Ta-yüan, the region containing several hundred cities of various sizes. The kingdom, which borders the Kuei River, is very large, measuring several thousand *li* square. Some of the inhabitants are merchants who travel by carts or boats to neighboring countries, sometimes journeying several thousand *li*. The coins of the country are made of silver and bear the face of the king. When the king dies, the currency is immediately changed and new coins issued with the face of his successor. The people keep records by writing horizontally on strips of leather. To the west lies T'iao-chih [Mesopotamia] and to the north Yen-ts'ai and Li-hsüan [Hyrcania].

T'iao-chih is situated several thousand *li* west of An-hsi and borders the Western Sea [Persian Gulf?]. It is hot and damp, and the people live by cultivating the fields and planting rice. In this region live great birds which lay eggs as large as pots. The people are very numerous and are ruled by many petty chiefs. The ruler of An-hsi gives orders to these chiefs and regards them as his vassals. The people are very skillful at performing tricks that amaze the eye. The old men of An-hsi say they have heard that in T'iao-chih are to be found the River of Weak Water and the Queen Mother of the West, though they admit that they have never seen either of them.[3]

[3] The Queen Mother of the West was an immortal spirit who was said to live in some fabulous region of the west. According to later writers the River of Weak Water was so called because it would not float even a goose feather.

Ta-hsia is situated over two thousand *li* southwest of Ta-yüan, south of the Kuei River. Its people cultivate the land and have cities and houses. Their customs are like those of Ta-yüan. It has no great ruler but only a number of petty chiefs ruling the various cities. The people are poor in the use of arms and afraid of battle, but they are clever at commerce. After the Great Yüeh-chih moved west and attacked and conquered Ta-hsia, the entire country came under their sway. The population of the country is large, numbering some million or more persons. The capital is called the city of Lan-shih [Bactra] and has a market where all sorts of goods are bought and sold.

Southeast of Ta-hsia is the kingdom of Shen-tu [India]. "When I was in Ta-hsia," Chang Ch'ien reported, "I saw bamboo canes from Ch'iung and cloth made in the province of Shu. When I asked the people how they had gotten such articles, they replied, 'Our merchants go to buy them in the markets of Shen-tu.' Shen-tu, they told me, lies several thousand *li* southeast of Ta-hsia. The people cultivate the land and live much like the people of Ta-hsia. The region is said to be hot and damp. The inhabitants ride elephants when they go into battle. The kingdom is situated on a great river.

"We know that Ta-hsia is located twelve thousand *li* southwest of China. Now if the kingdom of Shen-tu is situated several thousand *li* southeast of Ta-hsia and obtains goods which are produced in Shu, it seems to me that it must not be very far away from Shu. At present, if we try to send envoys to Ta-hsia by way of the mountain trails that lead through the territory of the Ch'iang people, they will be molested by the Ch'iang, while if we send them a little farther north, they will be captured by the Hsiung-nu. It would seem that the most direct route, as well as the safest, would be that out of Shu."

Thus the emperor learned of Ta-yüan, Ta-hsia, An-hsi, and the others, all great states rich in unusual products whose people cultivated the land and made their living in much the same way as the Chinese. All these states, he was told, were militarily weak and prized Han goods and wealth. He also learned that to the north of them lived the Yüeh-chih and K'ang-chü people who were strong in arms but who could be persuaded by gifts and the prospect of gain to acknowledge allegiance to the Han court. If it were only possible to win over these states by peaceful means, the emperor thought, he could then extend his domain ten thousand *li*, attract to his court men of strange customs who would come translating and retranslating their languages,[4] and his might would become known to all the lands within the four seas.

The emperor was therefore delighted, and approved Chang Ch'ien's suggestion. He ordered Chang Ch'ien to start out from Chien-wei in Shu on a secret mission to search for Ta-hsia. The party broke up into four groups proceeding out of the regions of Mang, Jan, Hsi, and Ch'iung and P'o. All the groups managed to advance one or two thousand *li*, but they were blocked on the north by the Ti and Tso tribes and on the south by the Sui and K'un-ming tribes. The K'un-ming tribes have no rulers but devote themselves to plunder and robbery, and as soon as they seized any of the Han envoys they immediately murdered them. Thus none of the parties were ever able to get through to their destination. They did learn, however, that some one thousand or more *li* to the west there was a state called Tien-yüeh whose people rode elephants and that the merchants from Shu sometimes went there with their goods on unofficial trading missions. In this way the Han, while searching for a route to Ta-hsia, first came into contact with the kingdom of Tien.

Earlier the Han had tried to establish relations with the barbarians of the southwest, but the expense proved too great and no road could be found through the region and so the project was abandoned. After Chang Ch'ien reported that it was possible to reach Ta-hsia by traveling through the region of the southwestern barbarians, the Han once more began efforts to establish relations with the tribes in the area.

Chang Ch'ien was made a subordinate commander and sent to accompany the general in chief Wei Ch'ing on expeditions against the Hsiung-nu. Because he knew where water and pasture were to be found in the Hsiung-nu territory, he was able to save the army from hardship. He was enfeoffed as Po-wang or "Broad Vision" marquis. This occurred in the sixth year of the *yüan-so* era [123 B.C.].

The following year he was appointed colonel of the guard and sent

---

[4] A stock phrase in Han rhetoric meaning that such people come from so far away that they have no knowledge of the Chinese language and their words must therefore be "translated and retranslated" through a number of intermediary languages before being put into Chinese.

with General Li Kuang on an expedition out of Yu-pei-p'ing to attack the Hsiung-nu. The Hsiung-nu surrounded Li Kuang's army and wiped out most of the men. Chang Ch'ien was accused of having arrived late at his rendezvous with Li Kuang and was sentenced to execution, but on payment of a fine he was allowed to become a commoner. This same year the Han sent the swift cavalry general Ho Ch'ü-ping against the Hsiung-nu. He defeated and killed thirty or forty thousand of the Hsiung-nu in the western region [5] and rode as far as the Ch'i-lien Mountains. The following year the Hun-yeh king led his barbarian hordes and surrendered to the Han, and the Hsiung-nu completely disappeared from the region from Chin-ch'eng and Ho-hsi west along the Southern Mountains to the Salt Swamp. Occasionally Hsiung-nu scouts would appear, but even they were rare. Two years later the Han armies attacked the *Shan-yü* and chased him north of the desert.

During this time the emperor occasionally questioned Chang Ch'ien about Ta-hsia and the other states of the west. Chang Ch'ien, who had been deprived of his marquisate, replied, "When I was living among the Hsiung-nu I heard about the king of the Wu-sun people, who is named K'un-mo. K'un-mo's father was the ruler of a small state on the western border of the Hsiung-nu territory. The Hsiung-nu attacked and killed his father, and K'un-mo, then only a baby, was cast out in the wilderness to die. But the birds came and flew over the place where he was, bearing meat in their beaks, and the wolves suckled him, so that he was able to survive. When the *Shan-yü* heard of this, he was filled with wonder and, believing that K'un-mo was a god, he took him in and reared him. When K'un-mo had grown to manhood, the *Shan-yü* put him in command of a band of troops and he several times won merit in battle. The *Shan-yü* then made him the leader of the people whom his father had ruled in former times and ordered him to guard the western forts. K'un-mo gathered together his people, looked after them and led them in attacks on the small settlements in the neighborhood. Soon he had twenty or thirty thousand skilled archers who were trained in aggressive warfare. When the *Shan-yü* died, K'un-mo led his people far away, declared himself an independent

[5] Following the reading in *Han shu* 61.

ruler, and refused any longer to journey to the meetings of the Hsiung-nu court. The Hsiung-nu sent surprise parties of troops to attack him, but they were unable to win a victory. In the end the Hsiung-nu decided that he must be a god and left him alone, still claiming that he was a subject of theirs but no longer making any large-scale attacks on him.

"Now the *Shan-yü* is suffering from the recent blow delivered by our armies, and the region formerly occupied by the Hun-yeh king and his people is deserted. The barbarians are well known to be greedy for Han wealth and goods. If we could make use of this opportunity to send rich gifts and bribes to the Wu-sun people and persuade them to move farther east and occupy the region which formerly belonged to the Hun-yeh king, then the Han could conclude an alliance of brotherhood with them and, under the circumstances, they would surely do as we say. If we could get them to obey us, it would be like cutting off the right arm of the Hsiung-nu! Then, once we had established an alliance with the Wu-sun, Ta-hsia and the other countries to the west could all be persuaded to come to court and acknowledge themselves our foreign vassals."

The emperor approved of this suggestion and, appointing Chang Ch'ien as a general of palace attendants, put him in charge of a party of three hundred men, each of which was provided with two horses. In addition the party took along tens of thousands of cattle and sheep and carried gold and silk goods worth a hundred billion cash. Many of the men in the party were given the imperial credentials making them assistant envoys so that they could be sent to neighboring states along the way.

When Chang Ch'ien reached the kingdom of the Wu-sun, the king of the Wu-sun, K'un-mo, tried to treat the Han envoys in the same way that the *Shan-yü* treated them. Chang Ch'ien was greatly outraged and, knowing that the barbarians were greedy, said, "The Son of Heaven has sent me with these gifts, but if you do not prostrate yourself to receive them, I shall have to take them back!"

With this K'un-mo jumped up from his seat and prostrated himself to receive the gifts. The other details of the envoys' reception Chang Ch'ien allowed to remain as before. Chang Ch'ien then delivered his message, saying, "If the Wu-sun will consent to move east and occupy the region of the Hun-yeh king, then the Han will send you a princess of the imperial family to be your wife."

But the Wu-sun people were split into several groups and the king was old. Living far away from China, he had no idea how large the Han empire was. Moreover, his people had for a long time in the past been subjects of the Hsiung-nu and still lived nearer to them than to China. The high ministers of the king were therefore all afraid of the Hsiung-nu and did not wish to move back east. The king alone could not force his will upon his subjects, and Chang Ch'ien was therefore unable to persuade him to listen to his proposal.

K'un-mo had over ten sons, among them one named Ta-lu who was very strong and skillful in leading the people. He lived in a separate part of the realm and had over ten thousand horsemen under his command.

Ta-lu's older brother, who had been designated as heir to K'un-mo, had a son named Ts'en-ch'ü. The heir apparent died early and on his deathbed he begged his father, K'un-mo, to make Ts'en-ch'ü the new heir. "Do not allow anyone to take his position away from him!" he pleaded. K'un-mo, moved by grief, gave his permission and designated his grandson Ts'en-ch'ü as the new heir apparent.

Ta-lu was furious that he himself had not been appointed heir and, persuading his other brothers to join him, led his forces in a revolt, planning to attack Ts'en-ch'ü and K'un-mo. K'un-mo, who was old and lived in constant fear that Ta-lu would attack and kill his grandson, gave Ts'en-ch'ü a force of over ten thousand horsemen and sent him to live in another part of the realm, while he himself kept over ten thousand horsemen for his own protection. Thus it happened that when Chang Ch'ien arrived the Wu-sun people were split into three factions, though the large part of them acknowledged the leadership of K'un-mo. K'un-mo for this reason did not dare make any promises to Chang Ch'ien on his own authority.

Chang Ch'ien dispatched his assistant envoys to Ta-yüan, K'ang-chü, the Great Yüeh-chih, Ta-hsia, An-hsi, Shen-tu, Yü-t'ien, Yü-mo, and the other neighboring states, the Wu-sun providing them with guides and interpreters. Then he returned to China, accompanied by twenty or thirty envoys from the Wu-sun and a similar number of horses which the Wu-sun sent in exchange for the Han gifts. The Wu-sun envoys thus had an opportunity to see with their own eyes the breadth and greatness of the Han empire.

On his return Chang Ch'ien was honored with the post of grand messenger, ranking him among the nine highest ministers of the government. A year or so later he died.

The Wu-sun envoys, having seen how rich and populous the Han was, returned and reported what they had learned to their own people, and after this the Wu-sun regarded the Han with greater respect. A year or so later the envoys whom Chang Ch'ien had sent to Ta-hsia and the other states of the west all returned, accompanied by envoys from those states, and for the first time relations were established between the lands of the northwest and the Han. It was Chang Ch'ien, however, who opened the way for this move, and all the envoys who journeyed to the lands in later times relied upon his reputation to gain them a hearing. As a result of his efforts, the foreign states trusted the Han envoys.

After Chang Ch'ien's death the Hsiung-nu learned that the Han had established relations with the Wu-sun and, infuriated by the news, decided to make an attack on the Wu-sun. By this time the Han had already sent envoys to the Wu-sun, as well as to Ta-yüan, the Great Yüeh-chih, and the other states to the south, and the Wu-sun, frightened by the threat of a Hsiung-nu attack, sent an envoy with a gift of horses to the Han court to ask that a Han princess be granted to the Wu-sun leader and an alliance of brotherhood concluded. The emperor referred the matter to his ministers for debate, and they all replied, "The princess should not be sent until the betrothal gifts have been duly received."

Sometime earlier the emperor had divined by the *Book of Changes* and been told that "divine horses are due to appear from the northwest." When the Wu-sun came with their horses, which were of an excellent breed, he named them "heavenly horses." Later, however, he obtained the blood-sweating horses from Ta-yüan, which were even hardier. He therefore changed the name of the Wu-sun horses, calling them "horses from the western extremity," and used the name "heavenly horses" for the horses of Ta-yüan.

At this time the Han first built fortifications west of the district of Ling-chü and established the province of Chiu-ch'üan in order to provide a safe route to the lands of the northwest, and as a result more and more envoys were sent to An-hsi, Yen-ts'ai, T'iao-chih, and Shen-tu. The emperor was very fond of the Ta-yüan horses and sent a constant stream of envoys to that region to acquire them.

The largest of these embassies to foreign states numbered several hundred persons, while even the smaller parties included over a hundred members, though later, as the envoys became more accustomed to the route, the number was gradually reduced. The credentials and gifts which the envoys bore with them were much like those supplied to the envoys in Chang Ch'ien's time. In the course of one year anywhere from five or six to over ten parties would be sent out. Those traveling to distant lands required eight or nine years to complete their journey, while those visiting nearer regions would return after a few years.

At this time the Han had already overthrown the kingdom of Yüeh in the southeast, and the barbarian tribes living southwest of Shu were all filled with awe and begged to be ruled by Han officials and to be allowed to pay their respects at court. The Han therefore set up the provinces of I-chou, Yüeh-sui, Tsang-ko, Ch'en-li, and Wen-shan, hoping to extend the area under Han control so that a route could be opened to Ta-hsia. The Han sent Po Shih-ch'ang, Lü Yüeh-jen, and others, over ten parties in the space of one year, out of these new provinces to try to get through to Ta-hsia. The parties were all blocked by the K'un-ming barbarians, however, who stole their goods and murdered the envoys, so that none of them were ever able to reach Ta-hsia.

The Han then freed the criminals of the three districts of the capital area and, adding to them twenty or thirty thousand soldiers from Pa and Shu, dispatched them under the command of two generals, Kuo Ch'ang and Wei Kuang, to go and attack the K'un-ming tribes that were blocking the Han envoys. The army succeeded in killing or capturing twenty or thirty thousand of the enemy before departing from the area, but later, when another attempt was made to send envoys to Ta-hsia, the K'un-ming once more fell upon them and none were able to reach their destination. By this time, however, so many envoys had journeyed to Ta-hsia by the northern route out of Chiu-ch'üan that the foreign states in the area had become surfeited with Han goods and no longer regarded them with any esteem.

After Chang Ch'ien achieved honor and position by opening up communications with the lands of the west, all the officials and soldiers who had accompanied him vied with one another in submitting reports to the emperor telling of the wonders and profits to be gained in foreign lands and requesting to become envoys. The emperor considered that, since the lands of the west were so far away, no man would choose to make the journey simply for his own pleasure, and so when he had listened to their stories he immediately presented them with the credentials of an envoy. In addition he called for volunteers from among the people and fitted out with attendants and dispatched anyone who came forward, without inquiring into his background, in an effort to broaden the area that had been opened to communication.

When the envoys returned from a mission, it invariably happened that they had plundered or stolen goods on their way or their reports failed to meet with the approval of the emperor. The emperor, who was very practiced at handling such matters, would then have them summarily investigated and accused of some major offense so that they would be spurred to anger and would volunteer to undertake another mission in order to redeem themselves. Thus there was never any lack of men to act as envoys, and they came to regard it as a trifling matter to break the law. The officials and soldiers who had accompanied them on a mission would in turn start at once enthusiastically describing the wealth to be found in the foreign nations; those who told the most impressive tales were granted the seals of an envoy, while those who spoke more modestly were made assistants. As a result all sorts of worthless men hurried forward with wild tales to imitate their example.

The envoys were all sons of poor families who handled the government gifts and goods that were entrusted to them as though they were private property and looked for opportunities to buy goods at a cheap price in the foreign countries and make a profit on their return to China. The men of the foreign lands soon became disgusted when they found that each of the Han envoys told some different story and, considering that the Han armies were too far away to worry about, refused to supply the envoys with food and provisions, making things very difficult for them. The Han envoys were soon reduced to a state of destitution and distress and, their tempers mounting, fell to quarreling and even attacking each other.

The states of Lou-lan and Ku-shih, though very small, lay right across the path that the envoys traveled, and they attacked and plundered the parties of Wang Hui and other envoys with extreme ferocity. In addition, raiding parties of Hsiung-nu from time to time appeared in the region to swoop down on the envoys to the western states and block their advance. The envoys hastened to the emperor with complaints of all the hardships which they suffered and suggested that, although the inhabitants of the western regions lived in fortified cities, they were poor in combat and could easily be attacked.

As a result of their complaints, the emperor dispatched Chao P'o-nu, the former Ts'ung-p'iao marquis, with a force of twenty or thirty thousand troops recruited from the dependent states and the provinces. He advanced as far as the Hsiung-ho River, hoping to attack the Hsiung-nu, but they withdrew.

The following year an attack was made on Ku-shih. Chao P'o-nu, with a force of seven hundred or more light horsemen, led the attack, captured the king of Lou-lan, and succeeded in conquering Ku-shih. At the same time he used his armies to intimidate the Wu-sun, Ta-yüan, and the other states in the region. On his return Chao P'o-nu was enfeoffed as marquis of Cho-yeh.

Wang Hui, who had several times acted as an envoy and been mistreated by the people of Lou-lan, took his complaint to the emperor. The emperor called out a force of troops and appointed Wang Hui as aide to Chao P'o-nu, in which capacity he attacked and defeated Lou-lan. He was enfeoffed as marquis of Hao. After this a series of defense stations was established from Chiu-ch'üan west to the Jade Gate Pass.

The Wu-sun sent a thousand horses to the Han as a betrothal gift for the Han princess whom they had been promised. The Han then sent a princess of the imperial family, the daughter of the king of Chiang-tu, to be the wife of the Wu-sun leader. K'un-mo, the king of the Wu-sun, made her his Bride of the Right. The Hsiung-nu also sent one of their women to marry K'un-mo, and he made her his Bride of the Left. Later, saying that he was too old, he gave the Han princess to his grandson Ts'en-ch'ü to be his bride. The Wu-sun have a great many horses, the wealthy men among them owning as many as four or five thousand.[6]

When the Han envoys first visited the kingdom of An-hsi, the king of An-hsi dispatched a party of twenty thousand horsemen to meet them on the eastern border of his kingdom. The capital of the kingdom is several thousand *li* from the eastern border, and as the envoys proceeded there they passed through twenty or thirty cities inhabited by great numbers of people. When the Han envoys set out again to return to China, the king of An-hsi dispatched envoys of his own to accompany them, and after the latter had visited China and reported on its great breadth and might, the king sent some of the eggs of the great birds which live in the region, and skilled tricksters of Li-hsüan, to the Han court as gifts. In addition, the smaller states west of Ta-yüan, such as Huan-ch'ien and Ta-i, as well as those east of Ta-yüan, such as Ku-shih, Yü-mi, and Su-hsieh, all sent parties to accompany the Han envoys back to China and present gifts at court. The emperor was delighted at this.

The emperor also sent envoys to trace the Yellow River to its source. They found that it rises in the land of Yü-t'ien among mountains rich in precious stones, many of which they brought back with them. The emperor studied the old maps and books and decided to name these mountains, where the Yellow River has its source, the K'un-lun Mountains.

At this time the emperor made frequent tours east to the seacoast, and at such times he would take all the visitors from foreign lands

---

[6] The purpose of this last statement is no doubt to indicate that a thousand horses was not by any means a very lavish betrothal gift to send in exchange for the Han princess. The parallel passage in *Han shu* 96B gives a much more elaborate account of the princess's attendants and her reception at the Wu-sun court and includes a famous poem supposedly written by her lamenting her exile to a strange and distant land.

along in his party, passing through large and populous cities on the way, scattering gifts of money and silk among the visitors, and supplying them with generous accommodations in order to impress upon them the wealth of the Han empire. He would hold great wrestling matches and displays of unusual skills and all sorts of rare creatures, gathering together large numbers of people to watch. He entertained the foreign visitors with veritable lakes of wine and forests of meat and had them shown around to the various granaries and storehouses to see how much wealth was laid away there, astounding and overwhelming them with the breadth and greatness of the Han empire. After the skills of the foreign magicians and tricksters had been imported into China, the wrestling matches and displays of unusual feats developed and improved with each year, and from this time on entertainments of this type became increasingly popular.

In this way party after party of envoys from the foreign lands of the northwest would arrive in China and, after a while, take their leave. Those from the states west of Ta-yüan, however, believing that their homelands were too far away from China to be in any danger, continued to conduct themselves with great arrogance and self-assurance; it was impossible to make them conform to proper ritual or to compel them to obey the wishes of the Han court.

The lands from that of the Wu-sun on west to An-hsi were situated nearer to the Hsiung-nu than to China, and it was well known that the Hsiung-nu had earlier caused the Yüeh-chih people great suffering. Therefore, whenever a Hsiung-nu envoy appeared in the region carrying credentials from the *Shan-yü,* he was escorted from state to state and provided with food, and no one dared to detain him or cause him any difficulty. In the case of the Han envoys, however, if they did not hand out silks or other goods they were given no food, and unless they purchased animals in the markets they could get no mounts for their riders. This was because the people considered the Han too far away to bother about. They also believed that the Han had plenty of goods and money and it was therefore proper to make the envoys pay for whatever they wanted. As may be seen, they were much more afraid of the Hsiung-nu envoys than of those from the Han.

The regions around Ta-yüan make wine out of grapes, the wealthier inhabitants keeping as much as ten thousand or more piculs stored away. It can be kept for as long as twenty or thirty years without spoiling. The people love their wine and the horses love their alfalfa. The Han envoys brought back grape and alfalfa seeds to China and the emperor for the first time tried growing these plants in areas of rich soil. Later, when the Han acquired large numbers of the "heavenly horses" and the envoys from foreign states began to arrive with their retinues, the lands on all sides of the emperor's summer palaces and pleasure towers were planted with grapes and alfalfa for as far as the eye could see.

Although the states from Ta-yüan west to An-hsi speak rather different languages, their customs are generally similar and their languages mutually intelligible. The men all have deep-set eyes and profuse beards and whiskers. They are skillful at commerce and will haggle over a fraction of a cent. Women are held in great respect, and the men make decisions on the advice of their women. No silk or lacquer is produced anywhere in the region, and the casting of coins and vessels was formerly unknown. Later, however, when some of the Chinese soldiers attached to the Han embassies ran away and surrendered to the people of the area, they taught them how to cast metal and manufacture weapons. Now, whenever the people of the region lay their hands on any Han gold or silver they immediately make it into vessels and do not use it for currency.

By this time a number of embassies had been sent to the west and even the lesser attendants who went along on the expeditions had become accustomed to appearing before the emperor and relating their experiences. "Ta-yüan has some fine horses in the city of Erh-shih [Sutrishna]," they reported, "but the people keep them hidden and refuse to give any to the Han envoys!"

The emperor had already taken a great liking to the horses of Ta-yüan, and when he heard this he was filled with excitement and expectation. He dispatched a party of able young men and carriage masters with a thousand pieces of gold and a golden horse to go to the king of Ta-yüan and ask him for some of the fine horses of Erh-shih.

But Ta-yüan by this time was overflowing with Han goods, and the men of the state therefore plotted together, saying, "The Han is far away from us and on several occasions has lost men in the salt-water wastes between our country and China. Yet if the Han parties go farther north, they will be harassed by the Hsiung-nu, while if they try to go to the south they will suffer from lack of water and fodder. Moreover, there are many places along the route where there are no cities whatsoever and they are apt to run out of provisions. The Han embassies that have come to us are made up of only a few hundred men, and yet they are always short of food and over half the men die on the journey. Under such circumstances how could the Han possibly send a large army against us? What have we to worry about? Furthermore, the horses of Erh-shih are one of the most valuable treasures of our state!"

In the end, therefore, they refused to give the Han envoys any horses. Enraged, the Han envoys cursed the men of Ta-yüan, smashed the golden horse with a mallet, and departed.

The nobles of Ta-yüan were furious, complaining that the Han envoys had treated them with the utmost contempt. After the Han party had left, therefore, they sent orders to the people of Yü-ch'eng on the eastern border of the kingdom to attack and kill the envoys and seize their goods.

When the emperor received word of the fate of the envoys, he was in a rage. Yao Ting-han and others, who had acted as envoys to Ta-yüan in the past, assured the emperor that the kingdom was militarily weak and that it would not require a force of more than three thousand Han soldiers equipped with powerful crossbows to conquer it and take the entire population captive. Earlier, when the emperor had dispatched Chao P'o-nu to attack Lou-lan, Chao had led an advance party of only seven hundred horsemen and had taken the king of Lou-lan prisoner. The emperor therefore believed the assurances of Yao Ting-han and the others and, wishing to have some excuse to enfeoff the relatives of his favorite, Lady Li, he honored her brother Li Kuang-li with the title of Erh-shih General and dispatched him with a force of six thousand horsemen recruited from the dependent states, as well as twenty or thirty thousand young men of bad reputation rounded up from the provinces and kingdoms, to launch an attack on Ta-yüan. The title of

Erh-shih General was given to Li Kuang-li because it was expected that he would reach the city of Erh-shih and capture the fine horses there. Chao Chih-ch'eng was appointed director of martial law for the expedition, and Wang Hui, the former marquis of Hao, was ordered to act as guide. Li Ch'e was made a subordinate commander and put in charge of various military affairs. This was in the first year of the *t'ai-yüan* era [104 B.C.]. At this time great swarms of locusts rose up in the area east of the Pass and flew west as far as Tun-huang.

General Li and his army passed the Salt Swamp and were advancing west when they found that the inhabitants of the small states along the way, terrified by their approach, had all shut themselves up tightly in their walled cities and refused to supply any food to the army. Even attacks on the cities did not always prove successful. The army was able to obtain provisions from some of the cities that submitted, but in the case of others, if a few days of attack did not bring capitulation, the army would move on its way. Thus by the time Li Kuang-li reached Yü-ch'eng he had no more than a few thousand soldiers left, and all of these were suffering from hunger and exhaustion.

He attacked Yü-ch'eng, but was severely beaten and a great many of his men were killed or wounded. General Li then consulted Li Ch'e, Chao Shih-ch'eng, and his other officers and decided that, if they could not even conquer the city of Yü-ch'eng, there was absolutely no hope that they could make a successful attack on Erh-shih, the king's capital, farther to the west. They therefore decided to lead their troops back to China. The journey to Ta-yüan and back had taken them two years, and by the time they reached Tun-huang they had no more than one or two tenths of their original force left.

Li Kuang-li sent a messenger to the emperor explaining that the distance had been so great and he had been so short of provisions that his men, though brave enough in battle, had been defeated by hunger and not enough of them had survived the journey to make an attack on Ta-yüan possible. He asked that the army be disbanded for a while and a larger force recruited for another expedition later on.

When the emperor received word of this, he was enraged and sent an envoy with orders to close the pass at Jade Gate, saying that anyone from General Li's army who attempted to enter the country would be cut down on the spot.

General Li, afraid to move, remained for the time being at Tun-huang. This same summer over twenty thousand Han soldiers under the command of Chao P'o-nu were surrounded by the Hsiung-nu and forced to surrender.

The high ministers and court advisers all wanted the emperor to disband the army that had been sent to attack Ta-yüan and concentrate the strength of the empire on attacking the Hsiung-nu. But the emperor had already undertaken to punish Ta-yüan for its outrage and he was afraid that if his armies could not conquer even a small state like Ta-yüan, then Ta-hsia and the other lands would come to despise the Han. No more fine horses could ever be obtained from Ta-yüan, the Wu-sun and Lun-t'ou people would scorn and mistreat the Han envoys, and China would become a laughingstock among the foreign nations. He therefore had Teng Kuang and the others who were most outspoken in their opposition to the Ta-yüan campaign handed over to the law officials for investigation, freed all the skilled bowmen who were in prison, and called out more young men of bad reputation and horsemen from the border states. By the end of a year or so he had sent sixty thousand new men to Tun-huang to reinforce the army there, not counting porters and personal attendants. The army was provided with a hundred thousand oxen, over thirty thousand horses, and tens of thousands of donkeys, mules, and camels, as well as plentiful provisions and a great number of crossbows and other weapons. The whole empire was thrown into a turmoil, relaying orders and providing men and supplies for the attack on Ta-yüan. Over fifty subordinate commanders were appointed to direct the army.

It was known that there were no wells in the capital city of Ta-yüan, the city drawing its water supply from rivers that flowed outside the walls. The emperor therefore sent water engineers to join the army so that when the time came they could divert the streams which flowed by the city and deprive the inhabitants of their water. A force of a hundred and eighty thousand soldiers was also dispatched to garrison the districts of Chü-yen and Hsiu-t'u, which had been established north

of Chiu-ch'üan and Chang-yeh in order to provide greater protection
for Chiu-ch'üan. All men in the empire who came in the seven classes
of reprobated persons [7] were called out and sent to transport supplies
of dried boiled rice to Li Kuang-li's forces. The lines of transport
wagons and marching men stretched without a break all the way
west to Tun-huang. In addition, two men who were skilled in judging
horses were appointed as commanders in charge of steeds so that, when
the conquest of Ta-yüan had been accomplished, they would be on
hand to select the finest horses to take back to China.

When all of this had been done, Li Kuang-li set off once again. This
time he had far more men, and in every little state he came to the
inhabitants came out to greet him with gifts of food for his army.
When he reached Lun-t'ou, however, the people there refused to submit. He besieged the city for several days and, after taking it, massacred
the inhabitants, and from there on west to Erh-shih, the capital of
Ta-yüan, his advance was unhindered.

He reached Erh-shih with a force of thirty thousand soldiers. The
men of Ta-yüan came forward to attack, but the Han soldiers overwhelmed them with their arrows and forced them to flee into the city,
where they mounted the battlements and prepared to defend the city.

General Li's men had wanted to attack Yü-ch'eng on the way, but
he was afraid that if he halted his advance it would only give the men
of Erh-shih more time to think up plots to save their lives. He therefore
pressed on to Erh-shih, where he broke down the banks of the rivers
and springs and diverted them from their courses so that they no
longer supplied water to the city. This move caused the inhabitants of
the city extreme distress and hardship.

After surrounding and besieging the city for over forty days, he
managed to break down the outer wall and capture one of the enemy
leaders, a noble of Ta-yüan named Chien-mi who was noted for his
bravery. The inhabitants were thoroughly terrified and fled within the
inner wall, where the nobles of Ta-yüan gathered to plot the next move.

---

[7] Petty officials who had committed crimes, fugitives, adopted sons-in-law,
resident merchants, those formerly registered as merchants, those whose fathers
or mothers had been registered as merchants, and those whose grandfathers or
grandmothers had been registered as merchants.

"The reason the Han has sent troops to attack us is simply that our king Wu-kua hid his best horses and killed the Han envoys," they said. "Now if we kill the king and hand over the horses, the Han troops will most likely withdraw. Should they refuse, that will be the time to fight to the death for our city!"

All having agreed that this was the best plan, they killed the king and sent one of the nobles to carry his head to General Li and ask for an agreement. "If the Han soldiers do not attack us," the nobleman said, "we will bring out all the finest horses so that you may take your pick, and will supply food to your army. But if you refuse to accept these terms we will slaughter all the best horses. Moreover, rescue troops will soon be coming to aid us from K'ang-chü, and when they arrive the Han will have to fight both our men within the city and their forces on the outside. You had better consider the matter well and decide which course to take!"

At this time scouts from K'ang-chü were keeping a watch on the Han troops, but since the latter were still in good condition, the K'ang-chü forces did not dare to advance against them.

Li Kuang-li consulted with Chao Shih-ch'eng, Li Ch'e, and his other officers on what to do. "I have received word," he said, "that the people within the city have just obtained the services of a Chinese who knows how to dig wells. Moreover, they still seem to have plenty of food. Our purpose in coming here was to punish the chief offender, Wu-kua, and now that we have obtained his head, our task has been accomplished. If under these circumstances we refuse to withdraw our troops, the inhabitants will defend the city to the last man. Meanwhile the scouts from K'ang-chü, seeing our soldiers wearied by the siege, will come with troops to rescue Ta-yüan and the defeat of our army will be inevitable."

His officers all agreed with this opinion, and General Li sent word that he was willing to accept Ta-yüan's proposal. The men of Ta-yüan then brought out their finest horses and allowed the Han officers to choose the ones they wanted. They also produced large stores of provisions to feed the Han army. The Han officers selected twenty or thirty of the choicest horses, as well as over three thousand stallions and mares of less high quality, and set up one of the nobles named

Mi-ts'ai, who had treated the earlier Han envoys with kindness, as the new king of Ta-yüan, promising that they would withdraw their troops. In the end the Han soldiers never entered the inner wall of the city, but withdrew according to their promise and began the journey home.

When Li Kuang-li first started west from Tun-huang, he considered that his army was too numerous to be provided with food by the lands along the way and he therefore divided it up into several parties, some of them taking the northern route and some the southern. One of these separate groups, comprising a thousand or more men and led by the subordinate commander Wang Shen-sheng, the former grand herald Hu Ch'ung-kuo, and others, arrived at Yü-ch'eng. The men of Yü-ch'eng withdrew into the city and refused to provide any food to Wang Shen-sheng's soldiers. Though he was two hundred *li* away from the main army of General Li, Wang Shen-sheng examined the city and, deciding that he had nothing to fear, began to berate the inhabitants for failing to give him any food. The inhabitants could see that Wang Shen-sheng's army was growing smaller day by day, and finally one day at dawn they sent out a force of three thousand men who attacked and killed Wang Shen-sheng and the other commanders and defeated his army. Only a few of the Han soldiers managed to escape and flee to the army of General Li.

General Li thereupon dispatched Shang-kuan Chieh, his chief commandant in charge of requisitioning grain, who attacked and conquered the city of Yü-ch'eng. The king of Yü-ch'eng fled to K'ang-chü, where Shang-kuan Chieh pursued him. When the men of K'ang-chü heard that the Han armies had already conquered Ta-yüan, they handed the king of Yü-ch'eng over to Shang-kuan Chieh. The latter ordered four of his horsemen to bind the king and take him under guard to the headquarters of the commander in chief, General Li.

The four horsemen consulted together, saying, "The king of Yü-ch'eng is the archenemy of the Han. Now we have been given the task of escorting him alive to the general's headquarters, but if he should suddenly escape it would go very badly with us!" They therefore decided to kill the king, but none of them dared to strike the first blow. Finally one of the horsemen from Shang-kuei named Chao Ti, the youngest of the group, drew his sword and cut down the king. Then, bearing the king's head, he and Shang-kuan Chieh and the rest of the group set out after and overtook General Li.

Earlier, when General Li started out on the second expedition against Ta-yüan, the emperor sent envoys to announce the fact to the Wu-sun and ask them to send a large force to cooperate in the attack. The Wu-sun did in fact send two thousand horsemen but, not willing to alienate either party, they held back and refused to join in the attack.

When General Li and his army returned east, the rulers of all the small states they passed through, having heard of the defeat of Ta-yüan, sent their sons or brothers to accompany the army to China, where they presented gifts, were received by the emperor, and remained at the Han court as hostages.

In General Li's campaign against Ta-yüan, the director of martial law Chao Shih-ch'eng achieved the greatest merit. In addition, Shang-kuan Chieh won distinction by daring to venture far into enemy territory and Li Ch'e by his skill in planning. When the army reentered the Jade Gate Pass, it numbered something over ten thousand men, with over a thousand military horses. During General Li's second expedition the army had not suffered from any lack of provisions, nor had many of the soldiers been killed in battle. The generals and other officers, however, were a greedy lot, most of them taking little care of their men but abusing and preying upon them instead. This was the reason for the large number of lives lost.

Nevertheless the emperor, considering that it had been such a long expedition, made no attempt to punish those who were at fault, but enfeoffed Li Kuang-li as marquis of Hai-hsi, and Chao Ti, the horseman who had cut off the head of the king of Yü-ch'eng, as marquis of Hsin-chih. He appointed Chao Shih-ch'eng as superintendent of the imperial household, Shang-kuan Chieh as privy treasurer, and Li Ch'e as governor of Shang-tang. Three of the officers who had gone on the campaign were appointed to posts ranking among the nine highest ministers; over a hundred were enfeoffed as marquises or appointed as chancellors, governors, or two thousand picul officials; and more than a thousand were appointed to posts paying a thousand piculs or less. Those who had volunteered to join the army were given posts which far exceeded their expectations, while the convicts who had been pressed into service were all pardoned and released from penal servitude. The common soldiers were rewarded with gifts valued at forty thousand catties of gold.

The expedition against Ta-yüan required four years to carry out, after which the army was disbanded. A year or so after the Han conquered Ta-yüan and set up Mi-ts'ai as the new king, the nobles of Ta-yüan, considering Mi-ts'ai a servile flatterer who had brought about the destruction of his own country, joined forces and murdered him. In his place they set up Ch'an-feng, the brother of Wu-kua, the former king. Ch'an-feng sent his son as a hostage to the Han court, whereupon the Han dispatched an envoy to Ta-yüan to present gifts to the new ruler and make sure that he restored peace and order to the kingdom. The Han also sent over ten parties of envoys to the various countries west of Ta-yüan to seek for rare objects and at the same time to call attention in a tactful way to the might which the Han had displayed in its conquest of Ta-yüan.

The government set up a chief commandant of Chiu-ch'üan in Tunhuang and established defense stations at various points from Tunhuang west to the Salt Swamp. A force of several hundred agricultural soldiers was sent to set up a garrison at Lun-t'ou, headed by an ambassador who saw to it that the fields were protected and stores of grain laid away to be used to supply the Han envoys who passed through on their way to foreign countries.

The Grand Historian remarks: The *Basic Annals of Emperor Yü* [8] records that the source of the Yellow River is in the K'un-lun Mountains, mountains over twenty-five hundred *li* high where the sun and moon in turn go to hide when they are not shining. It is said that on their heights are to be found the Fountain of Sweet Water and the Pool of Jade. Yet, since Chang Ch'ien and the other envoys have been sent to Ta-hsia, they have traced the Yellow River to its source and found no such K'un-lun Mountains as the *Basic Annals* records. Therefore, what the *Book of Documents* states about the mountains and rivers of the nine ancient provinces of China seems to be nearer the

[8] An ancient text now lost.

truth, while when it comes to the wonders recorded in the *Basic Annals of Emperor Yü* or the *Classic of Hills and Seas,*[9] I cannot accept them.

[9] A geography of ancient China filled with legends and descriptions of fabulous beasts and other wonders. This is the earliest mention of the work. It is from works such as these that Emperor Wu selected the name K'un-lun to apply to the range of mountains discovered by his envoys.

Shih chi 122: The Biographies of the Harsh Officials

The people scorned agricultural pursuits and turned more and more to deceit, flouting the regulations and thinking up clever ways to evade the law. Good men could not lead them to a life of virtue; only the sternest and most severe treatment had any effect in controlling them. Thus I made The Biographies of the Harsh Officials.

Confucius says, "If you lead the people with laws and control them with punishments, they will try to avoid the punishments but will have no sense of shame. But if you lead them with virtue and control them with rites, they will have a sense of shame and moreover will become good." [1] Lao Tzu states, "The man of superior virtue does not appear to have any virtue; therefore he keeps his virtue. The man of inferior virtue cannot forget his virtue; therefore he has no virtue." He also says, "The more laws are promulgated, the more thieves and bandits there will be." [2]

The Grand Historian remarks: How true these words are! Laws and regulations are only the tools of government; they are not the spring from which flows the purity of good government or the pollution of bad.

Formerly, in the time of the Ch'in, the net of the law was drawn tightly about the empire and yet evil and deceit sprang up on all sides; in the end men thought of nothing but evading their superiors and no one could do anything to save the situation. At that time the law officials worked to bring about order, battling helplessly as though against fire or boiling water. Only the hardiest and cruelest of them were able to bear the strain of office and derive any satisfaction from the task; those who cared for justice and virtue were left to rot in insignificant posts. Therefore Confucius said, "In hearing litigations, I am

[1] *Analects* II, 3.   [2] Lao Tzu, *Tao-te-ching* 38 and 57.

no better than anyone else. What is necessary is to make it so that there are no more litigations!"[3] And Lao Tzu said, "When the inferior man hears about the Way, he laughs out loud at it."[4] These are no empty words!

When the Han arose, it lopped off the harsh corners of the Ch'in code and returned to an easy roundness, whittled away the embellishments and achieved simplicity; the meshes of the law were spread so far apart that a whale could have passed through. The law officials were honest and simple-hearted and did not indulge in evil, and the common people were orderly and content. So we see that good government depends upon virtue, not harshness.

In the time of Empress Lü we find one instance of a harsh official, a man named Hou Feng who oppressed the members of the imperial family and committed outrages against the high officials, but when the Lü clan was overthrown, he and all his family were arrested and done away with. Again, in the reign of Emperor Ching, we have the case of Ch'ao Ts'o who, combining learning with natural ability, was noted for his sternness. When the leaders of the Seven Kingdoms rose in revolt, however, they used their resentment against Ch'ao Ts'o as an excuse, and in the end Ch'ao Ts'o was executed. After him came such men as Chih Tu and Ning Ch'eng.

Chih Tu

Chih Tu was a native of Yang. He served as a palace attendant under Emperor Wen, and in the time of Emperor Ching was made a general of palace attendants. He had no qualms about voicing his criticisms openly and contradicting the high ministers to their faces at court.

Once he was attending the emperor on an outing to the Shang-lin Park. Madam Chia, one of the emperor's concubines, had retired to the toilet when suddenly a wild boar rushed into the privy. The emperor signaled to Chih Tu to do something, but he refused to move, whereupon the emperor himself seized a weapon and was about to go to her rescue in person. Chih Tu flung himself on the ground before the emperor and said, "If you lose one lady in waiting, we will bring you another! The empire is full of women like Madam Chia. But what

[3] *Analects* XII, 13.   [4] *Tao-te-ching* 41.

about Your Majesty? Though you think lightly of your own safety, what will become of the temples of your ancestors and of the empress dowager?"

With this, the emperor turned back, and the boar also withdrew. When the empress dowager heard of the incident, she rewarded Chih Tu with a gift of a hundred catties of gold. From this time on the emperor treated Chih Tu with great respect.

At this time the Chien clan of Chi-nan, consisting of over three hundred households, was notorious for its power and lawlessness, and none of the two thousand picul officials could do anything to control it. Emperor Ching thereupon appointed Chih Tu as governor of Chi-nan. As soon as he reached the province, he executed the worst offenders among the Chien clan, along with the members of their families, and the rest were all overwhelmed with fear. After a year or so under Chih Tu's rule no one in the province dared even to pick up belongings that had been dropped in the road, and the governors of the ten or twelve provinces in the neighborhood looked up to Chih Tu with awe as though he were one of the highest ministers of the court.

Chih Tu was a man of great daring and vigor. He was scrupulously honest and public-minded, and would never deign even to break the seal on letters addressed to him by private individuals. He refused to accept gifts from others or to listen to special requests, but always used to say, "I turned my back on parents and kin when I took office. All that remains for me to do is to fulfill my duties and die, if necessary, to maintain my integrity as an official." To the end of his life he never gave a thought to his wife or family.

Later, Chih Tu was moved to the post of military commander of the capital. The chancellor Chou Ya-fu, the marquis of T'iao, was at the height of his power and behaved with great arrogance, but whenever Chih Tu appeared before Chou Ya-fu, he would only greet Chou Ya-fu with a low bow instead of the customary prostration.

At this time the common people were still simple-hearted and ingenuous; they had a genuine fear of breaking the law and took care to stay out of trouble. Chih Tu alone among the officials put sternness and severity above all other qualities and when it came to applying the letter of the law he made no exception even for the emperor's in-laws.

The feudal lords and members of the imperial family all eyed him askance and nicknamed him "The Green Hawk."

Liu Jung, the king of Lin-chiang, was ordered to come to Ch'ang-an and report to the office of the military commander of the capital to answer a list of charges which Chih Tu had drawn up against him. When he arrived, he asked if he might have a brush and scraper to write a letter of apology to the emperor, but Chih Tu forbade the clerks to give him any writing implements. Tou Ying, the marquis of Wei-ch'i, however, sent someone to slip the writing implements to the king in secret, and so he was able to write his letter of apology, after which he committed suicide.[5] When Empress Dowager Tou heard of this she was furious and managed to have charges brought against Chih Tu. He was obliged to resign his post and retire to his home. Emperor Ching then dispatched an envoy bearing the imperial credentials to honor Chih Tu with the post of governor of Yen-men Province on the northern border. Because of the empress dowager's anger, the emperor did not require Chih Tu to come to the capital to receive the appointment but allowed him to proceed directly from his home to Yen-men and to carry out his new duties as he saw fit.

The Hsiung-nu had long heard of Chih Tu's strict loyalty and integrity, and when he arrived in Yen-men they withdrew their troops from the border; as long as Chih Tu was alive they would not come near the province. The Hsiung-nu leaders even went so far as to fashion a wooden image of Chih Tu which they ordered their mounted archers to use as a target for practice; but none of them were able to hit it, such was the fear that he inspired in them. He was a constant source of worry to the Hsiung-nu.

Empress Dowager Tou, however, finally managed to find some legal pretext for bringing charges against Chih Tu once more. "Chih Tu is a loyal subject," the emperor said to her, "and I would like to pardon

[5] Liu Jung was the oldest son of Emperor Ching. Originally the emperor appointed him as heir apparent, but later removed him from that position because of his annoyance at the prince's mother, Lady Li, and made him king of Lin-chiang instead. From his biography in *Shih chi* 59, "Hereditary Houses of the Five Families," it is obvious that Chih Tu drove the prince to suicide by his threats and accusations. Empress Dowager Tou never forgave Chih Tu for this harsh treatment of her grandson.

him." But the empress dowager replied, "And the king of Lin-chiang—was he not a loyal subject too?" So in the end Chih Tu was executed.

Ning Ch'eng

Ning Ch'eng was a native of Jang. He served under Emperor Ching as a palace attendant and master of guests. He was a man of great spirit. As long as he was a petty official, he thought of nothing but how he could outdo his superiors, and when he himself became a master of others, he treated the men under him like so much soggy firewood to be bound and bundled into shape. By cunning, knavery, and displays of might, he gradually advanced until he had reached the post of chief commandant of Chi-nan.

At this time Chih Tu was the governor of Chi-nan. The men who had previously held the post of chief commandant of Chi-nan had always dismounted from their carriages and entered the governor's office on foot, requesting the clerks to grant them an interview with the governor as though they were no more than magistrates of districts; such was the awe with which they approached Chih Tu. When Ning Ch'eng took over as chief commandant, however, he soon made it clear that he was not only equal to Chih Tu but could outdo him. Chih Tu had long heard of Ning Ch'eng's reputation and was careful to treat him very well, so that the two became fast friends.

Some years later Chih Tu was executed, and the emperor, worried about the large number of outrages and crimes being committed by the members of the imperial family living in the capital, summoned Ning Ch'eng to Ch'ang-an and appointed him as military commander of the capital. In restoring order, he imitated the ways of Chih Tu, though he was no match for Chih Tu in integrity. It was not long, however, before every member of the imperial family and of the other powerful clans was trembling in awe of him.

When Emperor Wu came to the throne he transferred Ning Ch'eng to the post of prefect of the capital. The emperor's in-laws, however, were assiduous in pointing out Ning Ch'eng's faults and finally managed to have him convicted of some crime. His head was shaved and he was forced to wear a convict's collar about his neck. At this time it was customary for any of the high officials who had been accused of a capital offense to commit suicide; very few of them would ever submit to actual punishment. Ning Ch'eng, however, allowed himself to be subjected to the severest punishment. Considering that he would never again be able to hold public office, he contrived to free himself from his convict's collar, forged the credentials needed to get him through the Pass, and escaped to his home in the east.

"An official who can't advance to a salary of two thousand piculs or a merchant who can't make at least ten million cash is not fit to be called a man!" he declared. With this he bought a thousand or so *ch'ing* of hillside farm land on credit and hired several thousand poor families to work it for him. After a few years a general amnesty was issued, absolving him from his former offenses. By this time he had accumulated a fortune of several thousand pieces of gold. He did any sort of daring feat that took his fancy, since he knew all the faults of the officials in the area. Whenever he went out he was accompanied by twenty or thirty mounted attendants, and he ordered the people of the area about with greater authority than the governor of the province.

Chou-yang Yu

Chou-yang Yu's father was originally named Chao Chien. Because he was a maternal uncle of Liu Ch'ang, the king of Huai-nan, he was enfeoffed as marquis of Chou-yang and consequently changed his family name from Chao to Chou-yang. Chou-yang Yu, being related to the imperial family, was employed as a palace attendant and served under Emperors Wen and Ching. During the reign of Emperor Ching he became the governor of a province.

When Emperor Wu first came to the throne, most of the officials still governed with great circumspection and attention to justice, but Chou-yang Yu alone among the two thousand picul officials established a new record for violence, cruelty, and willfulness. In the case of people he liked he would twist the law around to have them set free; in the case of those he hated he would bend the law to any lengths to wipe them out. Whatever province he was appointed to he would not rest until he had brought about the destruction of its powerful families.

If he was acting as governor, he would treat the chief commandant of the province as though he were no more than a district magistrate; and if he was acting as chief commandant, it would not be long before he had gone over the head of the governor and seized the power of government right out of his hands. He was fully as stubborn as Chi An, and as good at utilizing the letter of the law for evil ends as Ssu-ma An; though all three of these men ranked equally as two thousand picul officials, if the other two happened to be riding in the same carriage with Chou-yang Yu, they would never venture to lounge side by side with him on the armrest.

Sometime later, when Chou-yang Yu was acting as chief commandant of Ho-tung, he became involved in a struggle for power with the governor of Ho-tung, Sheng-t'u Kung, each bringing accusations against the other. Sheng-t'u Kung was condemned to suffer punishment, but he cared too much for his honor to undergo the penalty and committed suicide instead. Chou-yang Yu was executed and his corpse exposed in the market place.

From the time of Ning Ch'eng and Chou-yang Yu·on, prosecutions became more and more numerous and the people grew very clever at evading the law. The officials for the most part were men of the same type as Ning Ch'eng and Chou-yang Yu.

Chao Yü and Chang T'ang

Chao Yü was a native of T'ai. He served originally as a clerk in his district and was later moved to a post in the capital. Because of his honesty he was appointed a clerk under the master of documents and served the grand commandant Chou Ya-fu. When Chou Ya-fu became chancellor, Chao Yü was made a secretary to the chancellor. Everyone in the chancellor's office praised Chao Yü for his honesty and fairness, but Chou Ya-fu put little trust in him. "I know perfectly well that Chao Yü would never do anything unfair," he remarked. "But he is too severe in applying the letter of the law. It would never do to appoint him to an important post such as chancellor!"

Under the present emperor, Chao Yü continued to work away as a brush-and-scraper clerk, piling up merit and gradually advancing until he became imperial secretary. The emperor considered him a man of ability and even appointed him as a palace counselor, setting him to work with Chang T'ang discussing and drawing up a number of new laws and statutes. They invented the laws that anyone who knowingly allows a criminal act to go unreported is as guilty as the criminal, and that officials may be prosecuted for the offenses of their inferiors or their superiors in the same bureau. From this time on the laws were applied with increasing strictness.

Chang T'ang was a native of Tu. His father worked as an aide in the city government of Ch'ang-an. Once his father went out and left Chang T'ang, who was still a young boy at the time, to mind the house. When he returned he discovered that a rat had stolen a piece of meat. He was furious and beat Chang T'ang for his negligence. Chang T'ang set about digging up the rat's hole, caught the rat, and recovered what was left of the piece of meat. He then proceeded to indict the rat, beat it until it told its story, write out a record of its words, compare them with the evidence, and draw up a proposal for punishment. After this he took the rat and the meat out into the yard, where he held a trial, presented the charges, and crucified the rat. When his father saw what he was doing and examined the documents he had drawn up, he found to his astonishment that the boy had carried out the whole procedure like a seasoned prison official. After this he set his son to writing legal documents.

After his father died, Chang T'ang became a clerk in the Ch'ang-an city government. Some years later it happened that the younger brother of Empress Dowager Wang, T'ien Sheng, who was only an official at the time, was arrested in Ch'ang-an. Chang T'ang did everything in his power to get T'ien Sheng freed and, after his efforts proved successful and T'ien Sheng had been released from prison and enfeoffed as marquis of Chou-yang, T'ien Sheng became fast friends with Chang T'ang and introduced him to all his acquaintances among the nobility.

Chang T'ang served in the office of the prefect of the capital, acting as aide to Ning Ch'eng, who held the post of prefect at that time. Ning Ch'eng, recognizing Chang T'ang's honesty and impartiality, recommended him for a post in one of the higher ministries. On the basis of this recommendation he was promoted to the position of commandant of Mou-ling and was put in charge of the construction work there.[6]

When T'ien Sheng's older brother T'ien Fen, the marquis of Wu-an, became chancellor, he selected Chang T'ang to act as his secretary. From time to time he praised Chang T'ang to the emperor, who appointed Chang T'ang to assist the imperial secretary and take over most of the latter's duties. He was responsible for investigating the charges of sorcery brought against Empress Ch'en and having her deposed, and he worked to root out and bring to justice all the members of her clique. The emperor, impressed by his ability, gradually promoted him until he made him a palace counselor and put him to work with Chao Yü drawing up a number of new statutes. Chang T'ang did his best to make the laws more severe and prevent the government officials from abusing their positions.

Later, Chao Yü was transferred to the post of military commander of the capital and then was appointed privy treasurer, while Chang T'ang was made commandant of justice. The two men were close friends, Chang T'ang treating Chao Yü like an older brother.

Chao Yü was a very parsimonious and arrogant sort of person. From the time he first became an official he never once entertained any guests at his lodgings. Though the other high officials would sometimes go to call on him, he never returned their calls. He did everything he could to prevent his friends and acquaintances from coming to him with requests and sought to act wholly on his own without any advice from others. If he saw that someone was breaking the law, he would have him arrested at once, but he did not extend his investigations or attempt to ferret out the secret faults of his subordinates.

Chang T'ang, on the other hand, was a very deceitful person who knew how to make use of his wisdom to get the better of others. When he was still a petty clerk he tried his hand at making a profit and was secretly friendly with T'ien Chia, Yü Weng-shu, and other wealthy merchants of Ch'ang-an. Later, when he had risen to one of the nine

[6] The construction work was the building of Emperor Wu's mausoleum at Mou-ling, but since Ssu-ma Ch'ien is writing during the reign of Emperor Wu, he avoids direct mention of the gloomy nature of the work.

highest ministerial posts in the government, he attracted some of the most eminent gentlemen in the empire to his side and, though he secretly disliked them, he made a pretense of admiring them.

The emperor at this time showed a great fondness for literature and learning, and Chang T'ang decided that when he was passing judgment in important cases it would be well to back up his decision with references to the Classics. He therefore asked some of the students and court erudits who were familiar with the *Book of Documents* and the *Spring and Autumn Annals* to act as his secretaries in the office of the commandant of justice and help in deciding on doubtful points of law. When he was presenting memorials to the throne concerning difficult cases, he would always inform the emperor beforehand of all the facts of the case. When the emperor had indicated what he thought was the right decision, Chang T'ang would then make a careful record of the emperor's decision and write it down among the statutes of the commandant of justice's office so that it could be used as a precedent in future cases and would make clear to all the wisdom of the ruler.

If the emperor happened to criticize his judgment in some case, he would accept the blame himself and apologize, claiming that he recognized the superior wisdom of the emperor's viewpoint. Then he would invariably mention the name of some worthy man among his aides or secretaries and say, "So-and-so expressed exactly the same opinion as Your Majesty, but I refused to listen to his advice and so I have committed this stupid blunder!" In such cases the emperor would always pardon him. At other times, when the emperor happened to praise him for some judgment, he would say, "I had nothing to do with preparing this memorial. It was drawn up by So-and-so" (mentioning the name of the one of his aides or secretaries). This was the way he worked to advance the officials in his office and make known their good points, at the same time covering up their faults.

In prosecuting cases, if he knew that the emperor was anxious to see the accused man condemned, he would turn the case over to his harshest and cruelest secretaries, but if he knew the emperor wanted the man pardoned, he would turn it over to secretaries who were more lenient and fair-minded. If he was dealing with a member of some rich and powerful family, he would invariably find a way to twist the law around and prove the man's guilt, but if it was someone from a poor and insignificant family, he would say to the emperor, "Although, according to the letter of the law, the man is guilty, I trust that Your Majesty will consider the matter in a generous light." As a result, many of the men whose cases Chang T'ang handled were pardoned.

After Chang T'ang became a high official he was very careful about his conduct.[7] He would entertain guests, dine and drink with his old friends, and look out for their sons and brothers who had become officials or their poor relations with extreme generosity. When it came to paying calls on others, he was not deterred by the hottest or the coldest weather. Thus, although he was severe in legal matters, suspicious and by no means impartial, he managed in this way to win fame and praise. Many of the sternest officials who acted as claws and teeth for him were students of the Classics who were studying under the erudits, and the chancellor Kung-sun Hung, himself a scholar, often praised his virtues.

Later, when Chang T'ang investigated the charges that the kings of Huai-nan, Heng-shan, and Chiang-tu were plotting revolt, he succeeded in ferreting out all the facts of the case. The emperor wished to pardon Chuang Chu[8] and Wu Pei, who were implicated in the case, but Chang T'ang objected, saying, "Wu Pei took the lead in planning the revolt, and Chuang Chu was one of your most trusted ministers, coming and going in the palace itself and carrying out your missions, and yet he engaged in secret doings with one of the feudal lords. If men such as these are not executed, there will be no way to control the officials hereafter!" As a result, the emperor approved the death sentence which Chang T'ang had recommended.

There were many instances like this in which Chang T'ang, in the course of his prosecutions, brought about the downfall of high officials and won merit for himself. Thus he continued to enjoy greater and

---

[7] As opposed to his earlier days, when he associated with merchants and tried to make a profit, conduct which was considered highly degrading for an official.

[8] Chuang Chu has appeared earlier in the accounts of Southern and Eastern Yüeh as the emperor's envoy to those regions. His surname is sometimes written Yen instead of Chuang. He later became a palace counselor and enjoyed great favor with the emperor. He was very friendly with Liu An, the king of Huai-nan, and was therefore implicated when Liu An was accused of plotting revolt.

greater honor and trust and was finally transferred to the post of imperial secretary.

It was at this time that the Hun-yeh king and his followers surrendered to the Han, and the government was busy raising large armies and sending them to attack the Hsiung-nu. The region east of the mountains was suffering from floods and droughts, and the poor and destitute were wandering from place to place, depending entirely upon the government for aid and sustenance, until the resources of the government were exhausted. Chang T'ang, acting on the suggestion of the emperor, proposed the minting of white metal coins and five-*shu* cash, and arranged for the government to take complete control of the salt and iron industries, removing them from the hands of the rich merchants and large-scale traders. He also drew up a law making it possible to confiscate the wealth of anyone attempting to evade the *suan* tax on his possessions and used it to bring about the ruin of the powerful families and great landowners, twisting the letter of the law around, devising clever ways to convict others, and patching up loopholes in the statutes. Whenever Chang T'ang would appear at court with some proposal and would begin to discuss the government's fiscal policy, the emperor would listen until sundown in rapt attention, forgetting even to take time out for meals. The chancellor soon became no more than a figurehead, all the affairs of the empire being decided by Chang T'ang.

But the common people continued restless and dissatisfied with their lot, and before the measures taken by the government to remedy the situation had had a chance to do any good, corrupt officials began utilizing them to snatch illegal gain. To prevent this, Chang T'ang made the punishments for violation of the law even more severe. Eventually everyone, from the highest officials down to the common people, was pointing an accusing finger at Chang T'ang.

Once, when Chang T'ang was ill, the emperor went in person to his bedside to see how he was: such was the respect and favor that Chang T'ang enjoyed.

When envoys from the Hsiung-nu came to court with requests for a peace alliance, the ministers deliberated their proposal in the presence of the emperor. One of the erudits named Ti Shan suggested that it would be best to conclude a peace alliance and, when the emperor asked him to state his reasons, he replied, "Weapons are the instruments of ill fortune; they cannot be lightly resorted to time and again! Emperor Kao-tsu wanted to attack the Hsiung-nu, but after the extreme difficulties he encountered at P'ing-ch'eng he finally abandoned the idea and concluded a peace alliance. Thus during the reigns of Emperor Hui and Empress Dowager Lü the empire enjoyed peace and security. When Emperor Wen came to the throne he tried again to deal with the Hsiung-nu by force and the northern border was once more thrown into turmoil and forced to suffer the hardships of warfare. In the time of Emperor Ching, when the kings of Wu and Ch'u and the other states raised the Revolt of the Seven Kingdoms, Emperor Ching spent several anxious and fearful months hurrying back and forth between his own palace and that of the empress dowager and planning how to deal with the situation, and once the revolt had finally been put down, Emperor Ching never again mentioned the subject of warfare. Thus under him the empire enjoyed wealth and plenty. Now, since Your Majesty has again called out the armies to attack the Hsiung-nu, the resources of China have become more and more depleted and the people on the border are troubled by severe poverty and hardship. In view of this situation, I believe that it would be better to conclude a peace alliance."

The emperor then asked Chang T'ang what he thought of this statement, and Chang T'ang answered, "This man is only a stupid Confucianist. He knows nothing about such matters!"

"It is quite true that my loyalty is the loyalty of the stupid," replied Ti Shan. "But the loyalty of the imperial secretary Chang T'ang is deceitful and meretricious! Look how he prosecuted the kings of Huai-nan and Chiang-tu, applying the law with the utmost severity and forcing the kings into a position of guilt, bringing about estrangement between the ruler and his own blood relations and filling the other feudal lords with anxiety! This is quite enough to convince me that Chang T'ang's so-called loyalty is meretricious!"

The emperor's face flushed and he said, "Master Ti, if I made you the governor of a province do you think you could keep the barbarian wretches from plundering the region?"

"No, I could not," replied Ti Shan.

"Suppose I made you the magistrate of a district?"

"No," Ti Shan replied again.

"Or the commander of a guard post on the border?"

Ti Shan realized that he could not argue his way out of the situation and that if he did not say yes he would be handed over to the law officials for trial. So he replied, "In that case I could do it."

The emperor then sent Ti Shan to take command of one of the guard posts on the border. A month or so after he arrived there the Hsiung-nu raided the post, cut off Ti Shan's head, and withdrew. After this the other officials were all too terrified to say a word.

Among Chang T'ang's friends was a certain T'ien Chia who, although a merchant, was a man of worth and upright in conduct. When Chang T'ang was still a petty official, he carried on various money dealings with T'ien Chia, but after he became a high minister T'ien Chia scolded Chang T'ang about his behavior and warned him of his faults in the manner of a truly virtuous man.

Chang T'ang's downfall occurred seven years after he assumed the post of imperial secretary and came about in the following way. There was a man from Ho-tung named Li Wen who had once had a falling out with Chang T'ang. Later he became an assistant in the office of the imperial secretary, but he continued to bear a fierce grudge against Chang T'ang and from time to time, whenever he was able to discover some point in the documents handled by the office that would reflect to Chang T'ang's discredit, he saw that it was made known and that Chang T'ang was given no opportunity to escape responsibility. One of Chang T'ang's favorite secretaries, a man named Lu Yeh-chü, knew that Chang T'ang was worried about the situation and therefore got someone to submit an anonymous emergency report to the emperor accusing Li Wen of disaffection and evil-doing. The case was referred to Chang T'ang, who conducted an investigation and ordered Li Wen's execution. Chang T'ang knew quite well that Lu Yeh-chü had engineered the move to relieve him from worry, but when the emperor asked Chang T'ang, "Who do you suppose it was that first brought the charges of disaffection against Li Wen?" Chang T'ang pretended to be completely at a loss and replied, "I suppose it must have been some old acquaintance of Li Wen's who had a grudge against him."

Some time after this Lu Yeh-chü fell ill and was put to bed in the home of a friend in his neighborhood. Chang T'ang went in person to see how he was and even massaged his legs for him.

The kingdom of Chao was the site of an important smelting industry, and the king of Chao on several occasions had brought suit against the iron officials of the central government for the way they were running the industry, but Chang T'ang had always dismissed the complaints. The king of Chao then began to look around for evidence of some secret doings of Chang T'ang that he could use as a weapon against him. In addition, Lu Yeh-chü had in the past once had occasion to draw up charges against the king of Chao, and the king hated him as well. The king therefore submitted a memorial to the throne accusing both Chang T'ang and Lu Yeh-chü and charging that Chang T'ang, although a high minister, had visited his secretary Lu Yeh-chü when the latter was ill and had even gone so far as to massage Lu's legs for him. There were grounds, he suggested, for suspecting that the two were plotting some major crime. The case was referred to the commandant of justice of investigation.

Lu Yeh-chü meanwhile died of his illness, but the investigations implicated his younger brother, who was arrested and imprisoned in the office of the grain selector.[9] Chang T'ang had occasion to cross-examine some other prisoner in the grain selector's office and at that time he saw Lu Yeh-chü's brother but, hoping to find some way to help him secretly, he deliberately pretended not to recognize him. The brother, not realizing this, was deeply resentful and got someone to send a memorial to the throne accusing Chang T'ang and Lu Yeh-chü of conspiring together to bring false charges of dissaffection against Li Wen. The case was referred to Chien Hsüan who, being on bad terms with Chang T'ang, was only too happy to have this opportunity to conduct a thorough investigation.

Before Chien Hsüan had had a chance to submit the results of his investigation to the emperor, however, it was discovered that someone

---

[9] Chang T'ang had managed to fill all the regular jails to capacity, and it became necessary to use the office of the grain selector to house the overflow.

had broken into the funerary park of Emperor Wen and dug up and stolen the offerings of money that had been buried in the mausoleum. When the chancellor Ch'ing Ti arrived at court, he and Chang T'ang agreed that, as the two highest ministers, they should both present their apologies to the emperor for the crime. After the two men appeared before the emperor, however, Chang T'ang indicated that, since it was the duty of the chancellor to make seasonal inspections of the funerary parks, it was proper for the chancellor alone to make the apologies for the crime. As he himself had nothing to do with such affairs, there was no reason for him to apologize, he said. The chancellor accordingly submitted his apologies and the emperor referred the case to Chang T'ang for investigation. Chang T'ang then set about trying to prove that the chancellor had deliberately failed to report the theft, until the chancellor became concerned about his own safety. The chancellor's three chief secretaries, Chu Mai-ch'en, Wang Ch'ao, and Pien T'ung, all hated Chang T'ang and began looking about for ways to trip him up.

Chu Mai-ch'en was a native of K'uai-chi. He was recommended to the emperor by Chuang Chu because of his knowledge of the *Spring and Autumn Annals;* he and Chuang Chu, who were both from the region of Ch'u and were versed in the *Elegies of Ch'u,*[10] enjoyed great favor with the emperor, serving in the palace and taking part in government affairs as palace counselors. At this time Chang T'ang was still only a petty clerk and used to get down on his knees before Chu Mai-ch'en and the others and take orders from them. Later, when Chang T'ang became commandant of justice and was put in charge of investigating the king of Huai-nan and his fellow conspirators, he brought about the downfall of Chuang Chu, and from that time on Chu Mai-ch'en hated Chang T'ang intensely. When Chang T'ang became imperial secretary, Chu Mai-ch'en, who was governor of K'uai-chi at the time, was made master of titles chief commandant, ranking among the nine highest ministers of the government. A few years later he was tried for some offense and removed from his post and made a chief secretary. Whenever he had occasion to visit Chang T'ang, the

[10] The collection of poems by the Ch'u poet Ch'ü Yüan and his disciples and imitators.

latter would receive him perched on a couch, treating Chu Mai-ch'en like a petty clerk and refusing to show him any respect. Chu Mai-ch'en, being a true man of Ch'u, burned with indignation and was constantly looking for some way to bring about Chang T'ang's death.

The second of the chancellor's three chief secretaries was Wang Ch'ao, a native of Ch'i who reached the post of right prefect of the capital because of his knowledge of legal matters. The third was Pien T'ung, a stubborn and violent-tempered man who studied the strategies of the Warring States period and twice served as prime minister of Chi-nan. Thus all three of these men had previously held higher posts than Chang T'ang but had later lost them and become chief secretaries. As a result they were forced to bow and scrape before Chang T'ang who, knowing that they had formerly been highly honored, never lost an opportunity to humiliate them in his frequent dealings with the chancellor's office.

The three of them plotted together and said to the chancellor, "Originally Chang T'ang promised to apologize with you, but later he betrayed his promise. Now he is trying to impeach you for what happened at the grave of Emperor Wen. It is obvious that he simply wants to get you out of the way so that he himself can replace you as chancellor. But we know all about his secret dealings!" Then they sent law officers to arrest T'ien Hsin and others of Chang T'ang's merchant friends, and got them to give evidence against Chang T'ang. "Whenever Chang T'ang was about to present some proposal to the emperor," T'ien Hsin stated, "he would let me know about it beforehand. In that way I was able to buy up whatever goods would be affected by the proposal and hoard them until the price had gone up. Then I would split the profits with Chang T'ang." T'ien Hsin also revealed other corrupt practices of Chang T'ang, all of which were reported to the emperor. The emperor said to Chang T'ang, "Whenever I do something, the merchants always seem to find out about it beforehand and start busily buying up the articles that will be affected. It would almost appear as though someone were deliberately informing them of my plans!" Chang T'ang made no admission of guilt but instead pretended to be completely taken aback and exclaimed, "Why yes, that must be what is happening!"

Meanwhile Chien Hsüan submitted his report to the emperor on Chang T'ang's involvements with Lu Yeh-chü and the other charges which he had investigated. The emperor finally became convinced that Chang T'ang was guilty of deceit and had been cheating him before his very eyes. He dispatched eight envoys with a list of charges to confront Chang T'ang. Chang T'ang denied all of them and refused to make any admission of guilt, whereupon the emperor sent Chao Yü to press the charges once more. When Chao Yü appeared, he began to berate Chang T'ang, saying, "After all the men you have tried and condemned to execution along with their families, don't you even realize what your own position is now? Every charge that people have brought against you is backed up by evidence! The emperor would hate to have to send you to prison. Instead he hopes that you will settle things for yourself! What do you expect to gain by denying the charges?"

Chang T'ang then wrote a letter of apology, saying, "I, though a man of no merit whatsoever, rose from the position of a brush-and-scraper clerk and, through Your Majesty's generosity, became one of the three highest ministers in the government. Though I have failed in my duties, it is the three chief secretaries of the chancellor who have plotted to bring about my ruin." Then he committed suicide [116 B.C.].

After his death it was found that he had no more than five hundred pieces of gold in his home, all of which he had received as salary or gifts from the emperor; outside of this he left no estate whatsoever. His brothers and sons wanted to give him a lavish burial, but his mother objected. "Although T'ang was one of the highest ministers of the emperor, he got a name for corruption and evil and had to kill himself. Why give *him* a lavish burial?" So in the end they carried his coffin to the graveyard in an oxcart and buried him with only an inner coffin and no outer one. When the emperor heard of the incident he remarked, "If she weren't that kind of mother she could never have borne that kind of son!"

The emperor then had charges brought against all three of the chief secretaries and executed them; the chancellor Ch'ing Ti committed suicide. T'ien Hsin was pardoned and released. The emperor felt sorry for what had happened to Chang T'ang and promoted his son Chang An-shih to a higher post in the government.

Chao Yü had once been deprived of his post but was later appointed as commandant of justice. Earlier in his career Chou Ya-fu had refused to trust him, saying that he was much too intent upon harming others and applying the law with severity; later, when Chao Yü became privy treasurer and ranked with the nine highest ministers of the government, he did indeed become one of the harshest of the officials. In his old age, however, as the number of criminal cases continued to increase and the other officials all worked to apply the laws with the greatest possible sternness, Chao Yü became more lenient in his prosecutions and won a reputation for fairness. Later, when men like Wang Wen-shu appeared on the scene, they were much harsher than Chao Yü. In his old age he was transferred to the post of prime minister of Yen, which he held for several years until he became senile and, committing some blunder, was forced to retire to private life. Some ten or more years after Chang T'ang's suicide Chao Yü died of old age in his own home.

I Tsung

I Tsung was a native of Ho-tung. When he was young he and a friend named Chang Tz'u-kung became highwaymen and formed a band of thieves. His older sister I Hsü had won favor with Empress Dowager Wang because of her knowledge of medicine, and one day the empress dowager asked her if she had any brothers who might be appointed to posts in the government. "I have a younger brother," she replied, "but he is worthless and could never be appointed." The empress dowager nevertheless reported her words to the emperor, who made her brother I Tsung a palace attendant and appointed him as magistrate of one of the districts in Shang-tang Province. He governed with great determination and little leniency, and no one in the district was behind time in paying taxes. Having won an outstanding record there, he was transferred to the post of magistrate of Ch'ang-ling and Ch'ang-an. He applied the laws with honesty and directness and made no exceptions even for the emperor's in-laws. When he arrested and tried Chung, the son of Lady Hsiu-ch'eng, Empress Dowager Wang's granddaughter, the emperor concluded that he was a man of ability and transferred him to the post of chief commandant of Ho-nei. When he reached Ho-nei he succeeded in wiping out the powerful Jung family that lived in that province, and the people of Ho-nei were soon too frightened even to pick up objects that had been dropped in the road.

Chang Tz'u-kung was also appointed a palace attendant and, being a brave and reckless man, joined the army and won merit by daring to fight his way deep into the enemy lines. He was enfeoffed as marquis of An-t'ou.

Ning Ch'eng was at this time living in retirement and the emperor wanted to make him the governor of a province, but the imperial secretary Kung-sun Hung said, "When I was still a petty official and living east of the mountains, Ning Ch'eng was serving as chief commandant of Chi-nan. He ruled the inhabitants like a wolf driving a flock of sheep—it would never do to let him govern the people of a province!"

The emperor instead appointed Ning Ch'eng as chief commandant of the Han-ku Pass. After he had been in this post for a year or so, the officials from the provinces and kingdoms east of the Pass who had had occasion to go in or out of the Pass used to say to each other, "Better to face a nursing tigress than the wrath of Ning Ch'eng!"

Later, I Tsung was transferred to the post of governor of Nan-yang. He had heard that Ning Ch'eng had retired and was living at his home, which was in Nan-yang, but when he reached the Pass he found that Ning Ch'eng had very politely come to greet him and escort him on his way. I Tsung, however, treated the matter very lightly and did not deign to return the courtesy. When he got to Nan-yang he proceeded to bring charges against the Ning family and had their houses completely destroyed. Even Ning Ch'eng himself was convicted of some offense. The members of the K'ung, Pao, and other powerful families all fled from the province, and the rest of the officials and people of Nan-yang went around on tiptoe for fear of breaking some law. Chu Ch'iang of P'ing-shih and Tu Chou of Tu-yen served under I Tsung, acting as his teeth and claws in applying the law, and were later transferred and made secretaries in the office of the commandant of justice.

The armies had from time to time marched out of Ting-hsiang Province to attack the Hsiung-nu, and the officials and people of that province had been thrown into turmoil by their presence. The emperor therefore transferred I Tsung to the post of governor of Ting-hsiang. When he reached the province he made a surprise visit to the jail, seized over two hundred prisoners accused of major and minor crimes, along with another two hundred or so of their friends and relatives who had slipped into the jail to visit them, and had the entire group arrested and tried at once. "These men were plotting to free prisoners who deserved to die!" he announced, indicating the friends and relatives of the prisoners, and in one day passed sentence on the entire group of over four hundred and had them all executed. Though the season was warm enough, the entire province shivered and trembled, and the more cunning and rascally among the people hurried forward to make themselves useful to the officials.

At this time Chao Yü and Chang T'ang had advanced to the highest posts in the government through their severe application of the law, but their ways were mild compared with I Tsung's and at least had a legal basis. I Tsung governed like a hawk spreading its wings and swooping down upon its prey.

Sometime later, when the five-*shu* and white metal coins were put into circulation, the people resorted to all sorts of evil practices to make a profit, those living in the capital being among the worst offenders. The emperor therefore appointed I Tsung as right prefect of the capital and Wang Wen-shu as military commander of the capital. Wang Wen-shu was one of the harshest officials. If he did not inform I Tsung in advance of what he was going to do, I Tsung would invariably use his influence to wreck Wang Wen-shu's plans and turn his successes into failures. Between them they executed an extraordinary number of people, but the effect of such measures was only temporary, and the offenders continued to increase until it became impossible to deal with them all. At this time the posts of imperial inquisitor were set up, the officials spent all their time arresting people and cutting off heads, and men like Yen Feng were appointed to office because of their severity. I Tsung was scrupulously honest and in this point resembled Chih Tu.

It was at this time that the emperor was taken ill while visiting Cauldron Lake and was forced to remain there for some time. After he had recovered, he made a sudden trip to the Palace of Sweet Springs and on the way he noticed that the road was in bad repair. "Did I Tsung think I would never have occasion to use this road again?" he remarked angrily, and seemed to be very upset by the incident.

When winter came, Yang K'o was put in charge of hearing accusations against men who had failed to report their possessions for the property tax. I Tsung believed that this procedure would throw the people into turmoil, and he therefore sent out his officials to arrest Yang K'o's agents. When the emperor heard of this, he ordered Tu Shih to investigate the case. I Tsung was convicted of disobeying an imperial edict and impeding the business of the government and was executed and his corpse exposed in the market place. This happened a year before Chang T'ang's death.

Wang Wen-shu

Wang Wen-shu was a native of Yang-ling. In his youth he robbed graves and committed similar evil deeds, but later he was given a trial post as village head in one of the districts. Though he was removed from this position several times, he finally managed to become an official and was made a secretary in the office of the commandant of justice, handling criminal affairs under Chang T'ang. He was transferred to the office of the imperial secretary and put in charge of suppressing robbers and bandits, in which capacity he had occasion to execute an extraordinary number of men. Sometime later, he was transferred to the post of chief commandant of Kuang-p'ing. There he selected some ten or more daring men from the powerful families of the province whom he believed worthy to be employed as his officials and had them act as teeth and claws for him. Meanwhile he ferreted out all of their secret crimes, but overlooked what he had found and put them in charge of capturing the bandits in the region. So long as they did as he wished and brought in the bandits he wanted captured, he did not press charges against them, even though they might be guilty of a hundred crimes. But if they allowed any of the bandits to escape, then he would utilize the information he had gathered to prosecute them and would not rest until he had wiped out their whole families. As a result of this policy, none of the bandits in the region of Ch'i and Chao dared come near Kuang-p'ing, and the province gained a reputation for being so strictly governed that people would not even pick up objects that had been dropped in the road.

The emperor, hearing of this, transferred Wang Wen-shu to the post of governor of Ho-nei. Wang Wen-shu had already learned during his stay in Kuang-p'ing who all the powerful and lawless families of Ho-nei were. When he reached his new post in the ninth month, he got together fifty privately owned horses from the province and had them disposed at the various post stations between Ho-nei and the capital for later use. In appointing his officials he followed the same strategy that he had used in Kuang-p'ing and had soon arrested all the powerful and crafty men in the province. By the time they had been investigated and tried, over a thousand families were implicated in their guilt. He then sent a letter to the throne asking that the major offenders be executed along with the members of their families, the lesser offenders put to death, and all their estates confiscated by the government to compensate for the illegal gains which they had gotten in the past. He forwarded the letter by means of the post horses he had stationed along the way, and in no more than two or three days an answer came back from the emperor approving his proposal. He proceeded to carry out the sentence at once, and the blood flowed for miles around. The whole province was astounded at the supernatural speed with which his proposal had been carried to the capital and approved, and by the time the twelfth month ended no one in the province dared speak a word against him. People no longer ventured out of their houses at night and there was not a single bandit left to set the dogs in the fields to barking. The few offenders who had managed to escape arrest and had fled to neighboring provinces and kingdoms found themselves pursued even there.

When the beginning of spring came Wang Wen-shu stamped his foot and sighed, "Ah! If only I could make the winter last one more month I could finish my work to satisfaction!" [11] Such was his fondness for slaughter and demonstrations of power and his lack of love for others. When the emperor heard of this he concluded that Wang Wen-shu was a man of ability and transferred him to the post of military commander of the capital.

He proceeded the same way in this post as he had in Ho-nei, summoning all of the most notoriously cruel and cunning officials to aid him in his work, such as Yang Chieh and Ma Wu of Ho-nei, and Yang Kung and Ch'eng Hsin from within the Pass. At this time I Tsung was acting as prefect of the capital, and Wang Wen-shu, who was rather afraid of I Tsung, did not dare to do everything he would have liked to do. Later, when I Tsung was executed and Chang T'ang fell from power, Wang Wen-shu was transferred to the post of commandant of justice and Yin Ch'i replaced him as military commander of the capital.

Yin Ch'i was a native of Shih-p'ing in Tung Province. From the position of a brush-and-scraper clerk he gradually advanced until he had become a secretary in the office of Chang T'ang, the imperial secretary. Chang T'ang often praised him for his integrity and fearlessness and put him in charge of suppressing bandits. When it came to ordering executions, Yin Ch'i did not make exceptions even for the emperor's in-laws. He was transferred to the post of chief commandant of the area within the Pass, where his reputation for sternness surpassed that of Ning Ch'eng. The emperor, concluding that he was a man of ability, made him military commander of the capital, and the officials and people under him were driven to even greater exhaustion and destitution.

Yin Ch'i was a boorish man with little refinement or learning. Under his administration the powerful and evil officials all went into hiding, while the good officials were unable to carry out his policies, so that things were continually going wrong in his office and he was even convicted of some fault. With this, the emperor transferred Wang Wen-shu back to the post of military commander of the capital. It was at this time that Yang P'u won the post of master of titles chief commandant because of his harshness and severity.

[11] Because capital punishments could not be carried out in the spring months.

Yang P'u was a native of I-yang. By purchasing the military rank of *ch'ien-fu* he managed to become an official and was recommended for his ability by the governor of Ho-nan. He advanced to a post in the office of the imperial secretary and was put in charge of suppressing bandits in the region east of the Pass, where he carried out his duties in the fashion of Yin Ch'i, swooping down upon his victims with the fierceness of a hawk. He continued to advance gradually until he became master of titles chief commandant and ranked among the nine highest officials. The emperor considered him a man of ability and, when the kingdom of Southern Yüeh rebelled, appointed him as General of Towered Ships and sent him to attack the rebels. He won merit in this campaign and was enfeoffed as marquis of Liang. When he was sent on another campaign, this time to Ch'ao-hsien [Korea], he was arrested by his fellow commander Hsün Chih and was reduced to the rank of commoner. He died some time later of illness.

As has been stated above, Wang Wen-shu was once more appointed to the post of military commander of the capital after the failure of Yin Ch'i. Wang Wen-shu was a man of little refinement, and when he appeared in court he acted rather stupid and confused and could never express himself clearly. When he reached the post of military commander of the capital, however, he seemed to find his element and set about suppressing thieves and bandits with great enthusiasm. Since he was a native of the area, he was thoroughly familiar with the customs of the people in the region within the Pass and knew all the powerful and evil officials. The latter for their part did all they could to assist him in carrying out his policies and kept a close watch for thieves, bandits, and young men of bad character. He put out boxes in which people could deposit accusations and reports of crimes, for which the accusers would receive a reward, and set up chiefs in the villages and rural communities to watch for and arrest bandits.

Wang Wen-shu was very much of a toady, playing up to people who had power and treating like so many slaves those who did not. In cases of really powerful families, although they had committed a mountain of crimes he would never bother them, but if he were dealing with people who had no real power, he would invariably impose upon them and insult them, even though they might be in-laws of the emperor himself. He would twist the law around in clever ways and bring about the ruin of all sorts of petty rogues in order to intimidate the more powerful families and show them what he could do if he wanted to. This was the way he carried out his duties as military commander of the capital.

Under his administration knaves and evildoers were subjected to the most thorough investigation; most of them were beaten to a pulp in prison, and none was ever known to have refuted the charges brought against him and gotten out of prison alive. The officials who acted as his teeth and claws were no better than tigers with hats on. In this way he forced all the lesser rogues in the area under his jurisdiction to their knees, while the more powerful ones went around singing his praises and commending the way he governed. During the several years of his administration many of the officials under him were able to utilize his authority to accumulate fortunes.

Later, he was sent to take part in the campaign against the kingdom of Eastern Yüeh, which had rebelled, and on his return the report he made did not entirely meet with the emperor's approval. He was accused of some trifling fault, tried, and dismissed from the post of military commander of the capital.

Just at this time the emperor was planning to construct the Terrace that Reaches to Heaven, but he had not been able to get together enough workmen. Wang Wen-shu then asked to be allowed to round up all the men under the jurisdiction of the military commander of the capital who should have been conscripted for service earlier but who had managed to evade their duty, and was able in this way to get together a force of twenty or thirty thousand men. The emperor was delighted and appointed him to the post of privy treasurer; later he transferred him to that of right prefect of the capital. Wang Wen-shu continued to carry out his duties in the same way as before, doing little to prevent evil and corruption, and was accused of some fault and removed from office. Later he was restored to office as right military commander, carrying out the same duties which he had earlier as military commander of the capital. He continued to behave as before.

A year or so later preparations were begun to send an army against

Ta-yüan [Ferghana] and an imperial edict was issued summoning various powerful officials to take service in the campaign. Wang Wen-shu contrived to hide one of his subordinates named Hua Ch'eng from the conscription. Shortly afterwards, someone sent in a report of disloyalty, accusing Wang of having accepted bribes from the regular members of his cavalry force in exchange for military exemption, and of other corrupt doings. Wang and his three sets of relatives were sentenced to execution; he himself committed suicide. At the same time, Wang's two younger brothers, along with their wives' families, were accused of some other crime and sentenced to execution. The superintendent of the imperial household Hsü Tzu-wei remarked, "Alas! In ancient times men were condemned to die along with their three sets of relatives, but Wang Wen-shu's crime was so great, it seems, that five sets of relatives had to be executed at one time!" [12] After Wang's death it was found that the fortunes of his family were equal in value to some thousand pieces of gold.

A few years later Yin Ch'i died of illness while holding the post of chief commandant of Huai-yang. He left behind him an estate of less than fifty pieces of gold. He had been responsible for the execution of a very large number of people in Huai-yang, and when he died the families which bore grudges against him planned to seize his corpse and burn it. The members of his own family were obliged to conceal the corpse and flee with it to his old home before they could bury it.

From the time when Wang Wen-shu demonstrated the way to rule by harshness, all the governors and chief commandants of the provinces, the feudal lords and two thousand picul officials who wanted to rule effectively began to imitate his ways. The lower officials and people more and more came to regard lawbreaking as a trifling matter, and the number of thieves and bandits continued to increase until there were men like Mei Mien and Po Cheng in Nan-yang, Yin Chung and Tu Shao in Ch'u, Hsü Po in Ch'i, and Chien Lu and Fan Sheng in the region of Yen and Chao. The more powerful of these gathered bands numbering several thousand men, assumed any title they pleased,

[12] The three sets of relatives are the families of the father, mother, and wife of the condemned man. In Wang Wen-shu's case two more families, those of his two younger brothers, were executed at the same time.

attacked cities, seized the weapons from the arsenals, freed the convicts, bound and humiliated the governors and chief commandants of the provinces, killed the two thousand picul officials, and circulated proclamations through the districts demanding that they be supplied with food. The lesser ones formed robber bands of a few hundred men, plundering the villages and hamlets in numbers too great to be counted.

The emperor first tried appointing the aides of the imperial secretary and chief secretaries of the chancellor to remedy the situation, but when they failed to achieve any success, he sent out Fan K'un (one of the lords under the superintendent of the imperial household), the military commanders of the capital, and men such as Chang Te, who had formerly been very high officials, dressed in brocade robes and bearing the imperial credentials and the tiger seals, to call out the troops and attack the bandits. They began cutting off heads in great numbers, sometimes as many as ten thousand or more at one time, and when they started arresting people for aiding and giving supplies of food to the bandits, the number of persons involved swelled at times to several thousand, the inhabitants of several provinces being implicated in one investigation.

After a few years of this most of the leaders of the robber bands had been caught and the others had scattered and fled into hiding. It was not long, however, before they began to gather again in the mountain and river fastnesses and to form new bands here and there. At a loss to know how to deal with them, the government promulgated the so-called concealment law, which stated: "If bandits arise and their presence is not reported, or if the full number are not arrested after their presence has been reported, everyone responsible, from the two thousand picul officials down to the lowest clerks, will be executed."

After this the minor officials, terrified of punishment, did not dare to report the presence of bandits, even though they were aware of it, for fear that they would not be able to capture them all and that the investigations would involve them with the provincial office. The provincial offices for their part were only too anxious to have the lower officials remain silent. As a result, the number of bandits began gradually to increase again, but both the higher and lower officials conspired to conceal the fact and sent in false reports to the central government in order to save themselves from involvement with the law.

Chien Hsüan

Chien Hsüan was a native of Yang. Having won a reputation for impartiality as a district secretary, he was promoted to service in the provincial office of Ho-tung. General Wei Ch'ing employed him to purchase horses for him in Ho-tung and, observing that he was very fair in carrying out his duties, recommended him to the emperor. Chien Hsüan was summoned to the capital and made an aide in the imperial stables, where he fulfilled his duties with great competence. He was gradually advanced to the post of secretary and then of aide to the imperial secretary. He was in charge of the prosecution of Chu-fu Yen and, later, of the conspirators involved in the king of Huai-nan's plans for revolt. He paid strict attention to the letter of the law and applied it with great severity, bringing about the death of a very large number of people, and at the same time achieved a reputation for his decisiveness in settling doubtful cases. He was occasionally dismissed from office, but was always reappointed, and served some twenty years as a secretary and aide under the imperial secretary.

When Wang Wen-shu was dismissed from the post of military commander of the capital, Chien Hsüan was appointed left prefect of the capital. He attended to every detail in the area under his jurisdiction down to the very grain and salt consumed; all matters, great and small, passed through his hands. He even doled out the supplies to the various district offices in person in order to prevent the district magistrates and their aides from drawing and handling supplies in any way they wished. He maintained order by applying the law with the utmost severity, and during his several years in office every affair in the province, down to the most trifling, was perfectly arranged. However, only a man like Chien Hsüan could have personally attended to every matter, from the smallest to the largest, in this way. It would be difficult to expect such behavior from all officials.

Later he was removed from his post and appointed supervisor of the right district of the capital. He bore a grudge against one of his subordinate officials named Ch'eng Hsin, who subsequently fled and hid in the Shang-lin Park. Chien Hsüan ordered the district magistrate of Mei to have Ch'eng Hsin sought out and killed, and when the magistrate's guards located him and shot at him, some of their arrows struck the gate of the emperor's garden in the park. Chien Hsüan was charged with the responsibility for the incident and was handed over to the law officials for trial. He was convicted of high treason and was sentenced to die along with the members of his family, but he anticipated the sentence by taking his own life. After this Tu Chou came to power.

Tu Chou

Tu Chou was a native of Tu-yen in Nan-yang. While I Tsung was acting as governor of Nan-yang, he employed Tu Chou as one of his subordinates. Later, Tu Chou was promoted to secretary in the office of the commandant of justice and served under Chang T'ang. Chang T'ang frequently commended him to the emperor for his impartiality, and in time he was appointed to the office of the imperial secretary and put in charge of investigating the losses of men, animals, and supplies that were taking place in the border regions. He was responsible for condemning a very large number of persons to execution. His proposals always won the approval of the emperor, and he enjoyed the same degree of confidence that Chien Hsüan did. He and Chien Hsüan took turns serving as aides to the imperial secretary for over ten years, and Tu Chou imitated Chien Hsüan's ways, though Tu Chou had a much more grave and sedate bearing. On the surface Tu Chou appeared to be tolerant, but at heart he had a severity that cut to the bone.

When Chien Hsüan was appointed left prefect of the capital, Tu Chou was made commandant of justice. He carried out the duties of this office in much the same way that Chang T'ang had, and in addition he was very skillful at divining the ruler's wishes. If the emperor wanted to get rid of someone, Tu Chou would proceed to find some way to trap the victim; if the emperor wanted someone let free, Tu Chou would keep the person bound in prison for an indefinite period awaiting further instructions, meanwhile doing all he could to make it seem that the person had been unjustly accused.

Once one of his guests chided him about this, saying, "You are supposed to be the dispenser of justice for the Son of Heaven, and yet you pay no attention to the statute books, but simply decide cases in any way that will accord with the wishes of the ruler. Do you really think that is the way a law official should be?"

"And where, may I ask, did the statute books come from in the first place?" replied Tu Chou. "Whatever the earlier rulers thought was right they wrote down in the books and made into laws, and whatever the later rulers thought was right they added as new clauses and stipulations. Anything that suits the present age is right. Why bother with the laws of former times?"

After Tu Chou became commandant of justice the flood of cases referred to his office by imperial command grew larger and larger. The number of officials of the two thousand picul class in prison, counting old and new arrests, never fell below a hundred or more men. All cases involving the provincial officials, as well as those of the high ministries in the capital, were referred to the commandant of justice, who handled over a thousand of them a year. In important cases, several hundred men would be arrested or called in to act as witnesses, and even in less important cases the number was twenty or thirty. Men living anywhere from several hundred *li* to several thousand *li* away were summoned to the capital for investigation. When a case was being tried, the prison officials would confront the accused with a list of charges, and if he refused to acknowledge his guilt they would beat him until they had forced a confession. For this reason anyone who heard that he was to be arrested would flee into hiding. Although several amnesties might have been issued in the meantime, men were held in prison for indefinite periods of time and not released. In other cases men who had been in hiding for over ten years were accused when they were found and were almost always tried for immoral conduct or some even more serious charge. In time, the commandant of justice and the other law officials of the capital had succeeded in arresting sixty or seventy thousand persons on imperial order, while the officials found legal grounds for bringing charges against another hundred thousand or more.

Later Tu Chou was dismissed from the post of commandant of

justice and then reappointed as military commander of the capital.[13] He worked to rid the area of thieves, and was responsible for the arrest and prosecution of Sang Hung-yang and the brothers of Empress Wei, whom he prosecuted with great severity. The emperor admired him for his untiring efforts and impartiality and promoted him to the post of imperial secretary. His two sons became governors of the provinces of Ho-nei and Ho-nan on either side of the Yellow River and governed with even greater harshness and cruelty than Wang Wen-shu or the rest.

When Tu Chou was first summoned to serve as a secretary in the office of the commandant of justice, he owned only one horse, and even that was maimed. But by the time he had worked in the government for a number of years and had advanced until he ranked among the three highest ministers, his sons and grandsons all held high offices and the wealth of his family ran to several hundred million cash.

The Grand Historian remarks: These ten men, from Chih Tu to Tu Chou, all won fame for their harshness. Nevertheless, Chih Tu had a certain stubborn frankness and strove to decide between right and wrong in order to provide a basis for justice in the empire. Chang T'ang knew how to be either stern or mild depending upon the will of the ruler, but his decisions on what was fitting and what was not were often of benefit to the nation. Chao Yü stuck to the letter of the law and was careful to be fair, but Tu Chou simply flattered the whims of the ruler and believed that gravity consisted in saying little. From the time of Chang T'ang's death on, the net of the law was drawn tighter and tighter, and harsh penalties became increasingly

---

[13] According to *Han shu* 19B, Tu Chou was relieved of his duties as commandant of justice and made military commander of the capital in the second year of *t'ien-han* (99 B.C.). This was the same year that Ssu-ma Ch'ien, having aroused Emperor Wu's anger by speaking in defense of General Li Ling, was sent to prison and condemned to suffer castration. It is quite possible, therefore, that Ssu-ma Ch'ien's case was handled by Tu Chou, or at least by the officials trained under Tu Chou. Ssu-ma Ch'ien's description of prison methods used at this time may accordingly be based upon personal experience. Certainly, from Ssu-ma Ch'ien's letter to Jen An describing his experience in prison it is obvious that he too was beaten and cowed by the prison officials into acknowledging guilt. See the translation of the letter in *Ssu-ma Ch'ien: Grand Historian of China*, p. 62.

frequent, so that the work of the government officials was gradually hampered and brought to a standstill. The high ministers went about their duties meekly and compliantly, and gave no thought to reforming defects in government policy. Indeed, they were so busy staying out of trouble that they had no time to think of anything but laws and regulations.

Yet among these ten men, those who were honest may serve as an example of conduct, and those who were corrupt may serve as a warning. These men, by their schemes and strategies, their teaching and leadership, worked to prevent evil and block the path of crime. All were men of strong character, combining in themselves both military and civil ability. And although they were known for their cruelty and harshness, it was a reputation that went well with their duties. But when it comes to men like Feng Tang, the governor of Shu, who violently oppressed the people; Li Chen of Kuang-han who tore people limb from limb for his own pleasure; Mi P'u of Tung Province who sawed people's heads off; Lo Pi of T'ien-shui who bludgeoned people into making confessions; Ch'u Kuang of Ho-tung who executed people indiscriminately; Wu Chi of the capital and Yin Chou of Feng-i who ruled like vipers or hawks; or Yen Feng of Shui-heng who beat people to death unless they bribed him for their release—why bother to describe all of them? Why bother to describe all of them?

Though only commoners with no special ranks or titles, they were able, without interfering with the government or hindering the activities of the people, to increase their wealth by making the right moves at the right time. Wise men will find something to learn from them. Thus I made The Biographies of the Money-makers.[1]

Lao Tzu has said that under the ideal form of government, "though states exist side by side, so close that they can hear the crowing of each other's cocks and the barking of each other's dogs, the people of each state will savor their own food, admire their own clothing, be content with their own customs, and delight in their own occupations, and will grow old and die without ever wandering abroad."[2] Yet if one were to try to apply this type of government, striving to drag the present age back to the conditions of primitive times and to stop up the eyes and ears of the people, it is doubtful that one would have much chance of success!

The Grand Historian remarks: I know nothing about the times of Shen-nung and before but, judging by what is recorded in the *Odes* and *Documents,* from the age of Emperor Shun and the Hsia dynasty down to the present, ears and eyes have always longed for the ultimate in beautiful sounds and forms, mouths have desired to taste the best in grass-fed and grain-fed animals, bodies have delighted in ease and comfort, and hearts have swelled with pride at the glories of power and ability. So long have these habits been allowed to permeate the lives of the people that, though one were to go from door to door

---

[1] The title of the chapter, *huo-chih,* literally "wealth increasing," is taken from Confucius' remark about his disciple Tzu-kung (discussed in this chapter): "Ts'e [Tzu-kung] does not acquiesce in his fate and his wealth increases" (*Analects* XI, 17). The chapter, containing as it does a great many technical terms and details of the economic life of the Han, is one of the most difficult in the *Shih chi,* and commentators differ on numerous points of interpretation.

[2] Lao Tzu, *Tao-te-ching* 80.

preaching the subtle arguments of the Taoists, he could never succeed in changing them. Therefore the highest type of ruler accepts the nature of the people, the next best leads the people to what is beneficial, the next gives them moral instruction, the next forces them to be orderly, and the very worst kind enters into competition with them.[3]

The region west of the mountains is rich in timber, paper mulberry, hemp, oxtails for banner tassels, jade and other precious stones. That east of the mountains abounds in fish, salt, lacquer, silk, singers, and beautiful women. The area south of the Yangtze produces camphor wood, catalpa, ginger, cinnamon, gold, tin, lead ore, cinnabar, rhinoceros horns, tortoise shell, pearls of various shapes, and elephant tusks and hides, while that north of Lung-men and Chieh-shih is rich in horses, cattle, sheep, felt, furs, tendons, and horns. Mountains from which copper and iron can be extracted are found scattered here and there over thousands of miles of the empire, like chessmen on a board. In general, these are the products of the empire. All of them are commodities coveted by the people of China, who according to their various customs use them for their bedding, clothing, food, and drink, fashioning from them the goods needed to supply the living and bury the dead.

Society obviously must have farmers before it can eat; foresters, fishermen, miners, etc., before it can make use of natural resources; craftsmen before it can have manufactured goods; and merchants before they can be distributed. But once these exist, what need is there for government directives, mobilizations of labor, or periodic assemblies? Each man has only to be left to utilize his own abilities and exert his strength to obtain what he wishes. Thus, when a commodity is very cheap, it invites a rise in price; when it is very expensive, it invites a reduction. When each person works away at his own occupation and delights in his own business then, like water flowing downward, goods will naturally flow forth ceaselessly day and night without having been summoned, and the people will produce commodities without having been asked. Does this not tally with reason? Is it not a natural result?

[3] A reference to Emperor Wu's economic policies, which put the government officials into competition with the people for profit. This whole chapter must be read in the light of the historian's earlier description of economic measures and conditions in *Shih chi* 30, "The Treatise on the Balanced Standard."

The *Book of Chou* says, "If the farmers do not produce, there will be a shortage of food; if the artisans do not produce, there will be a shortage of manufactured goods; if the merchants do not produce, then the three precious things will not circulate; if the foresters, fishermen, miners, etc., do not produce, there will be a shortage of wealth, and if there is a shortage of wealth the resources of the mountains and lakes cannot be exploited." [4] These four classes are the source of the people's clothing and food. When the source is large, there will be plenty for everyone, but when the source is small, there will be scarcity. On the one hand, the state will be enriched, and on the other, powerful families will be enriched. Poverty and wealth are not the sort of things that are arbitrarily handed to men or taken away: the clever have a surplus; the stupid never have enough.

At the beginning of the Chou dynasty, when the Grand Duke Wang was enfeoffed with Ying-ch'iu in the state of Ch'i, where the land was damp and brackish and the inhabitants few, he encouraged the women workers, developed the craft industries to the highest degree, and opened up a trade in fish and salt. As a result, men and goods were reeled into the state like skeins of thread; they converged upon it like spokes about a hub. Soon Ch'i was supplying caps and sashes, clothes and shoes to the whole empire, and the lords of the area between the sea and Mount T'ai adjusted their sleeves and journeyed to its court to pay their respects.

Later, the power of the state of Ch'i fell into decline, but Master Kuan Chung restored it to prosperity by establishing the nine bureaus for controlling the flow of money. As a result Duke Huan of Ch'i [685–643 B.C.] was able to become a dictator; nine times he called together the other feudal lords for conferences and set the empire to rights again. Moreover, Kuan Chung himself, though only a court minister, owned the mansion called the Three Returnings,[5] and his wealth exceeded that of the lord of a great feudal kingdom. Thus the

[4] No such quotation is found in the section of the *Book of Documents* devoted to the Chou dynasty or in the *I-chou-shu*. The "three precious things" are usually identified as the products of the other three classes, i.e., agricultural products, manufactured goods, and the products of mountains, lakes, etc.

[5] Meaning doubtful; some scholars would take it to mean that he had three wives.

state of Ch'i remained rich and powerful through the reigns of Wei and Hsüan [378–323 B.C.].

Therefore it is said, "Only when the granaries are full can people appreciate rites and obligations; only when they have enough food and clothing do they think about glory and disgrace." [6] Rites are born of plenty and are abandoned in time of want. When superior men become rich, they delight in practicing virtue; but when mean-minded men are rich, they long only to exercise their power. As fish by nature dwell in the deepest pools and wild beasts congregate in the most secluded mountains, so benevolence and righteousness attach themselves to a man of wealth. So long as a rich man wields power, he may win greater and greater eminence, but once his power is gone, his guests and retainers will all desert him and take no more delight in his company. This is even more the case among barbarians.

The proverb says, "The young man with a thousand catties of gold does not meet death in the market place." [7] This is no idle saying. So it is said,

> Jostling and joyous,
> The whole world comes after profit;
> Racing and rioting,
> After profit the whole world goes!

If even the king of a land of a thousand chariots, the lord of ten thousand households, or the master of a hundred dwellings must worry about poverty, how much more so the common peasant whose name is enrolled in the tax collector's list?

In former times when King Kou-chien of Yüeh [496–465 B.C.] was surrounded on Mount K'uai-chi by the armies of the state of Wu and was in great difficulty, he followed the advice of Fan Li and Chi-jan. Chi-jan said, "If you know there is going to be a battle, you must make preparations beforehand, and for ordinary use you must know what goods are needed in each season. When you understand these two

---

[6] The quotation is found in the opening paragraph of the *Kuan Tzu*, a text which purports to represent the sayings and theories of Kuan Chung.

[7] Commentators generally take this to mean that a son of a wealthy family has enough moral training to avoid breaking the law and thus incurring execution in the market place. Obviously, however, it may also be interpreted more cynically to mean that money can buy one's way out of any difficulties.

necessities clearly, then you can perceive how all kinds of goods should be disposed. When Jupiter is in the western portion of the sky, which is dominated by the element metal, there will be good harvests; when it is in the northern portion dominated by water, there will be destruction by floods; when it is in the eastern portion dominated by wood, there will be famine; and when in the southern portion dominated by fire, there will be drought. When there is a drought, that is the time to start laying away a stock of boats; and when there is a flood, that is the time to start buying up carts. This is the principle behind the use of goods.

"Every six years there will be a good harvest, every six years there will be a drought, and every twelve years there will be one great famine. If grain is sold as low as twenty cash a picul, then the farmers will suffer, but if it goes as high as ninety cash, then those in secondary occupations will suffer. If the merchants and others in secondary occupations suffer, then they will produce no goods, while if the farmers suffer they will cease to clear their fields. If, however, the price does not go over eighty cash nor fall below thirty, then both farmers and those in secondary occupations will benefit. If the price of grain is kept level and goods are fairly distributed, then there will be no shortages in the customs barriers and markets. This is the way to govern a country.

"The principle of storing goods is to try to get commodities which can be preserved for a long time without damage or depreciation [8] and can be easily exchanged for other things. Do not store up commodities that are likely to rot or spoil, and do not hoard expensive articles. If you study the surpluses and shortages of the market, you can judge how much a commodity will be worth. When an article has become extremely expensive, it will surely fall in price, and when it has become extremely cheap, then the price will begin to rise. Dispose of expensive goods as though they were so much filth and dirt; buy up cheap goods as though they were pearls and jade. Wealth and currency should be allowed to flow as freely as water!"

King Kou-chien followed this advice for the next ten years until the state of Yüeh became rich and he was able to give generous gifts to

[8] Following the reading in the So-yin and Cheng-i commentaries.

his fighting men. As a result, his soldiers were willing to rush into the face of the arrows and stones of the enemy as though they were thirsty men going to drink their fill; in the end King Kou-chien took his revenge upon the powerful forces of Wu, demonstrated his military might to the other states of China, and came to be known as one of the five dictators.

Fan Li, having helped to wipe out the shame of Yüeh's defeat at K'uai-chi, sighed and said, "Of Chi-jan's seven strategies, Yüeh made use of five and achieved its desires. They have already been put into practice in the state. Now I would like to try using them for my own family."

Then he got into a little boat and sailed down the Yangtze and through the lakes. He changed his family name and personal name and visited Ch'i, where he was known as Ch'ih-i Tzu-p'i, the "Adaptable Old Wine-skin." Later he went to T'ao, where he was called Lord Chu. He observed that T'ao, located in the middle of the empire, with feudal lords passing back and forth in all directions, was a center for the exchange of goods. He therefore established his business there, storing away goods, looking for a profitable time to sell, and not making demands upon others. (Thus one who is good at running a business must know how to select men and take advantage of the times.) In the course of nineteen years Fan Li, or Lord Chu, as he was now called, three times accumulated fortunes of a thousand catties of gold, and twice he gave them away among his poor friends and distant relations. This is what is meant by a rich man who delights in practicing virtue. Later, when he became old and frail, he turned over his affairs to his sons and grandsons, who carried on and improved the business until the family fortune had reached a hundred million cash. Therefore, when people speak of rich men they always mention T'ao Chu-kung, Lord Chu of T'ao.

Tzu-kung, after studying with Confucius, retired and held office in the state of Wei. By buying up, storing, and selling various goods in the region of Ts'ao and Lu, he managed to become the richest among Confucius' seventy disciples. While Yüan Hsien, another of the Master's disciples, could not get even enough chaff and husks to satisfy his hunger, and lived hidden away in a tiny lane, Tzu-kung rode about with a team of four horses attended by a mounted retinue, bearing gifts of bundles of silk to be presented to the feudal lords, and whatever state he visited the ruler never failed to descend into the courtyard and greet him as an equal. It was due to Tzu-kung's efforts that Confucius' fame was spread over the empire. Is this not what we mean when we say that a man who wields power may win greater and greater eminence?

Po Kuei was a native of Chou. During the time of Marquis Wen of Wei [403–387 B.C.], Li K'o stressed full utilization of the powers of the land, but Po Kuei delighted in watching for opportunities presented by the changes of the times.

> What others throw away, I take;
> What others take, I give away,

he said. "When the year is good and the harvest plentiful, I buy up grain and sell silk and lacquer; when cocoons are on the market, I buy up raw silk and sell grain. When the reverse marker of Jupiter is in the sign *mao*,[9] the harvest will be good, but the following year the crops will do much worse. When it reaches the sign *wu*, there will be a drought, but the next year will be fine. When it reaches the sign *yu*, there will be good harvests, followed the next year by a falling off. When it reaches the sign *tzu*, there will be a great drought. The next year will be fine and later there will be floods. Thus the cycle revolves again to the sign *mao*."

By observing these laws, he was able to approximately double his stores of grain each year. When he wanted to increase his money

[9] Since Jupiter takes approximately twelve years to complete one cycle of the heavens, the years of the cycle were designated by the twelve signs that marked the division of the horizon, depending upon which portion of the sky Jupiter was in. But because Jupiter appeared to revolve counterclockwise through the sky, and the order of the twelve signs ran clockwise, an imaginary marker, called *sui-yin* or *t'ai-yin,* was postulated, which revolved in the opposite direction from Jupiter. As this works out, when the reverse marker was in *mao* (east), Jupiter was in *tzu* (north); when the marker was in *wu* (south), Jupiter was in *yu* (west); when the marker was in *yu* (west), Jupiter was in *wu* (south); and when the marker was in *tzu* (north), Jupiter was in *mao* (east). Hence Po Kuei is saying that when Jupiter is in the north or south, there will be good harvests; when it is in the west there will be drought; and when it is in the east there will be a great drought. The reader may compare this with Chi-jan's laws above.

supply, he bought cheap grain, and when he wanted to increase his stock, he bought up high-grade grain. He ate and drank the simplest fare, controlled his appetites and desires, economized on clothing, and shared the same hardships as his servants and slaves, and when he saw a good opportunity, he pounced on it like a fierce animal or a bird of prey. "As you see," he said, "I manage my business affairs in the same way that the statemen I Yin and Lü Shang planned their policies, the military experts Sun Tzu and Wu Tzu deployed their troops, and the Legalist philosopher Shang Yang carried out his laws. Therefore, if a man does not have wisdom enough to change with the times, courage enough to make decisions, benevolence enough to know how to give and take, and strength enough to stand his ground, though he may wish to learn my methods, I will never teach them to him!"

Hence, when the world talks of managing a business it acknowledges Po Kuei as the ancestor of the art. Po Kuei tried out his theories in practice, and his experiments proved successful. He knew what he was talking about.

I Tun rose to prominence by producing salt in ponds, while Kuo Tsung of Han-tan made a business of smelting iron, and their wealth equaled that of the ruler of a kingdom.

Wu-chih Lo raised domestic animals, and when he had a large number, he sold them and bought rare silks and other articles which he secretly sent as gifts to the king of the Jung barbarians. The king of the Jung repaid him ten times the original cost and sent him domestic animals until Wu-chih Lo had so many herds of horses and cattle he could only estimate their number roughly by the valleyful. The First Emperor of the Ch'in ordered that Wu-chih Lo be granted the same honors as a feudal lord and allowed him to join the ministers in seasonal audiences at court.

There was also the case of a widow named Ch'ing of the region of Pa and Shu. Her ancestors got possession of some cinnabar caves and were able to monopolize the profits from them for several generations until they had acquired an inestimable amount of wealth. Ch'ing, although only a widow, was able to carry on the business and used her wealth to buy protection for herself so that others could not mistreat or impose upon her. The First Emperor of the Ch'in, considering her a virtuous woman, treated her as a guest and built the Nü-huai-ch'ing Terrace in her honor.

Wu-chih Lo was a simple country man who looked after herds, while Ch'ing was only a widow living far off in the provinces, and yet both were treated with as much respect as though they had been the lords of a state of ten thousand chariots, and their fame spread all over the world. Was this not because of their wealth?

After the Han rose to power, the barriers and bridges were opened and the restrictions on the use of the resources of mountains and lakes were relaxed. As a result, the rich traders and great merchants traveled all around the empire distributing their wares to every corner so that everyone could buy what he wanted. At the same time the powerful families of the great provincial clans and former feudal lords were moved to the capital.

The area within the Pass,[10] from the Ch'ien and Yung rivers east to the Yellow River and Mount Hua, is a region of rich and fertile fields stretching a thousand *li*. Judging from the tribute exacted by Emperor Shun and the rulers of the Hsia dynasty, these were already at that time considered to be among the finest fields. Later the ancestor of the house of Chou, Kung Liu, made his home in Pin in the region; his descendants Ta-wang and Wang-chi lived in the area called Ch'i; King Wen built the city of Feng; and King Wu ruled from Hao. Therefore the people of the region still retain traces of the customs they learned under these ancient rulers. They are fond of agriculture, raise the five grains, take good care of their fields, and regard it as a serious matter to do wrong.

Later, Dukes Wen and Mu [11] of Ch'in [765–621 B.C.] fixed the capital of their state at Yung, which was on the main route for goods being brought out of both Lung and Shu and was a center for merchants. Dukes Hsien and Hsiao [384–338 B.C.] moved the Ch'in capital to the city of Yüeh. The city of Yüeh drove back the Jung and Ti barbarians

[10] In the following description of the various geographical areas of the empire and the customs of the people in each, there are no indications of tense and it is not certain whether Ssu-ma Ch'ien is talking about the customs of older times or those of his own day. I have in most cases translated as though he meant the latter.

[11] Omitting the name of Duke Hsiao, which erroneously appears between Wen and Mu in present texts.

in the north and in the east opened up communication with the states that had been created out of the former state of Chin. It too was a center for great merchants. Kings Wu and Chao [310–251 B.C.] made their capital at Hsien-yang, and it was this site that the Han took over and used for its own capital, Ch'ang-an. People poured in from all parts of the empire to congregate in the towns established at the imperial tombs around Ch'ang-an, converging on the capital like the spokes of a wheel. The land area is small and the population numerous, and therefore the people have become more and more sophisticated and crafty and have turned to secondary occupations such as trade to make their living.

South of this region are the provinces of Pa and Shu, which also contain rich fields and produce large quantities of gardenias for making dye, ginger, cinnabar, copper, iron, and bamboo and wooden implements. In the south these provinces control the regions of Tien and P'o, the latter noted for its young slaves. Nearby on the west are the regions of Ch'iung and Tso, the latter famous for its horses and oxtails. Though the area is hemmed in on all four sides by natural barriers, there are plank roadways built along the sides of the mountains for a thousand *li* so that there is no place that cannot be reached. All these roads are squeezed together into one in the narrow defile running between the Pao and Yeh rivers. By means of such roads, areas which have a surplus may exchange their goods for the things which they lack.

North of the capital area are the provinces of T'ien-shui, Lung-hsi, and Shang, whose customs are the same as those of the area within the Pass. To the west there are profits to be gained among the Ch'iang barbarians, while to the north are the herds of the Jung and Ti barbarians, which are one of the riches of the empire. Nevertheless, the region is mountainous and inaccessible and the only route out of it is that which leads to the capital.

Thus the region within the Pass occupies about a third of the area of the empire. The inhabitants represent only three tenths of the total population, but they possess six tenths of the wealth of the nation.

In ancient times the men of the state of Emperor Yao made their capital in Ho-tung, those of the Yin dynasty established their capital in Ho-nei, and those of the Chou dynasty in Ho-nan. These three regions

stand like the legs of a tripod in the center of the empire and were
used as the sites of their capitals by the successive dynasties, each of
which lasted for several hundred or even a thousand years. The region
is narrow and constricted and the population large. Since the capitals
of the various dynasties served as gathering places for the feudal lords,
the people are very thrifty and experienced in the ways of the world.

Yang and P'ing-yang [12] in Ho-tung have customarily traded with the
area of Ch'in and the Ti barbarians in the west and with Chung and
Tai in the north. Chung and Tai are situated north of the old city of
Shih. They border the lands of the Hsiung-nu and are frequently
raided by the barbarians. The inhabitants are proud and stubborn,
high-spirited and fond of feats of daring and evil, and do not engage
in agriculture or trade. Because the region is so close to the territory
of the northern barbarians, armies have frequently been sent there,
and when supplies were transported to them from the central states,
the people were often able to profit from the surplus. The inhabitants
have mingled with the barbarians, and their customs are by no means
uniform. From the time before the state of Chin was divided into three
parts they were already a source of trouble because of their violent
temperament. King Wu-ling of Chao [325–299 B.C.] did much to encourage this trait, and the inhabitants today still retain the ways they
developed when they were under the rule of Chao. The merchants
of Yang and P'ing-yang roam through the region and obtain whatever
goods they want.

Wen and Chih in Ho-nei have customarily traded with Shang-tang
in the west and Chao and Chung-shan in the north. The soil in Chung-
shan is barren and the population large. Even today at Sandy Hill are
to be found the descendants of the people who took part in the decadent
revels of Emperor Chou, the last ruler of the Yin dynasty, who had his
summer palace there. The people are of an impetuous nature and are
always looking for some cunning and clever way to make a living. The
men gather together to play games, sing sad songs, and lament. When
they really put their minds to business, they go out in bands to rob
and kill, and in their spare time they loot graves, think up ways to
flatter and deceive others or, dressing up in beautiful array, become

---

[12] Omitting the place name Ch'en, which does not seem to belong here.

singers and actors. The women play upon the large lute and trip about in dancing slippers, visiting the homes of the noble and rich to sell their favors or becoming concubines in the palaces of the feudal lords all over the empire.

Han-tan, situated between the Chang and Yellow rivers, is a city of major importance. In the north it has communications with Yen and Cho, and on the south with the regions of the old states of Cheng and Wei. The customs of Cheng and Wei are similar to those of Chao except that, since they are located nearer to Liang and Lu, the people are somewhat more sedate and take pride in virtuous conduct. The inhabitants of Yeh-wang were moved there from their city on the P'u River when the latter was taken over by the state of Ch'in [207 B.C.]. They are high-spirited and given to feats of daring, traits which mark them as former subjects of the state of Wei.

Yen, situated between the Gulf of Pohai and Chieh-shih, is also a major city. The region of Yen communicates with Ch'i and Chao in the south, borders the lands of the Hsiung-nu in the northeast, and extends as far as Chang-ku and Liao-tung, a distant and remote area, sparsely populated and often subject to barbarian raids. On the whole the customs are similar to those of Chao and Tai, but the people are as fierce as hawks and exercise little forethought. The region is rich in fish, salt, jujubes, and chestnuts. On the north it adjoins the Wu-huan and Fu-yü tribes and on the east it controls the profits derived from trade with the Hui-mo, Ch'ao-hsien, and Chen-p'an peoples.

Lo-yang in the region of Ho-nan trades with Ch'i and Lu to the east and with Liang and Ch'u to the south.

The region south of Mount T'ai is the former state of Lu and that north of the mountain is Ch'i. Ch'i is bounded by mountains and sea, a fertile area stretching a thousand *li,* suitable for growing mulberry and hemp. The population is large and produces beautifully patterned silks and other textiles, fish, and salt. Lin-tzu, the capital, situated between the sea and Mount T'ai, is a city of major importance. The people are by nature generous and easygoing, of considerable intelligence, and fond of debate. They are very attached to the land and dislike turmoil and uprising. They are timid in group warfare but brave in single combat, which accounts for the large number of highway robbers among them. On the whole, however, they have the ways of a great nation. All the five classes of people [scholars, farmers, traveling merchants, artisans, and resident traders] are to be found among them.

Tsou and Lu border the Chu and Ssu rivers and still retain the ways which they learned when they were ruled by the duke of Chou. They are fond of Confucian learning and proficient in matters of ritual, which makes them very punctilious. Mulberries and hemp are grown to some extent, but no resources are to be gained from forests or lakes. Land is scarce and the population numerous, so that the people are very frugal; they are much afraid of committing crimes and give a wide berth to evil. In later days, however, as the state has declined, they have become very fond of trade and are even more assiduous than the men of Chou in pursuing profit.

East of the Hung Canal and north of the Mang and Yang mountains as far as the marsh of Chü-yeh is the region of the old states of Liang and Sung. T'ao and Sui-yang are the most important cities in the area. In ancient times Emperor Yao built his pleasure palace at Ch'eng-yang, Emperor Shun fished in the Lei Marsh, and King T'ang settled in Po, so that the people still retain traces of the customs they learned from these former sage rulers. They are grave in demeanor, devoted to agricultural pursuits, and include a large number of true gentlemen. Though there are no riches to be gained from the mountains and rivers, the people are willing to put up with poor clothing and food and even manage to store up a surplus.

The regions of Yüeh and Ch'u are divided into three areas which differ in their customs. From the Huai River north to P'ei, Ch'en, Ju-nan, and Nan provinces is the area of western Ch'u. The people are very volatile and quickly give vent to their anger. The land is barren and there is little surplus to be stored up. Chiang-ling occupies the site of Ying, the old capital of the state of Ch'u. To the west it communicates with Wu and Pa and in the east draws upon the resources of the Yün-meng lakes. Ch'en is situated on what used to be the border between Ch'u and the old empire of the Hsia dynasty and carries on a trade in fish and salt. The population therefore includes a large number of merchants. The people of the districts of Hsü, T'ung, and Ch'ü-lü are honest and strict and pride themselves on keeping their promises.

From the city of P'eng-ch'eng east to Tung-hai, Wu, and Kuang-ling is the region of eastern Ch'u. The customs are similar to those of Hsü and T'ung. From the districts of Ch'ü and Tseng on north, however, the customs are similar to those of Ch'i, while from the Che and Yangtze rivers on south, they resemble those of Yüeh. Ho-lu, the ancient king of the state of Wu [725–702 B.C.], the lord of Ch'un-shen [third century B.C.], and Liu P'i, the king of Wu in Han times, all did their best to attract wandering scholars and protégés to the city of Wu. The city enjoys the rich salt resources derived from the sea in the east, copper from the Chang Mountains, and the benefits from the three mouths of the Yangtze and the Five Lakes nearby, and is the most important city in the area east of the Yangtze.

Heng-shan, Chiu-chiang, Chiang-nan, Yü-chang, and Ch'ang-sha make up the region of southern Ch'u. The customs of the people are generally similar to those of western Ch'u. Shou-ch'un, which the Ch'u kings used as their capital after they moved from Ying, is the most important city in the area. The district of Ho-fei receives goods transported down both the Huai River in the north and the Yangtze in the south and is a center for the shipping of hides, dried fish, and lumber. The customs of the people have become mixed with those of the Min and Yüeh tribes. Thus the men of southern Ch'u are fond of fancy phrases and clever at talking, but what they say can seldom be trusted. Chiang-nan, the area just south of the Yangtze, is low and damp, and even hardy young men die early there. It produces large quantities of bamboo and timber. Yü-chang produces gold and Ch'ang-sha produces lead ore, but the quantity is so small that, though it exists, it seldom repays the cost of extraction.

From the Nine Peaks and Ts'ang-wu south to Tan-erh the customs are in general similar to those of Chiang-nan, though with a large admixture of the customs of the Yang and Yüeh people. P'an-yü is the most important city in the area, being a center for pearls, rhinoceros horn, tortoise shell, fruit, and cloth.

Ying-ch'uan and Nan-yang were the home of the people of the ancient Hsia dynasty. The Hsia people valued loyalty and simplicity in government, and the influence of the Hsia kings is still to be seen in the ways of the inhabitants of the region, who are warmhearted and sincere. In the latter days of the Ch'in dynasty the government moved large numbers of lawbreakers to the region of Nan-yang. Nan-yang communicates on the west with the area within the Pass through the Wu Pass, and with Han-chung through the Hsün Pass, and from the east and south it receives goods by way of the Han, Yangtze, and Huai rivers. Yüan is the most important city in the region. The customs are rather heterogeneous; the people are fond of business and there are many merchants among them. The local bosses in the area work in cooperation with their counterparts in Ying-ch'an. Even today people refer to the inhabitants of the entire region as "men of Hsia."

Various products are rare in one part of the empire and plentiful in another part. For example, it is the custom of the people east of the mountains to use salt extracted from the sea, while those west of the mountains use rock salt. There are also places in Ling-nan in the far south and in the deserts of the far north which have long produced salt. In general, the same is true of other products as well.

To sum up, the region of Ch'u and Yüeh is broad and sparsely populated, and the people live on rice and fish soups. They burn off the fields and flood them to kill the weeds, and are able to gather all the fruit, berries, and univalve and bivalve shellfish they want without waiting for merchants to come around selling them. Since the land is so rich in edible products, there is no fear of famine, and therefore the people are content to live along from day to day; they do not lay away stores of goods, and many of them are poor. As a result, in the region south of the Yangtze and Huai rivers no one ever freezes or starves to death, but on the other hand there are no very wealthy families.

The region north of the Che and Ssu rivers is suitable for growing the five types of grain, mulberries, and hemp, and for raising the six kinds of domestic animals.[13] Land is scarce and the population dense, and the area often suffers from floods and drought. The people therefore take good care to lay away stores of food. Hence in the regions of Ch'in, Hsia, Liang, and Lu agriculture is favored and the peasants are held in esteem. The same is true of Ho-tung, Ho-nei and Ho-nan, as well as Yüan and Ch'en, though in these regions the people also engage in trade. The people of Ch'i and Chao with their intelligence

---

[13] Horses, cattle, pigs, goats, dogs, and chickens. Dogs were raised to be eaten.

and cleverness are always on the lookout for a chance to make a profit. Those of Yen and Tai gain their living from their fields and herds of domestic animals, and also raise silkworms.

Judging from all that has been said above, when wise men lay their profound plans in palace chambers or deliberate in audience halls, guard their honor and die for their principles, or when gentlemen retire to dwell in mountain caves and establish a reputation for purity of conduct, what is their ultimate objective? Their objective is simply wealth. So the honest official after years of service attains riches, and the honest merchant in the end becomes wealthy.

The desire for wealth does not need to be taught; it is an integral part of all human nature. Hence, when young men in the army attack cities and scale walls, break through the enemy lines and drive back the foe, cut down the opposing generals and seize their pennants, advance beneath a rain of arrows and stones, and do not turn aside before the horrors of fire and boiling water, it is because they are spurred on by the prospect of rich rewards. Again, when the youths of the lanes and alleys attack passers-by or murder them and hide their bodies, threaten others and commit evil deeds, dig up graves and coin counterfeit money, form gangs to bully others, lend each other a hand in avenging wrongs, and think up secret ways to blackmail people or drive them from the neighborhood, paying no heed to the laws and prohibitions, but rushing headlong to the place of execution, it is in fact all because of the lure of money. In like manner, when the women of Chao and the maidens of Cheng paint their faces and play upon the large lute, flutter their long sleeves and trip about in pointed slippers, invite with their eyes and beckon with their hearts, considering it no distance at all to travel a thousand miles to meet a patron, not caring whether he is old or young, it is because they are after riches. When idle young noblemen ornament their caps and swords and go about with a retinue of carriages and horsemen, it is simply to show off their wealth. Those who go out to shoot birds with stringed arrows, to fish or to hunt, heedless of dawn or nightfall, braving frost and snow, galloping around the animal pits or into ravines without shying from the dangers of wild beasts, do so because they are greedy for the taste of fresh game. The reason that those who indulge in gambling, horse racing, cock fighting, and dog racing turn red in the face, shouting boasts to one another, and invariably quarrel over the victory is that they consider it a very serious matter to lose their wagers. Doctors, magicians, and all those who live by their arts are willing to burn up their spirits and exhaust their talents only because they value the fees they will receive. When officials in the government juggle with phrases and twist the letter of the law, carve fake seals and forge documents, heedless of the mutilating punishments of the knife and saw that await them if they are discovered, it is because they are drowned in bribes and gifts. And when farmers, craftsmen, traders, and merchants lay away stores and work to expand their capital, we may be sure that it is because they are seeking wealth and hope to increase their goods. Thus men apply all their knowledge and use all their abilities simply in accumulating money. They never have any strength left over to consider the question of giving some of it away.

The proverb says, "You don't go a hundred miles to peddle firewood; you don't go a thousand miles to deal in grain. If you are going to be in a place for one year, then seed it with grain. If you are going to be there ten years, plant trees. And if you are going to be there a hundred years, provide for the future by means of virtue." Virtue here means being good to people. Now there are men who receive no ranks or emoluments from the government and who have no revenue from titles or fiefs, and yet they enjoy just as much ease as those who have all these; they may be called the "untitled nobility." A lord who possesses a fief lives off the taxes. Each year he is allowed to collect two hundred cash from each household, so that the lord of a thousand households has an income of two hundred thousand cash. But out of this he has to pay the expenses of his spring and autumn visits to the court and pay for various gifts and presentations. Common people such as farmers, craftsmen, traveling traders, and merchants on the whole may expect a profit of two thousand cash a year on a capital investment of ten thousand. So if a family has a capital investment of a million cash, their income will likewise be two hundred thousand. Out of this they must pay the cost of commutation of labor and military services, as well as property and poll taxes, but with the rest they may buy whatever fine food and clothing they desire.

Thus it is said that those who own pasture lands producing fifty horses a year, or a hundred head of cattle, or five hundred sheep, or five hundred marshland swine; those who own reservoirs stocked with a thousand piculs of fish or mountain lands containing a thousand logs of timber; those who have a thousand jujube trees in An-i, or a thousand chestnut trees in Yen or Ch'in, or a thousand citrus trees in Shu, Han, or Chiang-ling, or a thousand catalpas north of the Huai River or south of Ch'ang-shan in the region of the Yellow and Chi rivers; those who own a thousand *mou* of lacquer trees in Ch'en or Hsia, a thousand *mou* of mulberries or hemp in Ch'i or Lu, or a thousand *mou* of bamboo along the Wei River; those who own farmlands in the suburbs of some famous capital or large city which produce one *chung* [14] of grain per *mou,* or those who own a thousand *mou* of gardenias or madder for dyes, or a thousand beds of ginger or leeks—all these may live just as well as a marquis enfeoffed with a thousand households. Commodities such as these are in fact the sources of considerable wealth. Their owners need not visit the market place or travel about to other cities but may simply sit at home and wait for the money to come in. They may live with all the dignity of retired gentlemen and still enjoy an income.

At the other extreme, when it comes to those impoverished men with aged parents and wives and children too weak or young to help them out, who have nothing to offer their ancestors at the seasonal sacrifices, who must depend upon the gifts and contributions of the community for their food and clothing and are unable to provide for themselves—if men such as these, reduced to such straits, still fail to feel any shame or embarrassment, then they hardly deserve to be called human. Therefore, when men have no wealth at all, they live by their brawn; when they have a little, they struggle to get ahead by their brains; and when they already have plenty of money, they look for an opportunity for a good investment. This in general is the way things work.

When it comes to making a living, the wise man will look around

[14] One *chung* is equal to ten *hu,* or about five and a half U.S. bushels. One *mou* at this time was probably about 0.114 acres. The units used in this list are often obscure, and commentators disagree on their interpretation. Throughout the chapter I have followed the interpretations given by Professor Miyazaki Ichisada in his article, in Japanese, "A Price-list in the Biographies of Millionaires in the *Shih-chi,*" *Miscellanea Kiotensia* (Kyoto University, 1956), pp. 451–74.

for some way to gain an income that does not involve any personal danger. Hence the best kind of wealth is that which is based upon agriculture, the next best is that which is derived from secondary occupations, and the worst of all is that which is acquired by evil means. But if a man is not a gentleman of unusual character who has deliberately sought retirement from the world, and if he grows old in poverty and lowliness and still insists upon talking about his "benevolence and righteousness," he ought to be thoroughly ashamed of himself.

As for the ordinary lot of tax-paying commoners, if they are confronted by someone whose wealth is ten times their own, they will behave with humility; if by someone whose wealth is a hundred times their own, they will cringe with fear; if by someone whose wealth is a thousand times their own, they will undertake to work for him; and if by someone whose wealth is ten thousand times their own, they will become his servants. This is the principle of things.

It is said, "If a man is trying to work his way up from poverty to riches, then farming is not as good as handicrafts, and handicrafts are not as good as trade; embroidering lovely patterns at home is not as good as lounging about the market gate." This means that the secondary occupations are the best source of wealth for a poor man.

Anyone who in the market towns or great cities manages in the course of a year to sell the following items: a thousand brewings of liquor; a thousand jars of pickles and sauces; a thousand jars of sirups; a thousand slaughtered cattle, sheep, and swine; a thousand *chung* of grain; a thousand cartloads or a thousand boat-lengths of firewood and stubble for fuel; a thousand logs of timber; ten thousand bamboo poles; a hundred horse carriages; a thousand two-wheeled ox carts; a thousand lacquered wooden vessels; brass utensils weighing thirty thousand catties; a thousand piculs of plain wooden vessels, iron vessels, or gardenia and madder dyes; two hundred horses; five hundred cattle; two thousand sheep or swine; a hundred male or female slaves; a thousand catties of tendons, horns, or cinnabar; thirty thousand catties of silken fabric, raw silk, or other fine fabrics; a thousand rolls of embroidered or patterned silk; a thousand piculs of fabrics made of vegetable fiber or raw or tanned hides; a thousand pecks of lacquer;

a thousand jars of leaven or salted bean relish; a thousand catties of globefish or mullet; a thousand piculs of dried fish; thirty thousand catties of salted fish; three thousand piculs of jujubes or chestnuts; a thousand skins of fox or sable; a thousand piculs of lamb or sheep skins; a thousand felt mats; or a thousand *chung* of fruits or vegetables —such a man may live as well as the master of an estate of a thousand chariots. The same applies for anyone who has a thousand strings of cash [i.e., a million cash] to lend out on interest. Such loans are made through a moneylender, but a greedy merchant who is too anxious for a quick return will only manage to revolve his working capital three times while a less avaricious merchant has revolved his five times. These are the principal ways of making money. There are various other occupations which bring in less than twenty percent profit, but they are not what I would call sources of wealth.

Now I should like to describe briefly the ways in which some of the worthy men of the present age, working within an area of a thousand miles, have managed to acquire wealth, so that later generations may see how they did it and select what may be of benefit to themselves.

The ancestors of the Cho family were natives of Chao who made a fortune by smelting iron. When the Ch'in armies overthrew the state of Chao, the family was ordered to move to another part of the empire for resettlement. Having been taken captive and plundered of all their wealth and servants, the husband and wife were left to make the move alone, pushing their belongings in a cart. All of the other captives who were forced to move and who had a little wealth left vied with each other in bribing the officials to send them to some nearby location, and they were therefore allowed to settle in Chia-meng. But Mr. Cho said, "This region is too narrow and barren. I have heard that at the foot of Mount Min there are fertile plains full of edible tubers so that one may live all his life without suffering from famine. The people there are clever at commerce and make their living by trade." He therefore asked to be sent to a distant region, and was ordered to move to Lin-ch'iung. He was overjoyed, and when he got there and found a mountain which yielded iron ore, he began smelting ore and laying other plans to accumulate wealth until soon he dominated the trade among the people of Tien and Shu. He grew so rich that he owned a thousand young slaves, and the pleasures he indulged in among his fields and lakes and on his bird and animal hunts were like those of a great lord.

Ch'eng Cheng, like Mr. Cho, was one of those taken captive east of the mountains by the Ch'in armies and forced to resettle in the far west. He too engaged in the smelting industry and carried on trade with the barbarians who wear their hair in the mallet-shaped fashion. His wealth equaled that of Mr. Cho, and the two of them lived in Lin-ch'iung.

The ancestors of the K'ung family of Yüan were men of Liang who made their living by smelting iron. When Ch'in overthrew the state of Liang, the K'ung family was moved to Nan-yang, where they began smelting iron with bellows on a large scale and laying out ponds and fields. Soon they were riding about in carriages with a mounted retinue and visiting the feudal lords, and from these contacts they were able to earn large profits in trade. They also won a reputation for handing out lavish gifts in the manner of noblemen of leisure, but at the same time the profits they derived from their business were surprisingly large—far larger, in fact, than those derived by more cautious and tightfisted merchants—and the family fortune eventually reached several thousand catties of gold. Therefore the traders of Nan-yang all imitated the K'ung family's lordly and openhanded ways.

Lu people are customarily cautious and miserly, but the Ping family of Ts'ao were particularly so. They started out by smelting iron and in time accumulated a fortune of a hundred million cash. All the members of the family from the father and elder brothers down to the sons and grandsons, however, made a promise that they would

> Never look down without picking up something useful;
> Never look up without grabbing something of value.

They traveled about to all the provinces and kingdoms, selling goods on credit, lending money and trading. It was because of their influence that so many people in Tsou and Lu abandoned scholarship and turned to the pursuit of profit.

The people of Ch'i generally despise slaves, but Tiao Hsien alone valued them and appreciated their worth. Most men worry in particular about slaves who are too cunning and clever, but Tiao Hsien gladly acquired all he could of this kind and put them to work for him, sending them out to make a profit peddling fish and salt. Though he traveled about in a carriage with a mounted retinue and consorted with governors of provinces and prime ministers of kingdoms, he came to rely more and more upon his slaves, and in the end managed by their labor to acquire a fortune of twenty or thirty million cash. Hence the saying, "Is it better to have a title in the government or to work for Tiao Hsien?" which means that he made it possible for his best slaves to enrich themselves while at the same time he utilized their abilities to the fullest.

The people of the old state of Chou have always been very close in money matters, but Shih Shih was an extreme example. With a couple of hundred cartloads of goods he traveled around to the various provinces and kingdoms peddling his wares; there was absolutely no place he did not go. The city of Lo-yang is situated right in the middle of the old states of Ch'i, Ch'in, Ch'u, and Chao, and even the poor people of the town study to become apprentices to the rich families, boasting to each other about how long they have been in trade and how they have several times passed by their old homes but were too busy to go in the gate. By making use of men like this in his business, Shih Shih was finally able to accumulate a fortune of seventy million cash.

The ancestor of the Jen family of Hsüan-ch'ü was an official in charge of the granary at Tu-tao. When the Ch'in dynasty was overthrown and the leaders of the revolt were all scrambling for gold and jewels, Mr. Jen quietly dug a hole and stored away the grain that had been in his charge. Later, when the armies of Ch'u and Han were stalemated at Jung-yang and the people were unable to plow their fields and plant their crops, the price of grain rose to ten thousand cash a picul, and all the gold and jewels of the great leaders soon found their way into the hands of Mr. Jen. This was the start of the Jen family fortune. But while other rich people were outdoing each other in luxurious living, the Jen family lived very frugally and devoted all their energies to farming and animal raising. And while most people try to buy the cheapest fields and pasture lands, the Jen family bought up only those that were really valuable and of good quality. Thus the family remained wealthy for several generations. Mr. Jen made all the members of the family promise that they would not eat or wear anything that was not produced from their own fields or herds, and that none of them would dare to drink wine or eat meat until their public services had been completed. Because of this rule they became the leaders of the community and, while continuing to be wealthy, enjoyed the respect of the ruler.

When the frontier was expanded and the border regions opened, only Ch'iao T'ao took advantage of the opportunity, acquiring resources calculated at a thousand horses, twice that number of cattle, ten thousand sheep, and ten thousand *chung* of grain.

When Wu, Ch'u, and the other kingdoms, seven in all, raised their revolt in the time of Emperor Ching, the feudal lords in Ch'ang-an made preparations to join the imperial armies in putting down the rebellion and began looking around for ways to borrow money to provide for the expedition. The moneylenders, considering that the fiefs and kingdoms of the feudal lords were all located east of the mountains and that the fate of that region was still a matter of grave doubt, were unwilling to lend them any money. Only one man, a Mr. Wu-yen, consented to lend them a thousand catties of gold at an interest of ten times the amount of the loan. By the end of three months the states of Wu and Ch'u had been brought under control, and within the year Mr. Wu-yen received his tenfold interest. As a result he became one of the richest men in the area within the Pass.

Most of the rich merchants and big traders of the area within the Pass belonged to the T'ien family, such as T'ien Se and T'ien Lan. In addition, the Li family of Wei-chia and the Tu families of An-ling and Tu also had fortunes amounting to a hundred million cash.

These, then, are examples of outstanding and unusually wealthy men. None of them enjoyed any titles or fiefs, gifts, or salaries from the government, nor did they play tricks with the law or commit any crimes to acquire their fortunes. They simply guessed what course conditions were going to take and acted accordingly, kept a sharp eye out for the opportunities of the times, and so were able to capture a fat profit. They gained their wealth in the secondary occupations and held on to it by investing in agriculture; they seized hold of it in times of crisis and maintained it in times of stability. There was a special aptness in the way they adapted to the times, and therefore their stories are worth relating. In addition, there are many other men who exerted themselves at farming, animal raising, crafts, lumbering, merchandising, and trade and seized the opportunities of the moment to make a fortune, the greatest of them dominating a whole province, the next greatest dominating a district, and the smallest dominating a village, but they are too numerous to be described here.

Thrift and hard work are without doubt the proper way to gain a livelihood. And yet it will be found that rich men have invariably employed some unusual scheme or method to get to the top. Plowing the fields is a rather crude way to make a living, and yet Ch'in Yang did so well at it that he became the richest man in his province. Robbing graves is a criminal offense, but T'ien Shu got his start by doing it. Gambling is a wicked pastime, but Huan Fa used it to acquire a fortune. Most fine young men would despise the thought of traveling around peddling goods, yet Yung Lo-ch'eng got rich that way. Many people would consider trading in fats a disgraceful line of business, but Yung Po made a thousand catties of gold at it. Vending sirups is a petty occupation, but the Chang family acquired ten million cash that way. It takes little skill to sharpen knives, but because the Chih family didn't mind doing it, they could eat the best of everything. Dealing in dried sheep stomachs seems like an insignificant enough trade, but thanks to it the Cho family went around with a mounted retinue. The calling of a horse doctor is a rather ignominious profession, but it enabled Chang Li to own a house so large that he had to strike a bell to summon the servants. All of these men got where they did because of their devotion and singleness of purpose.

From this we may see that there is no fixed road to wealth, and money has no permanent master. It finds its way to the man of ability like the spokes of a wheel converging upon the hub, and from the hands of the worthless it falls like shattered tiles. A family with a thousand catties of gold may stand side by side with the lord of a city; the man with a hundred million cash may enjoy the pleasures of a king. Rich men such as these deserve to be called the "untitled nobility," do they not?